The Passion of
Martin Scorsese

The Passion of Martin Scorsese

A Critical Study of the Films

ANNETTE WERNBLAD

McFarland & Company, Inc., Publishers
Jefferson, North Carolina, and London

LIBRARY OF CONGRESS CATALOGUING-IN-PUBLICATION DATA

Wernblad, Annette, 1958–
The passion of Martin Scorsese : a critical study
of the films / Annette Wernblad.
    p.   cm.
Includes bibliographical references and index.
Filmography: p.

ISBN 978-0-7864-4946-0
softcover : 50# alkaline paper ∞

1. Scorsese, Martin — Criticism and interpretation.
2. Motion pictures — Psychological aspects.
I. Title.
PN1998.3.S39W47   2011   791.4302'33092 — dc22   2010041093

British Library cataloguing data are available

© 2011 Annette Wernblad. All rights reserved

*No part of this book may be reproduced or transmitted in any form
or by any means, electronic or mechanical, including photocopying
or recording, or by any information storage and retrieval system,
without permission in writing from the publisher.*

On the cover: Leonardo DiCaprio in the 2010 film *Shutter Island*

Manufactured in the United States of America

*McFarland & Company, Inc., Publishers
Box 611, Jefferson, North Carolina 28640
www.mcfarlandpub.com*

To my mother,
Inge Wernblad

Contents

Acknowledgments ix
Preface 1

1. Something Being Done in Front of the Altar — 5
2. The Mask and the Mirror — 22
3. Down the Rabbit Hole — 58
4. Through the Looking Glass — 77
5. The Passion and the Pain — 100
6. To Be Without a Home — 118
7. Paying Out the Shadow — 139
8. To Beat the Devil — 177

Filmography 227
Notes 237
Bibliography 247
Index 253

Acknowledgments

To my incredible friend Jesper Abildgaard, for supporting me in the birth of this book. Thank you for sharing your time, your passion, your soul, and for sticking with me every step of the way, from the very beginning to the very end.

To Henrik Frederiksen, who generously gave me access to his vast knowledge of mythology. Thank you for sharing your wisdom, your brilliance and all those amazing ideas. Also a big hug to Ulla Madsen for keeping secrets.

To the luminous Debbie Ford. Thank you for making it possible for me to go even deeper into the darkness. And thank you to Julie Stroud and Pernille Melsted for supporting and cheering me on. I can't tell you how much that meant to me.

To Mads Haahr, my brilliant, enchanting friend. Thank you for giving me the elusive missing piece so that I could work instant magic. I'm still blown away!

To Katrine Ekman, the best friend, and Marianne Wernblad, the best sister. Thank you for holding the fort while I was finishing the manuscript. And a very special thank you to my lovely friend and cheerleader Anna-Frida Ekman.

To Thomas Rostock, whose steadfast faith in me made me go beyond what I thought I could. Thank you for never letting me get away with anything less than the very best I could do.

To the gifted and inspiring Cheryl Richardson who reminded me just how upsetting some of these films actually are when I had all but forgotten. Thank you for helping me take giant leaps of faith.

My heartfelt gratitude to my family: my nephew Tobias Wernblad for sharing keen insights into myths and monsters; my nephew Ronnie Wernblad for the inspiring times we've shared; my late grandmother for giving me the record that made me discover my true passion and purpose; my mother, Inge Wernblad, for tirelessly reading and inventing stories all through my childhood and for taking such good care of me.

Thank you to my treasured friends who have read parts of the book and offered their time and wisdom: Richard Pells, Molly Dougherty, Arun Dhundale, Maria Loizou, Margrethe Vadmand, Bettina Uma Knudsen, Pernille Nørregaard, and Yvonne Krogh.

To all the students, colleagues and others who have generously given me ideas, background material or encouragement over the years. There are too many of you to list, but I would especially like to thank Lene Estvad Christoffersen, Celeste Reumert Refn, Rikke Friis, Lene Hempel, the late Gitte Bertelsen, Jan Larsen, Lisbet Rasmussen, Lone Thomsen, Annette Biilmann, Anne-Birgitte Lieberkind, Lucienne Hartvig, Per Rasmussen, Morten

Vest Hansen, Lisbet & Morten Bagger, Thomas Vilhelm, Hanne Petri, Jan Mouritzen, Rikke Schubart, Claus Kjær, Søren Høy and Tinna Munk at UIP.

To my online peeps for support and encouragement during the very last stages, particularly Sebastian Robertson, Arturo Serrano, Juan Valenzuela, Thomas Stephen Quang, Jeff Fyke, Tim Quinlan, Christa Fuller, Adel Ganje, Gabe Bucsko, Jennifer Whiddon, Allison Maslan, Jayn Roberts Sadler, and Jill Bacharach.

To Anne McKevitt: Thank you for generously contributing your valuable time. I am deeply grateful. And to the fabulous Sandy Grason, Stephanie Gunning, Arielle Ford, Christine Kloser, and Ali Brown who have taught me so much.

To Mary Pat Kelly, Lawrence Friedman, David Thompson, Ian Christie, Thomas Sotinel, and Carrie Rickey—Scorsese scholars whose thorough and intelligent work has been a source of continual inspiration for me.

To my unwitting brothers in arms and traveling companions into the cold and holy darkness: Robert De Niro and the astounding Leonardo DiCaprio who took me through such a transformative change of heart.

To Thelma Schoonmaker, the best editor in the history of filmmaking. Thank you for offering your help and friendship, for believing in me, for paving the way, and for solving a few essential mysteries. I am deeply moved and honored.

Finally, to Martin Scorsese. Thank you for daring determinedly and courageously to keep holding up that mirror so that we have to see and accept our total selves. I will be forever grateful!

Preface

> Your vision will become clear only when you look into your heart. Who looks outside, dreams. Who looks inside, awakens.[1]
>
> Carl Gustav Jung

When I was a child, my grandmother bought me a record. It was a dramatized version of "Little Red Riding Hood"—a favorite story of mine. This is one of my most vivid childhood memories, and the reason, strangely enough, is that I could not stand listening to it. Every time someone played the record, I started screaming and crying, until finally my mother took it back to the store. My violent reaction puzzled everyone, because normally I loved scary books and movies.

I never managed to explain to them that what was so unbearable for me about that record was the terrified howling of the wolf at the end. He goes to the well to have a drink of water, but the rocks that Red Riding Hood, Grandmother and the hunter have sewn up inside him make him lose his balance, and he falls into the deep well and drowns, yelping in agony all the way down. It seemed to me that whatever the wolf had done to these people, this was much worse. After all, he only did what you would expect a wolf to do. He did not know any better. But these people with whom we were supposed to identify acted nefariously, I thought. The horror and rage I felt was all for the wolf.

This experience taught me that villains, dark characters, are extremely valuable—not just for the indispensable dramatic impact they have on the story, but even more so for the potential psychological impact they have on us, the audience. There were things, I vaguely felt even then, that one could learn about oneself by paying close attention to the wolves.

Later in my life I realized that filmic images often contain deep levels of meaning and affect us in ways we may not consciously understand. I began what would become my life's work: exploring works of art, and especially films, which depict the labyrinth of the human heart and mind, digging ever deeper in the hope of unearthing the treasures that master artists have hidden for us to discover in the innermost recesses of their work. I found that, intuitively, I still liked filmmakers who had the same interest in dark characters I did, and in the works of Martin Scorsese I recognized something deep inside myself that I had almost forgotten. Not until the early 1990s when I was in the throes of *Cape Fear* for the first time, however, did the full impact of this connection between Scorsese and my childhood experience with the wolf come to the surface and hit me with such force that it literally knocked the breath out of me. Watching that film made me decide on the spot that I absolutely had to write a book about this amazing, visionary director. I had—as Lionel Dobie says in *Life Lessons*—"no choice but to do it."

Although he is very modest about it, Martin Scorsese is indisputably one of the most gifted and insightful artists in the history of filmmaking.[2] His idiosyncratic filmic style is exhilarating and hypnotizing, distinguished by a dazzling energy and restlessness, and a musicality that goes way beyond just the use of music. He has an unequalled gift for getting under our skin, for deeply affecting, and sometimes enraging, his audience. Over the past decades he has presented us with a staggering array of dark, tormented and atrocious characters, and repeatedly he has managed to make us identify with them and even like them.

The experience of watching Scorsese's films is fascinating, but at the same time unpleasant and profoundly disturbing. One constantly has a sense that more is going on than meets the eye, that frightful and menacing things are lurking just beneath the surface. From the very beginning, when I decided to undertake the daunting project of writing this book, I wanted to explore the ways in which he reveals the inner workings and darker sides of the human mind. He consistently shows us things about ourselves that we would perhaps rather not see. The more I have scrutinized his work, the more convinced I have become that what it can teach us is similar to the valuable lessons fairy tales taught us when we were children. Like fairy tales and myths, Scorsese's works speak the language of the unconscious and convey deep psychological lessons in indirect, symbolic ways.

According to experts like Bruno Bettelheim, we were able to intuitively understand the profound implications of fairy tales when we were younger, but, unfortunately, we seem to lose that capacity as we grow up. My aim with this book is to gently open the door to that forgotten capacity by uncovering mythological and archetypal structures in Scorsese's films, symbolic layers that to some extent we do understand unconsciously, but which we need to become conscious of if they are to help us grow and evolve.

Scorsese frequently alludes to mythic material; ancient and Christian myths, children's stories, as well as literary and filmic classics. In this book, I will examine his films as mythological works and draw parallels to such material. In an attempt to get to the deepest symbolic layers, I will arrange them thematically rather than chronologically. As my theoretical foundation I will be using not film theory, but works by preeminent scholars: mythologists and psychologists including Joseph Campbell and Bruno Bettelheim, who spent their lives documenting how vital storytelling is for our psychological and spiritual development; and trailblazers like Carl Jung, Debbie Ford, and Robert A. Johnson, who have enlightened us about the essentiality of understanding and acknowledging our dark side, our own inner wolf. I sincerely believe that truly listening to and embracing the deeper lessons of Scorsese's work can help us do that.

Martin Scorsese is an extremely spiritual man and filmmaker who has been concerned with moral issues since childhood. The majority of his films concern characters who are forced through an ordeal, a mythical journey, and thereby offered a chance to face and embrace their whole selves. These characters reflect sides of all of us, and Scorsese's films touch us in places we may not necessarily like to be touched. They delve into caves where we have hidden things we do not want to look at. They hold up a mirror in which we are confronted with our darkest, most unflattering sides.

When you choose to deal with the powerful energy of the disowned sides of humanity that Jung called the shadow, there is a good chance of hitting raw nerves, and thus you always venture into potentially explosive territory. Predictably, Scorsese has repeatedly been the object of vehement outrage and controversy. Equally predictably, his detractors have an interesting tendency to take the imagined affront very personally, amputating and misrepresenting his films to the point where it reveals more about them than about the movie. They often manage to reduce his complex films to that which they themselves evidently abhor, choosing to see only the parts that offend and enrage them, and then holding Scorsese responsible for this. Although the following representative statements ought to be blatantly obvious, let me spell out that I am totally convinced that when Scorsese shows repulsive characters engaged in brutal behavior it does not mean that he advocates or encourages violence; when he shows misogynistic men who have an ingrown fear and hatred of women, who humiliate and abuse them, it does not mean that he believes women should be treated that way; when he shows Jesus Christ stepping down from the cross and living a normal human life with wives and children, it does not mean that he thinks that is what Christ should have done. In fact, as we shall see, his films (when regarded in their entirety) suggest the exact opposite.

That being said, the extreme reactions to Scorsese's work are perfectly understandable. His films touch upon deeply painful places inside us and affect us acutely. They *are* excruciating to watch, and they *do* prick at our most tender spots. They urge each and every one of us to accept that the darkness is inside ourselves; to surrender to the fact that only by owning our darkness can we truly claim our light and our magnificence. Whether we choose to get livid about his films, to dismiss them, reject them, or to take them to heart, use them as a mirror and take a long, hard look at ourselves, is up to each of us individually.

When asked why he wanted to make *The Last Temptation of Christ*, Scorsese said it was because he wanted to get to know Christ better. I initially started writing this book in an attempt to get to know Martin Scorsese better. This project has been with me for many years, and I have spent a significant part of my life exploring and analyzing his films, delving into and gradually internalizing the passion and the pain of Scorsese's work. Along the way on this quest I got to know myself better.

"The passage of the mythological hero may be over-ground, incidentally," said Joseph Campbell, but "fundamentally it is inward — into depths where obscure resistances are overcome, and long lost, forgotten powers are revivified, to be made available for the transfiguration of the world."[3] The central argument of this book is that Scorsese's films present us with an opportunity to look deep within ourselves and retrieve forgotten powers that we need if we are to transfigure and heal our lives and the world in which we live. It is my sincere hope that you will undertake this journey through the darkness and back into the light with me; that my work may provide you with a perspective to make the experience of Scorsese's films — and perhaps even your life — a more deliberate, conscious and joyful process.

It is as though movies answered an ancient
quest for the common unconscious.
They fulfill a spiritual need that people have
to share a common memory.
Martin Scorsese

Boris Lermontov: Why do you want to dance?
Victoria Page: Why do you want to live?
The Red Shoes

1

Something Being Done in Front of the Altar

> It is by going down into the abyss that we recover the treasures of life. Where you stumble, there lies your treasure. The very cave you are afraid to enter turns out to be the source of what you are looking for. The damned thing in the cave that was so dreaded has become the center.[1]
>
> Joseph Campbell

Throughout the history of mankind, stories, legends, and myths have been used to help us understand ourselves and the world in which we live. Often they speak the language of the unconscious, but the better we understand them consciously, the better we can use them to enrich our lives and develop into authentic human beings.

To illustrate their importance, mythologist Joseph Campbell uses the myth of Theseus who has to go into the labyrinth in Crete to fight the Minotaur. This is a double challenge: first, he has to slay the monster and survive; then, he has to find his way out. Fortunately, the king's daughter, Ariadne, is in love with him and gives him a thread that he can tie to the entrance of the labyrinth and unwind as he proceeds into it. When the time comes to leave, all he has to do is follow the thread back. If we compare the labyrinth to the journey, inner as well as outer, we all have to undertake in our lives, the stories we have heard or read are the equivalent of the thread. They enable us to go ever deeper without getting lost. "We have not even to risk the adventure alone," says Campbell, "for the heroes of all time have gone before us; the labyrinth is thoroughly known; we have only to follow the thread of the heropath."[2]

Storytelling is "older than the Pyramids, older than Stonehenge, older than the earliest cave paintings," one scholar says.[3] Martin Scorsese is a master storyteller who employs these ancient tools within that most distinctly modern art form: the moving image. His work manifests the sum total of his charismatic personality, his family history, his Catholic upbringing in Little Italy, and his seemingly endless knowledge of art, literature, mythology, music, and world cinema. Scorsese is more conscious of the power of stories than the majority of contemporary filmmakers, and his movies are deeply archetypal works that can help us face and embrace all aspects of ourselves — dark as well as light — if we dare to really see them. In this chapter we will examine some of the elements that form the basis of Scorsese's stories, laying out the various pieces of the puzzle, so to speak, in order to illuminate our journey through the deepest layers of each individual film.

The Dungeon Inside

"In the depths of every heart, there is a tomb and a dungeon, though the lights, the music, and revelry above may cause us to forget their existence, and the buried ones, or prisoners whom they hide," says Nathaniel Hawthorne in his story "The Haunted Mind."[4] In one way or another, all of Scorsese's films deal with those catacombs, the darker sides of the psyche. He ceaselessly forces us to look at those aspects of ourselves that, if disowned, turn into demons and ghosts which continue to haunt us until we find the courage to face them.

Hawthorne's description of the inner dungeon that most people constantly try to ignore is the perfect image of the psychological phenomenon that Carl G. Jung poetically named "the shadow" more than half a century later. During our early life we are urged by the conventions of the environment in which we grow up to repress the elements of our personality that are considered socially inappropriate. The rejected traits, thoughts, and feelings are stored deep inside us, and the shadow holds all the things we have been taught to consider unwanted. Our darkest, as well as our most brilliant, qualities are filtered off by the conscious ego because they are too painful or shameful or threatening to our surroundings and, therefore, to ourselves.

All over the Western world we tend to dismiss the irrationality of the unconscious in general and to ignore the shadow in particular. We prefer to think that if we just disregard it, it will go away. But, of course, it does not. Quite the contrary, because, as the saying goes, "What you can't be with, won't let you be." These undesired characteristics are still very much a part of who we are, and ignoring them not only makes us incomplete, but are potentially dangerous to ourselves and to our surroundings. Focusing all our energy on being acceptable to others entails extreme psychological instability and pain, and if we refuse to acknowledge our shadow self, there are powerful sides of us that we do not know and have no control over. The repressed shadow may then generate more energy than our ego and erupt suddenly and uncontrollably. And, as Jungian analyst Robert A. Johnson says, "The shadow gone autonomous is a terrible monster in our psychic house."[5]

Like all disowned unconscious elements, the negated shadow will express itself primitively, as we will see throughout this book. If we continually deny these perceived inner demons, they may end up possessing us in the sense that we *become* them, or we may project them onto others. Projection conveniently leads our attention away from ourselves. It allows us to deposit our shadows in the external world, blaming the things we do not want to believe ourselves capable of on others, instead of undertaking the painful process of knowing and accepting our total selves. The formation of the shadow is a healthy and necessary part of the civilizing process in our childhood. It is equally important, however, to learn to balance all sides of ourselves and restore wholeness later in life. If we neglect this process, according to Johnson, we are going to live "in a state of dividedness that grows more and more painful throughout our evolution."[6] The shadow is an integral part of our total self, and the light and the dark are necessary for each other to exist. Without light there would be no shadow to begin with, and without darkness the concept of light would make no sense.

The process of integrating the shadow is magnificently described in the prologue to the novel on which *The Last Temptation of Christ* is based: "Within me are the dark immemorial forces of the Evil One, human and pre-human; within me too are the luminous forces, human and pre-human of God — and my soul is the arena where these two armies have clashed and met."[7] The order in which this incessant battle is presented by Nikos Kazantzakis is significant: initially the powerful forces of light and darkness clash and then eventually a meeting takes place, which indicates consciously achieved harmony.

It is crucial to allow the dark side some time and space in which we face and accept it, and where it can do no harm to ourselves or others. This is referred to as "paying out the shadow" or "the shadow process." We can choose to do this in private, but a number of cultures have ceremonies or rituals which are used to that end. The Catholic Mass that Martin Scorsese attended zealously as a child is a perfect and rare example in Western culture of a ritual way of bringing light to the shadow.[8]

A large part of the entertainment industry — and, sadly, the most lucrative one — invites us to project our neglected shadow energy. Violent blockbusters continually provide us with convenient excuses to avoid the painful process of acknowledging our own darkness. This is doubly unfortunate because film as an art form is eminently suited as a modern ceremonial way of approaching the unconscious. Cinema in its very essence is an interaction between shadow and light. Like dreams, films consist of symbolic, ritual images that pass in front of us in the dark; images that we may, in part, understand unconsciously, but which we need to interpret if we want to know their full significance.

Joseph Campbell said that "dream is the personalized myth, myth the depersonalized dream."[9] Dreams belong in the realm of the individual unconscious, myths and films in the collective unconscious. Although dreaming entails a regression that the viewing of movies does not, in both cases we are exposed to images that are beyond the control of our conscious egos. Throughout his career, Scorsese has used the moving image to explore the unacknowledged shadow, and his films force us to look at ourselves and face those sides that we are most reluctant to admit to and accept.

Scorsese has often been criticized for his use of violence. Although the initial shock of watching the violence in his work may be sickening, there is nothing gratuitous about it.[10] It is a vital part of his concern with the dark side and the evil of man. In an attempt to explain this, Scorsese's late friend and mentor, British film director Michael Powell, once compared him to the painter Francisco Goya. After the Second May massacres, Goya spent the night walking through the streets of Madrid sketching mutilated corpses. His servant, who was holding the lantern, was horrified and asked Goya why he felt compelled to draw these terrible images. "To teach men forever not to be barbarians," was Goya's reply.[11] Scorsese never uses the horrifying images to get cheap thrills. Neither is violence in his films simply literal, physical violence. It belongs, to use Campbell's words, within "the labyrinth that we all know and visit in our dreams."[12] Like in the Catholic liturgy, blood-letting in Scorsese's work is part of a subtle, ritualized process meant to bring forth spiritual enlightenment, catharsis, and redemption.

Scorsese shows us that — like it or not — we all *are* barbarians somewhere inside. The sides of us that are hidden in the dungeon do not go away, and unless we acknowledge and own up to them, we will invariably *act* like barbarians. "Our shadows hold the essence of who we are," says Debbie Ford in *The Dark Side of the Light Chasers*. "They hold our most treasured gifts. By facing these aspects of ourselves, we become free to experience our glorious totality: the good and the bad, the dark and the light. It is by embracing all of who we are that we earn the freedom to choose what we do in this world. As long as we keep hiding, masquerading, and projecting what is inside us, we have no freedom to be and no freedom to choose."[13] Only when we are willing to face the darkest sides of ourselves can we accept full responsibility for them, and stop unconsciously acting out the same destructive scenarios over and over.

Needless to say, owning up to our dark sides is not something that happens automatically just by watching Scorsese's films — nor is it something we can do once and for all and be done with. It is a lifelong process that takes a lot of hard work. This is precisely the reason why we have an acute need for artists who can provide us with rituals for facing the dungeon, for aiding us in the process of consciously realizing who we are, and healing our wounds. Scorsese's work can be viewed as a modern, secularized counterpart to the Catholic Mass; a place where we can — and, in fact, are forced to — face and pay out the shadow. If we view his films from this perspective, they are extremely valuable, not only as great cinematic art, but as tools for us to understand and come to terms with ourselves and one another.

The Dark Night of the Soul

Let us begin our journey into the works of Martin Scorsese by learning "to think mythologically," as Robert A. Johnson says.[14] The most fundamental story in all cultures concerns the strenuous voyage of a boy or girl, man or woman, who has to leave home and venture into the unknown to face and overcome obstacles. This narrative structure has been used through all times in myths, religious scripture, fairy tales, epic poems, songs, novels, and moving pictures. The hero path leads into the realm of darkness where the protagonist is subjected to a grueling ordeal and has to look death in the face. After a symbolic death and rebirth, he or she is able to seize the magical object that is the reward — be it a treasure, grail, magical sword, or special knowledge — and to truly deserve it.[15]

The ultimate purpose of the hero's journey is always to enable him to become a better, more evolved person, and the tribulations he is faced with, however horrifying they may appear, are always precisely that which is needed to make him grow, as are the allies and enemies that await at each turn of the road.[16] The outer quest is a metaphor for a psychological or spiritual quest, and it echoes archetypal experiences known to all human beings. Cheryl Richardson defines grace as "a kind of spiritual intelligence." She says that if we have the courage to align ourselves with it "we wake up and suddenly become aware of signs, symbols, and messages that lead to our highest good."[17]

Martin Scorsese's work is deeply embedded in this basic mythical structure. Each of his films concerns a protagonist who has to go into unfamiliar territory and through a horrific trial. The outer landscape can be seen as a reflection of his mind or soul, and always the purpose of the journey is to expose the sides of himself that he has disowned and force him to face them. Grace is available for him, and he is offered a chance through his suffering to redeem himself, to face his shadow sides and embrace the totality of who he is.

In many of Scorsese's films there is a sense of circularity so that at the end the character is right back where he started. This echoes the basic structure of myths and fairy tales — home, away from home, back home again — and is inherently connected to one of Scorsese's central themes: death and resurrection. The climactic point of the hero path is the supreme ordeal — often referred to as "the inmost cave" or "the belly of the whale" — which St. John of the Cross called "the dark night of the soul." At this nightmarish stage one has to face one's darkest demons, and the ego is forced to surrender in order to bring about transformation and enlightenment. "When our day is come for the victory of death," says Campbell, "there is nothing we can do, except be crucified — and resurrected; dismembered totally, and then reborn."[18] At the end of the story when the resurrected hero returns home, he is a different person from the one who ventured out. The crucial question is whether or not he has acknowledged whatever it is he was denying. If so, he may move on to a higher level of spiritual awareness, if not, he is doomed to repeat the same pattern until he does.[19]

Martin Scorsese frequently plays with our perception of reality. Since he directed his first short films at New York University, Scorsese has always juxtaposed realism with various forms of non-realism. He provocatively plays off the outer, objectively verifiable, communal reality against the subjective, sometimes distorted inner reality of the individual. He counterpoints literal and physical reality with psychological, metaphysical and mythological reality, the conscious with the unconscious.

Considering his background, this is not all that surprising. Incorporating the fantastic and mystical into ordinary everyday life is done as a matter of course in the Roman Catholic Church, and the conflation of parallel realities, material and spiritual, realistic and mythological, has always been a part of Scorsese's life in the form of the ancestral stories from Sicily that were told in his childhood home.

Psychologist Dorothy Rowe says that we have to be able to "distinguish what goes on inside us from what goes on outside us and to knit together in some consistent way our inner and outer realities" so that we are able to relate to them but still perceive them as separate; to develop our own identities and still be able to coexist with others. Rowe says this process "is what psychologists call 'reality testing,' and the inefficiency of this process is their measure of madness."[20] Scorsese is well aware of this basic definition and its relevance for his work: "I don't think," he says, "that there is any difference between fantasy and reality in the way these should be approached in a film. Of course, if you live that way you are clinically insane."[21]

The term Gothic has been used to describe several of Scorsese's films by his collaborators, various critics and by Scorsese himself. Indeed, outer physical landscapes often reflect inner psychological landscapes in Scorsese's work as in a number of classic Gothic works. The concept of home—the physical space where the hero's journey conventionally begins and ends—is one of Scorsese's most central symbolic motifs. There is a general lack of domestic happiness in his work, and often a safe, loving home does not seem to be in the cards for his characters. Many of his characters do not have a home of their own, but still live with their mother. Some have left home and are permanent wanderers, constantly on the move. Some are searching for a new home, a place to belong, a family who will accept and applaud them. Some are stifled and restricted by their home and the rules of the tribe that prevent them from growing. Some have homes that are invaded by disruptive intruders. Some are forcibly expelled from home and into exile. Some are forced to make a painful choice between the domesticity that most people enjoy as a matter or course and their God-given vocation.

Architectural structures have always been important in Gothic literature and film. The classic tales were set in deserted castles or isolated abbeys in faraway regions in the comfortably distant past. Modern Gothic tales moved into the present, into relatively ordinary houses in cities, towns or suburbs that are uncomfortably familiar to the audience. Iconographical, architectural and geographical elements play a crucial role in Scorsese's films, too. Houses, rooms, hallways, basements, staircases, doors, locks, and keys have symbolic functions—always, if one looks closely, reflecting the minds of the main character. Doors, locks and keys logically signify the connecting point between outer and inner, conscious and unconscious. "There are things known and things unknown, and in between are the doors," said Jim Morrison. This image is double-edged: doors imply things that are hidden, that we cannot see or refuse to look at, in which case they prevent us from growing. At the same time, doors are crucial as partitions between the known and the unknown, as shields against looking at too much too soon, in which case it protects us from falling into the abyss of psychosis.

Cellars are the perfect graphic illustration of Hawthorne's dungeon, and underground spaces are used very effectively by Scorsese, notably in films such as *Cape Fear*, *After Hours*, and *Gangs of New York*. In *The King of Comedy*, Rupert Pupkin occupies a room that is situated in the basement. Although logically it must be surrounded by a whole house, we never see him in the rest of it. He seems to be living solely in this slightly unreal room that drastically changes appearance, which makes it apposite to read it as an internal landscape that reflects Rupert's inability to distinguish between inner and outer reality. In both *Taxi Driver* and *The King of Comedy* the camera stays focused on an empty hallway for an unnaturally long time — Scorsese says that this is the single-most important shot in *Taxi Driver*. The emptiness emphasizes the intense loneliness of the main character, and these shots confirm our suspicion that something is very wrong with his ability to communicate with other people.

Connected with the notion of doors and locks (and strongly suggesting the negated shadow trapped inside our inner dungeon) is the motif of prisons, which is used in a good number of Scorsese's films. In *It's Not Just You, Murray!*, *Mirror, Mirror*, *GoodFellas*, and *The Departed* the main character goes to jail. In *Raging Bull*, Jake's self-torment culminates in the Dade County Stockade. At the beginning of *Cape Fear*, Max Cady comes out of jail and the conflict is caused by the very fact that he was there. At the end of *The King of Comedy*, Rupert's celebrity status begins when he goes to jail, and at the end of *Taxi Driver* Travis Bickle's begins when, unexpectedly, he does not. At the end of *The Last Temptation of Christ*, Jesus is arrested in Gethsemane, and at the end of *Kundun*, the Dalai Lama escapes to India to avoid being arrested. In a slightly less literal manner, Mr. Sillerton Jackson in *The Age of Innocence* says of the Countess Olenska that her husband kept her a prisoner. At the beginning of *The Aviator* young Howard's mother enchants him into a life of self-imposed isolation by means of the word "quarantine." From beginning to end, the entire journey of Teddy Daniels in *Shutter Island* takes place on an insular treatment facility for the criminally insane.

The idea of the mirror as a gateway to the hidden, distorted side has been used effectively by artists like Lewis Carroll, Ingmar Bergman and David Lynch. Scorsese, too, uses mirrors and parallel realities extensively, as we shall see, manifestly in the iconic "You talkin' to me?" scene in *Taxi Driver*. This emphasizes the fact that on deeper levels, Scorsese's films concern each and every one of us: they are mirrors that are held up so that we are forced to take a close look at ourselves and our inner demons. Whether or not we own up to the troubling, dark sides Scorsese reveals, it is painful to watch them displayed, larger than life, on a gigantic screen in a theater filled with other people — so painful, in fact, that people frequently find it necessary to dismiss Scorsese's work using one excuse or another.

Hostile Brothers and Alter Egos

One of Scorsese's many memorable mirror scenes is the final moments of *Raging Bull* in which Jake La Motta is sitting in his dressing room, rehearsing the car scene from *On the Waterfront*. Like Terry Malloy, Jake used to be a boxer and feels betrayed by his brother who persuaded him to sell out and lose an important fight. Jake has not been able to work out his conflict with Joey in real life, and he is now trying to resolve it by acting it out in front of the mirror, talking to his real-life brother as well as to a brother inside himself.[22]

It is logical to associate our shadow with our mirror image: "The mirror," says Jung, "lies behind the mask and shows the true face."[23] Marie-Louise von Franz, one of his closest associates, calls our dreams "the realization of the shadow." The shadow, she says, "contains values that are needed by consciousness," and if we refuse to listen to its vital information, the shadow will appear in our dreams.[24] When it does, Dr. von Franz says, it is often personified, has the same gender as the dreamer, and invades the dreamer's house.

One of the ways in which Scorsese uncovers and illuminates the dark side is through his use of protagonist and antagonist. The majority of his films are centered around the relationship between two very different male characters. In the course of the film, one is led through tortuous tribulations by the other who functions as an annoying and inconvenient nemesis, a kind of twisted Jiminy Cricket who will not let him complacently lie to himself. It is pertinent to see these two characters as the conscious ego that is struggling with the shadow which has been repressed so long that it has materialized.

Jung says that we all have "a sinister and frightful brother, our own flesh-and-blood counterpart, who holds and maliciously hoards everything that we would so willingly hide under the table."[25] What he describes is the personified shadow and the related archetype, the hostile brothers. Examples of this archetype can be found in most cultures. In the Western world we see it in works such as the Bible, the novels of John Steinbeck, the plays of Sam Shepard, the music of Bruce Springsteen, Bob Dylan, and Kris Kristofferson.[26] The concept of the hostile brother, a distorted mirror image come to life as an independent person, forms a potent link between the abstract notion of the shadow and the troubled relationships between the protagonist and the antagonist in the films of Martin Scorsese.

Scorsese has often referred to the characters played by Harvey Keitel in *Who's That Knocking at My Door?* and *Mean Streets* as his alter ego. Throughout the opening of *Mean Streets*, we hear Charlie's thoughts as inner monologue. The voice we hear is extremely puzzling because it does not *quite* sound like Harvey Keitel. In actual fact, it was recorded as a scratch track, intercutting the voices of Scorsese and Keitel, resulting in an acoustic equivalent of the famous shot in Bergman's *Persona* when half of Liv Ullmann's face is superimposed over Bibi Anderson's. This accentuates Charlie's function as Scorsese's alter ego since we must assume that the thoughts expressed reflect both of them. Scorsese explains that for him, merging his own voice with Keitel's was "a way of trying to come to terms with myself, trying to redeem myself."[27]

One dictionary of psychology defines "alter ego" as "a person so close to oneself that he or she seems to be a 'second self.'"[28] This description precisely captures the Keitel characters who are extensions of Scorsese himself and reflect sides of his personality and his life. Like Scorsese, they are different from the neighborhood characters that surround them, and they do not quite fit into the street life of Little Italy. Charlie is torn between the rules of the street and the rules of the church, and like the characters played by Leonardo DiCaprio in Scorsese's later films, J.R. and Charlie truly endeavor to be good men against daunting odds.

The roles Robert De Niro has played in Scorsese's films are more diverse. On an immediate level, characters like Travis Bickle, Jake La Motta, Rupert Pupkin, and Max Cady are much more unsympathetic than Keitel's characters.[29] They are forces of destruction and seem mentally unhinged. Yet De Niro's position in Scorsese's work is so significant that it leads one to wonder whether these disagreeable characters do not in a less obvious way represent aspects of Scorsese, too.

Scorsese has acknowledged that in his life he has felt like both Jerry Langford and Rupert Pupkin of *The King of Comedy*, which makes it possible to assume that the other pairs of men, who in their structural function resemble Rupert and Jerry, are related to him as well. Steven Spielberg once said he believes that "Marty allows Bobby to do the violence — to lose control so Marty can stay *in* control."[30] De Niro regards his roles similarly, saying that they allow him to experience life through these twisted characters "without having to risk the real-life consequences."[31] Presumably, all art reflects sides of the artist, and the unpleasant characters Scorsese has created are expressions of things that he, like the rest of us, has inside; things that we cannot and should not live out in the outer world, but that we need to acknowledge and own up to. Interestingly, it is possible to characterize the abhorrent De Niro characters as alter egos, too, since the same dictionary defines "shadow" as "a complex of undeveloped feelings, ideas, desires ... the 'alter ego.'"[32] In other words, "alter ego" can mean an extension of the conscious ego as well as a manifestation of the shadow.

In Henrik Ibsen's play *Peer Gynt* there is a scene in which The Lean One tries to explain basic human psychology to Peer by using as a metaphor a newfangled invention called photography: "Remember, in two ways a man can be himself— there's a right and wrong side to the jacket. You know they have lately discovered in Paris a way to take portraits by help of the sun. One can either produce a straightforward picture, or else what is known as a negative one. In the latter the lights and the shades are reversed, and they're apt to seem ugly to commonplace eyes; but for all that the likeness is latent in them, and all you require is to bring it out."[33]

Scorsese has repeatedly used photography and negative images — inherently linked to film as an art form — for symbolic purposes. Like The Lean One, he is concerned with the relationship between the pictures that are straightforward and those that look so hideous to commonplace eyes merely because the lights and the shades have been reversed. Where the early Keitel characters represent the normal, positive photograph, the "right side to the jacket," the De Niro characters are often the distorted negative image that nevertheless has an undeniable likeness to our own face. Where Harvey Keitel is alter ego as second self, Robert De Niro is alter ego as shadow.

Mean Streets contains both alter egos — Scorsese's second self and the shadow. Charlie is the guilt-ridden young man who is trying to come to terms with his Catholicism and the Little Italy neighborhood, making feeble attempts at leaving. Johnny Boy is his semi-moronic tormentor, an important part of what is holding him back. The two of them are inextricably connected, almost as if they were two sides of the same person; the dubious saint and the importunate idiot. In that film, however, there is a third character who represents a significant piece of the overall picture, namely Teresa. Amy Robinson, who played the role, has intelligently pointed out that Teresa is closely related to Scorsese in that she is "a character who wanted to get out of the neighborhood. Harvey's character really didn't, and I think once you know Marty, you know his struggle to get out himself, I think the character of Teresa in a way has a lot in common with Marty."[34] Certainly, Teresa's epilepsy echoes Scorsese's asthma.

In the final scene, Charlie and Teresa try to help Johnny Boy escape from Michael, whom he has insulted and ridiculed. The three characters are in a car on their way to Brooklyn when Michael catches up with them. He has hired a professional killer who starts shooting at their car. This hit-man is played by Scorsese himself, and he has said about this scene that he was trying to kill off his alter egos, but that that is of course not possible. Since he is shooting not only at Charlie and Johnny Boy, but also at Teresa, in a sense he reveals that he, too, thinks of her as an alter ego, a side of himself and of an overall symbolic picture.

Teresa is a more mature, intelligent force that is urging Charlie to break free from his uncle and his friends and create a life for himself. She is intrinsically connected to Charlie by flesh (she is his lover) and to Johnny Boy by blood (she is his cousin). Where Johnny represents the shadow, Teresa (like most female characters in Scorsese's films) could be seen as representing the anima, the archetypically feminine side of the protagonist's personality that could help him take giant steps in his individuation process if he would only listen to her.

The animus is the male element in the female unconscious; the anima is the female element in the male unconscious. "In the Middle Ages, long before the physiologists demonstrated that by reason of our glandular structure there are both male and female elements in all of us," says Carl Jung, "it was said that 'every man carries a woman within himself.'"[35] The animus and anima are just as significant and potentially disruptive as the shadow. When the shadow appears in dreams, myths and stories, it is usually of the same gender as the dreamer or central character. When the animus or anima appears, it is by definition of the opposite sex. Many of the characteristics of the shadow are true of the anima as well. Like the shadow, she holds truths that can help a man grow and develop if he pays attention and attempts to establish a relationship with her, and she can become one of his strongest allies as the mediator between his conscious ego and his unconscious inner world. Also like the shadow, however, she can wreak havoc when she is ignored or repressed. Then she may turn into a dangerous or even deadly force, a demon or femme fatale, expressing herself primitively through complexes and projection.

We encounter the personified anima quite often in Scorsese's work, and his female characters are frequently related to "Mother" in the sense that, as Marie-Louise von Franz says, "The character of a man's anima is as a rule shaped by his mother."[36] The man who negates his anima may end up helplessly stuck in a mother complex or a Madonna/whore complex, or he may project his unacknowledged anima energy onto women outside himself, detesting or falling madly in love with women he hardly knows, incapable of seeing them as real persons separate from his own projection. "Were it simply the fact that the woman is so wonderful or so awful, we could either love her or leave her, but if we can do neither, then we are under the arresting spell of the archetype," says Edward Whitmont.[37]

The majority of Scorsese's male protagonists are trapped in a mother complex, and many are stuck in variations of the Madonna/whore complex. Some are even drawn to whores that they feel compelled to transform into Madonnas. A number of the films present us with girl-women who are seductive and strangely world-wise: Bertha in *Boxcar Bertha*, Iris in *Taxi Driver*, Vickie in *Raging Bull*, Marcy in *After Hours*, Paulette in *Life Lessons*, Danielle in *Cape Fear*, May in *The Age of Innocence*, Rose in *Bringing Out the Dead*, and Faith Domergue in *The Aviator*. These often mirror a split inside the protagonist who feels threatened by strong, self-reliant women.

Scorsese is sometimes accused of misogyny, but just as his use of violence reflects the shadow process of his characters (rather than a morbid fascination with barbarity on the director's behalf), so his female characters and the attitude toward them mirror the anima process, the emotional state of his male characters, which is often unhealthy and infantile. Just like the antagonist often represents the materialized shadow, so Scorsese's female characters frequently represent the materialized anima, and Scorsese's women are generally more intelligent, sympathetic and independent than his men.

In the final analysis "the projection can only be dissolved," Jung says, "when a son sees that in the realm of his psyche there is an image not only of the mother but of the daughter, the sister, the beloved, the heavenly goddess."[38] Newland in *The Age of Innocence* chooses the immature May over Ellen, the independent adult who is his equal. Paul Hackett is chased through Lower Manhattan by a whole pack of unruly women in *After Hours*. The philandering of Howard Hughes in *The Aviator* reaches epic proportions. The central character of *Shutter Island* sacrifices his sanity, indeed his very identity, rather than face the true nature of his wife and their relationship. Only in *Bringing Out the Dead* and *Gangs of New York* is harmony achieved at the end between the wounded male ego and the inner feminine power of the unconscious as well as the outer feminine aspect of a real woman.

Italianamerican

Before we begin our voyage into the fictional works of Martin Scorsese, let us briefly examine his origins and his personal background, which figure centrally in his films. Martin Marcantonio Luciano Scorsese was born on November 17, 1942, in Queens, New York, the second son of Charles and Catherine Scorsese. For thirty years, until their deaths in 1993 and 1997, respectively, his parents played an exceptionally active role in his career, playing cameo roles in his films and giving interviews that provide crucial information about the context out of which Scorsese's filmic style emerged. Their personalities and the family pattern they impart put into perspective important psychological mechanisms in Scorsese's work. Their most significant contribution is their starring parts in *Italianamerican*, a 45-minute film Scorsese made in 1974. It was shot over a weekend in the family's apartment on Elizabeth Street and is, Scorsese says, the documentary counterpart to *Mean Streets*. It shows us two remarkable human beings with their own gripping stories, but in addition it can be seen as a representative portrait of an entire ethnic community.

Italianamerican consists mainly of Catherine's and Charles's narratives about their background and their ancestors from the old country, to which Scorsese has added traditional Italian music, stills of family members, and old footage of anonymous immigrants arriving in America and working at hard physical labor. The film is a study in making the ultimate documentary. Catherine and Charles are obviously on friendly terms with the crew, and so they let go of whatever defenses people normally have in front of a camera. They are aware of being recorded, but it does not seem to bother or inhibit them. We thus get an unusually honest portrait of two people and their relationship, and the film is both touching and embarrassing to watch. From the moment the camera starts rolling, they bicker over things that on the surface appear to be trivialities, but which in fact concern extremely basic psychological and emotional issues known to all of us.

The unsurpassed star is the exuberant Catherine Scorsese, known to friends and relatives as Katie, and the film is structured around her cooking and serving her famous spaghetti sauce. Thus Mother and the family meal form the backbone of the film as of the Italian-American community. We cut back and forth between the voluble Catherine, fervently braising and boiling in the kitchen, and the soft-spoken Charles on the obligatorily plastic-covered sofa in the living room. Her vibrant emotional energy overshadows everyone else, and her husband, softly protesting, gets a chance to speak uninterruptedly only when she cannot hear him in the kitchen. In the rare glimpses we see of him, Marty is unusually reticent, trying gently to defend his father.

In the old days, Charles says, the telling of stories was very important, because there was no radio and no TV. Indeed, both parents are marvelously gifted storytellers, and their anecdotes give us clues to the origins of Scorsese's narrative craftsmanship and central motifs. Charles has a thick New York accent, and, like his son and many of his fictional characters, he speaks with machine-gun fire rapidity, repeating the key words of each sentence three or four times to make sure he is understood. He reminisces about the various immigrant groups in the neighborhood. The original inhabitants were the Irish, but when he was a boy, Italian and Jewish traders lived side by side, and he used to light the stoves for the Jews on Delancey Street on the Sabbath.

Many of the tales that were told ritually in Marty's childhood home take place in Sicily before Charles and Catherine were born. Most magnificent is the story about the silver ghost. After Catherine's father had left for America to create a new life for them, her mother was alone in Sicily with their firstborn baby. Once she woke up in the middle of the night, and at the foot of her bed was a man dressed in silver. "If you hit me with something, I will make you rich," he said. The young woman panicked and could not move, and the

Charles Scorsese and Catherine Scorsese in their living room on Little Italy's Elizabeth Street where Marty grew up. In the film *Italianamerican* (National Communications Foundation, 1974) he interviewed his parents about their life in New York and family history in Sicily.

mysterious man vanished as suddenly as he had appeared. Years later when they tore down the house, they found a fortune in silver coins in the ground underneath it. Catherine speculates about the veracity of this story. It sounds incredible, she knows, but she cannot believe that her mother would lie. Instead of the objectively verifiable reality commonly accepted as the truth, she chooses an alternative, metaphysical reality. This tendency, like the motif of seemingly frightening but potentially bountiful things hidden underneath the surface, is consistently found in the works of her son.

At one point Charles, hoping to get away with it, complains that Catherine is putting on airs for the cameraman in the kitchen. She instantly strides into the living room and sits down next to him with an amazingly friendly "Are you looking for a fight or something, dear?" evoking a distinct echo of Travis Bickle's "You talkin' to me?"

Implicitly and unconsciously, Scorsese's parents reveal deeply personal things about their repeated family patterns, and quite possibly about family patterns in general. They were both children of poor Sicilian immigrants and grew up in the crowded tenements on the Lower East Side of Manhattan, on Elizabeth Street, in the heart of Little Italy. Charles's father came to America around the turn of the century at the age of 19, and in Charles's childhood home, he tells us, nine people lived in four small rooms: the parents, five children, and two boarders. In Katie's home fourteen people were crammed into a three-room apartment. Both their fathers were physically absent from the home during the week and extraneous when they were present. Charles's father worked in the hull of a ship and only came home on weekends, or he worked at night and slept during the day. Catherine's father was a scaffold-maker in New Jersey. He left on Monday mornings and came home Friday nights, she tells us. Once he shaved off his mustache during the week, and when he came home his children started crying because they did not recognize him.

If the father was scarcely felt in the home, the mother was a vibrant and autocratic person. All through *Italianamerican* Charles and Catherine engage in seemingly innocent quibbles that have to do with Charles's mother, who was apparently even more formidable than his wife. We are told repeatedly how strong and capable and fierce this woman was. Charles proudly tells us that his father never got into arguments or fights because the men in this unbelievably tough neighborhood were afraid of his wife, Charles's mother. Toward the end of *Italianamerican*, when the three of them — Catherine, Charles and Marty — are feasting on the lavish spaghetti dinner comes the most shattering moment of the film. Charles tries to sum up his mother's personality: "My mother was a — she was a real whip!" After this ambiguous description, he is deeply moved, almost tearful, and a long silence, suffused with a dizzying mixture of overpowering emotions, follows. Two decades later Scorsese would explain this moment in the film: its real significance, he says, was "what he left unsaid about his family and his mother. That's why I let the camera roll. The silence implied much more than anything they could say."[39]

These patterns that they grew up in were repeated with variations in Marty's childhood home. More than once Catherine insists that Charles move closer to her on the sofa. "See, Marty," she laments, "every time I sit close to him, he moves away!" When Charles comes home from work, she says, he never talks to her: "Talk to me!" she both pleads and challenges him. Charles's response is a mumbled "What can you tell a person after you've been with them for 40 years?" At one point Charles boldly states that it is commonly known that men are better cooks than women. When Catherine wants to know why he is not doing the cooking then, he seems to know that he has gone too far and mutters, "Not supposed to!

Not my line!"⁴⁰ He timidly explains that when he comes home after a long day at work, all he wants is to sit in his chair and not be bothered with anything. She, on the other hand, has been by herself all day and craves intimacy and affection. Both their positions are perfectly understandable, and their honesty gives us a rare glimpse of something that is recognizable and familiar for many people: the wife and mother who is single-handedly responsible for keeping everything together, and the fatigued breadwinner who is reluctant to participate.

The father was frequently absent in the various Scorsese households, and when he was present, he was too passive or weak to be a match for the headstrong mother. These roles that Charles and Catherine Scorsese have inherited are typical of recently researched general family patterns in the twentieth century. The missing father is such a recurring phenomenon that he is now considered a new archetype, and Susan Faludi argues that the fatherless hero is one of the most prevalent figures in our society as well as our cultural expressions.

The way Scorsese uses parents in his films is fascinating. It has always been a favorite sport among Alfred Hitchcock's fans to try and spot his cameo appearances in his movies. Like the Master of Suspense, Scorsese appears regularly in his own films, but it pays off to look out for his parents as well. Catherine Scorsese's roles in her son's films are usually as a maternal figure. Her debut in *It's Not Just You, Murray!* is as the mother of the title character, and her sole function is to appear at regular intervals, often out of nowhere, bringing food. In the credits her character is listed simply as "Mother," which could be taken to mean several interrelated things. The nurturing Italian Mama represents not just Murray's mother, but the mother archetype. By extension, a number of Scorsese's male characters are not *men* so much as *sons*, and many of them still live with their mother well past the age when that is customary or healthy. The phrasing of this credit also calls to mind Hitchcock's films, and serves as a subtle reminder of the mother complex: the potentially dark and stifling aspects of Mother — especially when Father is weak or missing — if the caring and pampering is allowed to get out of control and the son allows himself to get stuck in it. The reference to Hitchcock is emphasized when Murray tells us that his mother only ever gave him one piece of advice: "Eat first!" We *see* Mother's mouth forming those words but the voice we *hear* is Murray's. As in Psycho, an unsettling symbiosis of mother and son is implied.

Mother is often present in Scorsese's work, and even when she is not she has a conspicuous influence over her son. As in *It's Not Just You, Murray!*, we have a feeling that she could appear at any moment without warning, so in a sense she is a constant presence. The mother in *The King of Comedy* is never seen but only heard (as Catherine Scorsese's voice) when she shouts admonitions to her son from someplace above, for all practical purposes a superego hovering over him. The male characters in the early films are thwarted sexually by this looming reprimand which is partly their own subconscious awareness of mother, and partly the influence of the Catholic faith of which Mother is the primary practitioner in the family. In *Who's That Knocking at My Door?* this is symbolized by a small white Madonna statuette that connects the Immaculate Mother with the physically manifested mother to whom it belongs. Father is less often seen or even mentioned in Scorsese's work. In fact, the main object of the hero's journey that many of his later characters have to undergo — notably in the DiCaprio films — is precisely coming to terms with the painful fact that Father is missing.

According to Martin Scorsese, *Italianamerican* made him see his parents as individuals rather than just parents. "I learned that they had a life before I was born. I guess that's what all children learn after a while. They didn't start with me." He continues: "Normally at a certain age you push your parents *away*," "but when I started making movies, it was more or less embracing the situation, saying, 'Look, this is where I come from.'"[41]

The Streets, the Church, the Movies

By the time Marty was born, the Scorseses, like many other second generation immigrants, had managed to escape the slummy tenements of the Lower East Side. The family — consisting of Charles, Catherine, Martin, and his older brother Frank — now lived in Corona, in Queens, in a two-family house with a yard that actually (Scorsese remembers) "had a tree in it."[42] When Marty was about six years old, the family had to move back to Little Italy because Charles Scorsese ran into business problems. For several months, they lived with Martin's grandparents on the very block on Elizabeth Street where Charles was born. Then they found a place of their own on that same street.

The streets of Little Italy were sharply divided, and Elizabeth Street, predominantly Sicilian, had its own set of laws. For a small boy, the move to the city was a terrifying experience, Scorsese says. The fact that he had contracted asthma and was not strong physically must have added to the shock. "I was old enough to realize that there were some tough guys around," he remembers. "You might be playing in a sandbox and something would fall behind you — not a bag of garbage, as you might expect, but a little baby that had fallen off the roof!"[43] This kind of experience has undoubtedly shaped Scorsese's attitude toward violence, which is always shown in his films as supremely appalling.

Several of Scorsese's films take place in the savage city streets — some in the actual streets where he grew up, some in other streets into whose innermost workings he seems to have an extraordinarily keen insight. A number of his characters, he says, are based on neighborhood types he used to know, and quite of few of his recurring themes and stylistic trademarks have their roots in this area, as does his use of street vernacular. His firsthand knowledge of the mentality of various mobsters in the old neighborhood has enabled him to give us the most unembellished and unglamorous portrayals of the masculine, Italian-American, urban subculture we are ever likely to see on film.

Often when his use of violence has been criticized, Scorsese has protested that it is neither possible nor morally defensible to represent organized crime without honestly showing how brutal it is. Actually, a main concern in his work which he got from his father is the question of how it is possible to "live a good Christian life" when "outside in the street, life is ruled by the gun."[44] Even as a child, he says, it was difficult for him to reconcile the beliefs he was brought up on with the bestiality he witnessed in the streets of Little Italy.

From an early age, he was concerned with such moral issues, and throughout his childhood the Roman Catholic Church was a powerful influence. His neighborhood church was the stunning and picturesque St. Patrick's Old Cathedral on Mott Street, in which he later shot scenes for *Who's That Knocking at My Door?* and *Mean Streets*. Father Francis Principe remembers that Marty was an altar boy "at a time when the liturgy was tremendously dramatic. Can you imagine a young boy — at midnight Mass on Christmas in this very large church with this absolutely mind-boggling, beautiful sanctuary, with these magnificent statues and magnificent organ and at midnight Mass? It has to be just overwhelming."[45] The Catholic Church and the streets of Little Italy, although antitheses, were inextricably connected in Scorsese's mind, and the juxtaposition of the sacramentalism of the Church with the ritualized rules of the streets play a central role in his early films. In *Mean Streets*, the first lines we hear are: "You don't make up for your sins in the church! You do it in the streets! You do it at home! The rest is bullshit, and you know it!"

When he was eight or nine years old, Scorsese decided that he wanted to become a priest. He had discovered that only three groups of people were respected in his neighborhood: wise guys, gang leaders, and priests. Because of his asthma the first two "career choices" were out of the question, and the Church was even more revered anyway. "The organized crime figures would tip their hats to a priest and watch their language, and they would have their cars and pets blessed."[46] So at the age of 14, he went to Cathedral College, a junior seminary on the Upper West Side of New York. After a year, however, he was expelled. He says that he was distracted by a young woman, whereas his parents maintain that he had difficulty with Latin. Whatever the reason, his grades were not good enough to get him into the Jesuit University at Fordham, and eventually he decided instead to attend New York University — taking Film Studies as his major and English as his minor — a decision that would change the course of his life as well as the history of film.

The period of the 1960s was seminal both in terms of the history of motion pictures and the way the United States of America regarded itself. Scorsese entered the film program at New York University in 1960, at the age of 17, when the movement known as the French New Wave was at its peak, and it would prove to be one of the most powerful influences on young filmmakers. Its revitalizing reinvention of film aesthetics, its emphasis on creative freedom and on the supremacy of the director as the artistic creator inspired new cinematic waves all over the world. Scorsese acknowledges the astounding impact of the New Wave in that it gave film students a sense of artistic freedom, of being able to do anything they wanted. For him, he says the first two minutes of *Jules and Jim* were "the most liberating of all; I still use it as an example to writers I am working with."[47] He further acknowledges the influence of François Truffaut on his films: "There are certain shots that Truffaut did," he says, "which I will never get out of my system. There's a shot in *Shoot the Piano Player* when the girl is pressing the door button, carrying the violin case. He cuts three times, coming in closer each time. That shot's in every picture I make, and I don't know why."[48]

Most of Scorsese's cine-literate contemporaries — among them Steven Spielberg, George Lucas, and Francis Ford Coppola — attended the renowned film programs in California, but Scorsese feels that staying in New York gave him several artistic advantages. Important plays and films were shown in New York that never made it to the West Coast: "In California you're cut off from everything, and that can be very destructive for a New Yorker," he says.[49] Paradoxically, he feels that his greatest advantage was the fact that N.Y.U. did not have the technical equipment that the West Coast schools did. One major reason his style is so different from that of his famous colleagues, he says, is that New York University was focused on ideas rather than technique "just because our cameras were older."[50]

The shaping influence during those years was Scorsese's teacher and mentor Haig Manoogian whose support and exceptional talents as a lecturer would have a lasting impact. Often they disagreed in their evaluation of films. Manoogian was of the old school and considered as artists only the masters among the European writer-directors. Scorsese, like the other emerging American directors, had a sense of the equal importance of his own cinematic heritage, the classic Hollywood movies he had watched while growing up. When Scorsese decided to write his thesis on *The Third Man*, Manoogian strongly questioned the artistic value of what he considered merely entertainment. Scorsese, however, was excited by the auteur theory formulated by the directors of the New Wave. "They told us in film school that we had to like only Bergman," he says. "Now Bergman's good, but he isn't the only one. I discovered that I had liked most of the films those auteurist guys were talking about." It was "like some fresh air," he says, because you no longer had to "reject totally the films you liked as a child."[51]

With a Supreme Court ruling in 1948, the Hollywood studios had lost their monopolistic position. As a result, and with the rising popularity of television, the power of the old studio system gradually declined during the 1950s, and no new structure was there to take its once-omnipotent place. A few pioneer directors — notably John Frankenheimer, John Cassavetes and Arthur Penn — had tried since the late 1950s to formulate a new American cinema, and their tremendous vision inspired Scorsese, because, as he says, "Cassavetes had used a lightweight 16 mm camera for *Shadows* in 1959, so there were no more excuses. If he could do it, so could we!"[52]

However, not until 1967, the year Scorsese finished his graduate studies, was the public ready for the ideas that had been fermenting for almost a decade. Major upheavals had taken place since the assassination of John F. Kennedy. The youth revolt and student unrest were incontestable factors, and young audiences were ready for films that reflected the world as they knew it. With the release of *Bonnie and Clyde* and *The Graduate*, the new American cinema became indisputable. The two films were critical successes as well as box-office hits; both were nominated for Academy Awards in all the major categories, firmly placing the new cinema within the mainstream.

As a result of the enormous success of these films, American directors gained a hitherto-unknown creative independence, and an overwhelming number of remarkable films followed. It was now possible for the young directors to explore their own ideas and direct their own visions in much the same way that the French directors had a decade earlier. At the same time, the concepts of storytelling were being challenged within the literary world as well, and the publication in 1966 of Truman Capote's *In Cold Blood* forever blurred the line between fact and fiction. This general climate of rebellion and reinvention was what Scorsese stepped right into when he finished film school.[53]

In retrospect, film seems like the only logical alternative to the priesthood as a calling for Martin Scorsese. Because he was a fragile, asthmatic child, he could not play in the streets very often, so to compensate his parents took him to the movies, sometimes several times a week. His first memory of his father, he says, is of the two of them in a movie theater watching a trailer for a Roy Rogers western that his father promised to take him to see the following week. He remembers watching the classics in movie theaters all over New York — something that made an enormous impression on his young mind and which he has never since forgotten. Scorsese's friends and colleagues have often enthused over his unbelievable memory for details about every single film he has seen since early childhood. Every little piece of information about the entire history of motion pictures seems to be stored indelibly in his mind.

Actor Peter Boyle, who played Wiz in *Taxi Driver*, has perceptively linked Scorsese's two overwhelming childhood experiences of St. Patrick's Old Cathedral and the cinema: "If Marty spent a lot of time in the movies as a kid, he also spent a lot of time in a church. They're both big and dark, and they're full of mystery, and the rites of purification and of life and death are acted out in the same way."[54] Scorsese says that the neighborhood kids used to compare the two and to "joke about Mass being the same show every day."[55] Paul Schrader, who has worked with Scorsese on some of his most acclaimed films, was brought up in a strict Dutch Calvinist home, and he stresses the ethical aspect of their partnership: "The essence of my collaboration with Marty was this: we approached a shared core from different directions. We are both quite moral, we believe decisions have consequences. There is right, there is wrong, and, in the end, there is a price to pay."[56]

Indeed, Scorsese's reverence for filmmaking has been described in religious terms by the late John Cassavetes. "Making films is an obsession," he said, "and very few people can put everything they have into it. They have other gods. But I think Marty has one god and that's film!"[57] Scorsese himself adds the most significant point about his perception of a connection between religion and film. When he was a child, priests and nuns would come to Old St. Pat's to tell about their experiences as missionaries around the world. "They would bring these giant crucifixes," he says, "and stand right in front of the altar and talk — scary hellfire-and-brimstone stuff. What they were doing was really *theater*. It was a holdover from the medieval period, when the church would have miracle plays that told about the lives of the saints, and dramatized tales from the Bible.... For me the important thing has always been this notion of theater — and, by extension, film — stemming from something being done in front of the altar."[58]

After giving up the idea of entering the priesthood, Scorsese says, "I soon realized that my real vocation, my real calling, was the movies. I don't really see a conflict between the church and the movies, the sacred and the profane." He elaborates: "I believe there is a spirituality in films, even if it's not one which can supplant faith.... It is as though movies answered an ancient quest for the common unconscious. They fulfill a spiritual need that people have to share a common memory."[59] The idea of the cinema as part of an ancient quest, of Martin Scorsese as a man with a vocation whose films are ritualized stories that take place in front of an altar and affect us on deep spiritual levels, forms the very essence of what this book is all about.

2

The Mask and the Mirror

> The mirror does not flatter, it faithfully shows whatever looks into it; namely, the face we never show to the world because we cover it with the persona, the mask of the actor. But the mirror lies behind the mask and shows the true face.[1]
>
> C.G. Jung

Since the beginning of his career, the city streets have been pivotal in Martin Scorsese's work. *Who's That Knocking at My Door?* and *Mean Streets* take place in the very streets where he grew up, and the rituals of the brotherhoods that rule them are their basic premise. *It's Not Just You, Murray!*, *Raging Bull*, and *GoodFellas* likewise concern the intricacies of male interaction, and even in *Casino*, which is set in Las Vegas, the city streets are constantly present as the underlying cause of the conflicts. These six films all deal with rigidly structured, subcultural male groups and with more or less organized crime. The protagonist does not quite belong in the tribal family and is either trying to move away or to be accepted as an equal so he can get further into it. In each film, he is burdened with a sidekick who exposes the things he is desperately trying to hide from the world. Repeatedly, the main character attempts to moderate and gloss over his story in the voice-over narration, but he is contradicted by the filmic images or thwarted when his friend takes over the narration and tells a different version. Try as he may, he cannot escape the shadow aspects of himself that the nemesis figure represents and reveals. The journey that is forced upon him is one of facing and admitting to those sides, and the more he resists, the more violent the struggle becomes.

These films have a characteristic use of female characters. A mother often appears (played by Catherine Scorsese), cooking and serving abundant meals, and the conflict between the men is intensified by the appearance of an attractive, usually blonde, woman.[2]

"He deals with the great archetypal themes of loyalty and treason, virtue and evil, heaven and hell, life and death, that spring from the collective unconscious," Robert A. Johnson once said. He was referring to Dante's *The Divine Comedy*, but he might as well have been talking about this group of films. "They are common to all of us, but this was his version of the archetypal themes," Johnson continues, "his individual way of living out the evolution that each of us must make."[3]

It's Not Just You, Murray!

It's Not Just You, Murray! is a 15-minute, black-and-white film that Scorsese made at N.Y.U. in 1964, and it is virtually a template for the rest of the films discussed in this chapter. It tells the story of two friends as seen in retrospect from Murray's perspective. It begins with a medium-shot of a balding, middle-aged man (Ira Rubin), who looks and talks straight at the camera. He manipulates its movements to show us his tie, his shoes, his suit and his car, telling us how much each cost. After several minutes of this, he tells the cameraman to stop filming because he realizes he has forgotten to introduce himself. His name is Murray, he says, "and, like, the reason I'm *here* is to tell you, like, how I got *here*!" He has already revealed that he primarily defines himself by means of his apparel and acquisitions, the outer persona he has assumed, and only secondarily by his real identity.

We soon learn that he is not a reliable narrator. His account is full of inaccuracies as he tries to dress up his life story. He tells us of his first arrest during the Prohibition era for bootlegging. We see the police chasing him around a basement while his friend Joe (Sam DeFazio) hides in a bathtub. Languidly and smugly, voice-over Murray tries to make us believe that it was a "misunderstanding in which, due to circumstances which I had no control, I was, ah, unfortunately I was misunderstood." He proudly tells us about the business that he and Joe started, and endlessly enumerates all the places, people and things that "have been affected" by them. Motel chains, politics, sports, and foreign aid have been affected, he says, while on the screen we see cheap hookers outside a motel, a man with a knife in his back, someone bribing a football player, and Arabs being handed rifles.

Even more flagrant are the discrepancies in his stories about Joe, as he himself gradually realizes. He claims that he owes all his success in life to Joe, who has stood by him through a history of crime, jail, Senate hearings, marriage and raising children. Without Joe, he says, "I wouldn't be where I am, I wouldn't be what I am, I wouldn't be who I am." In other words, Joe is supposedly responsible for Murray's entire life and personality.

Murray looks straight into the camera as he talks to us, but as soon as he mentions Joe, we shift to voice-over, as though he can no longer look us in the eye. Voice-over Murray says he wants to show us a picture of Joe as a child, and younger Murray in the image holds it up. In the photo Joe is six, Murray says, making him bigger than he is and reluctantly corrects himself, "or five." Next, he proudly shows us Joe's graduation photo: "There he is! With the hat!" No one in the picture is wearing a hat, and no one looks even remotely like Joe, whereas someone who resembles Murray is prominently placed in the center.

While Murray keeps giving Joe undeserved credit, we can clearly see that their friendship has been downright detrimental to Murray. Joe lets him take the rap and then visits him in jail, and — reversing the cliché — takes his only cigarette from him through the bars. Murray praises his friend so profusely that he demeans and belittles himself by comparison. This masochistic self-abasement culminates when he tells us about Joe's "excellent" advice: he has to learn to control himself when people abuse him or curse him or beat him up, because "one day you're gonna see somebody, some guy who's all those other guys rolled into one. And *then* you can give *him* all that he deserves!" As we hear Joe's advice, we see Murray looking at himself in a mirror. He then lifts his hand and smashes the mirror, destroying his own image, an act indicating intense self-loathing.[4]

The gravest example of Murray's misjudgment of Joe is in connection with his wife (Andrea Martin). She is a nurse Murray met at the hospital after the mirror incident, so he gives Joe the credit for his marriage, too. She is an "angel of mercy type," he says, while we see a jaded floozy who is openly flirting with Joe. Despite what is glaringly obvious, Murray (like so many later Scorsese protagonists) insists on believing his own fantasy. To enhance the irony, Murray's disapproving mother (Catherine Scorsese) repeatedly appears with dishes of food. Murray's epiphany comes when he proclaims that to his children "Joe is like a second father," showing us pictures of Joe and two children who look exactly like him. He finally sees the truth and asks Joe to come into his office. The sound is cut on Murray's insistence, and they have a heated discussion. Seconds later, however, Murray has resigned himself again. He keeps insisting that "we are very happy people," and that he is proud his wife still lives in his house. Like Sam Rothstein in *Casino*, he is willing to hang onto both his wife and his friend and the illusion of the happy home even after they have betrayed him.

A surreal Felliniesque ending is pasted on at the end: all the characters are dancing around in an open field to the sound of circus music. The dancing stops, and Murray and Joe are photographed together. The instant the photographer takes the picture, we hear what sounds like a gunshot. A flash of light illuminates Murray, the image freezes, and the film ends. We are left to wonder whether Murray was shot and whether this is connected with his discovery of Joe's perfidy. The idea that cameras and flashbulbs may be dangerous is repeated in many of Scorsese's later films.[5]

Aesthetically *It's Not Just You, Murray!* pays homage to the European art film of the late '50s and early '60s, but, more importantly, it is Scorsese's first take on the gangster genre. Despite what they seem to think, Murray and Joe are not in the least glamorous, and thus they form a marked contrast to the other gangsters of the new American cinema. Bonnie and Clyde are young and handsome, rebellious dropouts the audience can identify with while Coppola's Don Corleone is portrayed as a dignified patriarch and a just man. Scorsese's mobsters are more reminiscent of the classic gangsters from the 1930s, Tom Powers Enrico Bandello and Tony Camonte.[6] They are dull-witted borderline psychopaths who are obsessed with the emblems of their social ascent—clothes, shoes, and cars—to the point that it becomes comical. Unlike their classic forebears, however, they do not really rise to the top of the world. Most of them just stay in the old neighborhood and make a better living than everyone else. If we end up identifying with them, we do so in spite of ourselves. However, from the beginning of *It's Not Just You, Murray!* a certain reluctant sympathy for the protagonist is implied. The title suggests that we—the filmmaker and the audience—understand what is going on behind Murray's back and are supporting him: This is not all in your head, Murray—they really *are* double-crossing you, and we are with you on this!

Who's That Knocking at My Door?

In 1968 Martin Scorsese directed his final project at New York University, his first feature-length film, *Who's That Knocking at My Door?* It is a touching depiction of a troubled young man, J.R. (Harvey Keitel), an earlier, less philosophical version of Charlie of *Mean Streets*, who is torn between the caveman mentality of his numbskull buddies and his attraction to an intelligent and independent young woman. Its structure illustrates the conflict: scenes of J.R. with the smalltime hoods of Little Italy are intercut with his thoughts about and meetings with the girl, and these two mutually exclusive worlds never meet.

The film opens with Mother (Catherine Scorsese) cooking and serving a meal to a group of children seated around a table. She systematically prepares the food and passes it out one piece at a time, giving it a ritualistic, almost sacramental, significance. The image of Mother dissolves into shots of a small white figurine of the Holy Virgin with the baby, so that the two practically become synonymous and J.R.'s mother comes to represent the archetypal immaculate, nurturing Mother. We must assume, since these are the very first images in the film, that they form the basis of J.R.'s character; his pervasive Madonna/whore complex and antiquated expectations of what a woman should be.

The young woman he meets on the Staten Island Ferry (Zina Bethune) is given no name and is listed in the credits simply as "The Girl." She represents modern womanhood, an aspect of the anima that is completely ignored in J.R.'s tribe. Although she has her own apartment—whereas J.R. still lives with his mother—he takes her not only to Mother's home but to Mother's bed for their intimate moments together. In that space she is unavoidably held up against Mother and, by extension, the Holy Virgin for comparison. While they are kissing, J.R. suddenly stops, and we focus on the figurine in front of the mirror, implying that the immaculate representative (and Freudian reminder) of Mother is responsible for his inability to have sex. "I love you, and if you love me, you'll understand what I mean," he says, as we see their reflections in Mother's mirror. The girl is perfectly aligned with and of the same alabaster coloring as the figurine, which suggests different things: (1) J.R. expects the woman he marries to be pure, and so he cannot bring himself to have sex with her precisely because he loves her; (2) later we see him having casual sex with several women so his wish that the girl measure up to the standards of the Church which he does not bother to obey reveals him as a hypocrite; and finally (3) the fact that the girl is juxtaposed with the statuette may imply that she *is*, in fact, pure—despite J.R.'s condemnation when she turns out not to be a virgin because she was raped.

No other director has depicted the intricate mechanisms of male bonding with the excoriating truthfulness which Scorsese employs. In this early film, it is shown as frighteningly hermetic, coercive, and misogynistic, as well as both homophobic and homoerotic. The nucleus of the tribe is formed by J.R., Sally Gaga (Michael Scala) who owes everybody money, and Joey (Lennard Kuras) who is eager to keep the gang together and is thus extremely antagonistic toward J.R.'s girl.[7] Their so-called parties consist of a bunch of guys dressing up for each other, getting stinking drunk, and going out to pick up more or less professional tarts with whom they take turns having sex. Thus, they manage in one fell swoop to vilify women, to reinforce their belief that sexually active women are sluts, and for all intents and purposes to have sex with each other by proxy, getting as close as you possibly can without actually doing it.

The most appalling scene takes place during one such party. It is filmed in slow-motion which gives it a surreal quality, as if they are moving under water; Ray Barretto's "Watusi" is the only sound we hear. The guys are roaring drunk, and someone pulls out a loaded gun that they start playing with, screaming soundlessly with mirth as they hold down Sally Gaga and threaten to shoot him. After 95 horrifying seconds, the slow motion abruptly stops and we hear the sound of the gun going off. Scorsese then cuts to a still photo of John Wayne, testifying a connection between the dangerous prank and this timeless icon of rugged *machismo*.

Other stills from *Rio Bravo* follow, and it turns out that J.R. has taken the girl to see that film. *Who's That Knocking at My Door?* contains several allusions to Hollywood classics which illuminate the differences between the two worlds J.R. is torn between. He remembers walking on a roof and talking about pigeon coops with the girl, a scene which calls to mind Terry and Edie in *On the Waterfront*, and in fact J.R.'s girl physically resembles Edie. When J.R first meets her, the girl is reading a French film magazine featuring a picture from *The*

Searchers. The girl does not know that much about westerns, she admits, so J.R. tries to explain the fascination of John Ford's film: "Everybody should like westerns," he says. "Solve everybody's problems if they liked westerns."

The inserted stills from *Rio Bravo* mark the pivotal point of the film. They are placed at the dead center, preceded by the ultimate scene of mind-boggling male camaraderie, and followed by the most crucial scene with the girl, accentuating J.R.'s dilemma. As they leave the movie theater, the girl says she liked Feathers, the Angie Dickinson character, and J.R. gets upset: "She was a broad," he snaps. The girl does not understand. "There are girls and then there are broads," he explains. "A broad isn't exactly a virgin, you know what I mean? You play around with them. You don't marry a broad, you know what I mean?" The girl looks very uncomfortable, and the realization that he is serious prompts her to disclose that she was once date-raped, a confession that leads to their breakup.

Feathers is a sympathetic, intelligent modern woman in an antiquated, all-exclusive male setting, so it is no wonder the girl likes her and J.R. feels threatened by her. Although Sheriff Chance in *Rio Bravo* and J.R. are both attracted to the female intruder, she is regarded with suspicion. In this crucial scene, J.R. is perceptibly disturbed because it is the first confirmation that she comes from outside his die-hard, reactionary circle. She questions his misogynous and bigoted views, and indirectly reminds him that he ought to become conscious of his own behavior instead of unquestioningly staying in his restricting environment.

Indeed, the central symbols of *Who's That Knocking at My Door?* are rooms, doors, locks and keys, as well as various modes of transportation. Doors are contained in the title as well as the title song, which is played over the final scene. J.R.'s speculations about girls and broads are intercut with his memories of having sex with a number of different women, while on the soundtrack we hear the spoken section of "The End" by The Doors. By using this flagrantly Oedipal section of the song, Scorsese again weaves J.R.'s mother into his sexual encounters.[8] Doors, locks and keys signify J.R.'s closed mind, his being trapped inside the group that is so reluctant to grow, trying to shut out anyone who threatens or questions its complacency. Repeatedly they are locking themselves in. Joey constantly importunes the others to close windows or doors, and we focus in extreme close-ups on car windows slowly being rolled up, padlocks being snapped shut or keys being turned inside locks. Doors imply their locker-room mentality, and the closer J.R. comes to the girl, and the more his feelings are stirred, the more he is expected to compensate by participating in parties whose main point seem to be reinforcing the camaraderie by degrading women.

There are many indications that his relationship with the girl could lead to psychological and spiritual development for J.R., whereas the company of his friends involves nothing but stagnation and metaphoric death. The mode of transportation connected with the male group is a hermetically sealed car which, although it does take them a few blocks away from the neighborhood, only seems to reinforce their insularity and limited view of the world. The first encounter between J.R. and the young woman, on the other hand, takes place on the Staten Island Ferry. (In mythology, trips across water usually involve major development.) J.R. is on the ferry because he has to go down to his grandmother's house to pick up a parcel for his mother. The scene is thus a mirror version of "Little Red Riding Hood"— a story Scorsese refers to repeatedly in his work — suggesting that what J.R. has to learn on his trip across Upper New York Bay is similar to what Riding Hood had to learn on her trip through the forest: Just like the implicit eroticism of the wolf shatters the childhood world of Red Riding Hood, so that of the girl shatters J.R.'s, and he walks away from the encounter a changed person. Little Red Riding Hood, Bruno Bettelheim has proposed, is too little to understand the sexual implications of her red cape and cannot handle the situation it lands her in. J.R., on the other hand, is so old that this shift ought to have occurred much earlier, and it thus emphasizes the regressive traits in his personality.

J.R. still lives with his mother and has an extremely puerile relationship with a tribe that defines women as either virgins or broads. The modern feminine principle which this girl represents is precisely what is needed to provoke and tempt him if he is to move beyond the confines of the neighborhood and his own mind. His supreme ordeal and the ultimate test of his character would almost *have* to be a story of rape, being confronted with the involuntary defilement of the woman he loves. His initial reaction is denial ("How can I believe that story?"), but his main concern is what would happen "if anyone else heard this story." He goes out for a final, pathetic binge, an all-night orgy with his buddies, but he is not so thick-skinned that he can entirely block the girl from his mind, and the images of the rape are cut in as they keep appearing in his thoughts. Nevertheless, he cannot cope with the girl's confession, and he never really faces the monster of the inmost cave that it represents.

In the penultimate scene he goes back to her apartment very early the next morning. He makes an awkward effort at reconciliation: "I understand now, and I forgive you!" he says and offers to marry her "anyway." She says she does not want him to marry her "anyway," and he starts cursing her and calling her a whore. This is extremely painful because we are witnessing his conditioning triumph over his feelings and his potential for development: "You oughta be glad I'm gonna marry you," he yells. "Who do you think you are? The Virgin Mary or something?" The scene ends when she asks him to "go home" which testifies that on some level she realizes that home, the restrictive neighborhood, has overridden his individual progress. As J.R. leaves her apartment he falls down the stairs. Staircases often symbolize the interval between different levels of awareness and could well reflect the fact that he has not grown, but has degraded the girl as well as his own feelings.

In the final scene we see the first signs of the virtuoso director Scorsese was to become. As J.R. comes out of the confessional at St. Patrick's Old Cathedral, the 1959 song "Who's That Knocking?" by The Genies starts blaring on the soundtrack. Scorsese never uses music simply to underscore the emotional mood of a scene because, he says, "a love scene with love music is just mediocre."[9] Instead he hurls music at us which contradicts and counterpoints the image. Over the stunning statues of the Madonna with the baby and Christ on the cross we hear this amazingly irreverent, scratchy old 45 rpm doo-wop record. The camera glides across each iconic image, accompanied by the discordant song, and after tracking sideways for 4, 8, or 12 beats, we cut to the next image in mid-movement.

The ending is ambiguous, and it is unclear whether J.R. has learned anything at all. At the very end he is outside with Joey who more than anyone stands for the conformity of the tribe. "I'll see you tomorrow," Joey says, betokening that nothing has changed, and tomorrow things will be back to normal. All the way through, however, we see signs that J.R. has grown through his encounter with the girl. When he first meets her, he says he cannot breathe when he is away from the streets of Little Italy, but at the same time he tells her a story about a man who played golf during the blizzard in 1960. "The trouble with the world today," J.R. says jokingly, "is that if a guy wants to play golf in the middle of 14th Street and Broadway, people stare at you!" The fact that he finds sympathetic a man who

In the final scene of *Who's That Knocking at My Door?*, J.R. (Harvey Keitel) tries to find answers in St. Patrick's Old Cathedral on Mott Street where Scorsese used to be an altar boy (A Joseph Brenner Associates Inc. Release of a Trimod Films, 1968).

values his individuality over what his surroundings might think suggests that he may be eager for change. This is confirmed when we cut to the perpendicular extreme bird's-eye view that Scorsese uses in most of his films — which I call God's-eye view.

Later, J.R. and Joey go to the country with a man whom we only see in this one scene. After they come back the girl says, "I hear you climbed a mountain." The only way she could have heard this (since she does not know Joey) is if she knows the unnamed man. Whereas most scenes involving the tribe take place indoors and in the dark, those with the girl often take place outside and in daylight. This man takes J.R. out of the neighborhood and on a hill-climb, and the camera pulls back in a long, fast, backward zoom, whizzing through trees until the entire hill is visible. This stunning camera move draws attention to the moment and denotes radical upward movement. While Joey never stops *kvetching*, J.R. is awestruck when they reach the top of the hill. This implies that he reacts to the influence of the man who symbolically is an extension of the girl. He seems annoyed with Joey, who tries to restrain him within the confines of their usual behavior, and for the first time he is able to "breathe" outside the neighborhood.

Most indicative, however, is the final scene in Old St. Pat's. If we consider the use of the song for more than just shock value, the words "who's that knocking?" inside a church remind us that Christ, too, is traditionally connected with doors and locks: "Behold, I stand at the door and knock; if any man hear my voice, and open the door, I will come in to him, and will sup with him, and he with me."[10] This is often represented in paintings as Christ knocking on a door that only opens from the inside, meaning that Christ can only enter our lives if we open the door from the other side.[11] If Scorsese's startling combination of image and sound reflects J.R.'s mind, then it is implied that someone or something is indeed knocking, and that it is up to J.R. himself whether he will open that door or not.

Mean Streets

After Scorsese had finished making *Boxcar Bertha* for Roger Corman in 1972, John Cassavetes reportedly said to him: "You've just spent a year of your life making a piece of shit. You're better than that stuff, you don't do that again."[12] Cassavetes then asked his young colleague if he did not have a film he was really dying to make. Scorsese told him he was working on another project about his old neighborhood, but that it needed rewriting. "Well, rewrite it then!" was Cassavetes's only comment. That project would eventually become *Mean Streets* (1973), Scorsese's breakthrough picture. Like *Who's That Knocking at My Door?*, *Mean Streets* concerns the relationship between men, and it takes place in Little Italy during the San Gennaro festival in September.[13]

Discussing his exhilarating use of aesthetics, the pulsating musicality and relentless energy of the film, Scorsese has modestly claimed that "the economics dictated the style, and the style just happened to work."[14] The score is a medley of Neapolitan love songs, opera, and rock 'n' roll. Scorsese has explained that his astonishing musical sensibility has its roots in his childhood in Little Italy where music was constantly surging out of doors and windows. The jukeboxes contained an eclectic assortment of records: "When The Beatles came in, you had Benny Goodman, some old Italian stuff, Jerry Vale, Tony Bennett, doo-wop, early rock 'n' roll, black and Italian," he explains.[15] People's lives were in a sense scored by radios and jukeboxes, and he was amazed at the irony of certain records playing at certain times in a way that is quite similar to how he would later use music in his work. Once he looked out the window at two bums stumbling down Elizabeth Street, "one so drunk the other's stealing his shoes, and while this fight was going on I could hear from somewhere 'When My Dream Boat Comes Home' by Fats Domino."[16]

Scorsese has said that *Mean Streets* was "an attempt to put myself and my old friends on the screen, to show how we lived, what life was like in Little Italy. It was really an anthropological or a sociological tract."[17] In the same breath, however, he reveals that the real concerns of the film are penance and redemption. Indeed, the opening seems anything but sociological. We enter into total darkness, then over the black screen we hear the words: "You don't make up for your sins in the church. You do it in the streets. You do it at home. The rest is bullshit, and you know it!" We cut to a close-up of Charlie (Harvey Keitel) who wakes up from a nightmare in a bluish light. Right from the start we are catapulted directly into the darkest recesses of his mind. To the sound of a siren outside, he walks over to the mirror, looks at himself, then goes back to bed. As his head approaches the pillow, we see tears on his face, and as we cut closer, abruptly, the opening drumbeats of "Be My Baby!" begin at a volume that could wake the dead.

After the title sequence, we are introduced to the other main players.[18] Each of Charlie's friends is established in a short vignette and at the end his name is superimposed over the image. It is logical to assume that this vignette somehow sums up his character and his function in Charlie's drama. We cut from the brightly lit festival outside to a dark image of a man shooting up in the men's room of a bar that belongs to Tony (David Proval). Tony gets livid about finding drugs in his bar, which means either that he is a conscientious man or simply wants to keep his path clean.[19] Next we see Michael (Richard Romanus) unloading what he thinks are German lenses from parked trucks under a bridge, presumably buying them illegally from the drivers. Moments later he tries to sell them and is told that they are Japanese adapters and are practically worthless. He is revealed as being greedy, easily fooled where money is concerned, and not nearly as smart as he thinks he is. He takes himself extremely seriously and acts as if he is in complete control when, in fact, he is not.

We cut to Johnny Boy (Robert De Niro) who loiters down the street, drops a cherry bomb in a mail box, then ducks inside a doorway with a childishly satisfied look of accomplishment on his face when it explodes. He is Michael's complete antithesis. Michael is dapper, Johnny wears an old coat and a stupid porkpie hat.[20] He is feeble-minded, immature and proud of it. Throughout the film, Johnny refuses to pay back the money he owes Michael, and he is a constant reminder of Michael's weakness. Where Michael is presented as the well-dressed surface of the persona, Johnny Boy is presented as a disruptive shadow force who constitutes a threat to it, and the battle between the two is fierce and internecine.

Who's That Knocking at My Door? ended with Keitel's character searching for answers at St. Patrick's Old Cathedral, and when we return to Charlie that is exactly where he is, as if we were watching the same character half a decade later. He is now less adolescently concerned with what his buddies think and more engrossed in his spiritual battle with God.[21] He is talking to the Almighty about penance, saying that he does not want to atone for his sins with the usual Our Fathers and Hail Marys. "I do something wrong," Charlie says, "I just wanna pay for it *my* way. So I do my own penance for my own sins. What do you say?" He puts his finger into a lighted candle and continues: "That's all bullshit except the pain, right? The pain of hell. The burns from a lighted match increased a million times. Infinite. Now you don't fuck around with infinite. There's no way you do that. Pain and hell has two sides. The kind you can touch with your hand, the kind you can feel in your heart, your soul. The spiritual side. And you know, the worst of the two is the spiritual."

We cut from the House of God to an infernal, dark, red interior where people are eerily moving in slow motion. The music of the Rolling Stones pervades the scene, intensifying the hellish Hadean overtones.[22] As Charlie enters this landscape—which turns out to be Tony's bar—he continues his obsession with expiation. He ogles the black topless dancer and accepts stolen cigarettes from Michael, then again puts his hand into the fire, as if burning one's hand is a less hypocritical penance for casually committed sins than ten Hail Marys. Almost like a response, the unbridled Johnny Boy comes rambling in, the call to adventure of Charlie's journey. Charlie immediately picks up on the idea of Johnny as a penance sent by God and his reaction is blasphemous: "Thanks a lot, Lord! Thanks a lot for opening my eyes! We talk about penance and you send this through the door! Well, we play by your rules, don't we?"

Critics have tended to see Johnny Boy's disorderliness as aimless. Robert Philip Kolker describes him as "a character with no center who destroys himself with his own inarticulate desire to be a free spirit," while Ian Penman refers to him as "pure untrammeled id, doing its inexorable dance."[23] However, the tenacity and determination of Johnny's refusal to behave, and the way he flaunts his impenitence, suggests to me that he has a more profound function. From the start, Charlie realizes that Johnny is there as an ordeal for him, but what if he sees things the wrong way 'round? He considers himself a man with a mission, i.e., saving Johnny and straightening out his life. But what if the reverse were true? What if the film falls into place only if we choose the opposite approach? In Scorsese's mythological universe, it makes so much more sense to see *Johnny* as the man with the mission, and Charlie as the one whose life needs fixing.

"Charlie uses other people, thinking that he's helping them; but by believing that, he's not only ruining them but ruining himself," Scorsese says. Charlie's need to do good, be good, and especially look good may seem like Christian charity, but mostly it is a convenient excuse to further his own self-interest, to appear to others like a saint and ensure his own salvation. It is "a matter of his own pride — the first sin in the Bible," says Scorsese.[24] Johnny is thus the perfect moral and spiritual trial for Charlie, and he appears as God's compassionate response to Charlie's wish to do penance. This unruly, exasperating, frenzied character is virtually the prototype of Scorsese's annoying shadow nemesis, and he represents everything Charlie is trying to repress. The more Charlie refuses to accept him and the more he tries to force him into being respectable, the more Johnny acts up.

The very first thing we see in the film is Charlie looking at himself in the mirror after waking up from a nightmare. Where Michael represents the well-groomed persona, the mask we put on to hide our face, Johnny is the realization of the shadow, the mirror image who is constantly pulling in the opposite direction to counterbalance the ego and point out Charlie's hypocrisy. Like Michael, Charlie is well dressed and well behaved; Johnny Boy, on the other hand, is socially unacceptable in every way. Charlie always tries to placate; Johnny is only too eager to start fights. In the famous "mook" scene this becomes manifest. The gang enters a pool room to collect money for Joey, but Johnny begins to stir up the tempers. A tremendous fight breaks out because no one is sure exactly what a "mook" is, and while Charlie is lying on a pool table, stunned by the mayhem, Johnny is standing on another pool table having the time of his life, ecstatically swinging a cue with incredible energy. Even after the fight is over, he tries to annoy and provoke.

The motif of mirror images appears several places in the film. After the fight, Tony takes the others into the back room of his bar to show them his latest acquisition: a gigantic wild feline in a cage. He has always wanted a tiger, he says, "William Blake and all that." For one thing the animal is not a tiger, and for another it seems completely out of character for Tony to want something because of William Blake, let alone *know* who the English poet and mystic is. The reference to Blake's philosophical and religious poem "The Tyger" thus takes on a primarily symbolic significance. "Did he who made the lamb make thee?" the speaker of the poem wonders, referring to the tiger. The tiger and the lamb are seen as necessary antitheses that complement each other — the lamb representing the Savior, the tiger representing the dark side. One critic notes that this poem "illustrates Blake's belief that the fierce tiger is simply another manifestation of the Divine unity of all creation and that each element thereof is valid and necessary."[25]

Two things compel Charlie to suppress the shadow energy Johnny represents. Firstly, he wants to be a good man, but he goes about it by doing "the worst thing he could do," as Scorsese says, which is "to put everything off, put all the confrontations off, until everything explodes."[26] Charlie is in denial about the anger and violence that is in him and surrounding him, almost as if he thinks that by ignoring it, he can make it go away. What happens is, of course, the opposite, and the more he tries to keep conscious control of his shadow, the more havoc it wreaks. Secondly, and more dubiously, he is extremely concerned with appearances because he wants to be respected in the neighborhood by his buddies and by his Uncle Giovanni, the mafia boss for whom he works. He is less worried about what his friends think than J.R. was, but he is still subject to prejudices he is supposed to uphold and lines he is expected not to cross. The tribe is again characterized by homophobia, racism and misogyny; it fears outsiders and uses semantics to define and close off the group. Charlie, like J.R., is caught between the need to live up to its confining but comforting standards on the one hand and the need to develop as an individual on the other.

The more Charlie's ego and persona prompt him to gloss things over, the more wayward become Johnny and his cousin Teresa (Amy Robinson), with whom Charlie is having an intimate relationship. Charlie feels like he is being pulled at from all sides, but these are, in fact, merely external expressions of the war that is being waged in his mind and his soul: He has conflicting desires and needs, but he wants it all so he does not make a choice.

At one point, the gang goes to the movies to see John Ford's *The Searchers*, a film Scorsese repeatedly refers to in his work which likewise concerns a frantic attempt to keep things within the clan. The scene they are watching is the fight that erupts when Ethan and Martin return from the wilderness to find Martin's girlfriend about to marry another man. Instead of trying to win over the woman, the two rivals start fighting each other. The irony in the way Scorsese has set up this scene is unbelievable. At the back of the theater, a man starts feeling up another man and our guys start giggling. It does not occur to them that

Johnny Boy (Robert De Niro) and Teresa (Amy Robinson) refuse to behave until Charlie (Harvey Keitel) completely loses control in *Mean Streets* (Warner Bros., 1973).

on the screen in front of them, two guys are groping each other in an extremely physical tangle which is basically not that dissimilar from what is going on in the theater. The tendency in *The Searchers* to focus on the rival rather than, as might make more sense, the woman one is trying to win, is echoed toward the end of *Mean Streets* when Charlie leaves Teresa, who is in the middle of an epileptic fit, to run after Johnny Boy in order to beat him up.

The misogyny of the group obviously affects Charlie's relationship with and attitude toward Teresa. Like J.R., he divides women into girls and broads, so when Teresa asks him (in bed) if he loves her, he says that if there was even the slightest chance of that, he would not have had sex with her. It is clear, however, that he likes her more than he is willing to admit, that he feels torn between his feelings for her (which impel him to move out of the neighborhood, beyond the confines of the group) and his ambition to rise in rank within his uncle's hierarchy (which would mean giving up Teresa, of whom Uncle does not approve).

Significantly, Charlie's father is never mentioned. Instead we have a vaguely sinister, Hamlet-like setup of a mother and an uncle who is a powerful, sovereign ruler. Together they represent everything that keeps Charlie in a state of conflict. How can he be a good man and at the same time work for the mob? How can he be an authentic individual when he has to conform to Uncle's expectations? Uncle's power is explicit, but Mother's more subtle power should not be underestimated. Although we never *see* Charlie's mother, her presence is clearly felt, and, as we have seen, a mother's physical absence can make her all the more impending. Charlie still lives with his mother and she leaves him money and little love notes along with freshly laundered shirts. These manifestations of Mother's love touch upon powerful archetypal themes. In exploring the myth of Parcifal, Robert A. Johnson recounts that the one thing that prevents young Parcifal, whose father is dead, from living out his own destiny is the homespun garment his mother implores him to wear upon leaving home. The garment represents the mother complex in which Parsifal is encased, and if he is to continue his own individuation, it is imperative that he free himself from it restraints. "To get the mother's homespun off a youth is an arduous task," Johnson says. "Many never succeed in divesting themselves from their mother complex, for that is what is symbolized by the mother's homespun."[27] As Charlie sensuously caresses the monogram on the shirt Mother just ironed for him, on the soundtrack The Chantells are singing "I'm telling you darling, I'll never let you go."

Where the mother archetype, in Johnson's words, is "pure gold," the mother complex is "pure poison." It is a man's "regressive capacity which would like to return to a dependency on his mother and be a child again. This is a man's wish to fail, his defeatist capacity, his subterranean fascination with death or accident, his demand to be taken care of. This is pure poison in a man's psychology."[28] "No matter where he goes, he's lost," Scorsese says about Charlie, attributing this to his sense of guilt and unworthiness.[29] Those feelings might equally well be attributed to his wearing mother's shirts, because most likely they are the powerful source from which his sense of guilt springs.

Mother and Uncle represent regression. They want him to stay where he is and develop only within the confines they define and stake out. Teresa represents the opposite. She wants Charlie to take responsibility for his life, to move out of the neighborhood and free himself from its restrictions. She is the only one who sees through and deflates his pride and hypocrisy. His buddies ask him, "Art thou the King of the Jews?" and tell him to bless their pool paraphernalia, something which is profane to begin with, but which Charlie reacts to only when he is asked to bless their balls. Teresa on the other hand makes fun of him when he compares himself to Francis of Assisi: "St. Francis didn't run numbers!"

Where the girl in *Who's That Knocking at My Door?* was nice and bright, Teresa is a troublemaker, which indicates that Charlie may be even more dismissive towards the modern feminine principle she represents than was J.R. Like Johnny, the shadow nemesis, the repressed anima refuses to behave: "Between you and Johnny, you're gonna ruin everything for me," Charlie revealingly says to her. Teresa and Johnny contradict and disregard Charlie (the ego) and Michael (the persona) and deflate their complacency. They are constantly trying to force Charlie into a confrontation with Michael and Uncle Giovanni, making a change imminent.

Obviously, one does not become a good man by *playing* the saint and repressing anything unpleasant the way Charlie does. The true saint, Robert A. Johnson has said, is not someone who ignores his or her dark sides, but someone who has learned to live with them in a balanced way. If we ignore the shadow for too long, we can end up assuming its characteristics on the outside, in a sense being possessed by it. Toward the end of the film Charlie actually starts behaving like Johnny. He loses control and physically attacks Johnny (which is right up Johnny's alley) then tries to pick up a Jewish woman in the bar with an act that sounds exactly like something Johnny would pull: "I have loved you since that first day when I saw you playing basketball with the nuns." If we see Johnny Boy as representing the neglected shadow, Charlie is psychologically responsible for his antics, and in the penultimate scene, Johnny shows an insight into Charlie's character that only makes sense if we see things from that perspective. Charlie is at the end of his rope and criticizes Johnny for further enraging Michael by pointing a gun at him. Johnny just looks at him and says matter-of-factly, "You got what you wanted!"

Charlie's denial ends up nearly costing him his life. He never acknowledges his dark sides, and he refuses to make a choice between the assumed mask of false respectability that Michael and Uncle Giovanni represent and the mirror that Johnny and Teresa hold up, the authenticity of his total inner self. Naturally things come to a head: in the last scene Charlie is trapped in a car with the anima and the shadow, while the enraged persona has hired a killer who starts to shoot at them. What we see is a classic scene of death and rebirth. At the very end, the characters survive, after we were sure they had been killed. Michael and Johnny, the persona and the shadow, disappear into the night. We cut to Tony (who is literally washing his hands), and then to Uncle Giovanni whose withdrawal is represented metaphorically: he is leaning back in his armchair, resignedly watching a similar car accident on television in Fritz Lang's 1953 film *The Big Heat*. Charlie falls to his knees, a sign of surrender, but there's a striking difference between the real accident and the one Giovanni is watching: Fritz Lang's Dave Bannion is trying to pull his beloved wife out of the burning vehicle, whereas Charlie just abandons Teresa, her hand helplessly reaching out through the broken windshield, leaving it to the police to get her out. It is anyone's guess whether Charlie has learned from his ordeal, but the final images attest complete devastation: the persona and the shadow have withdrawn, and Charlie is completely oblivious to the mortally wounded anima.

Raging Bull

In the early fall of 1978 Martin Scorsese was hospitalized following a life of excess during and after the filming of *New York, New York*. While making *The Last Waltz*, he and

Robbie Robertson had discovered that they had a lot in common — the music they grew up on, Catholic guilt, and asthma — so when both their wives left them, Robertson moved into Scorsese's house on Mulholland Drive. Their lifestyle was chaotic, and for months on end they would stay up all night watching movies. "Marty had the house blacked out with shades, and he installed a soundproof air system so you could breathe without opening the windows," Robertson says. "We were like vampires," Scorsese confirms. "It was like, 'Oh, no, the sun is coming up.'"[30] They lived together under these circumstances "until Marty nearly died."[31]

Robert De Niro came to see him at the hospital on Labor Day weekend, fervently trying to persuade him to make a film based on the autobiography of middleweight champion Jake La Motta. Scorsese was depressed, in a state of total exhaustion and in no condition to take on a new project, especially one this emotionally demanding, so Robbie Robertson tried to force things into focus for him. "Do you have to do this movie? Because if you don't have to do it, don't do it," he told him. "Can you go on with your life without doing this?" Scorsese came to the conclusion that he could not go on with his life without making this movie, that he absolutely had to do it.[32]

Most critics seem to agree that *Raging Bull* (1980) is Scorsese's masterpiece, and it is still the most widely praised film of the 1980s. It takes place in the period between 1941, when La Motta started fighting professionally, and 1964, ten years after he retired. Remarkably for a film made in 1980, it is in black and white. Black-and-white photography has traditionally been associated with documentary realism, but, as Rudolf Arnheim argued, film is art precisely in the areas where it differs from reality. By definition, black and white resembles reality less than color photography and has a much darker, more dreamlike quality to it. By shooting it in black and white, Scorsese paradoxically makes *Raging Bull* more authentic as regards La Motta's life story, as well as more psychologically universal.

Most importantly, being black and white it automatically contains a subtextual reference to movie classics from the 1940s and 1950s. Scorsese says that he was inspired by noir films like *Force of Evil* and *Kiss of Death*, but more specifically *Raging Bull* invokes films about prizefighting such as *The Set-Up*, *Body and Soul*, *Somebody Up There Likes Me*, *The Harder They Fall*, *Requiem for a Heavyweight*, and *On the Waterfront*. Strictly speaking, boxing films do not constitute a genre, but they do have certain ritual traits in common, and *Raging Bull* is associated with this group of painful films and their characters, iconography, plots, and themes. Indeed, Pauline Kael has described *Raging Bull* as "a biography of the prizefight genre."[33] The prizefighting films all concern the manipulation, corruption, and degradation of the boxer, often because of mob involvement and corrupt ring practices, and his torment which is aggravated by the failure of a mentor or father figure.

One critic said about *The Harder They Fall* that it is "one of the most scathing indictments of boxing ever committed to film, ranking with such classic films as *Body and Soul*, *Champion*, *Requiem for a Heavyweight* and *Raging Bull*."[34] But in fact *Raging Bull* differs from the other great boxing films in that it is not really an indictment. Although Tommy Como has the role of the corrupter similar to that of Jackie Gleason in *Requiem for a Heavyweight*, Lee J. Cobb in *On the Waterfront* or even George C. Scott in *The Hustler*, Scorsese's prizefighter mostly inflicts his own pain. This is reflected in La Motta's trademark boxing style of always letting himself take a terrible beating before ferociously turning on his opponent.

The story of Jake La Motta (Robert De Niro) in *Raging Bull* is one of redemption through suffering, and it is perhaps Scorsese's most harrowing film. At the heart of it is

Jake's self-inflicted torment, humiliation, and martyrdom. Although he faces foe after foe in the ring, his main opponent is himself. Suffering is incidental for many of Scorsese's characters. Lionel Dobie requires pain to fuel his work. Christ has to endure pain to redeem mankind. But for Jake La Motta the pain itself is what matters, and he seeks it out ritually and obsessively. Pain is at the core of his profession, and for him it is the whole point of it. Quite simply, this is the story of a man whose philosophy of life is: "Hit me with everything you've got!"

Like so many of Scorsese's films, *Raging Bull* has a circular structure, so we begin in 1964 with the ending. Jake is inside a dressing room at the Barbizon Plaza in New York, rehearsing his one-man show. The first thing we notice is his obesity (rendering De Niro virtually unrecognizable), and his jokes have a propensity toward self-degradation which leads us to suspect that overeating may well be a symptom of his masochism. "One night I took off my robe, and what did I do?" Jake says, "I forgot to wear shorts."

La Motta's real-life bouts have been carefully selected, and emphasis has been added or removed in order to accentuate their symbolic nature. The structure of the film reflects his self-abasing attitude, skipping lightly over his victories — his many winning matches in the years from 1944 to 1947 are passed over in a three minute montage — to focus and dwell on the losses, the indignity, and the pain.[35] Finishing his opening monologue, he repeats the phrase — "That's entertainment!" — at the exact same time that we cut back to September 24, 1941, to see Jimmy Reeves's gloved fist smashing into his much younger and thinner face. "The Bronx Bull has taken a lot of punishment," the announcer says, describing him as "a man who doesn't know how to back up!" Interestingly, what distinguishes this fight (that Scorsese chooses to open with) is the fact that it was the first professional fight La Motta ever *lost*. Now begins the purgatorial journey back towards 1964, focusing on Jake's battle with his inner demons as personified in his flesh-and-blood brother, Joey (Joe Pesci); his professional nemesis, Sugar Ray Robinson (Johnny Barnes); his rival, Salvy (Frank Vincent); mob boss Tommy Como (Nicholas Colasanto); and his blonde child bride, Vickie (Cathy Moriarty).

Jake's journey is set in motion by two interconnected conflicts that represent the ordeals he has to go through: the mob wanting to buy a piece of him, and the siren call of the child temptress. Significantly, Joey is the middleman in both conflicts.

The first time we see him, Joey is walking in the street with Salvy, debating how they can persuade Jake to let mob boss Tommy Como take care of his career — something that would make anyone who has ever seen a classic boxing movie extremely apprehensive. However concerned Joey may seem about Jake's welfare throughout the rest of the film, he is established from the start as someone who is capable of deception and betrayal.

The first time we see Vickie, she is 15 years old, sitting at the edge of the Shorehaven Pool, beckoningly moving her legs up and down in the water. As soon as Jake lays eyes on the child goddess, he is entranced, and again, Joey is shown to be unreliable. Despite her age, Vickie looks worldly-wise, and when she goes with Jake to his father's apartment shortly afterwards it does not seem to be her first encounter with a man. Jake's obsessive jealousy rears its ugly head before he has exchanged a single word with her, and right from the start it is aimed at Salvy and Joey. Throughout, Joey encourages Jake to get rid of Vickie on the pretext that she is bad for him. His apparent concern is dubious, however, since he obviously has a hidden agenda in this matter too. Does she go with Salvy or the other mobsters, Jake wants to know as they are admiring her by the pool. Joey says she is only 15 so no one can take her out, but a few minutes later when Jake asks if he has had sex with her, he contradicts himself and says no, he has only been out with her.

The rest of the film revolves around these two themes — the pressure from the mob involving Tommy, Salvy, and Joey, and the question of Jake's insane jealousy involving Vickie, Salvy and Joey. The climactic scenes of the film are all connected to these conflicts, directly or indirectly. The second conflict culminates in the famous scene where Jake demands from his brother an answer to the question, "Did you fuck my wife?" People tend to think that Jake is just being paranoid, but the fact is that Joey constantly acts guilty around Vickie, whether because he *has* slept with her (maybe before she met Jake) or because he feels tempted to. We never get an unequivocal answer to Jake's question in the film, but the actors involved have their own views on it: "Jake goes after his brother, and he's right, the brother *was* with Vickie," De Niro insists. Joe Pesci does not agree: "No way, no way. Joey would not touch his brother's wife," and Cathy Moriarty concurs that "it was all in Jake's mind."[36]

Scorsese has never explicitly solved the mystery, but if one reads between the lines it seems quite evident that he supports De Niro's view. For one thing, the constellation of characters here is identical to that in *It's Not Just You, Murray!* and *Casino*, and in the other two films we know for sure that the wife is, in fact, sleeping with the nemesis. For another, and more importantly, in the scene in which Jake carries Vickie up the stairs to their new house on Pelham Parkway, Scorsese and editor Thelma Schoonmaker have inserted one sepia-toned frame of Joey's wedding. At an ordinary viewing, one only subliminally feels that something is wrong, but if you go through the shot frame by frame, Joey becomes clearly discernible. It makes no sense to meticulously insert this image unless it has meaning, and when I asked Schoonmaker about it in person, she assured me that it does. "We never thought anyone would catch us out," she said, seemingly pleased that after two and a half decades someone finally had. Literally what the frame shows, of course, is Joey invading his brother's new marriage. So we may have to concur with De Niro that Joey is guilty of *something*, that it's not just you, Jake!

Jake's suspicion in this scene is prompted by an event that took place three years earlier. One night in 1947 while Jake was away at training camp, Joey saw Vickie entering the Copacabana with Salvy and another couple on what looked suspiciously like a double date. When Vickie refused to go home, Joey responded by battering Salvy senseless, savagely pounding his head with a cab door. Jake now asks his brother what really happened that night, wanting to know if anything was going on between Vickie and Salvy. Joey looks uncomfortable, but keeps lying and accusing Jake of imagining things. Finally he blurts out that maybe Jake should just kill his wife and all the people he suspects her of having slept with: "Kill Vickie! Kill Salvy! Kill Tommy Como! Kill me while you're at it!" Jake may be unsympathetic and paranoid, but he is actually hits the nail on the head when he points out Joey's Freudian slip: "What do you mean kill *you*?" he insists, "You coulda said anybody, but you said you and them."

For the rest of their lives after this incident, Joey resents and avoids Jake, in the process covering up his own behavior of three years earlier. Even as he is assuring Jake that he is insane for imagining these things, he is concealing the fact that his own reaction to seeing Salvy and Vickie together was a lot more extreme than Jake's reaction. Joey's insane rage at the Copa went way beyond protecting his brother's interests. It revealed his innermost feelings, and when he smashed Salvy's head, he gave in to his own secret jealousy over Vickie.

To make matters even worse, and Joey's hypocrisy even more aggravating, the event at the Copa was also what led him to betray and sell out his brother, sacrificing Jake's dignity and integrity to save his own hide. Because Salvy is a made guy, Joey is called in for a conversation with Tommy Como after his transgression. He can make amends, it is implied, by delivering Jake to them. He convinces Jake to let Tommy buy his soul by throwing a fight in exchange for a shot at the title. Jake may be responsible for his own degradation, but his brother still is willing to sell him out at the drop of a hat.

The soul is the arena where the struggle between the forces of light and dark takes place, said Nikos Kazantzakis in *The Last Temptation*. Thus Jake's encounters in the boxing ring become a mirror of his soul. We see this most clearly in his fights with professional nemesis Sugar Ray Robinson. First, 30 minutes into the film, we see their second matchup on February 5, 1943, in which La Motta gained national recognition for breaking Ray's record and handing him his first defeat. The scene is placed right after Jake's first date with Vickie, suggesting that his feelings for her and his amazing victory are connected. Another scene with Vickie follows, this time explicitly sexual. Jake lets her arouse him, gets up from the bed — "I gotta fight Robinson. I can't fool around" — then goes to the bathroom and slowly pours a pitcher of ice water over his erection. Meanwhile, we focus on Vickie in a see-through nightgown, moving her legs up and down like she did at the pool. We then cut directly to the fight in which Jake loses to Ray, indicating that the seductive song of the school girl siren is connected to his defeat.

When Tommy, Salvy and Joey succeed in prevailing upon Jake to take a dive in the

Jake La Motta (Robert De Niro) is tempted by child siren Vickie (Cathy Moriarty) in his father's apartment in *Raging Bull* (United Artists, 1980).

fight against Billy Fox on November 14, 1947, it amounts to nothing less than a sacrifice. Although Jake refuses to be knocked down, the degradation of prostituting his gift reinforces his inherent masochism and contributes to his massive downfall. Repeatedly in the film we are presented with images and sounds that point to ritual bloodletting and present Jake as the bull that is to be ceremonially slaughtered. The title, *Raging Bull*, is superimposed over iconic slow-motion images of Jake alone in the ring, like the bull in the bullpen before the ritual offering. In the beginning he is called an animal by a neighbor, Joey constantly says he eats like an animal, he was nicknamed The Bronx Bull because of his endurance and ferociousness in the ring, he has a brutish and primitive character, and when he finally faces his shadow on the wall in the dark prison cell, he repeats over and over, "I'm not an animal."

In the Roman Empire in the early centuries of Christianity, the secret pagan cult of Mithras reenacted the mythological killing of a sacred bull by the ancient Persian divinity. The story of Mithras bears many parallels to the story of Christ, among them the fact that Mithras saved the world by sacrificing a bull, whereas Christ did it by sacrificing Himself. In both cases the redemption was symbolized by the spilling of blood. The Mithras myth might help make sense of the fact that Scorsese continually likens La Motta to Christ.

The offering of the bull in this film takes place in three stages, signified by three encounters in the ring. First he throws the fight against Billy Fox, defiling his talent and his own essence. Secondly, he gets his reward for doing so: the title shot against Marcel Cerdan in 1949. Interestingly, the match that makes La Motta World Middleweight Champion is shown as even more insidious and detrimental to his soul than the one he throws. We see him being led to the ring through dark, windowless, subterranean hallways which call to mind the Mithraea: for all practical purposes this is a bull being led passively to the slaughter. The Intermezzo from *Cavaleria Rusticana* that was played over the lone bull in the bullpen during the opening titles is repeated here. This has to be the quickest, most untriumphant victory in the history of boxing movies; the entire match takes a total of 90 seconds. Thirdly, he loses the title to Sugar Ray Robinson in their sixth and final matchup, the most memorable fight in the film and the very last one. It took place on February 14, 1951, but for the first time a date is not specified, which implies that the symbolic significance is more important now than historical facts.

Raging Bull is permeated with Biblical references that liken La Motta's suffering in the ring to the suffering of Christ on the cross, the sacrificial bull to the sacrificial lamb. These culminate in this final matchup with Robinson, the most intensely ritual scene in the film. The flashbulbs of the press photographers have an agonizing, piercing sound reminiscent of glass breaking, and over certain shots there is a roaring sound like the one Scorsese later used for the crucifixion in *The Last Temptation of Christ*. At one point Jake's trainer makes what looks like the sign of the cross with the ointment he rubs on him, and before the thirteenth and final round, he bathes him with a sponge that he dips into a bucket of bloody water, suggesting the Instruments of the Passion.[37]

During most of the round we focus on Jake standing perfectly still, urging Robinson to hit him. We hear a bullroar and Jake appears to be steaming. "Come on, Ray," he keeps repeating while taking the most astounding blows to the face. The blows are all filmed in excruciating slow motion which make then almost palpable to the audience. "How he can survive them nobody knows," says announcer Ted Husing. "No man can endure this punishment!" Rather than remaining the passive victim of Mithras, the bull at this moment offers himself up for slaughter. Rather than remaining the passive victim of Joey, Salvy and Tommy Como, Jake steps up and voluntarily lets himself be crucified. As with the crucifixion, what may appear to be only a senseless, barbaric sacrifice becomes the means through which redemption is possible. When it is proclaimed that the championship has changed hands, Jake points out that what seems like bloody defeat is actually a victory: "I never went down, Ray," he insists. "You never got me down!"[38] The camera then starts moving slowly and searchingly around the ring, until it finally rests on Jake's blood dripping from the ropes, the single most astounding shot in the film.

"*Raging Bull* is about a man who loses everything and then regains it spiritually," says Scorsese.[39] Jake's ultimate encounter with the dark night of the soul will have to reflect something deep inside himself. After his previous fight against Robinson, Jake responded to losing with a karmic thought that seemed inspired by his having an extramarital affair with a child: "I've done a lot of bad things, Joey. Maybe it's comin' back at me. Who knows?" Karma eventually catches up when he is arrested for "introducing" a 14-year-old girl "to some men" at his nightclub in 1957. This incident costs him everything he has left: his marriage, his championship belt, his club, his freedom, and his remaining sense of self.

When the wardens lock him up in the Dade County Stockade, it looks as if they are trying to cage a frantic, wild animal, and Jake is reduced to the most primitive state imaginable. His supreme ordeal is facing himself, facing the distorted shadow on the wall of the dungeon, so that he can reclaim his entire self, his humanity, and forgive himself. Inside the cell, however, he starts banging his head against the wall, heartbreakingly wailing, "They call me an animal! I'm not an animal!—I'm not that guy!"—discarding and forsaking the very side of himself for which he ought to feel compassion.

Redemption through boxing? In the final matchup with Sugar Ray Robinson in *Raging Bull* (United Artists, 1980), the sufferings of Jake La Motta (Robert De Niro) in the ring are likened to the sufferings of Christ on the cross. While these images are certainly brutal, they actually contain immense hope.

The penultimate scene is agonizing. Jake sees his estranged brother in the street and follows him into a garage. Jake prostrates and humiliates himself in asking Joey's forgiveness, whereas Joey remains detached and aloof, pushing Jake away as he tries to embrace him. Although Joey is guilty of the most inconceivable betrayal, he still projects all responsibility for their differences onto Jake, pathetically incapable of forgiving and owning up to his own significant share in them.

In the final scene Jake is sitting in front of the mirror. He is reciting the scene from *On the Waterfront* in which Terry Malloy blames his brother for his failure:

"It was *you*, Charlie!" Jake is looking at himself in the mirror when reciting these lines, however, and so it is feasible to assume that he is finally facing that dark shadow brother inside himself that he refused in the prison cell; that he is finally taking responsibility for the fact that his torment was self-inflicted, that he was his own only real opponent, and that he is finally capable of looking at the dark reflection, the demon brother inside the mirror with kindness and compassion.

"How can Scorsese possibly compare this repulsive, brutal man to Jesus Christ?" people have repeatedly asked me. The answer to that question, I believe, comes at the very end, when Scorsese quotes the Gospel According to St. John: "So, for the second time, [the Pharisees] summoned the man who had been blind and said: 'Speak the truth before God. We know this fellow is a sinner.' 'Whether or not he is a sinner, I do not know,' the man replied. 'All I know is this: once I was blind and now I can see.'"[40] The passage is followed by a dedication to Scorsese's mentor who, sadly, died before this masterwork was finished: "Remembering Haig P. Manoogian, teacher. May 23, 1916–May 26, 1980. With Love and resolution, Marty." Ending the film with these two texts, Scorsese likens himself to the man who was blind but now has achieved the ability to see — to feel love and resolution — thanks to He whom the Pharisees prejudged as a sinner, and Jake La Motta — whom we have prejudged as abhorrent — to Christ.

It is always hard to be faced with the darkest aspects of the shadow on a big screen, and *Raging Bull* probably remains Scorsese's most excruciating work. In real life, Jake La Motta mistakenly believed he had killed a man, and his guilt and remorse over this motivated his self-punishment. By deciding not to include this information in his film, Scorsese makes it less specific and more universal: Jake's need to suffer is fueled only by himself, and whether we will admit it or not, he comes to represent whatever masochistic and self-defeating shadow traits we all have deep inside us. This is what makes *Raging Bull* one of the most painful, at times almost unbearable, of Scorsese's films. Watching it, we are constantly faced with and reminded of our own most painful secrets.

This film not only reflects Scorsese's own darkest demons, however, but also his facing and surviving these demons. He has often admitted that making *Raging Bull* saved his life and helped him acknowledge and feel kindness toward Jake's self-destructive nature "after having gone through a similar experience."[41] Just imagine if we were able to truly listen to what Martin Scorsese is saying in this film. Imagine what *we* would be able to see, what would be available to us, what abundance could be at our disposal if we too had the courage to face that raging bull inside which this film ritually invites us to embrace. Imagine if we were to bring light to those sides of ourselves that we have ignored and imprisoned in the dark for most of our lives for being too disgusting, pitiful and unworthy, and to instead regard them as part of who we are, with love and resolution!

GoodFellas

GoodFellas (1990) is Martin Scorsese's scintillating adaptation of Nicholas Pileggi's bestseller *Wise Guy; Life in a Mafia Family*. The book tells the story of mobster Henry Hill, as narrated to Pileggi by Henry and his wife, Karen, in the early 1980s. After the book was published, Pileggi was contacted by Scorsese. "One day I answered the phone," Pileggi says, "and this guy said, 'My name is Marty Scorsese and I'm a movie director.'" Scorsese said that he was interested in doing a film version of the book, and Pileggi answered: "To tell you the truth, I've been waiting for this phone call all my life. If you want to do it, you can do it."[42]

The two of them worked together on the screenplay, and Scorsese was particularly interested in making a film that was different from the typical gangster film. *GoodFellas*, he says, is "the exploration of a lifestyle. It's about what it means to be in a life of that kind, minute-by-minute, day-by-day."[43] Despite its real-life origins and portrayal of the daily routines of the gangsters, the film is structured so that it moves inevitably toward tragedy, and even though Henry is based on a real person, in the film he becomes a fictional character with a distinct tragic flaw. Paul Sorvino (who plays Paul Cicero) says about his character that "he wields an awful lot of power. And yet he has a very vulnerable side, so much so that he treats Henry like a son. He really loves him — in fact, that love is his downfall."[44] *GoodFellas* is a masterfully directed film, an unrelenting bombardment of visual and auditory impressions and contradictory emotions. It is also the first film Scorsese made with Robert De Niro in the seven years since *The King of Comedy*.

In the opening scene, we see Jimmy (Robert De Niro), Tommy (Joe Pesci) and Henry (Ray Liotta) late at night in a car in 1970. "There was Jimmy and Tommy and me," says Henry later, as if to suggest that the three of them are the center of the universe. In addition to the three of them, however, there is Billy Batts (Frank Vincent) who is in the trunk of the car and turns out to be not quite as dead as they think he is. They stop the car and get out to solve the problem, each pulling from his coat an object that turns out to be an emblem of his nature and how we are to read him. Tommy has a gigantic butcher knife. He represents raw, mindless physical force. He likes to be close enough when he kills people so that he can feel it, and he proceeds to stab Batts so frantically that we can almost sense the spatter of blood. Jimmy has a gun. His nickname is "the Gent." He has the overview, kills when it is necessary, can wield his power from a distance, and he shoots Batts repeatedly. Henry has a key. He merely opens the trunk, then stands back and watches, letting the others do the dirty work.

The image freezes in a close-up of Henry and his voice-over narration begins: "As far back as I can remember, I always wanted to be a gangster," he says, rather startlingly after what we have just witnessed. We cut back 15 years, to 1955, to an extreme close-up of young Henry's eye as he watches the cabstand across the street where the gangsters hang out, while on the soundtrack his adult voice continues the story. The concept of the narrator is significant in many Scorsese films, but in *GoodFellas* it becomes the entire point. Henry is narrating in retrospect, which makes him omniscient and omnipotent as regards the story. Often the things he tells us make him seem slightly less violent or insensitive than his friends, but if we look closely, details in his narration (of which he may not be conscious) give him away.[45]

This raises an interesting question: what if this narrator is not just unreliable but actually a psychopath who can make us believe anything he wants to? Henry repeatedly lies in a deliberate attempt to mislead us and make us like him, and he is so good at it that we hardly notice or mind. His object in the opening scene — the key — signifies that it is, in fact, he who holds the key to the story, and it pays off to constantly keep in mind that he alone decides which doors, trunks and closets are opened for us to look into and which are not. The twisted Sid Vicious version of "My Way" that ends the film gives us a powerful hint that the entire story is Henry's attempt to exonerate himself, to wash his hands of the whole thing and disclaim responsibility. *GoodFellas* is a disconcerting and nauseating roller coaster ride, a choreographed dance of bamboozlement that takes us through the inner workings of Henry's mind, and the most frightening thing is that, judging by many reviews of the film, this master manipulator gets away with it.

Chronologically, Henry's story begins when he stands at the window in Brooklyn as a boy, looking longingly at the cabstand across the street.[46] This image calls to mind the photo of the view of Elizabeth Street from the Scorsese apartment where the asthmatic Marty would stand as a child, looking down at the hoodlums and gangsters below. Whereas the shot suggests a connection between Henry and Marty, the difference between them is, of course, that Marty did not cross the line that the street connotes. The extreme close-up of his eyes also connects Henry with Travis Bickle and emphasizes that what we are about to see is constantly filtered through his perceptions. Whereas Travis is a textbook example of the disorganized killer, Henry is a classic example of a different kind of criminal. FBI profiler John Douglas describes a typical psychopathic offender as "a sane individual with a character disorder such that, while he knew the difference between right and wrong, he wasn't going to let that moral distinction get in his way."[47] Although Henry tries to present himself as better than Jimmy and Tommy, he repeatedly reveals himself to be amoral and emotionless, to have an almost reptilian lack of empathy even for those who are supposed to be nearest and dearest to him.

Mythologically, this is the story of a boy who is yearning for a new family, a new glorious father to replace his humble working-class father. It is important for him to be treated with respect and like a grownup, he says, but "my father could never understand." What takes place is a transference of masculine authority. This is emphasized when Henry is beaten up by his father for missing school and we cut to the mobsters, under orders from the new father, finding and beating up a man whom we think is Henry's father until we realize that it is the mailman who delivered the letter about Henry's truancy to their house. A new paternal trinity — Tuddy (Frank DiLeo), Paulie, and Jimmy — is presented within the next couple of minutes. Through Henry's eyes we focus on close-ups of jewelry, clothes, dollar bills and expensive cars. What turns this child on is the persona, the demonstration of extreme external power. This is emphasized when he proudly shows his mother his new suit and is thrilled by her shocked reaction: "My God! You look like a gangster!" "To me, being a gangster was better than being president of the United States," Henry says, a statement which is in complete accordance with his character since a gangster has all the power without having to bother with the needs, feelings, or constitutional rights of other people. Immediately upon entering the new tribal family, the child is handed a significant symbol of power — the *keys* to a Cadillac he has to park.

Summing up what the new family meant to him, Henry says that now he was taken care of first at the baker's, glossing over the fact that the reason for this is not that he is respected but that he is feared. People pay tribute to Paulie so that he will protect them. "It is protection for people who could not go to the cops," Henry says, "that's all it is!" We then cut to a shot that negates this statement: the boy smashing car windows and blowing up a vehicle, something that can hardly be categorized as protecting people. "If anyone complained," he tells us shortly afterwards, "He was hit so hard he never complained again."

Soon the true nature of the young boy is shown: Henry is arrested for selling stolen goods and even though he knows fully well that it is illegal, he is totally convinced that it is all right for *him* to be doing it and keeps trying to assure the cops that "it's all right."

(From left to right) Henry Hill (Ray Liotta) in *GoodFellas* (Warner Bros., 1990) with his chosen family: Jimmy (Robert De Niro), Paulie (Paul Sorvino) and Tommy (Joe Pesci).

When he is released, the mobsters show up with presents to congratulate him. "Everybody gets pinched," Jimmy says. "But you did it right. You told 'em nothing and they got nothing. You learned the two greatest things in life. Never rat on your friends and always keep your mouth shut." Henry has passed his first test and is now literally shown at the center of the group. He has also acquired important knowledge and power: indirectly Jimmy has revealed to him that if you really want to hit this family where it hurts, you rat on them.

With the next cut, we jump to 1963. Henry has grown up, and soon we are pulled even further into his universe with a dizzying Steadicam shot. Traditionally, editing has been considered the most filmic device of all because it so obviously moves the film forward in time and cannot be copied in any other medium or art form, but Scorsese's idiosyncratic use of aesthetics has given the sense of time in cinema a whole new meaning. "There was Jimmy and Tommy and me," Henry begins and continues to introduce us to his friends at the Bamboo Lounge—Anthony Stabile, Frankie Carbone, Freddie No-Nose and Jimmy Two-Times. Not only do they come across as a solidly connected unit, but each member of the audience is personally included in this unit: I, represented by the camera (eye = I), walk through the room next to Henry, who informs me who each person is. The wise guy in question then looks straight into the camera—i.e., at me—and asks how I am doing. Rather than cutting and replacing one shot with another, Scorsese keeps moving the camera, staggeringly changing the framing and pulling the audience further and further into the filmic universe, until we are no longer capable of comfortably leaning back and disconnecting ourselves spatially, emotionally or morally.

The long, flexible framing shot has, of course, been used before, but rarely as consistently and with such a liquid sense of exhilarating energy as in the works of Martin Scorsese. A few minutes later, Karen (Lorraine Bracco) enters, and the next scenes are told from her point of view to the extent that she even takes over the narration. On her first real date with Henry, he pulls rank so they can jump the queue in front of the Copacabana and enter through the side door. We trail after them through the hallways and kitchen, and again our sense of identification is reinforced by the fact that the Steadicam allows us to share Karen's dizziness and excitement. In addition to moving the camera in complicated and magnetically fascinating maneuvers where we would have expected him to cut, Scorsese does it so that the movements of the camera fit the beats of the music — what I call "rhythmic framing." Instead of cutting, Scorsese has the camera turn a corner or change direction whenever we have heard 4, 8 or 12 beats of "And Then He Kissed Me."[48]

Karen is a nice Jewish girl, and she is flabbergasted over Henry's world. "I couldn't stand him," is the first thing we hear her saying. If we too feel that way — which well we might since this is right after the "funny guy" exchange — this gives us the illusion that now we have someone who is closer to us and our perspective with whom we can safely identify. She confirms our impressions of this tribal family and their insularity. These people did everything together and "there were never any outsiders around," she says. "Absolutely never. And being together all the time made everything seem all the more normal." So comforting is the sense of having someone we can identify with, that we hardly notice that Karen is only marginally less perturbing than Henry. From the beginning she seems to enjoy throwing tantrums in public, and later she repeatedly makes excessive scenes in front of her children, never paying any attention to the fact that she is frightening them. Once she uses the children as hostages when she brings them along for a confrontation with Henry's mistress, cursing and carrying on like a madwoman: later she throws a jealous tantrum when Henry is in jail while her children are watching. One night, after a violent altercation between Karen and Henry, the camera focuses on their little girl who is standing in the doorway in a nightgown, looking completely lost.

By her own admission, Karen decides to marry Henry because she sees him pistol-whip her neighbor, Bruce, to a pulp and then asks her to hide the gun: "I gotta admit the truth. It turned me on." We cut from Karen wrapping up the gun to the rabbi wrapping up the glass at the wedding ceremony as if one action leads directly to the other. "I didn't think there was anything strange about this," she confesses — she is just proud to have a husband "who would risk his neck to go out and get us the little extras." At one point Karen needs money to go shopping, and Henry gives her a bundle of cash. Her response to this is to get down on her knees to pay him back — a direct exchange of oral sex for money that makes her, for all practical purposes, a prostitute in her own home.

GoodFellas has a circular structure. The killing of Billy Batts does not mark the ending of the film, however, but a point slightly less than halfway into it. The scene begins at Henry's club in Queens, and the date is specified as June 11, 1970. Batts is celebrating his release after six years in prison, and he jokingly insults Tommy by reminding everyone that he used be a shoeshine boy. Finally, Tommy explodes and kicks Batts to death, aided by Jimmy and accompanied by Donovan's gentle song "Atlantis." All the while Henry is looking

Tommy's mother prepares an elaborate late-night dinner for her son and his friends in *GoodFellas* (Warner Bros., 1990). *(From left to right)* Henry (Ray Liotta), Tommy (Joe Pesci), Tommy's mother (Catherine Scorsese), and Jimmy (Robert De Niro).

on worriedly, and he continues to do so during the elaborate late-night dinner Tommy's mother (Catherine Scorsese) insists on cooking for them when they make an excursion to her house to borrow a knife so they can cut up the body.

Now we are back in the car, precisely where we started, and the circle closes with 80 minutes still left of the film. The fact that Henry begins the story with this event proposes that it is the major turning point. People were killing each other all the time, he explains, but "before you could touch a made guy, you had to have a good reason. You had to have a sitdown and you better get an okay, or you'd be the one who got whacked."

His narration leads us to believe that the events that follow are a direct result of the killing of Billy Batts, and since he claims to have been an innocent bystander to that, this would make him a victim of circumstance. However, things start snowballing as a consequence of Henry's own choices and actions, but we have to infer this for ourselves without any help from his narration. He starts seeing his mistress, Janice, openly until the temperamental Karen blows a fuse and becomes a nuisance and a potential threat to the tribal family. Henry is ordered to make up with his wife and to go down to Tampa with Jimmy on a job. As a direct consequence of this, they are all arrested and sent to jail. And *this* is what really marks the center point of the film. While serving his sentence, Henry starts taking and selling drugs clandestinely, knowing full well that Paulie would strongly disapprove — again, a deliberate choice. When he is released four years later, Paulie confronts him and says that while drugs may have been necessary in prison, he has to stop now. Henry unscrupulously denies everything and continues to sell cocaine on the sly, indifferent to the fact that he puts Paulie's business and life at risk doing so. And even though he has indeed stopped seeing Janice as he promised Karen, she has merely been replaced by another mistress.

In a mythological sense, this is a story of three sons who go against their father's wishes. In connection with the Air France caper in 1963, Henry pointed out that "we did the right thing, we gave Paulie his tribute." Now, more than a decade later, Jimmy, Tommy and Henry put a crew together for the Lufthansa heist, which turns out to be the biggest heist in history, and this time they greedily decide to do it behind Paulie's back. Throughout, Paulie Cicero, the father, is the stabilizing factor who keeps things under control. Doing it without him, then, intrinsically denotes infantile overindulgence. Predictably, things get out of hand and mayhem follows. Intoxicated by all the money, the members of their crew start spending and doing drugs like there is no tomorrow, and Jimmy starts having them liquidated, one by one. Then, and only then, does retribution for Billy Batts catch up when the mob kills Tommy.

As he did with the killing of Billy Batts, Henry tries to wash his hands of the Lufthansa aftermath: "It had nothing to do with me," he says. This obviously makes no sense, but even if we do believe him and disregard his participation in the heist, he and he alone is responsible for the final act, when he is arrested — *not* by the local police over Lufthansa, but by the narcs.

The overwrought third act is marked by a specific date — May 11, 1980 — and during this day Scorsese uses the aesthetics exhilaratingly to make us experience Henry's and Karen's coke-induced paranoia. Henry has to juggle a staggering number of projects. He is cooking an elaborate dinner for his handicapped younger brother, driving around frantically trying to unload some guns, getting a shipment of coke ready for a courier who is going to Atlanta, arguing with his wife and his mistress, and obsessing over a helicopter that is following him wherever he goes. At one point he goes to his mistress's apartment for more coke, and at the moment he sniffs it, the music cuts abruptly from George Harrison's upbeat "What is Life" to the heavy blues rhythm of Muddy Waters's "Mannish Boy" as the camera quickly moves in on Henry's deteriorating face, catapulting his experience into *our* systems. Finally, the shipment is ready and he goes out to his car with the babysitter/courier and is arrested. "For a second I thought I was dead," he says, but then he hears a sound and concludes that it must be the police and not the mob: "If they had been wise guys I wouldn't have heard a thing. I would have been dead."

He constantly tries to persuade us that Paulie wants to have him killed, but everything points to this being a deliberate lie or a drug-induced delusion. For one thing, taking Henry out would be the easiest thing in the world for Paulie, and it obviously does not happen. For another, Henry voluntarily goes to Paulie to ask for money after losing his stash. Paulie looks at him while continuing to cook sausages and says dejectedly, "You looked in my eyes, you lied to me. You treated me like a fucking jerk. Like I was never nothing to you." Then he gives Henry a wad of bills and sends him away. As if asking Paulie for help after betraying him and endangering his life is not insolent enough, Henry now complains that the money he gave him was not enough.

So convincing is Henry's claim that he is a victim of circumstance and that his life is in danger, that even the most perceptive members of his audience are bound, at least momentarily, to be seduced by it. Roger Ebert, in his review, took Henry's words at face value. "This kind of work," he wrote, "fills the soul with guilt and the heart with dread, and before long Henry Hill is walking around as if there's a lead weight in his stomach."[49] There is no doubt that Henry feels a substantial amount of dread as the film progresses, but I never see any sign of guilt. He keeps telling us that he did not have the stomach for this — he did not participate in killing Batts either time, he was sickened when they had to dig up the body six months later, he tried to talk Jimmy out of killing Morrie, etc.— but there is a serious discordance between what he says and what we actually see. Guilt would indicate that he has concern for the people who made his dream come true, a sense of remorse, or at least an awareness of having done something wrong, which he never does.

Like the classic tragic hero, the central character has a fatal flaw. Greed and indifference become Henry's downfall, and Henry's downfall becomes the downfall of everyone else when he does the only thing the psychopath knows to do: save his own hide. He negotiates with the FBI, and after striking an acceptable bargain, he rats out his friends. Where Karen's biggest worry about going into the witness protection program is that she cannot see her parents anymore, Henry's one concern is that he would like to be set up in a place where the climate is nice. Based on his evidence, his chosen father and mentor are arrested, and without batting an eye, Henry testifies against them in court.

It goes without saying that if we view Paul Cicero and Jimmy Conway from a normal real-life perspective, we would not be too crazy about what they stand for. The criterion here, however, should not be that of real life but that of Henry's fictional story since he himself eagerly chose them as his new father and mentor. From a mythological point of view the scenes of their arrest are heartbreaking, as is the scene in which Henry testifies against them. We zoom in on their angry and disappointed faces, and even Henry's own mother looks chagrined, as he flippantly reveals that his only concern is how all this affects him. "See, the hardest thing for me was leaving the life," he admits. "Anything I wanted was a phone call away. And now it's all over." At this moment the chronology of the narrative catches up with the narrator: Henry looks directly into the camera from the witness stand and continues his story on screen, still cavalierly dismissing the consequences of his actions: "It didn't matter. It didn't mean anything!"

Like the other films discussed in this chapter, *GoodFellas* concerns the archetypal themes of loyalty and treason, trust and betrayal, but in this film it is the central character who is the traitor. In the course of the film Henry Hill lets down his birth family, the family he creates with Karen, and the symbolic tribal family he himself has chosen. This remarkable moment in the courtroom shows that the entire story is told as an act of self-glorification from the witness stand, and that Henry's betrayal of the father, not the killing of Billy Batts, is the real pivotal point of the film.

Henry's perfidy takes the form of ratting, and the informer is regarded with contempt in most cultures. In Christianity the act is instantly associated with Judas, and "most people — including those who regard his act as the fulfillment of scriptural prophecy — would agree that he came to symbolize the most repellent of traitors," says Victor Navasky. "The Aramaic word for informer as found in the Book of Daniel is *Akhal Kurtza*, whose literal translation is 'to eat the flesh of someone else.'"[50] Henry only shows emotion when he feels cornered or trapped, when his own status or power is threatened, and, to me, his lack of empathy makes him more disturbing than any of Scorsese's other characters.

The image of the boy at the window looking longingly at Paulie Cicero's empire has an iconic quality to it. He wishes for a new father, and his wish is granted. While it pains the Irish Jimmy Conway that neither he nor Henry can ever become made guys and earn the approval of Father, it does not bother Henry in the least, and he thinks Jimmy is a bit silly for being overjoyed when Tommy is apparently being made. Henry only wants the persona, the status, power, and material wealth Paulie Cicero *represents*. He does not care one bit for the man himself. For Henry, there is no emotion involved in choosing a new father. For him the sole point is that when he is associated with Paulie, he does not have to wait in line at the bakery. Now "I have to wait around like everybody else," he laments at the end, "I am an average nobody." His money is gone, his power is gone, and he is living in an anonymous, suburban neighborhood where — when he orders spaghetti with marinara sauce at a restaurant — he is served egg noodles with ketchup.

The very last thing we see is Henry standing in the doorway to his new house. He looks healthier, but still has a devil-may-care grin on his face. We cut to an image of Tommy who shoots directly at the camera (and by implication at Henry and at us), and then back to Henry who shrugs, goes inside his new house and shuts the door. Tommy, the card-carrying psychopath, unequivocally personifies dangerous and aggressive shadow characteristics. If we see him as Henry's dark twin, he reveals the things Henry is trying to hide from us and points out his hypocrisy. One of the most unforgettable scenes in the film is the one in which Henry says to Tommy, "You're a funny guy!" The scene quite obviously illustrates how dangerous Tommy is, but it shows us something interesting about Henry, too. When he realizes that Tommy was just pulling his leg, he laughs unguardedly in relief — the revealing laugh that Debbie Ford calls the "shadow laugh" — and this is every bit as frightening as Tommy's menacing behavior. After the exchange, Tommy looks at him and says: "I wonder about you sometimes, Henry. You may fold under questioning!" The dark brother sees through Henry instantly and reveals the outcome of the story less than 20 minutes into the film. Tommy, the shadow brother, may be dead, but he is not gone. What he stands for still has to be reckoned with, and he comes back to haunt Henry and us, even now that Henry is apparently scot-free and we are about to leave the movie theater.

Casino

Catherine Scorsese died on January 6, 1997, at the age of 84. Her last appearance on film was as Artie Piscano's feisty mother in *Casino*. As usual, her two primary functions were cooking and acting as a moralizing superego, protesting profusely whenever her son swears. Even before we see her, attentive members of the audience will have guessed that she is on her way when Nicky tells us that "one of the guys made his mother do all the cooking." When she appears, she is teaching her granddaughter (played by Scorsese's oldest daughter, Catherine) how to cook, passing on her legacy. Shortly before her death, she published *Italianamerican: The Scorsese Family Cookbook* so that we can all have a go at Catherine Scorsese's legendary spaghetti sauce with meatballs and other favorites.

Like *GoodFellas*, *Casino* (1995) was a collaboration between Martin Scorsese and Nicholas Pileggi. *GoodFellas* was an adaptation of a book that Pileggi had already published. In the case of *Casino*, the book and the film were made simultaneously. Pileggi's book is based on extensive interviews with the real people behind the story and, again, the film maintains verisimilitude combined with deeply mythological layers. Real-life Frank Rosenthal is renamed Sam "Ace" Rothstein, Tony Spilotro becomes Nicky Santoro, and Geri McGee becomes Ginger McKenna.

When it was first released, *Casino* was superficially and unfairly tagged "*GoodFellas* removed to Las Vegas." "So striking are the films' similarities that *Casino*'s raison d'être seems unclear," says one critic.[51] Although the two films have many things in common — they are authentic works about the mafia, they contain some of the same actors, they have shifting narrators — they are actually quite different, on the explicit surface layer as well as the deeper symbolic layers, as we shall see shortly.

Like *GoodFellas*, *Casino* is about organized crime, a subcultural brotherhood, male interaction, and the city streets. It may take place in Las Vegas, but the tribal rules of the street are constantly present as an implicit and abstract principle. In the narration they are constantly referred to as the basis for the conflicts in the present, and apart from various profanities, the most frequently repeated words are "back home," "years ago," and "since then." Sam Rothstein (Robert De Niro) is an outsider who stands on the perimeter of the group and can never completely enter it. Clarence Henry's song about the lonely boy who "Ain't Got No Home" is played twice in the film, and is a perfect description of Sam.

Also like *GoodFellas*, this film is circular: it begins in 1983, cuts back to the early 1970s, then works its way back to 1983. In the pre-title sequence, Sam — dressed beyond immaculacy — exits a restaurant and walks toward his car. His retrospective voice-over narration begins: "When you love someone, you've gotta trust them. There's no other way. You've got to give them the key to everything that's yours. Otherwise, what's the point? And for a while that's the kind of love I thought I had." He gets into his car, turns the key in the ignition, and the car explodes. During the title sequence, we see his body flying in slow motion over red, purple, green and blue neon signs, the flames from the burning car at the bottom of the screen, accompanied by Bach's *St. Matthew Passion*. Because the background images move upward, it looks as if Ace's body is falling, connoting an expulsion from paradise and descent into Hell. The screenplay says: "His body twists and turns through the frame like a soul about to tumble into the flames of damnation." We are sure that Ace is killed by the explosion, so when he continues his story as we cut back to 1973, it would

Scorsese often refers to famous paintings in his visual compositions. In this stunning image of the pantheon of Midwest bosses in *Casino* (Universal Pictures, 1995) — with Remo Gaggi (Pasquale Cajano) solidly planted in the center — there is a clear nod to Caravaggio. Other actors not identified in cast list.

seem that he is narrating from the hereafter. Knowing Scorsese's fondness for classic Hollywood movies, this might be a tongue-in-cheek reference to *Sunset Blvd.*, in which the narrator turns out in the end to be dead.

Shortly after the title sequence, the narration is temporarily taken over by Nicky Santoro (Joe Pesci), Ace's childhood friend. Ace has just told us that he was "given paradise on earth" when he was entrusted with running a casino for the Midwest mob bosses. Nicky immediately reveals the darker sides of the same story: "In the end we fucked it all up," he tells us, "it turned out to be the last time that street guys like us were ever given anything that fuckin' valuable again."

It is indicated that the film concerns sin, trust and betrayal, penance and potential redemption, death and potential resurrection, and during the first few minutes we are given significant implications regarding the nature of Sam's mythological journey. The films discussed in this chapter are all about treachery, and Sam reveals himself to be so obsessed with the fear of betrayal that he is bound to attract it. His opening words may refer to Nicky, on whose initiative he is blown to kingdom come, or to Ginger (Sharon Stone). He falls in love with a woman who is openly undependable, marries her against his better judgment, and then insists on trusting her. "I have to be able to trust you with my life," he keeps saying. "Can I trust you?" I always have a strong urge to shake my head whenever he asks this, and the very fact that he feels the need to repeat it so often reveals that he knows he cannot and should not trust her. Nevertheless, he gives her the key to a safe deposit box containing two million dollars: "My shakedown and kidnapping money. And, since I'd either be in jail or locked in a closet when I needed the money the most, I gave Ginger the only key to the cash that could get me back alive."

The answer to why he feels compelled to trust her and set himself up for certain failure is contained in his immaculate appearance. Throughout, Sam is impeccably dressed to the point where at times he looks involuntarily comical. His self-invented persona may be consummately perfect, but it is only a thin veneer over what is underneath: the slum kid who has come up in the world, the past he is trying to escape from, the real Sam Rothstein. He admits as much between the lines: "Anywhere else in the country, I was a bookie, a gambler, always lookin' over my shoulder, hassled by cops, day and night. But here, I'm 'Mr. Sam Rothstein.' I'm not only legitimate, but running a casino." We cannot, of course, run away from the past or our true self, and paradoxically, the more Sam relies on symbols of external power in an attempt to mask it (money, clothes, the casino, physical violence, an abundantly luxurious house, expensive Bvlgari jewelry to hang on a trophy wife), the more frightened and disempowered he feels inside. At various points, we see him demonstrating his power over trifles precisely because he feels extremely powerless.

His dilemma touches upon both Gatsby's fear of having his true origins exposed in F. Scott Fitzgerald's *The Great Gatsby* and Arthur Dimmesdale's spiritual agony in Nathaniel Hawthorne's *The Scarlet Letter*. Just like James Gatz is always present underneath the self-made Jay Gatsby, so Ace Rothstein is terrified that the façade of the casino manager will rip to reveal the street kid he is trying to run away from. But as Hawthorne says: "No man, for any considerable period, can wear one face to himself and another to the multitude, without finally getting bewildered as to which may be the true."[52]

Sam's obsession with appearing respectable and relying on people who cannot be trusted points toward different things. He is terrified of being exposed for who he is and tries furiously to impose conscious control on his surroundings. At the same time he has a strong

No matter how airtight Sam Rothstein of *Casino* (Universal Pictures, 1995) tries to make his persona, it cannot protect him against Nicky and Ginger or the street kid he is trying to run away from. *Top:* Sam (Robert De Niro) and Nicky (Joe Pesci). *Bottom:* Nicky (Joe Pesci) and Ginger (Sharon Stone).

subconscious urge to *be* exposed. Like so many Scorsese characters, he has an all-pervading masochistic and self-defeating tendency at the center of his being and so he creates a vicious cycle: he does not feel he deserves the splendid mask and sets himself up for exposure; because he is also terrified of that exposure, he tries to control Ginger and exert power over her. Finally, his need to be exposed could be caused by a real spiritual longing to be forced back into a life that is less overblown and more authentic, less dependent on external symbols of power and more truly empowered from the inside.

What brings about the loss of Sam's paradise at the end is not primarily the wrath of Remo Gaggi (Pasquale Cajano), the stupidity of Artie Piscano (Vinny Vella), or even the betrayal of Nicky and Ginger, but the fact that he is trying to hide his true face. On an outer level, the explosion of his car may be instigated by Nicky, but on an archetypal level, the father, the jinx, the nemesis and the blonde woman are reflections of something that goes on deep inside Sam himself, and what brings about his death is his mask and obsession with betrayal.

The more inflated the ego and the more impenetrable the persona, the more dark power the shadow invariably accumulates. Nicky, in this sense, exists *because* Sam looks so immaculate. As Sam spends most of his energy trying to hide the darker sides, Nicky gets more and more dangerous. By definition, Nicky reminds Sam of the things he is trying to hide, because, literally as well as symbolically, he comes from "back home."

Mirroring the two of them is the image of the glittering lights of Las Vegas, the landscape Sam is trying frantically to control, and the surrounding desert that one cannot see at night, where Nicky knows all the rules and reigns supreme. While Ace's casino and the Vegas strip are the lights, music and revelry above, which Hawthorne described in "The Haunted Mind," Nicky's desert is the tomb and the dungeon. "Got a lot of holes in the desert, and a lot of problems are buried in those holes," Nicky informs us. "You gotta have the hole already dug before you show up with a package in the trunk. Otherwise, you're talkin' about a half-hour or forty-five minutes of diggin'. And who knows who's gonna be comin' along in that time? Before you know it, you gotta dig a few more holes. You could be there all fuckin' night." As the film progresses, Nicky becomes associated more and more with the desert, with rooms and houses being invaded, holes being blown and drilled into walls and cut into floors, and things oozing through those holes. At one point the camera is placed inside a cavity in his bedroom floor to which eventually he closes the trapdoor, in effect leaving *us* locked in and buried.

At one point Sam suggests to Andy Stone (Alan King) that they send Nicky on vacation. This so infuriates the dark brother that he orders Sam to meet him in the desert. Going to the shadow territory is obviously terrifying for Sam because it represents everything he is trying to keep at bay: "Meeting in the middle of the desert always made me nervous. It's a scary place. I knew about the holes in the desert, of course, and everywhere I looked, there could have been a hole. Normally, my prospects of comin' back alive from a meeting with Nicky were ninety-nine out of a hundred. But this time, I gave myself fifty-fifty." Shortly after this meeting, Nicky indeed orders Frank Marino (Frank Vincent) to dig a hole in the desert so they have it ready for Sam later.

Nicky Santoro represents the raw, socially unacceptable energy of the shadow. He is the flip side of Sam's attempts at control, and the two are inextricably connected: "Every time you're on television I get mentioned," Sam complains to Nicky, and shortly afterward he laments to Andy Stone, "Every time they mention my name in the papers, these cocksuckers, they mention Nicky, too!" The war between the two gets more and more internecine. "Vegas was like a dream for me," Sam says. "Trouble was Nicky was dreamin' his own kind of Vegas." Nicky makes so much of a spectacle of himself that he is finally banned from the casinos and relegated to the desert altogether. Banishing the shadow only makes it more dangerous, and before long he has a business up and running with the help of some "desperados from back home."

It is fascinating from a psychological point of view *how* Nicky gets himself expelled: Instead of going to other casinos, which would have been easier and safer, he makes trouble right in his own backyard. By openly cheating the casino owned by his own people, Nicky erodes the place from within — mirroring the work of the shadow that erodes us from within when it is ignored.

If we repress the shadow for too long, we can end up assuming its characteristics. That is precisely what happens when pressure is applied and Sam feels threatened. The Gaming Control Board starts investigating him because he has no license. At first he tries to persuade them of his respectability by flaunting his perfect façade. When that does not work, he cracks up and gradually becomes as embarrassing as Nicky. Paradoxically he first loses control at the Control Board Hearing. He feels unjustly treated and starts repeating "Was I at that dinner?" with the same lurking menace as Travis Bickle's "You talkin' to me?" The mask cracks and the dark side clearly shows through. All along he has *felt* unworthy of his persona and now someone else officially states that he is, and so he starts seeking satisfaction with a near-pathological fierceness. As Sam struggles to get his mask back on, the battle with Nicky gets even more intense.

Equally ferocious is his relationship with Ginger, who has a sexual relationship with Nicky. As in *Raging Bull*, the De Niro character suspects his wife of having an affair with his closest friend, the Pesci character. As in *Mean Streets*, it is possible to take the view that the shadow and the anima are, in fact, putting the protagonist through tribulations from which he could learn. Ginger and Nicky are both connected with keys and having access to places that other people cannot get to, and at the precise point that Sam entrusts Ginger with the key that symbolizes life and death, he informs us that Nicky had his own plans for Las Vegas.

The very first time Sam sees Ginger is on a surveillance monitor. She is throwing dice, winning big-time for a high roller while at the same time stealing from him. She ends up creating complete pandemonium at the casino: when the man tells her to get lost, she gleefully tosses thousands of dollars' worth of chips into the air. "I fell in love right there," Sam says. While Ginger is stunning and luminous, she is also a prostitute, a thief, and a troublemaker, and one has the impression that this is why he falls in love with her.[53] "Ginger's mission in life was money," Ace says. She had "the hustler's code." She is interested in him for his money, wanting his persona while not really caring who he is. Ginger, too, has a dark friend from her past who will not go away, her old pimp boyfriend, Lester Diamond (James Woods), whom she has "been with" since she was a kid (which connects her with Iris in *Taxi Driver* and Vickie in *Raging Bull*). While Ginger seems to be on pretty straight terms with her nemesis, accepting him with all his flaws, Sam tries to deny and demolish Lester as well as Ginger's affection for him.

It becomes apparent that Sam suffers not so much from a Madonna/whore complex, as from a Magdalene complex, wanting the whore to be penitent so he can transform her into a saint. His urge to save Ginger is bound to fail since she does not seem to want saving.

His insistence on changing her into a respectable, trustworthy person is actually a subtle form of abuse, and the story becomes one of boy meets girl, boy marries girl, boy destroys girl. When Sam asks Ginger to marry him it is clear that she is a symptom of his masochism and that the eventual loss of paradise is partly self-induced: "The gods were happy, or as happy as the gods can ever be. And I, I decided to complicate my life. For a guy who likes sure things, I was about to bet the rest of my life on a real long shot." By profession Sam is a handicapper, and when he starts his proposal Ginger says: "What, are you trying to handicap me?" The word is significant because Sam literally handicaps her after they are married. When she is a self-reliant whore she looks radiant, but after she becomes "Mrs. Sam Rothstein" she begins gradually to look more and more emaciated and unhealthy until she finally dies of an overdose, alone and destitute.

Whereas money may not be the answer to every question posed in the film, it is certainly important here, as in much of Scorsese's work. Symbolically money represents vital life energy. In *After Hours* his money is the first thing Paul loses. Betsy in *Taxi Driver* raises money for a living, whereas Iris and Matthew sell sex for money. In *Cape Fear*, Sam tries to pay off the shadow with money which makes him very angry. In *Raging Bull*, people keep talking about making money off Jake and buying a piece of him, and the central motif in *Mean Streets* is Johnny Boy owing everybody money. Interestingly, we never see Johnny borrowing money. What we *do* see is all the other characters desperately trying to get money out of *him*. Johnny is the repressed shadow that eats up energy, and we constantly see everyone chasing this dynamo, endlessly trying to get him to pay up.

Before Sam and Ginger are married, she constantly gives everyone money, having plenty of energy to spare. After they are married, she is gradually drained, and Sam is holding her hostage by withholding money. Ironically, although he gives her the key to everything he has, she has to humiliate herself whenever she actually needs cash, and whatever she gets out of him is instantly taken away by Lester. "Look, Sam," Ginger says, "I've been independent my whole life. I never had to ask anybody for anything. Now you're making me beg you for this. You're embarrassing me. Why do want to make me feel so bad?" Ace's only reply is his fearful, manipulative song and dance: "You're askin' me for twenty-five thousand. I'm not out to make you feel bad. I want to just be able to trust you. You know, it's about trust. I have to be able to trust you with my life. Do you understand? Can I trust you? Can I trust you? Can I trust you? Answer me."

For Sam, money symbolizes the external power upon which he is so dependent. It can buy the things that make up the persona which he believes protects him from the past, and when he gives Ginger the key to his money, he expressly hands over his entire life and his freedom. When she violates his trust and runs off with Lester, her perfidy obviously runs a lot deeper than the cash she has taken, but the $25,000 she has squandered is all Sam is capable of focusing on when they go out to dinner after she comes back. He keeps nitpicking on the exact amount she has spent with such overwhelming hatred and disgust that he makes her withdraw even further. He is emotionally incapable of expressing that he is devastated and wants her to acknowledge her enormous betrayal and give him back some of his dignity, so his sole focus is on the money.

Coming out to Vegas in the first place is only about money. "What do you think we're doing out here in the middle of the desert? It's all this money," Sam says. "It's all been arranged just for us to get *your* money. That's the truth about Las Vegas. We're the only winners. The players don't stand a chance. And their cash flows from the tables to our boxes, through the cage and into the most sacred room in the casino, the place where they add up all the money, the holy of holies, the count room."

As in *GoodFellas*, it is possible to see Remo Gaggi — the top boss — as a symbolic father figure, and Sam and Nicky as the sons. When Sam and Ginger cannot seem to talk about love without talking about money, this is no wonder since, for Sam, Father's love is directly contingent upon it. Whenever we are told how the bosses really see the Jewish outsider son, it is by Nicky, the insider son. "To them he was a cash register," Nicky says. "He was a money machine. A tremendous earner for these guys. As soon as he took over, he doubled the fuckin' drop. With Ace the casino never saw so much money. And the bosses, they couldn't be happier." Sam's obsessive need for respectability is probably connected to his wanting to be accepted by Father and the family to which he does not belong. He constantly uses religious imagery. "I was given paradise on earth," he begins his tale. He calls the count room "the holy of holies," "the cardinal rule is to keep them playing," and "Ginger's mission in life was money." "The eye in the sky is watching us all," he says about the surveillance system at the casino. "For guys like me, Las Vegas washes away your sins. It's a morality car wash. It does for us what Lourdes does for humpbacks and cripples." The imagery he uses is constantly connected with Catholicism and not Judaism. This accentuates his wish to belong in the Italian group, but he reveals a superficial understanding of absolution and miracles which only reinforces his being an outsider who knows very little about these concepts.

Whereas Nicky was born an insider and does not have to do anything to earn his position, Sam has had to work for whatever respect he gets, and it is always dependent on how much money he makes. When Remo worriedly asks Frankie, "The little guy, he wouldn't be fuckin' the Jew's wife, would he?" it is not personal. He is concerned only in terms of Sam's earning potential. At this point the image freezes and Frankie takes over the narration briefly: "What could I say? I knew if I gave the wrong answer, I mean, Nicky, Ginger, Ace, all of 'em could've wound up gettin' killed. Because there's one thing about these old-timers: They don't like any fuckin' around with the other guys' wives. It's bad for business."

The fact that Frankie, a minor character, is allowed to take over the narration, even if only for a few sentences, gives him a much more prominent place in the story than he would have otherwise had. Time literally stops for a few seconds when the image freezes in total silence, which draws enormous attention to him. Frankie is the one Remo confides in which shows us that he has an even higher status than Nicky. On a mythological level, *Casino* is a film about a father who has three sons, Sam, Nicky, and Frankie, and the significance when Frankie later beats Nicky to death in a cornfield back in the Midwest goes way beyond this film. In three Scorsese films — *Raging Bull*, *GoodFellas*, and *Casino* — we have a troika of characters played by Robert De Niro, Joe Pesci, and Frank Vincent. In all three films these characters are defined by their relationship to a mob boss and symbolic father figure. The De Niro character (Jake La Motta, Jimmy Conway, Sam Rothstein) is the outsider who does not belong in the group and does not have Father's respect. The Joe Pesci character (Joey, Tommy, Nicky) is an insider who does not have to earn his status, but who is also not trusted because he tends to lose his temper and cause embarrassment. The Frank Vincent character (Salvy, Billy Batts, Frankie) is the true insider, a made guy, the legitimate son who is trusted and cannot be touched without there being serious repercussions.

The second brother, the Joe Pesci character, is the nemesis of the protagonist, as we have seen. The third brother, the Frank Vincent character, could then be viewed as the nemesis of the nemesis. Just as Nicky ordered Frankie to dig a hole for Sam to be buried in earlier, so Frankie now has a hole dug for Nicky. In *Raging Bull*, Joe Pesci smashes Frank Vincent's head with a cab door outside the Copacabana. In *GoodFellas*, Pesci kicks Vincent to death and later stabs him repeatedly. In *Casino*, Vincent finally gets to beat Pesci to death with a baseball bat. Karma catches up with Nicky at this point as does the narrative. His voice-over is cut off in mid-sentence when he is hit by a baseball bat that terminates his narration for good.

The execution of Nicky is connected to the beginning and the ending of the film. Just before the scene in the cornfield, we see Ace leaving the restaurant again (a repetition of the opening), go to his car, turn the key in the ignition and blow up. "The bombing was never authorized, but I suspect I know who lit the fuse. And so did the power that be," Ace's voice-over tells us, overlapping Nicky's murder, and thus indicating that Nicky is responsible. We cut back to the parking lot and see the explosion one more time, now with a different outcome. Engulfed in flames, Ace makes it out of the car before it explodes. We were sure at the very beginning of the film that he was killed, so rather than just a narrow escape these different versions betoken death and resurrection, and the real question becomes whether he has learned whatever it is he is supposed to learn.

The explosion destroys Sam's car and his beautiful clothes, literally tearing his persona to shreds. We then see the old Las Vegas being demolished, emphasizing that his entire mask goes up in flames. "The town will never be the same," he tells us nostalgically as we see hotels and casinos being wrecked. Nicky represented erosion from within, and the old Vegas, like the old Sam, is destroyed by implosion, suggesting that the impetus for the destruction comes from within rather than without.

"The bosses had had enough of Nicky," he says. "So, they made an example of him and his brother. They buried them while they were still breathing." Sam is, of course, spared only because he can still make money. "In the end I wound up right back where I started," a much older Sam Rothstein ambiguously informs us. "I could still pick winners, and I could still make money for all kinds of people back home. And why mess up a good thing?" We see him in a new luxurious house, back to being a handicapper. This might suggest that he has not budged an inch, that he is back to square one, and that the old persona has simply been replaced with a new one. Or it might suggest that he has finally come to terms with "back home," acknowledged who he really is underneath the mask and accepted it.

The faculty of seeing is often used symbolically in Scorsese's films to reflect a character's ability to see in a psychological or moral sense. *Raging Bull* ends with the passage from the Bible about the man who was blind and now can see. At the end of *GoodFellas*, Jimmy Conway suddenly wears very strong glasses after the Pesci nemesis is killed. The older Sam Rothstein seems more balanced and at peace, albeit with a hint of resignation about him, and he, too, wears thick glasses after Nicky's death.[54] The glasses might imply that, now when the persona is shed and the hostile brother is gone, Sam has had to learn to see with his own eyes the things that Nicky used to disclose for him, that he has learned to assimilate the dark sides of himself that he used to disown. After all, one cannot get rid of one's shadow by beating it to death with a baseball bat, and Nicky *was* still breathing when they buried him.

3

Down the Rabbit Hole

> How queer everything is to-day! And yesterday things went on just as usual. I wonder if I've changed in the night? Let me think: *was* I the same when I got up this morning? I almost think I can remember feeling a little different. But if I'm not the same, the next question is "Who in the world am I?"[1]
>
> Alice's Adventures in Wonderland

At first glance, *After Hours* and *Alice Doesn't Live Here Anymore* may seem extremely dissimilar. One takes place in the streets of lower Manhattan late at night, the other takes place in Arizona in broad daylight. But both are existential films that concern very ordinary people who feel compelled to leave home and, as a result, are hurled into unfamiliar territory where they know no one. Everything they have is taken away from them, and they have to completely reinvent themselves. The main character of one is a man whose journey forces him to examine his relation to women and the anima principle; the main character of the other is a woman whose journey forces her to examine her relation to men and the animus principle. Both films, like *Alice's Adventures in Wonderland* and *The Wizard of Oz*, are turbulent rites of passage during which the main character is constantly yearning to go home.

After Hours

After Hours (1985) is a disquieting black comedy about a computer programmer who meets a young woman late one evening and ventures out of his safe surroundings on the Upper East Side of New York to go visit her in SoHo. He ends up being trapped for the entire night when all he wants is to get home. The film was made after several strenuous and exhausting years for Scorsese, both personally and professionally, and it was his attempt to get back to basics. "What *After Hours* really is," he says, "is a reaction against my year and a half in Hollywood trying to get *The Last Temptation of Christ* made."[2] *After Hours*, a delightfully simple picture (Scorsese's first feature film in ten years without Robert De Niro), was a small independent project produced by Griffin Dunne (who plays the central character) and Amy Robinson (who played Teresa in *Mean Streets*). Its budget was a mere $4 million, and it became Scorsese's first commercial success since *Taxi Driver*.

It is set in New York where anything can happen, and so it is almost possible to take it literally, but it is much more rewarding to see it as an existentialist tale, a mythological journey into the realm of Hades. "The film is like playing a game, and if you're going to see this movie, you've got to be willing to play the game," says Scorsese, "you've got to be willing to suspend belief and have fun with the coincidences, kinda watching the outsider trying to make his way through the maze of the underworld."[3]

The film follows the outline of the basic hero path very closely, and the points where it deviates become significant. It calls to mind a number of classic tales, from the ancient Greek myth of Orpheus who ventures into the underworld, to *Alice's Adventures in Wonderland* and *The Wizard of Oz*, to the modern, anxiety-ridden world of Franz Kafka and John Fowles's *The Magus*— all of which likewise concern a traumatic, yet often preposterous, journey into psychedelic territory where the safe, rational rules of the ego no longer apply, and where conscious control is not an option.

After Hours starts with what is presumably a typical day in the life of Paul Hackett (Griffin Dunne). He is instructing a younger colleague in front of a computer, and passionately, although somewhat presumptuously, the man starts telling Paul about his dreams for the future. Paul looks bored and inattentive, shown by contrast as completely dispassionate. "It is only those who know neither an inner call nor an outer doctrine whose plight truly is desperate," writes Joseph Campbell, which prefigures that Paul's journey through the maze will be grueling.[4] When he leaves the building at the end of the day, two men close a pair of iron gates of mythical proportions behind him, as if ending his life as he knows it.

Paul spends the evening in his blandly neat, impersonal apartment (which we later learn is on East 91st Street), frantically switching the remote control of the TV. Those two words — remote and control — perfectly describe his demeanor and might well be the key to why he has to be forced through the traumatizing journey if he is to reclaim what is missing in his life and his personality. He typifies the young, urban, professional, single male of the mid–1980s, just as the nameless, anal-retentive main character in David Fincher's *Fight Club* typifies the same species at the turn of the millennium. Paul is lying on a sofa in this scene, and so it is possible to assume that he falls asleep and that his journey — like that of Alice, Dorothy and Professor Wanley in Fritz Lang's 1944 film *The Woman in the Window*— is a dream. This would explain the unreal, nightmarish feel of the journey, but unlike the two fabled girls and Lang's middle-aged protagonist, Paul is never seen waking up.

Bored, he goes to a coffee shop, bringing along a copy of Henry Miller's *The Tropic of Cancer*, and the call to adventure is presented in the shape of Marcy (Rosanna Arquette), an attractive, somewhat ditzy young woman. Using the book as an excuse to talk to him, she gives him the phone number of Kiki, an artist friend of hers who makes plaster of Paris paper weights in the shape of bagels with cream cheese. The veiled sexual invitation is, as Lang's Professor Wanley says, a "siren call," and indeed Paul's entire journey is centered around sexuality and women, whereas the absurd paper weights, although oddly evoking female genitalia, are primarily a McGuffin.[5] The only other customers in the place are Charles and Catherine Scorsese, so in a sense the parents are the last people to see Paul in his old incarnation.

When he gets home, Paul calls Kiki's number and, as he was hoping, Marcy is there. She has had a terrible fight with her boyfriend and asks Paul to come down, despite the fact that it is close to midnight. He now leaves his safe yuppie haven and takes a taxi into the bohemian strangeness south of Houston.

The long trip downwards is a dizzying, surrealistic affair that is filmed in fast motion. Like Dorothy's cyclone and Alice's rabbit hole, it signifies the descent into the unconscious. The cab is tearing though the streets of Manhattan at such a breakneck speed that Paul is flung around, holding on for dear life, and his $20 bill flies out the window. It slowly falls to the pavement, accompanied by fervent Flamenco music, exaggeratedly emphasizing that he will not be able to pay for the ride. Additionally, it thus evokes the River Styx which connects the upper and the nether worlds in Greek mythology. When crossing into the realm of the dead on the ferry of Charon, one had to pay him a coin or be condemned to wander the banks for a hundred years. The glower of the cabdriver when he is informed that Paul has no money poignantly mirrors that of Charon in Michelangelo's *The Last Judgment*, and Paul is doomed to failure before his trip through the maze even begins. One suspects that Scorsese may even be conscious of the analogy since he holds the image of the cab driver's piercing gaze for an astounding twelve seconds.

Paul is now standing at the entrance to a building, literally on the threshold to the unfamiliar world. The name of the first character he encounters, Kiki Bridges (Linda Fiorentino), is symbolically indicative. Her first name, which Marcy pronounces key-key, as well as her last name strongly argue that she is a gatekeeper: the name on the buzzer is Franklin, Marcy had told him on the phone, "Bridges is crossed out." The bridges to Paul's past have been burned, and having crossed into Hades without paying for the ride, he will be stuck there. Kiki controls the entrance to the unknown territory ahead, and she tosses her keys out of the window. As they fall to the ground they are filmed in a portentous upward angle from Paul's point of view, and they land to a clap of thunder, emphasizing that Paul himself has to assume the responsibility for opening the first gate.

Paul's journey consists of repeated motifs and ordeals that gradually begin to form a pattern, showing us the nature of what he has to learn in the underworld. Like Alice's Wonderland it is inhabited by strange creatures — most of them women or sexually nonconforming men — who may at first seem friendly, but who turn malicious and hostile at the drop of a hat. We constantly see clocks, and the music sounds like direful ticking, reflecting Paul's acute concern with time passing. When Marcy proposes that he come down to see her, he looks worried, and we cut to a close-up of a digital alarm clock which informs us that it is 11:32, as we hear the illogical, roaring sound of ticking. His obsession with time connects our yuppie with Alice's White Rabbit who is constantly late for no reason other than that the seeming respectability of it gives him some sort of perverse pleasure.[6] Also, since we now know there is a clock close to his sofa, this might support the theory that Paul falls asleep at the beginning, and that the rest is a dream which might then be triggered by what Freud calls "external sensory stimuli" or "internal sensory excitations," i.e., the real or imagined sound of ticking close to Paul's head.[7]

The few possessions Paul has brought along on his journey are powerful symbols, and, gradually, they are taken away from him. On the way down he loses his money, representing energy and payment for the ride there and back. When he enters Kiki's loft, she asks him to work on her sculpture, and when he gets glue on his shirt, she persuades him to let her wash it. He never gets his own shirt back, so for the rest of the night he wears one Kiki gives him. His persona is ripped off him and his appearance is determined by someone else. Later he loses his keys, representing access to both physical space (the ability to get into his home, should he be lucky enough to ever get back) and mental space (someone other than himself now has control over his home and his mind). He loses a good deal of his hair, another bit of his protective persona as well as (by way of the Old Testament story of Samson) potency and masculinity.[8] Finally he becomes aware that he could lose his life, and, symbolically, he does.

Paul Hackett (Griffin Dunne) frantically tries to hold on to his thick protective shell. At the end he is trapped inside the papier-mâché sculpture that he helps create at the outset of his journey through Hades in *After Hours* (Warner Bros., Double Play/The Geffen Company, 1985).

Paul is forced to shed layers of his thick protective shell in order to get to the raw nerves and sensitive areas. His losses deprive him of the ability to protect his old incarnation and get back to his home, the very foundation of his ego. His journey, like little Alice's, is a rite of passage that has to do with identity. Whenever he enters a new locale, he ritually, almost compulsively, goes to the bathroom to check himself in the mirror and wash his hands. As things are being stripped away, he is trying desperately to wash off the residue of Hades and hold on to his old identity. As if the whole story is taking place on the other side of the mirror, he seems to be glancing back into whatever is left of his old world. Gradually, his mirror image deteriorates and he is finally forced to surrender. He has to be robbed of the illusion of safety that seemed so important to him in the first scenes, and his ego has to be shattered, and only then is he able to go home.

Bathrooms are never safe places in Scorsese's work. In Tom's apartment, Paul flushes the toilet and it starts to run over, a horrifying moment since we can all imagine his embarrassment at flooding the floor in a stranger's home with whatever is in a toilet. Once he clutches his head and bangs it against the bathroom mirror, a subtle act of self-hatred that calls to mind similar scenes in other Scorsese films.[9] When he enters the men's room in the Terminal Bar, he sees a graffiti drawing of a shark attached to a man's erect penis. Indeed, images of castration and mutilation permeate the film. Often they have to do with fire or burning, and usually they appear in connection with female sexuality. There are many indications that Paul's journey might be connected with an intense, almost pathological fear of this issue. Scars and burns are constantly brought up. When Paul massages Kiki's shoulders at the beginning, he tells her a traumatizing childhood story. He went to the hospital to have his tonsils removed and afterwards was taken to the burn ward, blindfolded and with strict instructions not to remove the blind. His curiosity got the better of him, and he finally loosened it: "And I saw—" Paul says confidentially, only to find that Kiki is snoring loudly, which of course means that *we* never get to hear the rest of the story, and are left to wonder what exactly it was in Paul's childhood that so affected him.[10]

It is more than suggested that Marcy's body is disfigured by burns. When Paul arrives at the loft, she has gone to the drugstore to get something for a condition which, Kiki says, is "under control." A few minutes later he compliments Kiki on her body, and she replies that at least she does not have a lot of scars, unlike some women she knows who are "covered with them head to toe." The label on Marcy's prescription medicine is for second degree burns, in her room Paul finds a book with gruesome pictures of burn victims, and he sees an alarming shadow on her inner thigh. The object of desire that is placed in proximity of Marcy's inner thigh which made Paul come down here in the first place, is perceived now as potentially horrifying, and, in fact, most of his encounters on this nightmarish journey are with more or less attractive women who gradually turn frightening. Later we realize that there are no burns or scars on Marcy's body at all, so the horror of female sexuality exists only in Paul's head.

After Paul convinces himself that Marcy is disfigured, he is no longer interested in her, and he escapes to the Spring Street subway station only to learn that the fare, surreally, went up to $1.50 at midnight.[11] He did not pay Charon his coin for the journey down, so he is stuck inside Hades. From this point on, Paul's only goal is getting home, and his obstinate opposition to the journey only makes the experience more violent and grueling.

Although virtually penniless, he goes into a bar to get out of a sudden torrential downpour. Here he meets Julie (Teri Garr), an eccentric waitress, and Tom (John Heard), a sympathetic-looking bartender. Tom is masculine and apparently sane so Paul confides in him. "I just wanna go home," he says, and Tom instantly offers to give him money.

That Tom is only deceptively reassuring comes out in several ways. When he cannot open the cash register, he starts kicking it frenziedly. He surrounds himself with skulls and bones, emblems of mortality, and the name of his establishment, the Terminal Bar, is so ominous that one might even suspect that he represents Hades himself, the one who is in charge of the nether world. Later, we find out that his full name is Thomas Schorr, so that in effect he is Tom Ashore; the one who is to lead Paul ashore, away from the banks of the Styx and into the inmost cave where he has to face death.[12] Throughout one has a feeling that the other characters are actors in a game, that someone is deliberately toying with Paul, and repeatedly we hear mysterious giggling in the background. It is entirely possible to see Tom as the Godhead and puppet master, the constantly felt presence who is staging Paul's tribulations. Because Paul resists the experience through most of the night, his mentor turns into a tormentor and the landscape of the unconscious turns into the realm of Hell.

Like the Wizard of Oz, Tom creates an illusion of competence and promises to get Paul home only to send him on an impossible mission instead. There have been a series of burglaries in the neighborhood, he says, and if Paul goes to his apartment to check that his alarm is on, he can get the key to the cash register. Tom gives him his keys, and, moved by this act of apparent confidence, Paul hands over his own keys with an excessive "if I don't come back everything I own is yours." For all intents and purposes he hands over control of his inner and outer space to Hades, forfeiting everything he owns.

The visit to Tom's apartment becomes fateful. Paul is accused by the neighbors of *being* the infamous burglar, then moments later he sees the actual burglars, Neil and Pepe (Cheech Marin and Thomas Chong), who appear to have stolen Kiki's TV and sculpture. At this point halfway through the film, Paul makes an important choice that drastically changes the nature of his journey. He could now actually go back to the Terminal Bar, give Tom the keys, get some money and his own keys, and go home. Instead he chooses to steal the sculpture from the thieves and go back to Kiki's place with it. In Greek mythology the abducted Persephone was tricked by Hades into eating some pomegranate seeds and thus was bound to the realm of the dead forever. When Paul is likewise seduced into interacting with the underworld, things begin escalating. From being mildly disturbing and slightly weird, his encounters become grotesque and frightening, and, gradually, Paul begins to realize that he may not even survive.

He finds Kiki bound and gagged, and assumes that the burglars tied her up, but it turns out to be part of a sexual game. Her lover, Horst (Will Patton), commands Paul to go and apologize to Marcy, whom he had sneaked out on earlier. Paul obediently goes and sits by Marcy's bed for some time before he realizes that she has taken her own life. The synchronicity is mind-boggling when the burn he thought he saw on her thigh earlier now turns out to be a tattoo which is an exact replica of the skull on Tom's key chain in Paul's pocket, and the bottle of Seconal she has ingested has Tom's name on it. Paul contacts the police, finds a note saying that Kiki and Horst have gone to the Club Berlin, and leaves the loft for the second time.

As a result of his own actions the Terminal Bar is closed when he finally gets back: Tom got worried when he did not return and has gone looking for him. Not only can he not go home now, he does not even have his keys anymore. As if by magic Julie, the waitress, appears and offers Paul shelter against the rain until Tom returns. Her apartment across the street contains the perfect "props" to connote dangerous femininity. Her bedspread has a chessboard pattern, and her bed is surrounded by mousetraps, connoting castration and death. While talking to her, Paul is playing with a pair of huge, inflated, pink plastic lips — female sexuality literally blown all out of proportion — and just before he leaves, his hand mysteriously gets stuck in her hair while we hear the sound of a siren outside. He finally extricates himself, but Julie manages to make him promise that he will return.

At the Terminal Bar Paul confides to Tom that he does not want to go back to Julie's, so Tom tells him not to do it: "What's she gonna do? Kill herself?" At this precise moment the phone rings and Tom is informed that his girlfriend, Marcy, has committed suicide. Paul, reactive and polite as ever, does not want to seem insensitive, and instead of asking for his keys, he goes back to Julie who presents him with a gift for keeping his promise. "Do you know what this is?" she asks, showing him the preposterous bagel with cream cheese paperweight that was his pretext for coming down to SoHo in the first place. There is little doubt by now that all the players in this game know one another, and at the exact moment she shows him the bagel, a mouse is caught with a loud bang in one of the spotlighted mousetraps that surround her bed. Both bagel and mousetrap now have lethal vaginal overtones and Paul flees while Julie yells a threat after him.

Now Tom's apartment really *has* been robbed, and a frantic vigilante mob decides that Paul must be the burglar and starts chasing him. "Every corner represents a turn for the worse," one reviewer said, "and by the end of the night, he's got to wonder, like Kafka's K, if he might not actually be guilty of something."[13] Indeed, Paul now discovers that the two burglars had not stolen but bought and paid for the sculpture he took from them, so in the perverse logic of Wonderland, Paul actually *has* committed a theft. At this point he has lost his money (energy/power/payment for the passage over the river), his shirt (persona/protection of his old ego), and his keys (control over his physical and mental space), and when he goes to find Kiki at the Club Berlin, it turns out to be "Mohawk Night" and he is chased by a group of people who cut off a substantial part of his hair (strength and manhood).

For the third and last time he goes back to Kiki's place, and in a last desperate attempt to get money for the trip home he takes a $20 bill he saw earlier, glued onto her papier-mâché sculpture. At the precise moment he snatches the bill the vigilante mob appears in the street below, suggesting a connection between his act and the retribution (again, he actually does steal), and reminding us that you cannot cheat your way out of the inmost cave, you have to earn it. As the film goes into the third and final act, Paul ventures downstairs, and the cab driver who took him there, the ferryman whom he cheated out of his coin at the start, pulls up, triumphantly snatches the stolen money out of his hand and drives off.

Emerging from the cab is yet another blonde woman, Gail (Catherine O'Hara), who against all logic injures his arm badly with the car door. Gail is scatterbrained like Marcy and wears yellow and black clothes like Julie. She insists that he come home with her so she can dress his wound, and as she removes the shirt she sees a scrap of newspaper that apparently stuck to him when he was working on Kiki's sculpture earlier. On the tiny piece of paper, she manages to read an entire story about a man who was torn to smithereens by an angry crowd, and what particularly fascinates and repels her is the fact that the man had "his face pummeled."

This moment is crucial for several reasons. The scrap of newspaper, pasted papier-mâché fashion to his physical frame, logically connects the sculpture he worked on at the start and later stole with the sculpture he ultimately becomes. The newspaper story seems to portend that being dismembered by the vigilante mob might in fact be the fate of Paul Hackett. Gail disgustedly asks what a man has to *do* to get his face pummeled, again suggesting some form of responsibility on Paul's part. Furthermore, being torn limb from limb by furious women was the fate of Orpheus, one of the few people to escape and return from the underworld alive. Orpheus crossed the River Styx to charm Hades into resurrecting his beloved Eurydice, and it makes sense to assume that the real purpose of Paul's journey is similar: this tediously respectable, bourgeois man has to face and embrace the darkness inside himself in order to resuscitate his symbolic feminine side. Indeed, the anima is inherently connected with the trip into the abyss because it "represents the abysmal Yin element," says Edward Whitmont, "the psychic aboriginal sourceground, the world of Goethe's 'Mothers,' which has existed in man prior to his experience of himself as an 'I,' an ego."[14]

The fact that Orpheus disobeyed the rules of Hades and Persephone and lost his wife forever does not augur well for Paul. Returning to the world of the living, Orpheus renounced women in favor of pederasty, which makes the next stage of Paul's journey hilariously ironic. When Gail turns against him and joins the neighborhood mob, he escapes, and as he stops for breath on a fire escape, he sees a woman shooting a man in an apartment across the street, the culmination of his fear of the feminine annihilating the masculine. "I'll probably get blamed for that," he says, and finally lets go of his control. We cut to a perpendicular God's-eye view as he drops to his knees, looks upward and shouts: "What do you want from me? I'm just a word processor for Christ's sake!" Now the ultimate joke is delivered: at the exact moment that he surrenders to the Godhead, an insecure homosexual man appears across the street. "Would you please help me?" Paul pleads. "Can you take me home?" "I have never done this with a man before," the stranger admits, and Paul has to reject him and go back downstairs where the mob is closing in on him.

Then a woman hands him his final summons, an invitation to a "Conceptual Art" show at the Club Berlin. Paul is chased by the mob into the inmost cave to stare death in the face and encounter his supreme ordeal. The club is a totally different place now. When Paul left an hour ago, it was a punk club filled with Mohawked people, now it is practically empty. Nothing is going on, no one is there, there is no sign of an art show, and they are closing in a few minutes, the bartender says. The dictionary definition of conceptual art is: "Art that is intended to convey an idea or a concept to the perceiver and need not involve the creation or appreciation of a traditional art object such as a painting or a sculpture."[15] Very likely Paul's arrival *is* the conceptual art show, and shortly he will be turned into a work of art.

He sees a sad-looking woman sitting alone who seems quite a bit older than the women he has encountered so far. Her name is June, he is told, and *she is always there.* June represents the primal, permanent feminine force, the original anima, the ultimate archetypal female principle, namely Mother. This assumption is supported by the fact that she is played by Verna Bloom, whom Scorsese also chose to play Mary, Mother of Christ.

In John Fowles's *The Magus*, the Godhead is assisted by two women who constantly shapeshift in order to keep the main character in a state of uncertainty and powerlessness, and in one incarnation they are actually called Julie and June. All the women Nicholas encounters on the island are really the same two women in different guises. In *After Hours* it, likewise, is pertinent to wonder whether all the women represent different sides of the anima principle. Like Marcy, June seems to have something wrong with her skin, like Kiki, she is an artist who makes papier-mâché sculptures and, like most of the women Paul encounters, she has blonde hair. At the gay man's apartment, Paul recaps the night. He sees Julie downstairs and shouts "That's *her*!" which logically makes no sense since he has mentioned several different women, but not actually Julie. It attests that there is only one *she*— the feminine principle—in the first place. Like the shadow, the anima becomes furious when ignored and repressed, which might account for the fact that the women Paul meets in the maze invariably turn hostile.

For the last time Paul goes to the bathroom at the Club Berlin and checks himself in the mirror, but he looks so disheveled by now that he surrenders and gives up trying to fight the disintegration of his old identity. When he comes back, he hesitates for a second, then drops his last quarter into the jukebox — voluntarily and consciously giving up the last morsel of control, and the last thing that connects him to the past — and embraces June in a dance.

Within minutes the vigilante mob invades the club, and June takes him to her home and studio in that most Gothic of spaces, the basement underneath the club. The inmost cave where the terrifying monster lives turns out to be Mother's cave, i.e., the womb. For a while the two of them sit on the sofa, June holding Paul against her chest in a position that suggests a Pietà which again connects her with the Holy Mother. By the time the angry mob forces its way into the basement, she has enveloped him in papier-mâché so that he has become a work of art. Whereas this saves his life, she refuses to set him free once the vigilantes have left because "you're safe like this!" she says.

The sculpture that he has encountered repeatedly, that he has co-created and then stolen, now turns out to be himself. At the stage where the hero is supposed to seize the grail, the magic sword, the philosopher's stone, Paul is completely immobilized. The mother creator has turned into the mother destroyer, mother archetype has become mother complex, and Paul is encased and imprisoned in the shell of her safety. His unwillingness to let go of security has led back to the womb and that equals living death. Scorsese originally wanted the film to end with a literal inverted birth where Paul disappears up into June's body and returns to the womb. What Paul gets instead of this permanent regression is an intimation of what returning to the womb would be like, and at the same time a chance, if he dares, to make the sacrifice and finally let his old controlled identity die so that a new one can be born.

Eventually the basement is invaded again, this time by the two burglars. Thinking that Paul is their sculpture, they take him and put him in the back of their van. It is now dawn and the journey back to the normal world begins. The burglars drive uptown, and this drive out of Hades is every bit as frantic as was the journey down with Charon. As they turn the corner in front of Paul's office building, the back door of the van opens, the sculpture falls out, the shell breaks open, and Paul is free.

For Paul, as for Dorothy, the grail seems to be knowledge. Not the realization that "there's no place like home," but rather the wisdom contained in the very act of letting go, letting himself be "crucified—and resurrected; dismembered totally, and then reborn," as Joseph Campbell says.[16] "Spiritually," says Deepak Chopra, "no action is more important than surrender."[17] At the beginning of Paul's journey, Marcy told him that her husband, a movie freak who was obsessed with *The Wizard of Oz*, would yell "Surrender Dorothy" whenever he climaxed sexually. This absurd story might thus be the central piece of advice that is customarily given to the hero to help him get through the maze, and the scatterbrained Marcy is then the instrument of the mentor, the Godhead, the man behind the curtain.

The journey for Alice and Dorothy, both prepubescent girls, concerns growing up. For John Fowles's Nicholas Urfe and Martin Scorsese's Paul Hackett, both grown men convinced of their own superiority, the journey has to do with their pride, with owning up to the unacknowledged darkness inside themselves, and with their relation and attitude to women, sexuality, femininity and the anima. "I just wanted to meet a nice girl," Paul says to the gay man, "and now I have to *die* for it?" However unfair this may seem on a realistic level, spiritually he is right. Most of the characters he encounters are blonde women and shapeshifters, and thus by definition connected with anima. Most of the men he meets are overt threats to his masculinity and sexuality: Horst who is into bondage and discipline, the leather-clad gay men making out at the Terminal Bar, the threatening doorkeeper and castrating men at the Club Berlin, and the sulking, closeted homosexual. The only two exceptions to the pattern of blonde women and sexually nonconforming men are "Key-Key Bridges" and "Tom Ashore"—the ones who hold the keys—and it makes a lot of sense to see the two of them as the masterminds and puppet masters in control of Paul's journey: Hades and his Iron Queen.[18]

The ending of *After Hours* is ambiguous. Despite the grueling voyage he has been on, Paul has resisted it all the way, and there is no sign that he has made the sacrifice that is necessary to be resurrected and redeemed and move on to the next level. The return to the ordinary world is an important part of the hero path, but for Paul it, too, is involuntary and passive. At the end of the journey, the hero is supposed to return triumphant, but Paul just staggers into a deserted office landscape and turns on a computer which bids him good morning. The residue of the realm of death is supposed to be cleansed off before the hero reenters the upper world, but at the very end when we leave him, alone in front of his computer, Paul is still covered in the plaster and glue placenta of the Mother Goddess.

Before Paul left home at the beginning, we focused on the words "Faces West" that were branded on his clock. Geographically, Paul travels south, but he himself "faces west," symbolically representing the worldliness, defeat, and living death of Babel. The journey is not completed, and the only way out of this unremittingly painful state is to go through it again at some point. The man may be out of Hades, but Hades may not be out of the man.

Alice Doesn't Live Here Anymore

The period of the new American cinema in the 1970s was one of the most dynamic and prolific eras in motion picture history. However, one very unfortunate tendency during this time of increased creative freedom for the young directors (as always, predominantly male) was the way in which women were depicted. Molly Haskell has traced the portrayal of women throughout film history in her book *From Reverence to Rape*, and notes that this period was "the most disheartening in screen history."[19] Women were profusely beaten, raped and murdered onscreen in a way which had hitherto been prohibited by The Motion Picture Production Code. Although there *were* memorable performances by female actors, the women's roles of the decade were "whores, quasi-whores, jilted mistresses, emotional cripples, drunks. Daffy ingénues, Lolitas, kooks, sex-starved spinsters, psychotics. Icebergs, zombies, and ballbreakers."[20] Women's roles were marginal to the plot, and with the emergence of buddy films and road movies there were fewer of them than ever. "The growing strength and demands of women in real life," says Haskell, "obviously provoked a backlash in commercial film: a redoubling of Godfather-like machismo to beef up man's eroding virility."[21]

It is ironic that Martin Scorsese, who has often been reviled for his alleged misogyny, was one of the first to challenge this overwhelming, and in many cases violent, male chauvinism. He made the first commercially and critically successful film of the '70s in which the main character was a woman trying to define herself and her own life. In the wake of *Alice Doesn't Live Here Anymore* (1974) a handful of films—notably Herbert Ross's *The Turning Point*, Claudia Weill's *Girlfriends*, Paul Mazursky's *An Unmarried Woman*, Martin Ritt's *Norma Rae*—would help turn things around.

Alice Doesn't Live Here Anymore was Scorsese's first real Hollywood film, and its budget was three times that of *Mean Streets*. The opening scene alone cost 2.5 times more than *Who's That Knocking at My Door?* Originally the film was Ellen Burstyn's idea, and she approached Scorsese. "What I wanted to do in *Alice*—and what nobody was doing at the time—was to tell a story from a woman's point of view," Burstyn says. She felt that "most scripts need to be polished, but this one needed to be 'roughed up.'" She asked Francis Coppola if he knew a director who could do that, and he told her to watch *Mean Streets*. She knew immediately that Scorsese would be the perfect guy and set up a meeting. "I was very impressed with him," she remembers. "We talked for a few minutes. I told him how much I like *Mean Streets*. Then I asked, 'What do you know about women?' And he said, 'Nothing. But I'd like to learn.' I thought that was a wonderful answer."[22]

The demeaning treatment of women in the movies of the early 1970s has led many critics to see *Alice Doesn't Live Here Anymore* as a feminist film. In addition to its sociopolitical implications concerning sexual politics and gender issues, which have been discussed often enough, the film is a mythological and psychological tale of one woman's individuation, and in my opinion, Alice's development as a human being is much more interesting than her status as a spokeswoman and feminist icon.

Like *After Hours*, this film contains parallels to Carroll's books about Alice and *The Wizard of Oz* and concerns a very strange journey. Like many films of the road movie and western genres, it takes place in that most masculine of landscapes, the American Southwest. The opening scene contains classic cinema references. The titles are written in ornate red letters over white satin while on the soundtrack Alice Faye sings "You'll Never Know." Then we cut to "Alice as a young girl" (Mia Bendixsen), a child of about ten who is walking at dusk through a Hollywood version of a childhood farm filmed through a slightly ominous red filter. The stage set evokes *The Wizard of Oz* and is constructed as a replica of Auntie Em's and Uncle Henry's farm. The girl continues the song from the title sequence, although badly out of tune. Then she makes a stunning statement that is discordant with the dreamlike innocence of the set: "I can sing better than Alice Faye. I swear to Christ I can," she says. "And if anybody doesn't like it, they can blow it out their ass!"

Alice is presented as a headstrong, willful, rather angry child, with an unrealistic but inspiring faith in her own talent. The red filter calls to mind Atlanta after the fire in *Gone with the Wind*, and this girl is an obvious descendant of the fiercely determined Scarlet O'Hara who likewise swears with God as her witness that she will never go hungry again. Then a big dog barks ferociously and Alice's mother calls her, introducing another menacing element that clashes with the Hollywood idyll: "Alice Graham," she yells, "you get in this house before I beat the living daylights out of you. Do you hear me?" As the child continues to sing undauntedly, slowly moving toward the house, one cannot help but wonder if her toughness and her need to cling to her dream with such fierceness may have something to do with her mother's excessive brutality.

As she sings the last words of the Alice Faye song, the sound freezes in a horrifying echo, and as she bolts into the house, the word "now, now, now, now, now," is repeated, increasing in volume. Then the entire image is catapulted to the sound of jet engines into the center of the screen. This violent transition suggests the end of childhood innocence. In effect, Alice is hurled into the rabbit hole of adulthood so suddenly and abruptly that she does not have time to prepare for it. It thus makes sense to see Monterey (rather than Socorro) as the starting point of the journey. The rest of the film is her odyssey through the strange territory of adulthood which she neither understands nor quite feels she belongs in — always hoping, like Dorothy and Alice, that she will eventually be able to go back home.

We now meet Alice as a wife and mother (Ellen Burstyn), 27 years later in Socorro, New Mexico. We move across the town, then enter a house through a window, trailing after Mott the Hoople's "All the Way from Memphis." The house is totally covered by vines and thus invisible and it seems like a reflection of Alice herself. Astonishingly, she is now a colorless, submissive doormat in her mid-thirties, albeit still with a certain sense of irony. She is married to Don (Billy Green Bush), a truck driver who is sullen bordering on abusive, and she seems to spend most of her energy trying to please him and make sure that their eleven-year-old son, Tommy (Alfred Lutter), does not upset him. Later, she confesses to a

Alice Hyatt in *Alice Doesn't Live Here Anymore* (Warner Bros., 1974) with her disgruntled husband and uproarious son before the call to adventure. *(From left to right)* Don (Billy Green Bush), Tommy (Alfred Lutter), and Alice (Ellen Burstyn).

certain masochism when she says that she likes having a strong and dominating husband who orders her about and to whom she has to respond, "Yes, master!" At first glance, one might say that nothing in the headstrong child in the first scene prepares us for the adult that Alice has turned into, but the husband whose first act is a hollered off-screen threat is a logical continuation of the voice of Mother. Consequently, Alice seems much more comfortable and on equal terms with 11-year-old Tommy than with her husband.

Then suddenly Alice magically is set free. She tells her girlfriend that she could easily live without a man, and dreamily imagines what it would be like to be married to Robert Redford instead of the ill-tempered Don. At that precise moment the phone rings and she is informed that her husband has been killed in an accident. Critics have complained that Don's demise is too convenient to be believable (although in real life coincidences like that happen all the time), but this merely connects *Alice Doesn't Live Here Anymore* less with feminist social realism and more with the mythological magic of *Alice in Wonderland*, *The Wizard of Oz* and *Peter Pan*. It happens *because* Alice wishes it. She is now free, not because she has seen the light of women's liberation, but because of an accident that her wish invokes. As Scorsese says: "If her husband hadn't been killed, she would never have left him. She would not have moved unless the hand of God came down and said, 'Bang. That is it. Make your decision. What are you going to do.'"[23] For the second time within 12 minutes of screen time, Alice is flung into a situation in which she is at a loss.

Theoretically, she can now do anything and go anywhere she wants, but she chooses to go back to where she came from, back to Kansas in a sense. Unlike Dorothy, Alice and Wendy, however, she is no longer a little girl, so this is neither appropriate nor possible. She obviously wants to leave Socorro and that whole part of her life behind, but instead of moving forward and becoming an independent adult woman, she is trying to move backwards, to evade her divinely enforced individuation by regressing to a state of innocence — a state which, as was obvious from the flagrant Hollywood set with the threatening undertones, was an illusion to begin with. Furthermore, she wants to go back not only to her childhood home but to her dream of being a singer. Whereas a child can have a wild dream of fame and fortune, it is more problematic for an adult to cling to that dream in the face of reality, and initially she even admits that she "ain't no Peggy Lee" when she sits down to play and sing for the first time in years. Her regressive journey is constantly sabotaged so she never makes it to Monterey nor to fame and fortune. Although various feminist critics have found this very disappointing, psychologically it is quite as it should be: what Alice is prevented from doing is going back to the womb.

Where Carroll's Alice travels alone, Scorsese's Alice has a sidekick on her trip through New Mexico and Arizona, namely Tommy. This plants the film solidly within the road movie genre and makes it even more unusual since in the mid–1970s that genre was reserved solely for men. One critic noted that women in road moves "are usually depicted as weak, stupid or wretched." They are "essentially along for the ride, and are not part of what is constantly being redefined as an exclusive male enclave. The road movie is therefore virtually a locker room on wheels for men to indulge their camaraderie as well as their misogynist tendencies."[24] "As in real life," says another critic, "men in road movies are considered the natural helmsperson of vehicles. The potent car (or motorcycle) is the man's private phallus symbol and a woman behind the wheel will evoke castration anxiety and is in any case threatening to patriarchal conventions. Thus the women in film history who have traveled alone are few and unfortunate, as for instance in Hitchcock's *Psycho*."[25]

The traveling companion connects Scorsese's Alice with Dorothy (whose sidekick, her dog, Toto, is a dependent) and Wendy (whose sidekick, her male counterpart, Peter Pan, is an equal). Alice's sidekick is also a dependant, yet she often seems more dependent on Tommy than he on her, and frequently she expects him to be the responsible one. After the funeral the child asks his mother, "What are you going to do now?" to which she replies, "What are *you* going to do now? We're in this together, you know!" However lightly it might be meant, this puts an inordinate burden on an 11-year-old boy who has just lost his father. Later, after being removed from the only world he knows, Tommy is worried about how they will survive, a totally understandable and rational fear. Alice responds by screaming at him and forces him to sit down and write a list of all the things with which he is dissatisfied. Later, when they have to flee the motel after her aggressive lover Ben (Harvey Keitel) threatens them, she is so busy crying and assuring the boy that she is okay (rather than asking if he is), that she would have forgotten to bring all the money they have in the world if he had not reminded her to do so.

They both often behave as if he is the parent and she is the child or as if they are a couple. Like an annoyed father or jealous husband, Tommy sits up and waits for her when she stays out late at night, and questions her about where she has been. When he picks her up after work, he says, "I came to escort you home," and she replies, "Well, thank you, sir!" The slightly Oedipal undertones are emphasized when Alice's colleague, a timid woman named Vera (Valerie Curtin), is picked up by a man on a motorcycle whom some critics have described as her lover, but who Vera specifically tells Alice is her father. Later we cut directly from an overhead shot of Alice lying side by side in bed with her lover to an identical overhead shot of her lying side by side in bed with her son.

Carroll's Alice physically keeps getting bigger and smaller, not able to find her right size. Scorsese's Alice does so emotionally. The night before Tommy's birthday — when they are still only a four-hour drive closer to Monterey than they were at the outset — Alice says to him: "Tomorrow you are twelve years old. Fully grown. You can do what you want." While she says the words, she is looking not at him, but at her own reflection in the mirror. This again suggests that she herself was forced prematurely to be an adult. It also affirms the sense one has that Tommy is an extension of the Alice we saw in the first scene.

Their relationship is closer to that of Wendy and Peter than to that of Dorothy and Toto. Although she is not always acknowledged as such, Wendy is actually the protagonist of *Peter Pan*, and the conflict that is established at the beginning is between her and the grownup world which she is expected, but not ready, to enter.[26] As a subconscious protest she invokes Peter Pan, the boy animus, in her dream, and in the mythical landscape of Neverland *he* can do all the things she longs to do in London. Traditionally, the same actor has always played Wendy's father and Captain Hook, and Peter's battle with Hook is a symbolic reflection of Wendy's unspoken rebellion against her domineering father. Almost a century later, Thelma in *Thelma and Louise* goes on a similar journey of initially timid rebellion against her father/husband. On a realistic level the charming seducer and thief J.D. may be bad news, but on a symbolic, psychological level, he is the boy animus who removes her wedding band and is assimilated into her body and soul through the sexual act.

In many ways Alice's marriage resembles Thelma's, and presumably it prompted her to tuck away the defiance, determination, and belief in herself that we saw in the opening scene. Like Thelma on her journey through the Southwest, Alice meets a number of men who reflect her own development, and she gradually allows herself to reassume the characteristics that we traditionally associate with masculinity, which she had so plentifully as a child. Like Thelma needed J.D. and like Wendy needed Peter Pan, so Alice needs her son and the surrounding landscape of the Southwest in order to move on to the next level in her individuation. The headstrong son represents the boy animus, the male counterpart to young Alice. This might be the reason that getting to Monterey before his birthday is so crucial for Alice—much more so than it is for him.

Many of Alice's encounters have a strangely surreal quality to them, often with allusions to Wonderland. Her very journey is related to the question of the caterpillar: "Who are you?" When looking for a job in Phoenix, she stands at a crossroads saying, "Quo vadis?" which are virtually the words of Carroll's Alice: "Which way?" She goes into a bar called Joe's & Jim's, calling to mind Tweedledee and Tweedledum, only to learn that they do not exist in real life. She meets people with strange names and is repeatedly moving through dark corridors. Finally, after unsuccessfully applying for a job as a singer, she starts crying in front of a friendly bar owner who assures her that her problem can be solved by drinking something, and endearingly but absurdly he keeps repeating "I don't even have a piano in here."

Like the original Alice, our Alice gets through the first gate because she cries. She gets the job not because of her talent or perseverance, but as an act of mercy from a paternal man. Weeping got her a modicum of affection from her husband and now it gets her her

In *Alice Doesn't Live Here Anymore* (Warner Bros., 1974), when Alice (Ellen Burstyn) meets Ben (Harvey Keitel), his face is overshadowed by a huge hat which suggests that, like the Hatter, he is probably mad and potentially violent, as indeed he turns out to be.

first job as a singer. When they leave the bar so that she can audition for him at a piano bar down the street, the bar owner tells his bartender, "Don't burn it down," which is less preposterous if we recollect the fate of the white rabbit's house. When Alice meets Ben shortly afterwards, his face is overshadowed by a huge hat which suggests that, like the Hatter, he is probably stark raving mad and potentially violent, as indeed he turns out to be.

Much like the men Thelma encounters, Ben reflects Alice's own life. The relationship between Ben and his wife is like the relationship between Alice and Don, blown all out of proportion. Ben is not the Robert Redford she wished for, but the exact same kind of man as her husband, only worse. Alice was a weepy doormat with a child and a passive-aggressive man. Ben's wife, Rita (Lane Bradbury), is so dependent and frightened that she is barely articulate — and she has a child that is very sick. Rita's husband cheats on her, threatens her with a switchblade knife, then kicks her out the house in front of Alice. Although Alice cries again, now it solves nothing and she is forced to take action.

She flees to what becomes the final destination of her journey, Tucson. She cannot get a job as a singer there, so she settles for a job as a waitress, although she considers it humiliating and degrading. This is quite understandable since in road movies diners, brothels, and motels are in essence replicas of the home in which women provide men with food, sex and a bed in which to sleep. What Alice is doing now is merely an extension of what she was doing in the first place, although now she is doing it in a public space and getting paid. At the diner she meets Flo (Diane Ladd), a waitress with a mouth like a sewer. At first Alice finds her offensive, but gradually they become friends. Apparently Flo has some of the *chutzpah* Alice lacks, but eventually we learn that for all her apparent defiance, Flo is merely sporting a pinned-on façade, as symbolized by the piece of jewelry she has made out of safety pins which holds her together, as she says.

Alice also meets David (Kris Kristofferson), a handsome and intelligent farmer who takes an interest in her and Tommy. She allows herself to fall for him, but then he holds her responsible for her son's lack of discipline. David eventually slaps Tommy (after the kid has yelled "Shitkicking" into his face three times at the top of his lungs and hit him with a plate of birthday cake), and Alice storms out of David's house and out of the relationship. Significantly, this altercation takes place on Tommy's birthday, the very date by which she had solemnly promised him that she would have gotten them to Monterey.

Alice is, in reality, sabotaging her own journey back. Geographically, Monterey is less than 1,200 miles from Socorro, which one could easily drive in a couple of days, so if getting there was really her one true goal the way she claims, the logical thing would have been to stop in Phoenix for the night and then immediately move on. Instead of spending what little money they have on food and gas to keep going, she chooses to stay in Phoenix and buy a whole new wardrobe. Furthermore, after being chased out of their motel room by the psychopathic Ben, she drives to Tucson which is actually moving backwards. By going toward Socorro rather than toward California, she herself in a sense invokes the waitress job which is an extension of who she was in her marriage, and she is now trapped in an eternal loop of her own regressive wish so that no matter "which way" she chooses, it will always be a road going backwards; back towards Socorro or back towards Monterey.

At one point David asks her the logical question, "You wanna go home or you wanna sing?" When she maintains that she wants to do both, he says, "You think they're the same?" In the climactic scene he shows up at the diner to try and patch things up between them, and Alice still insists that going to Monterey and becoming a singer is what she wants out of life. Immediately, he offers to leave everything and take her there so she can live out her dream. We have no reason to assume that he would not actually go if she were to take him up on it, but she does not. Despite his offer, she is still in Tucson when the film ends. There are, however, signs that she may have accepted that being a singer does not necessarily entail going to back to her childhood. When David asks her how good she is, she defiantly says, "I'm as good as I am. That's how good I am!" indicating that she no longer feels she has to be better than Alice Faye, but can simply be Alice Hyatt — whatever that turns out to mean.

Although, atypically of its time, *Alice Doesn't Live Here Anymore* concerns a woman's struggle for independence, many critics have found the outcome disappointing. "The conventional ending of the film betrays the feminist aspiration its first half indicated, and the implicit message remains that woman cannot succeed on her own," one critic says. "Alice's road trip is not completed, but cut off half way without her obtaining either of the two things she set out for."[27] Personally, I find it unfair that one movie is supposed to make up for the overwhelming misogyny of the entire period; and what Burstyn and Scorsese intended to make was a film about a modern woman, not necessarily a radically feminist one.

The question becomes whether staying with David and possibly giving up her dream of Monterey is good or bad for Alice's own development. She does not have much talent as a singer, as we have plenty of opportunity to witness, and clinging to the illusion prevents her from moving on with her life. Furthermore, the Monterey she is after is not the geographical place that is located a few hours drive from where she is, but a Chimera. This is reinforced in the final scene when Alice and Tommy admit to each other that they would both rather stay in Tucson, and then — when walking off into the horizon — pass under a gigantic billboard sign that reads "Monterey," implying that Alice's fantasy of Monterey has all the credibility and authenticity of an advertisement. It is not a real place anymore (if indeed it ever was), but a state of mind.

In *The Last Temptation of Christ* Jesus says to Judas that revolt only on the physical plane with no change on the spiritual plane does not really work. While you may be able to get rid of the Romans that way, they will soon be replaced by something similar or worse if you are not transformed within. For Alice, Don is replaced almost immediately by Ben, and she can never be free as long as her attempt at getting away from her husband consists of going back to the time *before* him. Until she is ready to let go of her regressive dream, she will be as trapped as she ever was with him.

As far as staying with David is concerned, Roger Ebert points out that "most women in Alice's position probably wouldn't run into a convenient, understanding, and eligible young farmer, but then a lot of the things in the film don't work as pure logic. There's a little myth to them."[28] David is, in fact, the second half of her initial wish come true, a gentle and interested man, just as Don's death fulfilled the first half, and this is a wish that she made as an adult rather than one retained from childhood.

Scorsese says: "I remember we had some criticism from some feminist groups because Alice winds up going with a man at the end. I just thought she'd decided she'd, you know ... just like to have a man!"[29] Alice admits to Flo that she cannot see herself without a man, but David — as played by Kris Kristofferson — is not just any man by a long shot. Being a Western male of the old mold, a Rhodes Scholar, and one of the world's most gifted poets and songwriters, Kristofferson signifies an entirely separate branch of desirable manhood. "Next to his easy masculinity, Norman Mailer seems like a man who is trying too hard," Blanche McCreary Boyd said about Sam Shepard, but might equally well have said about

Kristofferson.³⁰ And after all, David virtually repeats Scorsese's endearing words to Burstyn when he says to Alice at the end: "I think I understand you. I wanna try!"

All this is even more interesting because of the way the ending of the film was conceived. In the original script, Alice chose to go her own way, but Warner Bros. objected to that. They wanted a traditional happy ending that would sell. "Marty and I were disgusted," Burstyn remembers. "The ending they wanted was a *movie* ending, not a *real* ending — which was why Marty had everybody in the restaurant applaud, because that was *his* way of acknowledging that this was the *movie* ending. But then Kris Kristofferson made the contribution that saved us all. We were all very disgruntled, because she was giving up her dream of singing to live on Kris's farm. Then Kris came up with the idea of his character saying, 'Hey, come on. You want to go to Monterey? I'll take you to Monterey, let's go!' He sprung that on me in an improvisation during rehearsal. I said, 'You will?' And I just fell in love and was disarmed. It got me off the hook. It resolved everything."³¹ As if to acknowledge Kristofferson's crucial contribution, Scorsese used the chorus of his song "The Pilgrim (Chapter 33)" in his next film, *Taxi Driver*.

When I find this ending satisfying, it is obviously not because Alice stays with a man instead of pursuing her own dream, but because she chooses the present and the future instead of voluntarily staying stuck in the past, which makes any road she takes a road backwards. Several other Scorsese characters (notably Charlie in *Mean Streets* and Newland in *The Age of Innocence*) are given a chance at getting out of their self-imposed prison through the love of a woman, just as Alice is given that chance through the love of a man. Unlike her male counterparts, Alice accepts that opportunity. She may or may not give up her dream of a career as a singer, but there is every indication that if she *were* to pursue it, she would be better off with David than without him. By giving up the old dream, she now has a chance, from a mature, conscious starting point, at being a singer or at least verbalizing what she actually wants now.

Many lament Alice's giving up her dream and independence, but I have always found that dream and the way she goes about trying to realize herself selfish and irresponsible. Leaving Tommy alone in motel rooms, knowing nobody and with nothing to do, may be necessary to keep him fed, but I would hope that most single parents would not choose a job where they get off at 1:30 A.M. in order to live out a 27-year-old dream that they have no noticeable talent at. Additionally she starts dating and sleeping with men literally days after his father's death, leaving him alone even longer. She spends Tommy's birthday making out with David on a couch, while the boy, dressed in the cowboy outfit she has given him, has only his mirror image for company which is about the loneliest birthday party for a child one could imagine.

Tommy's much more mature and realistic view of her life and behavior is seen when they drive away from David's house after the fight. Alice absurdly reiterates that she will eventually get them to Monterey, to which Tommy replies that this will only be possible "*if* you don't get involved with another maniac." At this point the circle is completed when Alice, with a verbal violence that matches that of her mother in the opening scene, tells him that if he does not close his mouth, "I swear to God I'm gonna nail it shut" and then forces the boy out of the car and drives off into the nightfall leaving him alone in the middle of nowhere.

Only at the very end does Alice seem to acknowledge that Tommy is a child and allow him to be one. For the first time she appears concerned about what *he* wants. Throughout

Alice (Ellen Burstyn) and David (Kris Kristofferson) get cozy on the couch while her son tries to entertain himself on his birthday in *Alice Doesn't Live Here Anymore* (Warner Bros., 1974).

the film she has been repeating that they are "in this together"—meaning not so much that they should both try to create the life they want, but that he has to share the responsibility and the cost so that she can live out her dream. Only in the very last scene, when she has taken on her own adulthood and let go of the outdated fantasy—and with it all the self-defeating luggage she has been carrying around—can she allow some space for what the boy wants. For me that is a much more fulfilling ending than any feminist vision. Hilariously, the film ends when Alice playfully wraps her arm around Tommy's throat and the last words we hear are: "Mom, I can't breathe!" Although she has reached a higher level of maturity, the conflict is certainly not perfectly solved in typical Hollywood fashion.

4

Through the Looking Glass

> Let's pretend the glass has got all soft like gauze, so that we can get through. Why, it's turning into a sort of mist now, I declare! It'll be easy enough to get through.[1]
> *Through the Looking Glass*

In 1985 Martin Scorsese directed "Mirror, Mirror," a 24-minute installment for NBC's *Amazing Stories*. The film is inspired by the stories of Edgar Allan Poe and the British Hammer horror films, and concerns a writer, Jordan Manmouth (Sam Waterston) whose fortified, fastidious home is invaded by a phantom (an unrecognizable Tim Robbins) that comes out of the mirror. Although his girlfriend, Karen (Helen Shaver), covers up every reflecting surface to protect him, the phantom eventually devours him, emerging from a reflection in Karen's eye.

Most of Scorsese's films concern a character who has to go through a learning process, often a turbulent and upsetting one. Paul Hackett and Alice Hyatt were normal, average people who fell into a "rabbit hole" and landed in a strange world where the rules they knew no longer applied. In this chapter we will encounter characters who are neither average nor, probably, clinically sane. Their world is not just irrational but seriously distorted or downright psychotic. They slip or crash through to the other side of the looking glass, and they are beyond the point where they can learn from the experience. The shadow can no longer teach them anything, it can only devour, destroy and annihilate, and several of them are swallowed up by their mirror image. Paul's shell breaks at the very end so he can continue with his life; these characters stay trapped inside the repressed shadow beyond redemption.

Like most people, Scorsese's protagonists usually try to avoid the darkness of the shadow (most vehemently Teddy Daniels of *Shutter Island*), but these characters are mesmerized by it and compulsively seek it out. They are incapable of heeding Nietzsche's warning that "if you gaze for long into an abyss, the abyss gazes back into you."[2] They can all be compared to Narcissus, not because they love their own outer beauty, but because they are so fascinated by the hideousness of the twisted mirror image that they drown in it. Thus their destruction is to some extent self-induced.

The hero's journey is usually instigated by someone or something outside the main character. Even if we view the archetypal figures he encounters — the herald, the mentor, the shapeshifter, and the shadow — as representing sides of himself, they are personified and are generally regarded as separate characters. In these films, the journey is provoked solely by something beastly inside the protagonist. The thing that haunts Jordan Manmouth exists only in the mirror and it comes at him from the inside. Or as Travis Bickle's mirror image says: "I'm the only one here."

What's a Nice Girl Like You Doing in a Place Like This?

What's a Nice Girl Like You Doing in a Place Like This? is a nine-minute short that Scorsese made as part of the summer program at New York University in 1963, and it is his first film. It was inspired by a story by Algernon Blackwood and was influenced by the French and Italian New Wave cinema as well as Mel Brooks's "The Critic." Scorsese finds it "kind of young, kind of silly," but it is a remarkable debut for a 20-year-old.[3] Like many of his other films, it is simultaneously absurdly humorous and deeply disturbing, and it contains many elements that will be central in the later works. It is also the first of many Scorsese films in which we have an explicit narrator who cannot necessarily be trusted.

The offscreen voice of the main character (Zeph Michaelis) tells us that he just moved into a New York studio apartment, and he is obviously very proud of his new bohemian lifestyle. We see still images of skyscrapers and an empty room that is abruptly furnished by means of jump cuts. It may occur to us that both the apartment and the visual style is a reflection of the mind of the narrator. He tells us that he is a writer, and we see his new bookcase, an important part of his identity, collapse without warning. The narrator repeatedly ignores (or is ignorant of) the boundaries between the metaphorical and the literal: "I was hanging around the house," he tells us, and we see him actually hanging by his arms. These hints of a frail ego continue when he tells us that his name is Algernon, but that his friends call him Harry. His identity is determined not by himself but by others. "Why, even my friends said it," he constantly assures us whenever he expresses an opinion, and we cut to a straight-faced man (Fred Sica) sitting in a dark room who repeats verbatim what Harry has just told us. It is as if the things Harry tells us are not real to him, or he thinks they will not be credible to us, unless they are repeated by someone else.

The fatal moment for this brittle and suggestible mind comes when he buys a picture for the new apartment. He did not really like it, he tells us, but the man in the store was very persuasive. As he is saying this, we see the man in question sitting quietly with a book, indicating that the pressure is all in Harry's mind. "It was really nothing to look at," he says (and his armchair friend repeats it), but as soon as he hangs it on his wall, he becomes transfixed and feels compelled to stare at it constantly. "I was drawn to it," he says, and we see him literally being drawn across the floor. He cannot eat or sleep or write.

The photo depicts a man (Martin Scorsese) standing in a boat in a creek. When Harry tells us that it is nothing to look at, the man and the boat are removed so that we see only water. "There was a man," he says, and the man is cut in, suspended above the water, "and a boat," the man is taken out and the boat is cut in, establishing that what we are seeing is a reflection of Harry's mind rather than objective outer reality.

Because he cannot sleep, he sits up all night watching TV. *King Kong* comes on, and while Carl Denham describes Kong as something big and monstrous that is "holding that island in a grip of deadly fear," we focus on Harry's face, staring in a hypnotic trance at the picture on his wall which obviously represents the same dark and frightening things as Kong. Commonly, when islands appear in our dreams they represent the conscious ego while the surrounding water represents the unconscious. This would imply that Harry's ego is held in a similar "grip of deadly fear," and that what he is really terrified of is the water, i.e., his own unconscious.

Then what seems like a miracle happens. His friends tell him to throw a party and a woman guest (Mimi Stark) starts kissing him. Harry seems more overwhelmed than enamored, but he decides that "she was really a great catch," and when his friend repeats it, he decides to marry her. Now, he says, he was able to eat (we see him eating), to write (we see him typing away, still surrounded by people dancing), to sleep (we see him on the floor amid the partiers, soundly asleep). He is saved from the damaging influence of the picture for the time being.

Their married life is very happy, he tells us. He writes and she paints naïve pictures. She loved to paint nature, he says: flowers, trees, birds. But then disaster strikes in the form of "water, water, more water!" Whereas Harry all but says directly that his wife *paints* water, what we see now is a photograph of an ocean that apparently awakens the demon inside him again. He goes to an analyst (Sarah Braveman) who tells him to "stare it down!" His armchair friend starts repeating, word by word, what the analyst told him, but before he finishes, we hear a splash when Harry falls into the picture. We see him waving from inside it, in the middle of the ocean, and the film ends as he yells to his friend that the analyst also told him that "life is fraught with peril!"

The photograph now mysteriously seems to be in the friend's apartment rather than Harry's, evidencing again that what we experience is reflected through Harry's warped mind. The analyst, a maternal-looking woman, is seated in an isolated chair in an otherwise empty and dark room, just like Harry's friend. The friend looks much older than Harry, and when he starts asserting his authority by repeating the words of the analyst, it becomes a symbolic battle of wills between Father and Mother. This is the precise point at which Harry finally loses his grip on reality and disappears back into the preconscious state inside the ocean, i.e., Mother. The fear of being devoured is one of our most primal fears, says Bruno Bettelheim, and Harry is indeed swallowed up whole at the end as his ego is shattered. When he falls into the picture, he disappears from the face of the earth and ceases to exist as a separate individual. Like Norman Bates in *Psycho*, Harry becomes "all Mother" at the end of the film, and possibly, as the analyst says of Norman, "He only half existed to begin with."

The Big Shave

In 1967 Scorsese made *The Big Shave*, another short that contains references to Hitchcock and specifically to *Psycho*. It has been said that it was meant as a protest against the Vietnam War, but Scorsese has stated that it says a lot more about his own mental state at the time than about politics. Certainly, it seems timeless and much more ambiguous than a simple political allegory would be, and now, several decades later, it still has a very powerful effect on audiences. It deals with self-immolation, symbolic crucifixion, ritual bloodletting and repeating an act until it becomes virtually lethal. Thematically, it is closely connected with Scorsese's other works.

The Big Shave is Scorsese's first color film, and it begins with a series of close-ups of spotlessly, almost obsessively, clean bathroom fixtures. For any film buff, and certainly for a cinephile of Scorsese's stature, these connote the shower scene in *Psycho* and contain a premonition that something extremely violent might happen here. The color scheme is white and chromium-gray, portentously broken only by a blood-red nailbrush. Like Hitchcock's film, *The Big Shave* turns a bathroom — an ordinary place that we visit several times a day — into a place of sacrificial slaughter, and an everyday procedure like shaving ends in carnage through mutilation with a knife. In *Psycho* the knife was wielded by Mother/Norman on Marion; in *The Big Shave* it is wielded, even more horrifically, by the central character on himself.

A man (Peter Bernuth) enters the immaculate bathroom while Bunny Berrigan's "I Can't Get Started with You" plays matter-of-factly over most of the six-minute film. An obsessive-compulsive ritual begins when we see the man taking off his undershirt three times. He proceeds to take shaving cream and — irony of ironies — a *safety* razor from the medicine cabinet and starts shaving. Whereas it has often been said that he accidentally cuts himself but continues shaving anyway, in point of fact he finishes shaving without ever cutting himself and puts on after shave. *Then* for some reason he starts over again, and only now does he start mutilating himself, finally cutting his throat three times. He deliberately repeats the act *until* he injures and symbolically kills himself, and there seems to be something sacramental in the repetition itself, as if it were an act of penance and hurting himself the real objective.

His overwhelming masochism and self-imposed martyrdom connects this nameless man with many of Scorsese's later protagonists, from Charlie in *Mean Streets*, to Jake in *Raging Bull* and Sam in *Casino*, to Frank in *Bringing Out the Dead* and Howard Hughes in *The Aviator*. For all practical purposes, he shaves himself to death without batting an eyelid. He stands in front of his mirror image and carves away at himself as if it were the most natural thing in the world, and, fascinatingly, he takes the Instruments of the Passion, the objects that he uses for his own torture and symbolic crucifixion, from behind the looking glass.

Finally the song ends, and the camera focuses on the man's feet, then on his chest over which the blood rolls down in ropes. The screen turns red, and the film ends. The final shots make comparisons with the crucifixion unavoidable. They make us aware that there is a fine line between trying to get redemption through self-flagellation and complete psychosis, and they leave us wondering which side of the mirror this particular man is on.

Taxi Driver

In a central scene in *Taxi Driver* (1976) it is said of the main character that like the eponymous pilgrim of Kris Kristofferson's song, he is partly truth, and partly fiction.[4] The description is uttered more or less as a platitude, but it captures the essence of Scorsese's masterpiece. *Taxi Driver* is a deeply symbolic, mythological and religious film, and at the same time a horrifyingly precise psychopathological study of a psychotic killer.

So much has been said about this amazing film already, and parallels have been made to the works that inspired Paul Schrader and Scorsese when they made it — existential novels like Jean-Paul Satre's *Nausea* and Fyodor Dostoevsky's *Notes from the Underground*, diaries of real-life assassin Arthur Bremer, classic noir movies, and John Ford's western *The Searchers*. One contribution that could perhaps still be added to the vast array of analyses is a slightly more systematic journey into this devastating work — a difficult task, to be sure, since the film itself is rather like the abyss Travis Bickle (Robert De Niro) falls into: bottomless, pitch dark, and mercilessly confusing.

Toward that end, I will concentrate on the constantly overlapping levels of meaning that the film contains: the literal level (the study of Travis's psychosis and what FBI profilers call a "disorganized offender"); the religious level (Travis's perception of himself as an avenger sent by God to clean up the filth of the city); and the mythological level (*Taxi Driver* as a captivity myth, a story in which a hero ventures into the realm of Hell to save a fair maiden who is held captive there). Both of the latter levels and Travis's savior complex are, of course, part of his psychosis to begin with, but far from everything can be explained by examining the main character's mental state.

One reviewer said that the film "refuses to try to explain his insanity. Did it happen to him at birth? Did he pick it up in Vietnam, along with that horrible scar down his back? Or is it something he acquired in Manhattan, some sort of madness he breathed in with all the other pollutants? Scorsese and Schrader don't tell us because, frankly, they don't care. Neither, they imply, should we."[5] More than the "walking contradiction" that Betsy labels him, Travis Bickle (like Norman Bates) remains an enigma. We all have a tendency to feel more comfortable when we can categorize and rationally explain what is "wrong" with someone, but in this case, giving in to that desire only leads to a dead end. *Taxi Driver*, like *Psycho*, presents us with "a world and a state of mind so enclosed and so unknowable that we, as observers, are fooled for attempting to understand it," as Robert Phillip Kolker put it.[6]

Although no explanation is given for Travis's mental state, the first key to understanding this convoluted film is the realization that everything we experience (with a few notable exceptions) is filtered through his distorted perceptions, and his quixotic tunnel vision is all we are allowed to see. Travis insists that he will go "anywhere, anytime," but the fact remains that he does not. He never drives through the romantic Woody Allen areas of New York, but cruises Harlem, Times Square, 8th Avenue, and the East Village. He sees only what he chooses to see, and he seeks out the places that fuel his rage and reinforce his obsession.

Many of the vehement objections to the film (its alleged glorification of violence, misogyny, racism) can be dispelled by regarding it from this perspective. It is obviously misleading to assume that because a film focuses on sordidness, ugliness and aggression, its director is ghoulishly fascinated by those things. The whole point is that *we* see only these things because *Travis* sees only these things. The film is undeniably upsetting, but what is really disquieting is the fact that, for the better part of two hours, we are forced to experience the world from inside the inflamed mind of a man who is probably on the other side of the mirror from the beginning. Not only do we recognize and even sympathize with many of Travis's reactions, we also have to admit that he may not be as different from the rest of us as we would prefer to believe. Maybe we are even a bit afraid that his madness and loneliness are contagious when we are this close.

In most works about homicidal maniacs, there are other characters present — for instance, a sane person who is trying to solve the crime — with whom we can identify and against whom we can measure the sickness of the killer, and usually we get some kind of comforting denouement. In *Psycho*, Lila and Sam are trying to solve the mystery and at the end the "lunatic" is behind bars. In Michael Powell's *Peeping Tom* we get very close to the killer and experience things from his point of view, but by the end he is on the verge of being captured by the police *and* he kills himself *and* we get extensive Freudian explanations for his behavior. In *Taxi Driver* we have no one else with whom to identify. At the end, the killer is loose on the street, is lusted after and revered as a cultural hero and, frankly, we still have no clue why he did what he did.

Where Paul Hackett in *After Hours* was forced into a mythological underworld, Travis himself *transforms* New York into an inferno. Because of his obsession with the squalor of the city, he precipitates a scenario in which he can become a hero and savior, a modern equivalent of Orpheus who descends into Hades to recall to life his beloved Eurydice, or Theseus who attempts to retrieve the abducted Persephone, or Ethan Edwards of John Ford's *The Searchers* who goes out to rescue his young niece who has been kidnapped by Comanches. Unlike J.R. and Charlie, both of whom idolize John Wayne, the antisocial and alienated Travis does not "follow" politics or music or movies, and he has presumably never heard of any of his legendary forebears or of the captivity myth.

Even though *Taxi Driver* reflects the mind of a deranged individual, its structure can be outlined fairly simply:

1. Prologue
2. Travis's character and life are established
3. Travis is searching for a mission
4. Travis finds his mission
5. Travis goes out on his mission
6. Epilogue

The film is set during a six-month period: the first date we hear is May 10, and the ending takes place 17 days before the presidential election. During the first half we focus on Travis's disgust, impotent rage, and powerlessness as he searches for "a sense of some place to go" and tries to reach out and establish relationships with other people. "Then suddenly there's a change," catalyzed by Betsy's rejection and the macabre back-seat passenger played by Martin Scorsese, and Travis actively takes up arms to go on his newfound mission as a divine instrument. He prepares for battle and goes to war to redeem the human race. Finally comes the bewildering epilogue which suggests that he has fallen even deeper into the abyss and can erupt again at any moment.

The first thing we see is smoke billowing from an unknown source for slightly longer than feels comfortable. Then out of the poisonous-looking steam, filmed from a worm's-eye view, a yellow taxi slithers into view. It is presented like a lurking animal emerging from the fumes of Hell, accompanied by Bernard Herrmann's haunting jazz drums. Then we cut to an extreme close-up of Travis's feverish eyes, the focal point of the movie, that move back and forth in barely discernible slow motion. Then finally we cut to what he sees: people moving grotesquely through a red and blue cityscape, likewise in slow motion, while rain water on the windshield blurs distinctions. Finally, we cut back to Travis's eyes, and by now we have slipped imperceptibly into his inflamed mind.

This prologue exists outside of time and space and is a symbolic distillation of the main idea: for the next couple of hours we are forced to experience things from Travis's point of view — sharing his gaze as well as his distorted interpretation of what he sees — and his perception which is, at best, extremely distorted and, at worst, psychotic. Scorsese says about the way he filmed the movie: "There would be a certain look in his eyes, a certain close-up of his face, shot with a certain lens. Subtle — not too wide, not to destroy it, not to nudge the audience into, 'Hey, this guy's a whacko.' Not that sort of thing. But rather to let it sneak up on the audience, like Travis does, and move the camera the way he sees things — all from his point of view."[7]

Then the story begins when Travis goes into a 57th Street office, applying for the job as a taxi driver. Our first impression of him is not unlike our first impression of Norman Bates in *Psycho*: he seems boyishly innocent and awkward (he does not know what "moonlighting" is), and he is not very good at verbal communication. Yet, at the same time, there is something almost subliminally disturbing about him. Although he seems innocuous, the man who interviews him for the job feels provoked, and when the man tells him off, the camera moves closer to Travis's face as it stiffens with repressed rage.

We also learn that Travis suffers from chronic insomnia and was a Marine, "honorable discharge, May '73." Critics have argued about whether Vietnam is important for our understanding of his character. Paul Schrader seems to believe that it is peripheral. Travis's malaise, his loneliness and rage are, he says, existential in origin and not "societally imposed."[8] Scorsese, on the other hand, has said that it is essential that Travis had "experienced life and death around him every second he was in southeast Asia," this memory was "held in him and then it explodes."[9] The truth probably lies somewhere in the middle: Vietnam does not hold the entire answer to Travis's character (nothing does) and does not fulfill our desire for an explanation, but Travis's reflex actions undeniably seem related to the experience. Certainly, this motif connects *Taxi Driver* to *The Searchers* in that Travis, like Ethan, has been through the traumatizing experience of war, and at the start of the film he pops up out of nowhere leaving us to wonder where he has been in the meantime.

We cut to Travis's apartment and track slowly across it, while in voice-over he reads fragments of a diary entry: "May 10th. Thank God for the rain which has helped wash the garbage and the trash off the sidewalks." This introduces the obsession with filth that makes him perceive of the city as Hell. At this point Travis is passive, waiting for the divine intervention that he is convinced will somehow purge the world. The inner monologues which reveal his thoughts all through the film are significantly more articulate than his conversations with people. "It is as if," objects one critic, "Schrader is willing to sacrifice Travis's believability on the altar of literary influence."[10] But the schism makes sense: as part of his delusion Travis is more eloquent when we hear how he *thinks* he sounds than when we witness how he *actually* sounds. Also, the diary connects Travis with Scorsese's other voice-over narrators. Unlike most of them, however, he is not aware of speaking to an audience, and when we cannot trust what he tells us it is not because, like Henry Hill, he lies to manipulate us, but because, like Harry in *What's a Nice Girl Like You Doing in a Place Like This?*, his own sense of reality is warped.

As soon as he starts driving around in the taxi, Travis's obsession with filth and putrefaction increases. We see slow-motion close-ups of the car driving through Times Square, while Travis tonelessly lists all the "animals" that "come out at night," as part of an obsessive ritual, feeding his frighteningly subdued rage. "Some day a *real* rain will come and wash all the scum off the streets," he says, and again the Biblical overtones reveal his belief in purging through apocalyptic annihilation.

Travis's diary and psychopathology connects him with various real-life killers, notably Arthur Bremer and John Hinckley. He is virtually a textbook example of the so-called disorganized killer, which is extremely ironic because repeatedly he talks about getting "organizied" [sic] and honestly believes that he is succeeding. He is an uneducated, virtually inarticulate loner who lives in a squalid, ugly room. His verbal and social skills are so bad that he never really connects with other people. His only contact with his parents is through greeting cards in which he lies about his life to make up for being an underachiever. Retired FBI profiler Robert Ressler gives this definition of the typical disorganized offender which might be a verbatim description of Travis: "The disorganized offender grows up to internalize hurt, anger, and fear. While normal people also internalize these emotions to some degree — that's necessary in order to live together in a society — the disorganized offender goes far beyond the norm in his internalization. He is unable to let off steam, and lacks the verbal and physical skills for expressing these emotions in the proper arenas." These offenders, continues Ressler, "act in an inadequate manner, thus reinforcing their hurt, anger, and isolation. Disorganized offenders tend to withdraw from society almost completely, to become loners. Whereas many organized killers tend to be reasonably attractive, outgoing and gregarious, the disorganized ones are incapable of relating to other people at all.... Such offenders actively reject the society that has rejected them."[11]

While moralizing about the depravity of others, Travis abuses his body. We see him repeatedly drinking, popping pills and eating junk food, and like many violent offenders he is a habitual user of pornography. He associates sex and emotions with violence: he tells us that some mornings he has to clean sperm off the back seat of his car and some mornings he has to clean blood off, and toward the end he goes to a porn theatre and shoots his finger at the screen like a gun. On two occasions he sits in front of the TV nuzzling his .44 Magnum while watching human affection. First he sees couples dancing on *American Bandstand*, then on a soap opera a man is rejected by a woman because of a rival, at which point Travis unbalances the TV set with his foot so that it smashes.

Travis lives in total isolation; he has no phone, his record player is broken (or so he tells Betsy, although I doubt whether he even has one), and he smashes the TV which is his only link to the world and defines how he sees it. All through the film, Bernard Herrmann's haunting score seems to surround and envelop him and emphasizes the hermiticism of his existence. The absence of familiar music underscores Travis's loneliness. Like Scorsese's other early films, *Taxi Driver* is set in his native New York City, so, realistically, music from radios and jukeboxes should be surging out of doors and windows, and probably does. The point is that Travis does not hear it, and thus, neither do we. Some critics have complained that the other characters in the film seem flat and clichéd, but again that is because we experience them filtered through Travis, so that they are "the reflections of a junk food mind," as Kolker puts it.[12] As is often the case in Scorsese's work, the physical surroundings mirror the character's mind, and Travis's empty, squalid room is a powerful metaphor, at the same time that it accurately resembles the typical real-life habitat of this type of offender.

"All my life needed was a sense of some place to go," says his next diary entry — mysteriously in the past tense. Betsy (Cybill Shepherd) is introduced like a response, appearing "like an angel out of this filthy mass." "She is alone!" Travis says, projecting himself onto her, "They cannot touch her!" We see Betsy dressed in white, floating across the screen in slow motion, and we might have taken Travis's Madonna vision at face value were it not for the fact that Scorsese himself is sitting in the background, looking positively mischievous, as if to warn us that he has serious objections to this canonization. That Betsy is indeed not the luminous, virginal soulmate that Travis perceives her to be is revealed in the next scene, one of only two that we experience independently of Travis. We are inside the Palantine Campaign Headquarters while Travis is sitting outside in the cab. Betsy is talking with Tom (Albert Brooks), a co-worker with whom she is possibly intimately involved, but certainly stringing along. At the same time she is expressing a sexual interest in the senator for whom they work. Contrary to Travis's celestial vision, she seems to be reasonably intelligent, extremely flirtatious, and not particularly deep.

Travis (Robert De Niro) in *Taxi Driver* (Columbia Pictures, 1976) insists that he will go "anywhere, anytime," but mainly he cruises places that fuel his rage and reinforce his obsession. Here he is parked outside the Palantine Campaign Headquarters.

Shortly afterwards Travis walks up to Betsy's desk and offers to volunteer, but he soon reveals his true purpose. He has been watching her, he says, and has decided that she is "not a happy person," so he wants to take her out for coffee. He tells her not to be afraid: "I'm here to protect you." While *he* is out to rescue a damsel in distress, Betsy does not seem unhappy or particularly distressed, so we can already predict that his mission will fail.

In the next scene he takes her to a coffee shop on Columbus Circle on May 26th, and they are all but incapable of communicating with each other. When he says he wants to get a sign that reads "One of these days I'm gonna get *organizized!*" [sic] she does not get the joke. When she describes him by paraphrasing the Kris Kristofferson song as a tongue-in-cheek compliment, he is offended because he thinks she calls him a pusher. During most of the conversation, and especially when Travis seems to think he is profound, Betsy looks as if she is trying hard not to laugh. "I don't think I have ever met anyone quite like you," she says, but instead of looking friendly and happy the way she is described in Schrader's script, she looks like she is pulling his leg.

We cut back and forth between close-ups of Betsy and Travis sitting across from each other at the table. Whenever we see Betsy she is filmed over Travis's shoulder, whereas Travis is alone in the frame, as he is through most of the film. The fact that he is always alone in the frame reinforces his intense loneliness and disconnectedness, while our seeing everybody else over his shoulder reinforces the idea that we experience everything through him and not objectively. We sometimes cut out to a neutral two-shot from the side. In these shots, Betsy is sitting with her legs spread wide apart underneath the table in a way that looks singularly vulgar and implies that she is certainly not the virgin Travis would have her be.[13]

Between the coffee scene and their date come two scenes that are crucial because, after

Betsy's rejection, they determine where Travis's attention goes. First, he coincidentally picks up as his passenger Senator Palantine (Leonard Harris). Travis confides in him that the smells of the city give him headaches that will not go away, and says that if Palantine is elected he should "flush it right down the toilet." Then Iris (Jodie Foster), the child prostitute, gets into his car and asks him to take her away from her pimp, Matthew (Harvey Keitel).

Travis's big date with Betsy has, I think, been slightly misread over the years. Although it contains sexually explicitly material, the film he takes her to is *not* a porn flick but, as the sign outside says, a semi-documentary called *Swedish Marriage Manual*. This means that he has actually given this some serious thought rather than just taking her to one of the sleazy hardcore porn theatres he himself frequents. This is the very best this man — at one and the same time completely warped and completely innocent — can come up with. He genuinely believes this is where one might go on a first date, which makes the scene significantly more harrowing. Most critics say that Betsy leaves the theatre in disgust as soon as she realizes what kind of film this is, but I do not believe that for a minute. There is no way she does not know exactly what she is getting into before she enters that theatre. She has seen the explicit signs outside on Times Square and chooses to enter anyway, which makes her the less innocent of the two. Whereas Travis takes her there in good faith, she does not enter in good faith. As in most of her scenes, she is playing games, and only when she realizes that she may be in over her head does she leave.

The next scene contains the most important shot in the entire film, according to Scorsese. Travis calls Betsy from a phone in a hallway, and while he is being rejected, the camera moves away from him and focuses for the longest time on the empty hallway. Robert K. Ressler and his colleague John Douglas explain that people who turn into killers often have a violent fantasy that they turn into reality when some stressor tips them over the edge. In Travis's case the fantasy is cleaning the filth off the streets, playing knight in shining armor to an unhappy damsel and eliminating his male rival, and Betsy's rejection is the stressor that eventually makes him go on a killing mission.

Now the physical and verbal violence escalates, markedly so in the next scene in which Scorsese appears as the unusual backseat passenger who utters what Lawrence S. Friedman has called "one of the most misogynistic outbursts in screen history."[14] The scene is closely connected with the concept of the shadow. The man is shadowing his wife who is having an affair with a black man, and we see them as shadows on the window. The man asks Travis: "D'ya see the woman in the window?" and since Scorsese often plants significant references to movie classics in his work, this could be an allusion to Fritz Lang's *The Woman in the Window*, which is about the physical manifestation of our darker sides in connection with adultery. Is the man saying, "Do you see the woman in the window?" or, "Did you see *The Woman in the Window*?"

This nightmarish passenger then starts fantasizing about what one could do to various parts of a woman's anatomy with a .44 Magnum. We are so incredulous over his frenzied speech that our first impulse is to simply conclude that he must be demented. What he is doing by saying these shocking things, however, is paying out the extreme hurt and rage in his shadow so that, hopefully, he does not have to act on it. Admittedly, it is very inappropriate to do this in semi-public, but his horrifying words are just words, and he puts into perspective Travis's inability to express his emotions, verbally or in any other remotely socially acceptable way. For Travis, these words serve as a catalyst to *act on* his pent-up rage, to *become* his shadow, almost as if it emerges from the rearview mirror. Influenced by the stories of his colleagues that contain every form of bigotry imaginable, he goes out and buys guns, able to find release only through extreme violence.

Travis's mind is so feeble and impressionable after Betsy's rejection that every single thing he experiences becomes part of his rampage, and apparently minor scenes inspire the violent climax. He watches the primaries on TV, and the senator's repeated catchphrases "the people are rising" and "the people are beginning to rule" inspire Travis's claim that he is the man "who stood up." He sees Iris again and starts following her and accepts what he perceives as his divine calling: "Loneliness has followed me everywhere," he says. "There is no escape. I am God's lonely man." He can now actively assist God rather than passively waiting for the apocalyptic torrent of rain.

"My life has taken another turn," says a diary entry on June 8th, marking the midpoint of the film, and he meets up with Easy Andy (Steven Prince) to buy a whole arsenal of weapons, among them the .44 Magnum that the backseat passenger was talking about.[15] He has decorated his room with the senator's campaign posters as well as the sign that reads: "One of these days I'm gonna get organized [*sic*]!" Apparently he is convinced that he actually is *getting* organized. He vows that he will stop abusing his body and starts working

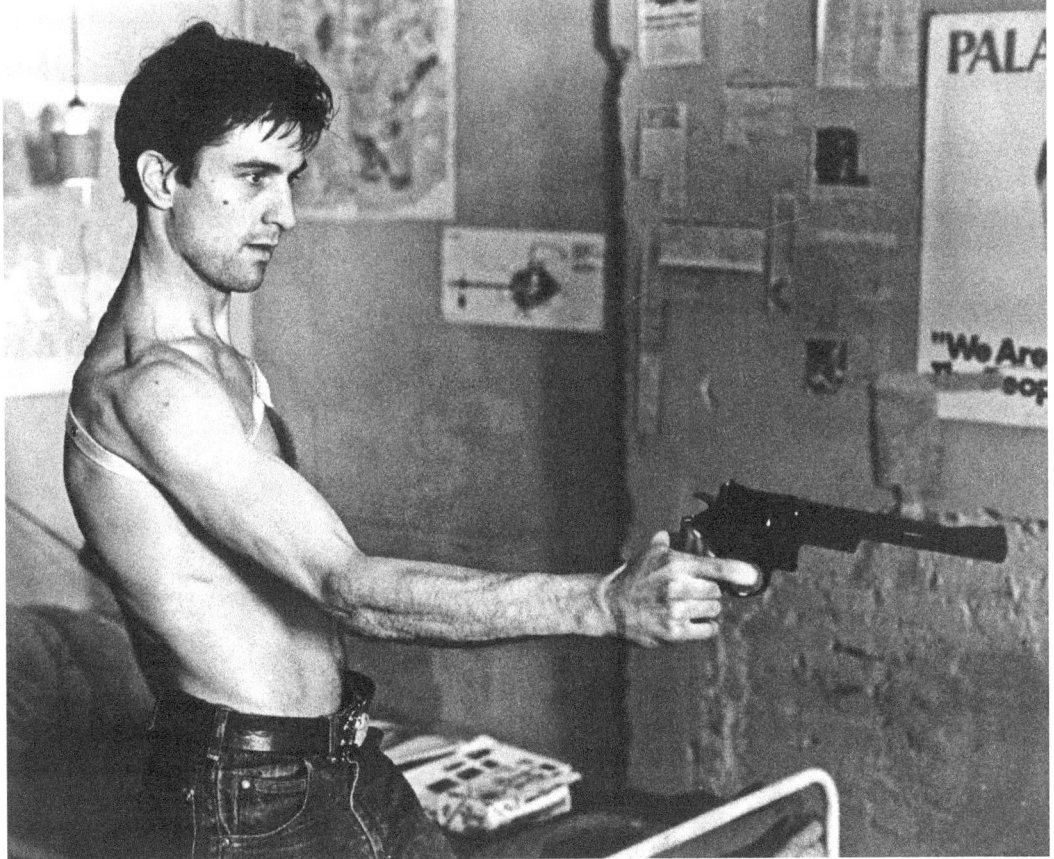

Travis Bickle (Robert De Niro), "God's lonely man" in front of Senator Palantine's campaign poster in *Taxi Driver* (Columbia Pictures, 1976).

out fanatically, but he is still popping pills and looks singularly unhealthy. His thoughts still make no sense in any rational or sane way, even though he clearly thinks they do. "The idea," he says, "had been growing in my brain for some time," not specifying what idea he is talking about. He rambles on about "true force" and "all the king's men" not being able to "put it back together again" while standing in front of posters of Palantine, so we have to assume — by way of Robert Penn Warren — that he means to assassinate the senator.[16] How that, according to normal logic, would further his plan of getting the scum off the streets is not at all clear.

Within minutes of this comes the famous and constantly quoted mirror scene — presumably the single-most famous scene from any Scorsese picture. Whenever it is quoted the focus is always on the repetition of: "You talkin' to me?" But actually the next line — "Well, I'm the only one here!" — is a lot more interesting, as is the fact that the one speaking these lines is not really Travis himself, but his mirror image. It affirms that at the center of this film is Travis's duel with his own psychotic self, and *it* has the upper hand. The man who "stood up against the scum, the cunts, the dogs, the filth," who is walking around armed to the teeth, is totally psychotic, like a bomb just waiting to go off.

Travis now seeks out the 12-year-old prostitute, and the parallels to *The Searchers* — in which Ethan goes out to find his niece who has been abducted by Comanches — become palpable. Iris's pimp has long, black hair and a head band, and calls to mind Chief Scar. As interested as Travis is in saving Iris, he is every bit as interested in savaging the pimp, just as Ethan is, in fact, more obsessed with butchering Scar than with rescuing Debbie. The scene in which Travis and Iris meet for breakfast is precisely analogous to the coffee scene with Betsy. He keeps harping on the rival (Tom, whom he was trying to get Betsy to criticize, and Matthew, whom he wants Iris to realize is "scum"). Both conversations pave the way for the climactic scene in which Travis acts out his knight in shining armor complex, and his real objective turns out to be annihilating the dragon/rival, rather than rescuing the princess.[17]

In their article about *Taxi Driver*, Patricia Patterson and Manny Farber furiously try to prove that the film is not realistic. They complain that Iris "has the shiny complexion, hair, and bright eyes of neither Lower East Side nor a baby prostitute."[18] That is very possibly true. In fact, there is something decidedly cherubic about Iris's playful manner, chubby face and curly hair, and the hat that frames her curls at times looks like a halo. But considering that we are experiencing everything in the film through Travis's distorted perception — something Patterson and Farber never even consider — does that not make sense? Saving Iris is his proclaimed mission and, therefore, he obviously sees her not as a whore who has been sullied beyond salvation, but as "sweet Iris," as he preposterously insists on calling her. Travis's Madonna/whore complex manifests itself in a need to take on the questionable project of redeeming the whore and turning her into a saint, like Christ did with Magdalene.

Accordingly, Iris's room is not the sleazy brothel one would expect but easily the nicest and coziest space in the entire movie. It looks rather like a devotional shrine, complete with dozens of lit votive candles. That is, of course, in perfect keeping with the fact that this is the space where Travis's ultimate mission, his avenging battle against evil, will eventually be played out, and it reflects his distorted perception of himself as a divine instrument. Although Iris assures him that she likes being with Matthew, that there is a reason why she left home in the first place, and that she really has nowhere else to go, Travis keeps insisting that she has to get out of there. He needs his mission so badly that he does not care that

4. Through the Looking Glass 89

As interested as Travis (Robert De Niro, right) is in rescuing the fair damsel in *Taxi Driver* (Columbia Pictures, 1976), he is every bit as interested in getting even with the rival. Iris's pimp, Matthew (Harvey Keitel), is dressed to look like Chief Scar in John Ford's *The Searchers*.

Iris may not want to be saved. Like Charlie in *Mean Streets*, as Scorsese has pointed out, Travis wants to help people so much that he does not care that he may be harming them in the process.[19]

To emphasize that Iris may feel differently about getting away than Travis supposes, Schrader and Scorsese added a scene which they refer to as "the Scar scene." They feel a scene was missing from *The Searchers* that would describe how Debbie felt about the Indians that had been her only family for years, and particularly about Chief Scar. Travis is standing outside the building so we are free to experience the relationship between Iris and Matthew without his filter. Ironically, this scene — a pimp tries to seduce a teenage hooker into staying with him — is the tenderest scene in the movie. Iris softly protests: "I don't like what I'm doing." Matthew cleverly undermines her protest by saying that he loves her and never wanted her to *like* turning tricks. He holds her tight and reassures her. Clearly this is one big manipulation, but as Friedman points out, it calls into question "any easy assumption we might have that *anything* would be preferable (for a 13-year-old girl) to prostitution: with Matthew, Iris shares an equivocal tenderness, whereas there is no indication that 'home' offers her anything at all."[20] This does not mean that the film advocates teenage prostitution, but simply that Travis does not know how Iris feels or what she ran away from to begin with. By taking out the captor at the end, Travis, like Ethan, takes out the closest thing to a father figure the girl has.

Travis now starts ritually preparing for the grand finale. He goes to the firing range, burns the decaying flowers Betsy sent back, polishes his boots, and leaves money and a letter for Iris: "By the time you read this, I will be dead," the note reads, which proves that this last act is meant as a suicide mission.[21] "My whole life has pointed in one direction. I see that now. There never has been any choice for me," his voice-over tells us, while we see the senator arriving for the rally. What Travis is expressing is a delusional conviction of a fixed, holy purpose that does not exist outside his head. In retrospect we know that the final act will not at all be pointing in one direction but haphazard and coincidental: when he reaches clumsily inside his coat for the gun at the rally, dressed in army fatigues and with a Mohawk haircut, he is spotted by agents immediately, so he ends up transferring his rage to Iris's pimp. Ironically, if he had succeeded in assassinating the senator, he would have gone to jail, but instead he kills various lowlifes and is hailed as a cultural hero.

Changing his mind at the last minute is in perfect accordance with his psychopathology, because "the disorganized killer doesn't choose victims logically, and so often takes a victim at high risk to himself," says Ressler. He "has no idea of, or interest in, the personalities of his victims.... The disorganized offender's actions are usually devoid of normal logic; until he is caught and tells us his version of the crimes, chances are that no one can follow the twisted reasoning he uses to pick his victims or to commit his crimes."[22] By this time, however, we are so far inside Travis's mind that mostly his reasoning seems perfectly natural to us, and that is the really frightening thing about this film.

When his mission fails, Travis instantly decides to rescue Iris instead, but interestingly, he makes no attempt to protect her during the entire shootout — in fact, he hardly even looks at her. All his attention is focused on the rivals. His warped sense of predestination can easily be undermined. He wants to help Betsy but she does not want to be helped, then he transfers his feelings onto Iris. "He tries," says Paul Schrader, "to kill the surrogate father of the first and fails, so he kills the surrogate father of the other."[23] Presumably, if he had not succeeded in that, either, he would have simply picked a third target.

The climactic scene is excruciating and bloody. It takes only a few minutes of screen time, but feels like several hours. After the massacre, Travis picks up a gun at random and shoots himself five times, and since the weapon is not his, he has no way of knowing it is empty. When the police arrive, he smilingly makes a symbolic gesture of shooting himself three times in the head with his index finger. These expressions of self-hatred can only be read as a symbolical suicide — which corresponds with his goodbye note to Iris — and for the last time we cut to the God's-eye-view shot that is used whenever he tries and fails to connect with people. This time it suggests the final disconnection of his spirit leaving his body and floating, to the sound of harps and drums, in a slow reverse-tracking shot down the stairs and into the street. This shot lasts almost four minutes and is actually much longer than the shootout.

When we see Travis again he turns out, grotesquely and anticlimactically, to have been hailed as a hero. His walls are covered with newspaper clippings — among them a photo of Iris's parents (which is, in reality, a picture of Charles and Catherine Scorsese in their living room) and a letter from Iris's father in Pittsburgh where she has been returned. The letter is read in the droning, apathetic voice-over of a man who sounds much too old to be the father of an adolescent girl, and it has a grim undercurrent when he reads that they have "taken steps to see she has never cause to run away again." Like Ethan's words at the end of *The Searchers*—"Let's go home, Debbie!"—this is at best superficially comforting. Although Travis has saved the girl, we cannot really be sure what he has sent her back to and, significantly, we never learn how Iris feels about being home, just as we did not with Debbie.

One might assume that Travis's symbolic death would entail resurrection and cathartic renewal, but I do not believe it does. Herrmann's haunting music is still played at the end, and if Travis's new room is a reflection of his mind the way his old room was, things have not improved—quite the contrary. Significantly, we never see Travis *in* this room, which is even more squalid and naked than the last one, attesting that his mental state, too, has deteriorated. It could even be a prison cell or a room in a mental hospital, which might mean that the subsequent scene takes place only inside Travis's head.

We see Travis back on the street and as he is standing with his colleagues, who are still telling stupid stories, Betsy gets into his cab. While he drives her home, the fair maiden who rejected him earlier tells him that he is a hero, and she has a dreamy, libidinous look on her face. She makes it clear that now that he is a celebrity she is interested in him, which is probably the sickest thing in the film. When she gets out and Travis drives off, she looks after him longingly, the way Joey's mother looked at Shane riding off into the sunset. We see her mainly in the rearview mirror, however, which might indicate that she is not really there.

Up until this point we may still debate whether Travis has undergone a transformation and been reborn after his symbolic suicide, whether the shootout, as some critics claim, has made him suddenly (and unbelievably) sane. But in the last few moments there can be no more doubt. We hear a sudden high noise, and with a jerk of the head Travis assumes an expression precisely like the one Norman Bates gets whenever he snaps into the personality of Mother. Whatever Travis is startled by is inside the mirror, because that is the only place he looks. The image is sped up, and we hear the subliminally disturbing sound of a cymbal played in reverse, which emphasizes Travis's psychotic movement and the sense that we are on the other side of the mirror. After that, the picture cuts to the view through his windshield as it did at the beginning of the film.

What we see now is even more grotesquely distorted and feverish than it was at the start when at least we could make out what it was. Now we have two or more images bleeding into each other, and all we can be sure of is that Travis is still driving through the exact same neighborhoods. The three last notes we hear are precisely the same notes that end Herrmann's soundtrack for *Psycho*. The sum total of all these things tell us beyond any doubt that Travis, like Norman, is as deranged as ever. He has fallen hopelessly into the mirror, beyond rescue and repair, and he might erupt again at any minute. This time, however, he knows for sure that he can get away with murder and, thus, he might be slightly more confident and dangerous.

As with Norman Bates, any attempt at finding ultimate answers to Travis's mental state are bound to sound ludicrous. Similarly ludicrous was the facile assumption that the entire explanation for the Hinckley shooting could be found in his obsession with *Taxi Driver*. On March 30, 1981, John W. Hinckley shot and wounded President Ronald Reagan, later offering as his defense that he wanted to attract the attention of Jodie Foster, whom he had watched in *Taxi Driver* innumerable times. Clips from the film were shown repeatedly in the courtroom. It is, says Scorsese, like "the end of [Truffaut's] *Fahrenheit 451*, where the guy is chased, and they just pick up anybody at random, so they can tell people at home, 'It's okay. We caught him. You can rest.' It's okay; he did it because of our picture. Now you can all sleep."[24]

Some people would obviously be more comfortable if Scorsese's films did not insist that we look at these troubling things. It is almost as if they truly believe that he, Schrader and De Niro invented them, and that Hinckley would be perfectly sane if only they had not made this film. But whether we like it or not, Norman Bates, Travis Bickle, and John Hinckley are there, both in the outer world and as a reflection of parts of ourselves, and trying to ignore the destructive shadow impulses and pretend that if we refuse to look at them they do not exist is infinitely more dangerous than depicting and trying honestly to understand them.

The King of Comedy

In 1981, The Academy Awards ceremony was originally planned for March 31st, but because of the Hinckley shooting, it had to be postponed for a day. Martin Scorsese was nominated for *Raging Bull* and arrived at the ceremony not knowing that a connection had been made between the attempted assassination and his film, *Taxi Driver*. He only became aware that special FBI protection had been arranged for him and Robert De Niro when he went to the bathroom and three other guys came with him. "I'm not kidding," Scorsese remembers. "I think they had radios, they certainly had wires and things hanging out of their ears. I remember thinking, 'Gee, this security is remarkable.'"[25] He did not learn about the connection until he went to congratulate De Niro on his Best Actor Award for the role as Jake La Motta.

The next film the two of them made after the unpleasant experience of being held partly (and completely unreasonably) responsible for the shooting was *The King of Comedy* (1983). This film concerns a man, Rupert Pupkin (Robert De Niro), who is obsessed with a Johnny Carson–like talk-show host and is so desperate for his attention and for instant fame that he is willing to commit a crime to get it.

Scorsese often sounds weary when asked to talk about the film. An imminent directors strike forced him to shoot it before he was ready and under strenuous circumstances for which he was in no condition physically as he was recovering from pneumonia. But also, this is without comparison his angriest film, and this modest, controlled man might possibly feel retrospectively self-conscious about how clearly his bitterness shines through.

Despite Scorsese's ennui and critics generally regarding it as a minor work, *The King of Comedy* is an absolutely astounding film. Although it is at times funny, it is, as Scorsese has pointed out, by no means a comedy. At first glance it may appear lighter than most of his work, but actually it is one of the most painful and purposefully embarrassing films ever made. In the light of the Hinckley shooting and of John Lennon having been killed by a fan a few months before that, it is much more harrowing than it might seem. It contains scathingly ironic comments on the Hinckley case and on the phenomenon of celebrity. As regards the mythological hero's journey, it is Scorsese's most provocative film.

The King of Comedy has a lot in common with *Taxi Driver*, and Rupert Pupkin (De Niro's best performance according to Scorsese) is closely related to Travis Bickle.[26] He, too, has serious problems with reality testing, and the line between outer objective reality and inner subjective reality is seriously blurred from the beginning. He has no sense of boundaries, which is hilariously shown in the way he constantly uses public spaces for private purposes, such as when he stakes a claim on the only functional public phone on Times Square and creates complete pandemonium. Where *Taxi Driver* is primarily an expressionistic work, *The King of Comedy* is Scorsese's most aesthetically straightforward film. In the former we were forced to *enter* the psychosis; in the latter we *watch* it from a distance. Whereas Travis's distorted world is extremely disconcerting, the deceptively safe distance between us and Rupert serves to make us relax, and perhaps even feel superior to him. So when Scorsese eventually lays bare that Rupert Pupkin is no worse than any one of us, that shocking slap in the face becomes almost unbearable — one reason, I suppose, why many people cannot stand watching this film.

Rupert's inability to distinguish between fantasy and reality is pervasive, and it often makes us unsure of whether the things we see are real or delusional, since he is only marginally less embarrassing in his fantasies. It is possible to view the film as a seriously distorted version of the hero's journey, the title emphasizing the mythological aspects: Rupert wants to become the new king of comedy, and celebrity is the coveted grail. The plot takes place over six days — Tuesday night to Sunday night — and concerns his frantic attempt to cajole his way into show business, trying to get through the stages of the hero path by trickery or force rather than going through the ordeals that are necessary to deserve the passage.

In the opening scene, Rupert is waiting at the stage entrance, among other fans, for Jerry Langford (Jerry Lewis) to arrive after his show late at night. Rupert manages to manipulate his way into Langford's car, thinking, like the Sorcerer's Apprentice, that the mere contact with a celebrated master will make him one, too. Like all good mentors, Langford admonishes him that he must make his own journey. He has to start at the bottom and work his way up, honing his talent, Langford says. Rupert's reply is that he *is* at the bottom and does not have time to work his way up because he is 34 years old. In other words, he basically wants to skip the journey and have the grail bestowed upon him.

His dream began, he says, when he saw Jerry achieve instant fame one night on *The Ed Sullivan Show*. He fails to realize that, although Langford's celebrity may have come overnight, he had been working on his talent for decades before that. Later, in Langford's country home, Rupert shows Rita pictures of Jerry's career from boyhood on, still missing the implication that Jerry has worked on his craft since he was no more than a child. The old king has spent his entire life earning his position, yet Rupert wants to have the same thing handed to him. He is not interested in the hard work of being a comedian. He wants stardom, he wants it now, and he wants it for free.

Celebrity is Rupert's dubious grail, and the two things he chooses to do on Tuesday night when he is convinced that his fame is imminent are interesting indications of *why* he wants it so much. From their forced conversation in the car, we cut abruptly to Sardi's and see a frazzled Jerry pleading a suddenly famous Rupert to take over his show for six weeks. As we crosscut between the two of them at the table, Rupert mysteriously changes appearance, until finally we realize that he is actually alone in his room in his mother's basement, acting out the conversation, playing the role of both his own adored fantasy self and the obeisant and powerless Jerry. The bubble pathetically bursts when his mother starts yelling at him to be quiet.[27] Later that night, he looks up the beautiful Rita (Diahnne Abbott) with whom he used go to school and who seems completely out of his league. Again, we cut to the two of them at a restaurant and suspect that this takes place in Rupert's head also, but this time it is really happening. Like Travis, Rupert approaches the princess because he does not think she is happy. "I'm offering you a way out," he says, "I wanna help change your life." He is about to be king and he wants Rita as his queen, he says, preposterously offering her his autograph. He is already reaping the fruits of his imagined renown, and in his mind he is a knight in shining armor while Rita is a damsel in distress.

It is significant that Rupert's fair maiden is someone from his school days, since everything about his demeanor and appearance is infantile and/or connected to childhood. He and his friend Masha (Sandra Bernhard) behave and dress like children who are trying to imitate adults — specifically, Rupert tries to look and behave the way he immaturely thinks that Jerry Langford looks. Rupert and Masha constantly have fights in public which are extremely puerile in nature and content. Rupert's comedy routine, which is the crux of the film, describes a small boy whose life is so miserable that it becomes tragicomic. His mental state seems to have its origins in his childhood, and he is still stuck there.

The mere fact that he still lives with his mother in his mid-thirties suggests a regressive personality. Throughout the film, Mother yells admonitions to him, but, in fact, we never see her. The reason for this, I would propose, is that she is dead and the voice from above is only in Rupert's head. In his comedy routine he says: "If she were only here today, I'd say, 'Hey, Mom, what are you doing here, you've been dead for nine years.'" Even after Mother has been gone for almost a decade, Rupert needs her to be present to the point where we can hear her, always criticizing him, the same way we could hear the late Mrs. Bates yelling at Norman.[28] The idea is substantiated repeatedly. When Rupert is making a tape for Jerry, Mother starts hollering at him to turn down the sound. Rupert stops the

Liza Minnelli, Robert De Niro, and Martin Scorsese are entertained by Jerry Lewis in the room in Mother's basement on the set of *The King of Comedy* (Twentieth Century–Fox, 1983).

tape, argues with her, then turns it on and continues. The normal procedure, one would think, would be to rewind, erase her voice, and start over. The fact that he does not bespeaks an awareness that there is nothing *to* erase because the voice is not really there.[29]

The knight in shining armor in fairy tales often starts out as an insignificant boy who goes out into the world, saves a fair damsel, and makes a great success of his life. On a psychological level this concerns very basic motifs. "In the throes of Oedipal conflicts," says Bruno Bettelheim, "a young boy resents his father for standing in his way of receiving Mother's exclusive attention. The boy wants Mother to admire *him* as the greatest hero of all; that means that somehow he must get Father out of the way."[30] These thoughts create feelings of anxiety and guilt, but the fairy tale of the young hero who slays the dragon (Father) and frees the princess who is held captive against her will (Mother) and would rather be with the hero if she were free to choose, gives him a safe place to play out these fantasies.

On the basis of Rupert's comedy routine, it is safe to venture that his dream is to be just such a boy. Being neglected and victimized, he has powerful fantasies about making it *so* big that the school principal would have to apologize to him on national TV, asking his forgiveness on behalf of the entire school, and thanking him for the meaning he has given to all their lives. Also, Rupert's relationship to his mother strongly suggests unresolved Oedipal conflicts: he wants to become the king of comedy in order to get the attention of the "beautiful, blonde, intelligent, alcoholic" mother with whom he used to laugh after school, until she would throw up, and he would have to clean up her vomit.

The damsel in the fairy tale makes the fantasy less shameful, says Bettelheim, by implying that "it is not Mother the child wants for himself, but a marvelous and wonderful woman" he will meet when he grows up.[31] Thus, Rita is part of the prize: the beautiful princess Rupert must rescue and win to make his kingdom complete. She is an extension of Mother, the fabulous woman whose exclusive attention Rupert can get only by disposing of Father and becoming "the greatest hero of all." Thus one condition in his ransom demands, and, in fact, the whole point of his wanting to be on the show in the first place, is that *he* get to watch *Rita* watching him on TV.

Similarly, Father — a man who in real life only ever paid attention to Rupert by kicking him in the stomach — is represented in Rupert's drama by Jerry Langford. The Boy (= Rupert) wants Father's (= Jerry's) position and status in order to get Mother's (= Rita's) attention. Rupert states repeatedly that he wants to be the *new* king of comedy, a phrase that implies that not only does he want the power and the glory of that title, but specifically he wants to usurp them from the old king. Underneath his adulation of Jerry smolders a barely suppressed aggression that comes out in his fantasies which are subtly, but invariably, about a shift in power and picture Jerry as emasculated, deflated and envious of Rupert. In these symbolic castration fantasies, Jerry is expressing the hostility that Rupert is feeling, although comfortably masked as jokiness.

While Rupert fits Bettelheim's reading of the young Oedipal hero in almost every detail, the problem is, of course, that he is not a small child, but a 34-year-old man. This is what makes *The King of Comedy* a deranged version of the hero path. Rupert frantically struggles for the grail while diligently evading every step of the journey, instead using ever-increasing force to cross the thresholds.

He meets the first gatekeeper shortly after talking to Langford for the first time, namely Langford's assistant, Miss Long (Shelley Hack). She listens to his tape and tells him in a friendly but decisive way that he is not ready for the show, but that he can call them next time he is performing somewhere, saying in effect that he cannot cross the threshold until he has deserved it. Rupert has no intention of making this kind of effort, and his response to the rejection is to remain passively by the gate and finally crash his way through it. He is expelled from the building, but rather than making him consider earning the passage, this only makes him crank it up a notch: in one of Rupert's fantasies Jerry has asked him to visit for the weekend, and the following day, Saturday, Rupert takes him up on the imagined invitation, bringing an unsuspecting Rita along.

The scene at Jerry's country home took two weeks to shoot, Scorsese says, because it was "so excruciating."[32] It parallels the scene in *Taxi Driver* in which Travis takes Betsy to the movies. In both instances we see that the main character is both warped and completely innocent. In both instances we initially feel relieved to have another person who is apparently sane—Betsy and Rita respectively—who can put into perspective the main character's twisted behavior, and with whom we can identify. But in both scenes, the sane character turns out to be as bad as the delusional one. Whereas Rupert (like Travis) is acting in good faith, Rita (like Betsy) turns out not to be. One might ask what her motives are for going on the weekend date in the first place, since she is obviously not romantically interested in Rupert. When they parted after the disastrous dinner on Tuesday night, she seemed to find Rupert irredeemably ludicrous, until he convinced her that he knew Jerry Langford personally. Without a doubt, Rita accompanies him on this outing so that she can get to meet a celebrity, a reason most of us can probably recognize. When she realizes that Rupert does not know Langford, and that they are not welcome, she starts apologizing so profusely that she becomes as embarrassing as Rupert. All through, he and Masha are like children that imitate grownups, and in this scene Rita is dressed up in a copy of the provocative dress Marilyn Monroe (Rita's professed favorite celebrity) wore in *The Seven Year Itch*. This "costume" is clearly a sexual proposition, and clearly not to Rupert. In her apology to Langford there is an implicit invitation: "If there is *anything* I can do to make it up to you," she says, "*anything*." Furthermore, we know that her outrage is feigned, because a few seconds earlier she stole a trinket as a souvenir from her visit to the famous man's house.

We can no longer conveniently hide behind Rita with the excuse that Rupert is just a gatecrashing madman, because the sane person who represents us is as warped as he is. At this point, halfway through the film, Scorsese pulls the rug out from under us by pointing out that Rupert Pupkin is no worse than any one of us, the only real difference between him and us is that he knows no better. The truly frightening thing is not that one mentally unhinged man believes he can win fame and fortune and gain the favors of a fair damsel and the adulation of the entire kingdom without doing anything at all to deserve it. The truly frightening thing is that he is right.

The scene closes with a major turning point to take us into the second half of the film. Jerry irrefutably rejects Rupert who responds with childish defiance. He is glad this happened, he says: "I'm gonna work 50 times harder, and I'm gonna be fifty times more famous than *you*." Again Rupert reveals that he measures himself against Father, and that he is interested not in becoming better or funnier or more skilled than him, but merely in becoming more famous. Normally one would expect that working 50 times harder would entail actually *working*, but for Rupert it means crashing his way through the next gate with 50 times more force, and we cut to him and Masha sitting in a car in front of Jerry's building, armed and disguised, and ready to kidnap him.

It becomes even more pronounced now that they resemble children who are trying to pass for adults. They seem to be *playing* at abducting someone, endlessly squabbling over who knows more about Jerry's habits. Their disguises are preposterously unconvincing, they wear immense sunglasses that make them look exactly the way children look when wearing the glasses of a grownup, and the gun they use to hold up Jerry is a toy gun that Rupert immediately drops so that it flies across the sidewalk.

They come across as a grotesque, overblown version of Hansel and Gretel, two children who have been rejected by their parents and left to fend for themselves in a world they are too immature to understand. Hansel and Gretel are driven by excessive, uncontrolled oral cravings that demand instant gratification, caused by their disappointment over Mother for failing to gratify their needs as fully as they expected, says Bettelheim.[33] They perfectly reflect Rupert's infantile conviction that immediate fame should be handed to him with no effort on his part.

They take the kidnapped Jerry to Masha's house and, in effect, play house with the helplessly immobilized man whom they dress and undress as if he were a doll/baby. Later, Oedipal overtones shine through, as Robin Wood points out: Rupert wants to *be* Father, Masha wants to *have* Father and tries to seduce him.[34]

At the end Rupert finally gets his chance to perform on Jerry's show, and his comedy routine turns out to be nothing but an exaggerated retelling of his sad life. He grew up in a low-income household in New Jersey, his alcoholic parents neglected and abused him, he was systematically victimized in school, and his mother has been dead for nine years. Combined with his fantasies, this more than implies that for him, celebrity is simply a "substitute for love," as Madonna puts it.

When Rupert reaches out for the grail of celebrity without having gone through the journey to deserve it, he hurts himself the same way the Fisher King did when, as a young boy, he reached out prematurely for his divine nature.[35] Rupert has forced his way through every gate, never facing the monster, and thus he is devoured by it and is stuck inside it at the end. To all appearances he gets everything he has craved: an admiring look from Rita (similar to the one Travis got from Betsy), instant celebrity, cover stories in every major magazine, a bestselling autobiography, and a ready-made audience when

"Better to be king for a night, than shmuck for a lifetime." Rupert Pupkin (Robert De Niro), in *The King of Comedy* (Twentieth Century–Fox, 1983), finally gets his chance to perform on Jerry's show as part of his ransom demands after kidnapping him.

he is released from jail two years and nine months later. The last scene, however, suggests differently. Rupert is standing on a television stage facing his audience. The presenter cheerfully says that here is the man "we've all been waiting for. *And* waiting for." The camera slowly moves in on Rupert, and the annoying voice endlessly repeats "Rupert Pupkin, ladies and gentlemen. Let's hear it for Rupert Pupkin," until the film ends. Rupert is caught in the hell of repetition that invariably is the price for evading or failing one's journey. He is standing inside a small circle of light that encloses him, completely fenced in by his undeserved fame, trapped in a loop of a few seconds that are repeated over and over.[36]

In this scene Rupert is dressed all in red, a color that has been associated with Langford throughout the film. In Scorsese's work, as we shall see shortly, red is usually connected with the concept of vocation, so logically it is Jerry's color. Like other characters in Scorsese's films who have a calling, Jerry Langford has paid an exorbitant price: He is shown as intensely isolated and his luxurious apartment is sterile and echoingly empty. The pictures in his country home indicate that he does not have a life to put on display but only a career. In the course of the film, Rupert assumes the red color proportionally to his usurpation of the sovereignty of Langford, the old king. In the lunch scene at Sardi's at the beginning he has a red tie, when he kidnaps Jerry he wears a red shirt, and now when he has achieved his goal and become the new king, his entire outfit is red.

In mythology, young Parsifal desperately wants to become a knight. King Arthur tells him that he must learn many things and do noble works first, but Parsifal is impatient so he kills the Red Knight and dons his stunning red armor. Because Parsifal has not gone through his own journey, and because he wears it over the homespun garment that represents his ties to his mother, he becomes trapped in it. The red armor of manhood, valor and vocation is of no use "when it only covers a mother-complexed man," Johnson says.[37] Red is not really Rupert's color, but something he has stolen from the old master, so it only reinforces his entrapment. He may be the new king of comedy, but he is, as his name betokens, merely a puppet king.

The King of Comedy is about "the extremism of fans determined to play a part in their idols' lives — even if it means appearing as executioners," Mary Pat Kelly says.[38] As always, however, this Scorsese film is not simply and conveniently about *them* — it is about *us*. It concerns Rupert's personal psychosis but also the mass hysteria over celebrity of the entire Western World. However painfully embarrassing Rupert Pupkin may seem, he merely represents ugly sides of all of us blown out of proportion. In a central scene, Jerry Langford goes down a bustling Manhattan street around lunchtime, and people constantly yell and wave at him. A perfectly normal, average lady is talking on a public phone, sees Jerry, and starts adulating loudly. She asks him to talk to her nephew on the phone, and when he refuses, she starts screaming that she hopes he gets cancer. All you have to do is "follow the logic of her hostility, as Scorsese knows at least as well as the rest of us," says Jean Callahan, "and you get Mark Chapman lying in wait for John Lennon outside the Dakota or John Hinckley shooting at Ronald Reagan in an attempt to impress Jodie Foster."[39]

Celebrity worship, like romantic adoration, is a form of shadow projection where we project the negated gold in our shadow; those brilliant aspects of ourselves that we are even more afraid to own than the dark sides, because it may cause others to reject us. This form of shadow projection is inherently ambivalent because it is connected to the rest of those obscure, unconscious traits and can instantaneously turn around. Just underneath what masks as veneration and devotion, lurks aggression, hostility, anger, and envy. However happy we may be about the success of famous people, an ugly part of us rejoices when they fail or feels betrayed when they do something other than what we expect.

Daniel Boorstin famously described the synthetically produced instant celebrity of the twentieth century as someone who is "well-known for his well-knownness."[40] In the past, he says, "a man's name was not apt to become a household word unless he exemplified greatness in some way or other. He might be a Napoleon, great in power, a J.P. Morgan, great in wealth, a St. Francis, great in virtue, or a Bluebeard, great in evil." However, in the last century "we seem to have discovered the processes by which fame is manufactured," and now "a man's name can become a household word overnight" even if he has never done anything at all.[41]

The King of Comedy was a prophetic film in many ways: the embarrassing way in which Rupert invades the public space is now an everyday occurrence with people having intensely private conversations in public on cell phones. Celebrities are now ground out like linked sausages in the staggering array of TV shows that guarantee the participants instant fame for surviving on a desert island or being locked up in a house. "We can fabricate fame, we can at will (though usually at considerable expense) make a man or woman well known; but we cannot make him great," says Boorstin. "The household names, the famous men who populate our consciousness are with few exceptions not heroes at all, but an artificial new product."[42] The closing line of Rupert's routine, that he would rather be "king for a night than shmuck for a lifetime," may sound deceptively sympathetic, but it is nothing more than Andy Warhol's "fifteen minutes of fame" gone haywire.

In most of Scorsese's films we have to own our responsibility for what happens on the screen. In *The King of Comedy* this is triply the case. We all know the feeling of wanting the instant gratification of the grail without going through the journey to deserve it; we all project unacknowledged shadow energy onto famous people; and we are all responsible for creating the mechanisms of celebrity worship and their sometimes fatal consequences. As always, Martin Scorsese and Robert De Niro force us to look at these sides of ourselves, to question our beliefs and behaviors, and to own our shadow traits, dark as well as light, instead of repressing and projecting them.

5

The Passion and the Pain

> If you, who are organized by Divine Providence for spiritual communion, refuse, and bury your talent in the earth, even though you should want natural bread, sorrow and desperation pursue you through life, and after death shame and confusion of face to eternity.[1]
>
> William Blake

Martin Scorsese once said that Michael Powell, his late friend and mentor, is the key to understanding his theology. He frequently mentions Powell's *The Red Shoes* as one of his favorite films, and like so many of Scorsese's own works, that film concerns the concept of the God-given vocation. Carl Jung said that vocation "destines a man to emancipate himself from the herd and from its well-worn paths." Like William Blake, Jung sees vocation as a law of God from which there is no escape, and the one who is called "must obey his own law, as if it were a daemon whispering to him of new and wonderful paths."[2] "Why do you want to dance?" Boris Lermontov asks Vickie at the beginning of *The Red Shoes*. "Why do you want to live?" is her reply. In Hans Andersen's fairy tale, the red shoes symbolize sexuality. In Powell's film they represent Vickie's passion, her calling, her entire being. Lermontov uncompromisingly considers his art "a religion," and Scorsese has admitted that he feels a kinship with him to the point where he dreams about him at night on a regular basis. Like Scorsese, Lermontov believes that however painful a divine calling may be, refusing it is infinitely more excruciating.

Scorsese uses the color red in a more consistently sublime manner than most living directors—equaled only by Italian master of horror, Dario Argento—and always it refers to his Catholic background as well as to Michael Powell. In Christianity, red signifies the blood and heart of Jesus Christ, the Son of Man who died on the cross; whereas blue, the holiest of colors, signifies God, the Father, and by extension faith, joy, truth, insight, and wisdom. In the films of Martin Scorsese, as in *The Red Shoes*, red is connected with the passion and the pain of the God-given vocation. It is the color of blood, the color of renouncing worldly matters in order to completely embrace one's own calling and "wait upon the Lord without distraction," as St. Paul wrote.[3]

When Vickie falls in love with Julian, Lermontov warns her: "You cannot have it both ways. A dancer who relies upon the doubtful comforts of human love can never be a great dancer! Never!" Julian, on the other hand, asks her to give up dancing, in effect asking her to amputate her soul. At the end of the film Vickie is torn apart by Lermontov, who begs her to obey her calling, and Julian, who wants her to renounce it so she can be his wife exclusively. Because she does not choose, the red shoes, the symbol of her holy gift, take

In the stunning Powell/Pressburger classic *The Red Shoes* (The Archers, 1948), which has inspired so much of Scorsese's work, Vickie must choose between her God-given vocation, represented by the red shoes, and domesticity.

over and destroy her. The color of vocation becomes dangerous when she considers sacrificing her true purpose in life on the altar of love and marriage. In Scorsese's films, the red color carries the exact same meaning, and it takes on ominous overtones whenever a God-given vocation is compromised or refused.

The increasingly popular tendency to consider Jesus Christ merely as a historical person is unfortunate and impoverishing because it robs the New Testament of its valuable archetypal significance and power, its enduring spiritual importance. "Wherever the poetry of myth is interpreted as biography, history, or science, it is killed. The living images become only remote facts of a distant time or sky," Joseph Campbell said. "When a civilization begins to reinterpret its mythology in this way, the life goes out of it, temples become museums, and the link between the two perspectives is dissolved."[4]

At the center of *The Last Temptation of Christ*, as of all Scorsese's films, are the eternal and universal aspects. The trials Christ has to go through resemble the trials of countless heroes of myths and fairy tales. You see the mythological journey "reflected everywhere you look, not just in your own career but also in literature like the *Odyssey*, in the Hindu and Buddhist scriptures, in the Koran," says Catholic scholar Kevin Orlin Johnson. "And you find the same view of the universe revealed in the Bible. It's the major theme of the Church's art and ceremonies, too. From the Church's point of view, this journey through life is governed by God's plan of creation, sanctification, and salvation: what you might call the 'Cycle of Redemption.'"[5]

The Last Temptation of Christ and *Life Lessons* both concern the choice between vocation and domesticity, and the schism between the two reflects the difference between realism and myth: do you opt for the ordinary everyday life most people take for granted, or do you feel compelled to choose the painful and lonely road less traveled that goes ever so much deeper? Real art, as Lionel Dobie says to Paulette, is "not about talent, it's about no choice but to do it." For many of Scorsese's characters, the comfort of a home, a family, and an ordinary human life is not possible if they are to fulfill their divine purpose.

The Last Temptation of Christ

One of Martin Scorsese's childhood dreams was to become a painter, and — inspired by the movies his parents took him to see — he started meticulously drawing films at a young age. Later, when he began making real films, he kept the habit of drawing them, always making sketches in the margins of the script, laying out the editing, shot by shot, in advance. "Without those little drawings," he says, "and without working out that cutting pattern beforehand, anything could happen on the set and I would be dead."[6] Many of the movies he drew as a boy were colorful Biblical epics, so one might say he had been planning to make such a film since childhood. In the early 1970s when he was shooting *Boxcar Bertha*, Barbara Hershey gave him a copy of Nikos Kazantzakis's novel *The Last Temptation*, a complex fictional account of the life, death and resurrection of Jesus Christ.

The Last Temptation of Christ (1988) would turn out to be one of the most controversial works not only in Scorsese's career but in the history of cinema. It caused such vehement protests from various extremist and Protestant fundamentalist groups that Universal Pictures was forced to let it open several months before scheduled. What so enraged these groups — who had not actually *seen* the film, although they had been invited to do so — was a sequence at the end where Christ is told that he can come down from the cross and live a normal human life with Mary Magdalene. In Scorsese's film, as in Kazantzakis's book, the last temptation is not, as the fundamentalists revealingly imagined, sexuality, but having a home and a family. Jesus, like Scorsese's other main characters, goes through a violent learning process, and the painful choice he is faced with at the end is the choice between vocation and domesticity.

After many mishaps, Scorsese managed to complete *The Last Temptation of Christ* in 1988. Having tried and abandoned the idea of a grandiose big-budget production, he eventually made the film on a modest budget of $6.5 million. In different ways the film challenges the earlier versions of the Passion of Christ. About Cecil B. De Mille's *The King of Kings* Scorsese has argued that if Christ was always surrounded by a glorious white light, why did people doubt his divinity? In Scorsese's version, Jesus looks and acts like a human being, and he and his disciples do not wear startlingly clean, off-white robes all the time.

One of the keys in making the story believable was to avoid the stilted, archaic language that makes the other versions so remote and difficult to relate to. Scorsese wanted, he says, "to have him speak like we speak," so Christ speaks in everyday, modern language, and different accents are used symbolically in the film.[7] Ancient Galilee becomes a flux of different cultures not all that different from the contemporary New York City in Scorsese's other films, and Peter Gabriel's score mixes different musical traditions into a constantly changing kaleidoscope of cultures and sound.

The film, like the novel, deals with the duality of Christ. We are to regard him as fully human *and* fully divine. At the heart of *The Last Temptation of Christ* is the struggle of the human side trying to come to terms with the divinity he does not understand. Initially he does not believe he is the son of God, and thinks the voice that keeps telling him he is belongs to Satan. Even when he accepts his calling, he never knows more than God chooses to reveal at any given moment. As he tries to come to terms with his anger and confusion, he comes across as a torn and troubled, even neurotic, human being who is familiar to us.

In the opening, Scorsese quotes from the prologue to the novel: "My principal anguish and the source of all my joys and sorrows from my youth onward has been the incessant, merciless battle between the spirit and the flesh," says Kazantzakis, echoing the primary concern in so much of Scorsese's work. "Within me are the dark immemorial forces of the Evil One, human and pre-human; within me too are the luminous forces, human and pre-human of God — and my soul is the arena where these two armies have clashed and met."[8] The meeting of the "luminous forces" and the "dark immemorial forces" correspond precisely to the shadow process we all have to go through in our lives, and this quotation is vital for understanding the film.

From the opening shot, Scorsese uses visual symbols that add symbolic layers which go beyond those of the novel. The first image is a close-up of a clear, vibrantly red background with a black pattern on it. As the camera pulls back, the overwhelming red fills the screen, and we see that the black pattern is formed by thorns, foreshadowing the crown of thorns. Red is used to show Jesus as the Son and instrument of God. Later, blue is used to indicate his divine nature, but since he does not understand his divinity, he is much more at ease in the red scenes than in the blue scenes. Then the camera rushes through bramble, and we see a young man, Jesus (Willem Dafoe), lying on the ground, filmed from the God's-eye view angle that Scorsese uses consistently. In the context of *The Last Temptation of Christ* the meaning of this angle finally becomes manifest. It is quite simply the point of view of God: rather than being just a camera angle, it is a narrative point of view, God being the ultimate omniscient narrator. After sharing the point of view of God, we go down to share the point of view of Jesus. He is a tormented young man who is struggling with a harrowing inner pain and a voice that keeps telling him he is the son of God. He makes crosses for the Romans, hoping that this will make God hate him and leave him alone.

Then his friend Judas (Harvey Keitel) enters, speaking in Keitel's familiar New York vernacular which at first seems strangely anachronistic, but gradually turns out to have meaning. Judas represents the political point of view, as opposed to Christ's spiritual point of view, and he is connected with the Zealots whom it makes sense in the film to associate with Scorsese's Little Italy. At times the conversations between Judas and Jesus call to mind the hilarious discussion between Charlie and Johnny Boy at the back of the bar in *Mean Streets*, with Keitel still in the role of the frustrated protector who has to put up with his friend's antics: "Every day you have a new plan," Judas complains when Jesus gives him half-baked explanations about messages from God. The Zealots evoke the hoodlums and mobsters of Scorsese's early films: they form a subcultural brotherhood who "armed with crowbars, ropes and knives" terrorizes everyone else, and has its own rules and laws which are markedly different from those of society.[9] They ask Judas to kill his best friend, Jesus, because he is in their way, and later they stab the resurrected Lazarus (Tomas Arana) for the same reason.

Throughout, Jesus and Judas have discussions about making the world a better place. Judas wants a revolution and believes that first you must free the body and the masses by revolting against the Romans, and then you can worry about freeing the soul. Jesus answers that this way of thinking creates a vicious cycle. If you have political revolt without any spiritual change in the individual, the Romans — while you may get rid of them — will soon be replaced by something similar or worse, he says. Physical freedom for the masses is of no use without spiritual freedom for the individual.

We are constantly presented with polarities, opposing aspects that form the dialectic principle which is at the center of the film: metaphysical phenomena as opposed to physical phenomena; the divine point of view of the Father as opposed to the human point of view of the Son; Christ as fully divine and Jesus as fully human; the spirit versus the flesh; spiritual freedom as opposed to physical freedom; love as opposed to politics; the axe versus love; and chastity as opposed to sexuality.

To illustrate how he first became conscious of the shadow, Carl Jung recounts a dream he had. He was walking on a foggy and windy night, his hands "cupped around a tiny light which threatened to go out at any moment." Suddenly, he felt something coming up behind him. "I looked back and saw a gigantic black figure following me."[10] The point of this dream is that the dark figure, the shadow, was brought into being *by* the light. Good and evil, shadow and light are complementary, they need each other in order to exist in the first place, they lend meaning to each other, and make each other possible. "Everything is from God," says Jesus in the film, "and everything has two meanings." Indeed, all Scorsese's dialectic pairs eventually lead up to the ultimate duality of the film, namely the choice between vocation and domesticity.

The idea of celibacy, and of domesticity as a hindrance to the divine calling, is not, as we see in *The Red Shoes*, a moral one. In the First Letter to the Corinthians, St. Paul explains: "The unmarried man cares for the Lord's business; his aim is to please the Lord. But the married man cares for worldly things; his aim is to please his wife; and he has a divided mind. The unmarried or celibate woman cares for the Lord's business; her aim is to be dedicated to him in body as in spirit; but the married woman cares for worldly things; her aim is to please her husband."[11]

The character of Mary Magdalene (Barbara Hershey) is vital for this duality. Before going to the desert, Jesus visits the house of ill repute where she works, asking her forgiveness. She rejects his request and offers him her body which he refuses. Later that night, Jesus has a mystical experience. An old master (Robert Blossom) says he knows who Jesus is and leads him to a monastery, where it turns out that he, the old master, is actually dead. During the night Jesus has a vision of snakes that speak to him in Magdalene's voice, saying that she forgives him. Jeroboam (Barry Miller) says the snakes came from inside him, and now that he is purified it is time to go back and speak to people. On his way back from the monastery, Jesus sees Magdalene being dragged to a stoning pit because she has broken the law of Moses and slept with Romans on the Sabbath. Thus, Christ's first speech about love is motivated by her. He confronts the aggressors, saying that he who has never sinned may throw the first stone. The Sermon on the Mount ends with Jesus kneeling and kissing Magdalene's foot, a potent image that is repeated in other Scorsese films like *Life Lessons* and *The Age of Innocence*.

Shortly afterwards, John the Baptist (André Gregory) tells him that his weapon should not be love but the axe. Confused, Jesus again goes to the solitude of the desert to search for answers. He tells God that he is tired of signs and of pain. "Just speak to me in human words," he says. "I'll take any path; love, the axe or anything else." But again he is met by signs and temptations that he must interpret for himself. First a snake appears, speaking as before in Magdalene's voice and signifying the part of him that she represents. The snake says it is his spirit (the literal meaning of the word "anima") and it wants him to give up the notion of saving the world with a spiritual revolution. "Save yourself instead," it says, "go home and start a family, just like Adam." The reference to the Fall from Eden is the first mention of the temptation of domesticity, and already it is implied that a home and family and a divine calling are mutually exclusive. Second, ten days later, a lion appears. It is his heart, it says in the voice of Judas, signifying the part of him that Judas represents. It tempts him with the lust for worldly power, and it, too, is rejected. Third comes fire. It claims to be an archangel, but Jesus recognizes it to be Satan and it disappears.

Finally comes a tree with apples, and when Jesus takes a bite of one, blood oozes out. Again we are reminded of the *first* temptation in the Garden of Eden, as well as of the Baptist saying that his weapon should be the axe so he can cut down the rotten tree the world has become. When an axe appears at the foot of the tree, Jesus accepts it. He cuts down the tree and goes back to Nazareth to "baptize with fire" and to invite the waiting disciples to join him in a "war." He has rejected the temptations of sexuality, domesticity, worldly power, and evil, and the scene is filmed through a red filter, indicating that he has accepted and embraced his vocation. We see images of dripping blood, Jesus takes out his heart and offers it to the disciples, he talks about bloodletting and about cutting the devil's throat, and Judas kneels before him and calls him *Adonai*.[12]

The imagery of the tree and the axe is explained in the Gospel of Matthew. John the Baptist says: "Already the axe is laid to the roots of the trees; and every tree that fails to produce good fruit is cut down and thrown on the fire. I baptize you with water, for repentance; but the one who comes after me is mightier than I. I am not fit to take off his shoes. He will baptize you with the Holy Spirit and with fire."[13] Later, in the Sermon on the Mount Jesus adds: "Beware of false prophets, men who come to you dressed up as sheep while underneath they are savage wolves. You will recognize them by the fruits they bear. Can grapes be picked from briars, or figs from thistles? In the same way, a good tree always yields good fruit, and a poor tree bad fruit. A good tree cannot bear bad fruit, or a poor tree good fruit. And when a tree does not yield good fruit it is cut down and burnt."[14]

The preaching of war is likewise elucidated in Matthew: "You must not think that I have come to bring peace to the earth; I have not come to bring peace, but a sword," Jesus says. "I have come to set man against his father, a daughter against her mother, a son's wife against her mother-in-law; and a man will find his enemies under his own roof. No man is worthy of me who cares more for father or mother than for me; no man is worthy of me who cares for son or daughter; no man is worthy of me who does not take up his cross and walk in my footsteps. By gaining his life a man will lose it; by losing his life for my sake, he will gain it."[15] In an archetypical sense, walking in the footsteps of Jesus means breaking away from the safe confines of the group to follow your own inner voice, shape your divine path, and find your God-given talent. Again, vocation and domesticity are seen as mutually exclusive.

That following your own voice is likely to produce hostile feelings in the group you are breaking away from is demonstrated almost immediately. Jesus asks the disciples to give away their sheep and leave their families, and shortly afterwards he meets his mother whom he rejects by saying, "I have no mother!" Mary (Verna Bloom) is devastated, but another woman tells her not to be, because "there were thousands of blue wings behind him!" Mary's reply, understandable as it may be, exemplifies the attitude of the family that is abandoned in favor of the calling: "I wish there weren't!"

With the blue wings of divinity behind him, Jesus proceeds to heal the poor, the blind, and the crippled, eventually resurrecting Lazarus. The scene is filmed from inside the cave, and Jesus is standing in the opening. Behind him is the most astounding blue sky, indicating the presence of God, but Jesus does not understand what is happening and is understandably terrified, as he is by most of the miracles he performs. We cut to outside the cave to see that the frightened and overwhelmed Jesus is almost pulled into it by Lazarus rather than pulling him out, calling to mind the horrifying dream sequence in Bergman's *Wild Strawberries* where Professor Borg tries to pull himself out of a coffin while his dead self tries to pull him down into it. As Lazarus comes to life and the shroud falls from him, Jesus gives vent to his bewilderment by quietly saying: "God help me!"

Gradually Jesus begins to realize the nature of the inmost cave into which his journey is leading: that "like a lamb led to the slaughter" the full acceptance of his vocation implies being sacrificed. "I am the lamb," he tells Judas. "I have to die on the cross, and I have to die willingly." In the scene prior to the Last Supper, Jesus tries to convince Judas to betray him. He assures him that he must play his part: "God gave me the easier job," he says, but "without you there can be no redemption." In Scorsese's version of the Passion, Judas's betrayal forms an integral part of the crucifixion and the redemption. He finds this a powerful reading of Judas's role, because only thus do their friendship and Judas's actions make sense. Scorsese points out that the ultimate sacrifice Jesus makes is the leap of faith: he does not understand why he has to be crucified, yet he chooses to be anyway.

After the crucifixion, Jesus is alone on the cross. This is the dark night of the soul, the time when he has to look death in the face, and he cries out, "Father, why have you abandoned me?" The startlingly clear blue sky surrounding him attests that he has not been abandoned at all, but that he is in fact on the verge of the ultimate consummation of his purpose. This is emphasized by the tracking movements of the camera around the cross and a deafening roar, reminiscent of jet-engines, that seem to indicate that the sky is opening. At this point an angel appears. She says that God has sent her to tell him he has suffered enough and that, like Abraham's son, Isaac, he is being spared. She persuades him to get down from the cross and to go and live an ordinary life with Magdalene. Later when Magdalene dies, Jesus, again prompted by the angel, goes to live with both of Lazarus's sisters.

Toward the end of the human sequence Jesus is an old man. In the last apocalyptic scene the destruction of Jerusalem and the Second Temple take on symbolic meaning. The scene is filmed through a red filter which, now that Jesus has relinquished his divine calling, seems only ominous. His life is drawing to a close, and we see him from the God's-eye view on his deathbed. The apostles come to say goodbye, but Judas is furious with Jesus for renouncing his vocation. Judas did his part as Jesus asked and has lived his life with the consequences, in degradation and as an outcast. "Your place was on the cross," Judas says. "What business do you have here with women, with children?" Jesus objects that God sent an angel to give him permission to end the suffering and get off the cross, but Judas points out that the girl is not an angel, but Satan (which we might have realized because, like Satan and Pilate, she speaks with a British accent).[16]

Jesus is devastated that he fell for Satan's trick and begs God to take him back. "I am

The excruciating acceptance of vocation on Golgotha Hill as Jesus Christ (Willem Dafoe) is crucified in *The Last Temptation of Christ* (Universal Pictures, 1988).

the lamb," he says, "help me go through the door." Instantly he is back on the cross, and the decades of human life he has just lived vanish like a hallucination. Satan's last temptation, which makes Jesus succumb and give up his divine place on the cross, is domesticity. The loneliness and pain of the vocation is so overwhelmingly excruciating that the promise of relief becomes too alluring even for Christ to resist. The implication here, as in all of Scorsese's work, is that having a home and a family may assuage the suffering, but you cannot fulfill your God-given vocation, be crucified and resurrected, if you compromise your mission for creature comforts, as Lermontov told Vickie. Indeed, if you *are* "organized by Divine Providence for spiritual communion," as William Blake says, refusing that and denying your calling leads to even greater pain, sorrow and desperation.[17]

In reviewing the film, we see that Mary Magdalene, the sexual temptress, is by no means the only one who has been trying to entice Christ away from his calling. At the beginning, Jesus doubts his divinity and the voice that tells him he is the Son of God. This doubt is actually planted by his mother who proposes that it is Lucifer's voice. Mary questions his vocation and manages to fundamentally unsettle him. She also clearly states that she would rather have an ordinary human son than a son of God with a purpose and blue wings behind him. Furthermore, on the way home from the desert, Jesus seeks shelter in the house of Mary and Martha of Bethany.[18] He speaks to them of love, but Mary starts flirtatiously talking of the love between husband and wife: "Don't you miss all this," she asks, "having a home?" God "wants you to make children," she assures him. The snake that speaks in Magdalene's voice tells him to give up his idea of saving the world and instead to love a woman and start a family. The point here is not that women are dangerous temptresses who lure men away from their calling. Rather, the understandable impetus to seek relief in human love, the urge to step down from the cross to alleviate the pain of the Passion, comes from inside Jesus himself.

Interestingly, the dream sequence, a long life of ordinary humanity (although boiled down to about 20 minutes of film) seems extremely boring and anticlimactic. Where the torn and neurotic Christ spoke passionately and movingly, the fully human Jesus speaks in clichés. Ironically, this further undermines the criticism of the Protestant fundamentalist groups, because not only is the film much less sexually explicit than they were apparently able to imagine, but it ends up by unequivocally concluding that Christ's place is in fact, as Judas says to him, on the cross and not with women and children. The film ends with the words "It is accomplished!" which now make perfect sense. We cut to the sound of bells ringing over an abstract image of blue, red and yellow — the colors of the Holy Trinity — melting together into whiteness, as light triumphs over darkness.

Life Lessons

Martin Scorsese directed *Life Lessons* (1989) right after *The Last Temptation of Christ*, and this exquisitely structured forty-minute film is, in fact, one of his finest works.[19] The basic idea for the plot was inspired by the relationship between Polina Suslova and Fyodor Dostoyevsky as described in Suslova's diary, and the film contains references to Dostoyevsky's novel *The Gambler*. The premise in the diary, as in *Life Lessons*, is that a young woman and aspiring artist sends word to her much older lover — a recognized master within her field — that she wants to end their relationship. He pretends not to have received the message and shows up so that she has to humiliate him in person by telling him she is in love with another man who does not love her. He is mortified, but keeps a straight face and suggests that they stay together on a platonic basis for the sake of their art.

Unlike Suslova's realistic and straightforward diary, *Life Lessons* is a complex and captivating tale whose deeper themes are much more related to *The Red Shoes* and to Scorsese's other work. It consists of a multitude of intricately interlaced allusions to fairy tales, Gothic stories, and the New Testament. Scorsese's version of this twisted love story has two main players: the central character Lionel Dobie (Nick Nolte), a brilliant and celebrated neo-expressionist painter, and his much younger assistant and lover, Paulette (Rosanna Arquette), who provides the conflict. Lionel is under tremendous pressure because he has to get a show ready in three weeks — the mythological time span which the film covers. He cannot paint when Paulette is not there, she is threatening to leave him, and they are constantly taunting and provoking each other which results in innumerable confrontations. In addition, there are three minor players who appear at different times to add perspective and further dimensions: Gregory Stark (Steve Buscemi), the performance artist Paulette has gone off to Florida with at the beginning; Reuben Toro (Jesse Borrego), the aspiring and handsome young artist whom she brings home from a party; and an unnamed young woman (Brigitte Bako) whom Lionel meets at the end, and to whom he offers the job as his new assistant.

In the pre-title sequence we are presented with Lionel, his home/studio, and the basic dramatic conflict. We see parts of his body in extreme close-ups, he is alone in the gigantic loft in the Southern part of Manhattan, pacing the floor like a caged lion, smoking a cigarette and drinking expensive cognac out of a glass that is smeared with paint. On the soundtrack is Procul Harum's "A Whiter Shade of Pale," a song which turns out to contain some of the basic meanings of the film. We hear the opening verse of the song, each line corresponding precisely to the image: When the song refers to feeling seasick, Lionel steps on a tube of blue paint that is spewed out over a white pillar; when it mentions a crowd that calls out for more, the doorbell rings and we cut to a tiny iris of Lionel standing very far away, forced into a corner and trapped by the invasion. The caller turns out to be Lionel's agent, Phillip Fowler (Patrick O'Neal), the embodiment of the hungry crowd of the song. He wants to see Lionel's work and to remind him that "the show's in three weeks," but Lionel does not respond to the pressure: he is picking up his assistant at the airport, he says unenthusiastically, and sends Phillip away with a puzzling parable about chocolate pudding.

When Lionel goes to the airport, we realize that despite the reluctance he expressed earlier, he is apprehensive and nervous as he is waiting for Paulette to arrive. We experience everything in slow motion, that "subliminal stretching of time," Barbara Hershey once said of Scorsese's use of slow motion, that "you have in an emergency."[20] When Paulette finally appears in the distance, she, too, is isolated in an iris, testifying that Lionel's entire being is in suspense and focused on her. We hear the chorus of the song about the ghostly face that turned a whiter shade of pale, and like Chaucer's "The Miller's Tale" that it refers to,

In *New York Stories: Life Lessons* (Touchstone Pictures, 1989), Lionel Dobie (Nick Nolte) picks up Paulette (Rosanna Arquette) at the airport, trying to persuade her to move back in with him while he finishes the work for his show in three weeks.

this story is about a young woman who has been cheating on her much older lover. Additionally, Paulette is associated with the pale female face in the song, and at this point (only a few minutes into the film) our attention has already twice been drawn to people who are being drained: a depleted man from whom the crowd keeps wanting more, and a woman whose face mysteriously grows paler. This is the first indication of a vampire motif that runs through the film.

In *The Last Temptation of Christ*, Jesus said, "Everything is from God, and everything has two meanings." This insight seems to be the governing principle of *Life Lessons*. Most elements in the film can be seen from two diametrically opposed points of view, and their meanings change radically depending on which view we consider. This is particularly true of the two paintings that are featured prominently—one on which Lionel is consistently working, fueled by his pining for and anger toward Paulette; and one Paulette has finished and about which she feels insecure. Each artist has a preferred interpretation of his/her own work, but there is another meaning present in each painting, which might indicate that unconsciously they have a deeper understanding for the other than they are willing or able to express verbally.

Lionel's painting constitutes the central dramatic tension, since we learn at the beginning that he has only three weeks to get ready for the show. This work of art is multilayered and larger than life, and it changes drastically throughout the film. It contains a multitude of colors that he slaps on with an incredible dynamic force. The basic structure, which he has outlined on the immense canvas before Paulette comes back, is a series of dark vertical lines connected by a horizontal line about one third down. In between we glimpse many smaller images, the most clearly accentuated ones being the arched, tawny back of something that resembles a lion, and a small, tormented, pale face. It is logical to assume that the pale face represents Paulette while the lion represents Lionel. He refers to himself as "the lion" and his name connotes lion, as do his shaggy beard and tousled hair. For all intents and purposes, he is a large nocturnal animal who by turns looks lethargic and ready to pounce, and his restless pacing calls to mind a lion in a cage.

There are many possible readings of Lionel's painting, but two of them lend perfect meaning to the lion, the pale face, and the rudimentary structure, placing it centrally in Scorsese's total body of work.[21] The vertical and horizontal lines bear a resemblance to the Colosseum in Rome, commonly regarded as the site of the martyrdom of early Christians, and calling to mind Kazantzakis's metaphor of the soul as the arena in which the struggle between good and evil takes place. Within this context, the carnivorous lion would be an aggressor and the anguished white face would belong to a victim. Seeing Paulette as a martyr who is devoured by the lion is consistent with her paleness, the fact that she always wears a crucifix around her neck, and her desperate remark to Lionel during their last fight: "Sometimes I feel like a human sacrifice!" It also connects her to the Apostle Paul—her name meaning "little Paul"—who, it is assumed, was martyred in Rome. Since her character is inspired by a woman named Polina, one might wonder why her name is Paulette and not Pauline. Both names connote Paul, pall, and pale, but Paulette also resembles palette, one of the essentials of Lionel's trade. Although she has a great influence on his work (he cannot start painting until she is home), it is not the elusive, spiritual influence of the muse. Rather, like his palette, she is essential, but ultimately replaceable, as we see in the final scene.

The second interpretation of Lionel's painting is the reverse of the first one, the lion here being a symbol of Christ, the Lion of Judah. While Lionel is waiting for Paulette at

Art as crucifixion? Martin Scorsese (left) directs Nick Nolte in *Life Lessons*, standing in front of Lionel's masterpiece with the impressive brown crosses on Golgotha as the central structure in *New York Stories: Life Lessons* (Touchstone Pictures, 1989).

the airport, we track sideways across his face, hearing the deafening roar of jet engines. This is an echo of the shot of the crucified Christ. Jesus told Judas that all his life he has been feeling a shadow hanging over him. "Do you know what the shadow is?" he asks. "The cross!" If the shadow is the cross, then the shadowy structure of dark lines in Lionel's painting is Golgotha, the place of the skull, where Jesus was crucified. In the few seconds before we really see the picture for the first time, Lionel's entire loft becomes Golgotha. We track across the studio where every wooden object is cruciform: frames at the back of canvases, window bars, exposed beams and rafters, and even a stick of wood on which hangs a stained piece of fabric that calls to mind St. Veronica's legendary cloth.

Lionel obviously is not likened to Christ in the sense of being the Redeemer of the world, but in the sense that he has a calling, and his main battle is the one between the spirit and the flesh. Like Lermontov, Lionel seems to have definitively chosen his vocation over domesticity a long time ago. Everything he does is connected to it, his loft is primarily a studio and barely a home at all, and his concern over Paulette's threatening to leave is motivated by the fact that he cannot paint without her there. When we track across an early version of his painting, at the extreme right-hand side we see some painted letters which spell NIFIN or NILFIN, which suggests a never-ending circular process (as well as recalling the letters INRI which were written over the top of the cross on which Jesus was crucified).

From this point of view, *Life Lessons* becomes the story of the passion and pain of the lion, living out his vocation as a painter. He often provokes his own suffering over Paulette and seems masochistically to revel in it; it gives him a chance to renounce temptation, and at the same time it provides fuel and energy for his work. Paulette constantly wants things he cannot give her, and she is the temptress who is spurned in favor of his vocation. The pale, painted face, then, is the anguished face of the rejected Magdalen, the spectator at the crucifixion. The scene in which we see the small, painted face most clearly is one in which Paulette is trying to get Lionel's attention. He is totally immersed in his work and does not hear her, and gradually she, the spectator, becomes enchanted and mesmerized by the sight of the master at work, and we cut to the God's-eye view, indicating that what we see is indeed Lionel's true purpose.[22]

During their final showdown, Lionel reveals that he considers his art and their relationship to be mutually exclusive when in a last desperate effort to keep Paulette there, he stammers out: "Maybe I should stop painting and just be a nice person for you." The fact that he chooses his work over Paulette does not mean that he does not have feelings for her or does not lust after her, but simply that feelings are personal and thus for him, as for Boris Lermontov, subordinate to his vocation. This is emphasized in a scene in which Lionel looks at Paulette's foot and says that he has an overpowering urge to kiss it. In Suslova's diary, this moment is an expression of love and submission, but Lionel insists that "it's *nothing personal*." Rather than expressing his veneration for Paulette, it substantiates his vocation, being a parallel to Christ kissing Magdalene's foot. In *Life Lessons* as in *The Last Temptation of Christ*, domestic harmony is only possible in a dream sequence: In an early scene we cut from a close-up of Lionel looking lasciviously at Paulette to a two-shot of the two of them together in a tender and intimate moment to a close-up of Paulette looking dreamily at Lionel. The two-shot is filmed through a blue filter which makes it come across more like a fantasy than a memory. Because it is sandwiched between close-ups of Lionel and Paulette, it is not possible to determine whose fantasy it is, and it makes sense to assume that this moment is a shared, but impossible, dream.

Whether we see Lionel as the carnivore at the Colosseum, or as the heir to Christ who chooses vocation over domesticity, Paulette is exploited and depleted in their relationship because she is primarily there to provide him with fuel for his work. This is expressed in her work, represented by one finished painting. Significantly, we never see her in the active and painful process of creating. Her picture is a simple, achromatic composition. On a dark gray background are two figures, one luminously white and one ashy gray. They are facing in the same direction, the white figure in front of and facing away from the dark figure. Their hands meet, and it looks as if the white figure is trying to walk away, while the dark figure is holding on to it.

The painting obviously refers to their relationship, but depending on our point of view it can mean two radically different things. If we see Paulette as the white figure — as *she* obviously does — she is a luminous but pale and ghostly individual trying to walk away from a grizzled one who is holding her back and draining her of light. This view is supported by the framing of the opening shot of the scene in which she asks Lionel's opinion of her picture: she is standing in front of the white figure wearing a white, paint-stained shirt, whereas Lionel is standing in front of the gray figure wearing brownish gray. As soon as the shot moves out of its original composition, however, it becomes necessary to take into account the opposite view: during the rest of the scene Paulette chases after Lionel who is trying to walk away, begging him to tell her whether the painting is any good. Lionel is now the luminous force, the celebrated master artist out of whom Paulette, the would-be painter, is trying desperately to suck brilliance and energy.

These two interpretations of the paintings, and by extension of the film, exist side by side. We cannot and should not choose one; Lionel and Paulette are in this together, they are both trying to exploit the other, and this is where the double-edged vampire motif that was introduced by the song in the pre-title sequence becomes significant. In Edgar Allan Poe's story "The Oval Portrait," a wounded man seeks refuge in a gloomy, deserted chateau. During the night he becomes fascinated by an old portrait that is extremely lifelike and haunting, and he finds a book that describes the horrifying story of the painter and his young wife: "She was a maiden of rarest beauty, and ... evil was the hour when she saw, and loved, and wedded the painter. He, passionate, studious, austere, and having already a bride in his Art." The painter wants to do a portrait of his beloved, and against her better judgment she agrees to sit for him. As the painting evolves and becomes more and more beautiful and alive, the young bride becomes less and less so. The painter "*would* not see that the light which fell so ghastlily in that lone turret withered the health and spirits of his bride, who pined visibly to all but him.... And he *would* not see that the tints which he spread upon the canvas was drawn from the cheeks of her who sat beside him."[23]

Lionel uses his confrontations with Paulette as fuel for his work and seems to get his energy and incentive to paint from the self-imposed torment of having her so close and yet totally out of reach. Throughout the film he stalks her as if she were a prey, and it is indicated that as his work progresses, she becomes paler and paler as if he is draining her of blood. Red and blue are essential colors in this film; red signifying blood, the fluid of life and passion; blue connoting a lack of blood, strength and life. In *Life Lessons* blue becomes the "whiter shade of pale" of the face that was "at first just ghostly" but has been completely depleted. The dream sequence is shot through a blue filter, so that even the only scene of harmony seems cold and anemic. At one point during this dream sequence, Lionel lowers his mouth toward Paulette's neck — a gesture which in the light of the vampire motif seems horrifying — and over the whole scene is played "A Whiter Shade of Pale."

In the final scene, the exhibition of his work, Lionel goes to get a drink and looks with satisfaction at his completed masterpiece, which is hanging behind the bar. We see him in close-up and a hand suddenly reaches into the frame and touches his. It turns out to belong to an astonishingly beautiful young woman, who is approximately the same age as Paulette. She wants to touch his hand, she says, to see if it will bring her luck in her budding career as a painter. She flatters him and blushes when he responds. Lionel's tired face immediately lights up and he slips into his old routine that he gave Paulette earlier, and which he has presumably given many times before: He needs a new assistant, he says, and he can offer room and board and a salary, as well as "life lessons that are priceless."

Lionel's eyes move over the young woman and we see a montage of extreme close-ups of her lips, eyes, and ear, as well as her nervous hands clasped tightly across her stomach. Most importantly, we see her head tilted playfully and coyly down, toward her shoulder, while the neck is totally exposed. Lionel's next prey has volunteered, and he is smacking his lips and virtually drooling. This woman has all the color Paulette lacked. Her hair is lustrous and dark, and her black eyes are sparkling with life. She is wearing jewelry with little blood-red gems, and we can literally see the blood being pumped around in her body through her exposed veins.

At the end of *Life Lessons* (Touchstone Pictures, 1989), the story starts over in the never-ending process implied by the letters "NIFIN" on the painting right next to Lionel's (Nick Nolte) shoulder.

As in a number of Scorsese's films, a circle is completed at the end, and the story is starting over in the never-ending process that was implied by the letters — NIFIN — on Lionel's painting. We have a distinct feeling that his relationship with Paulette must have started in a similar manner and with the exact same sales pitch, which suggests that she too had more blood at the beginning. At the very end Lionel and the new woman are isolated in an iris in the upper left-hand corner, and "A Whiter Shade of Pale" begins again, implying that although she is the one who starts the ball rolling, eventually this lovely woman, too, will be bled white.

The vampire motif is double-edged, however, and, like Jerry Langford, Lionel Dobie is the victim of his lionization. Everyone wants something from him, the celebrity and master artist, and they think they can extract his talent by touching him and being near him. *Life Lessons* is filled with celebrity hunters. At every party Lionel goes to, people flatter him and whisper about him. The young woman in the final scene wants to touch him for good luck, and Paulette needs his endorsement before she can approve of her own work. Her relationship to Gregory Stark, the performance artist, is also that of a fan with a schoolgirl crush and she has a publicity poster of him in her room. Conversely, Gregory Stark is in awe when Peter Gabriel turns up at the party after his show.

Most interesting in this connection is Reuben Toro, the gorgeous young artist whom

Paulette brings home from a party and sleeps with to annoy Lionel. Toro, the bull, is clearly brought into the arena to twist the lion's tail and is thus exploited by Paulette, but on closer scrutiny he, too, is after something. At the party Paulette is talking to a group of middle-aged men who seem vaguely interested in her work. One of the men asks, "Do you live with Lionel Dobie?" and another man answers, "She works for him." While hearing this offscreen we see Toro's face in close-up, substantiating that he, too, hears it, and seconds later he makes a move on Paulette. That Toro's seduction is motivated by her connection to Lionel rather than her loveliness is confirmed moments later. Lionel feels threatened by this sudden interest in Paulette and walks over to get her away from the young hunk. "Mr. Lionel Dobie," Toro says with adolescent reverence in his voice, "You know you, sir, are like my Willie Mays!"

Toro, like the girl at the end, is a voluntary, even eager, player. They both step into the arena of their own free will, but presumably neither one of them will be able to hold their own against the lion in the long run. Even though Toro gets to spend the night in Paulette's bed, Lionel manages to wipe the floor with him professionally. The next morning Lionel asks if Toro is a graffiti artist, then walks over to work on his gigantic masterpiece with a gloating, childish grin on his face, the lion looking victoriously at the defeated bull.

Life Lessons contains countless allusions to fairy tales which form an integral part of the basic structure. In fact, it can be read as two different fairy tales, one centered around Paulette and one centered around Lionel. Paulette's room is situated upstairs and resembles a tower underneath which Lionel repeatedly stands in worship. The tower is the inverted mirror image of the dungeon, and with its red flowered curtain, her room suggests both the harlot, the captive fairy tale princess, and the cold, unreachable fairy tale princess. Paulette's fairy tale resembles "Beauty and the Beast." Physically the two of them resemble the characters of that story: Lionel with the shaggy mane and beard, and Paulette with her pale skin and long, golden hair. Like Beauty, she wants to go home and feels trapped because Lionel will not let her. During an argument he mockingly concludes from her accusations: "So, I'm the monster, right?"

The fateful events in "Beauty and the Beast," says Bruno Bettelheim, are brought about because a father inappropriately steals a rose, a symbol of sexuality, to bring to his beloved youngest daughter. While her sisters go to parties, Beauty stays home with her father. Later she takes his place as the captive of the Beast, sacrificing herself for the sake of her father to whom she constantly longs to go home. The beast is Father's first rival for Beauty's amorous attention, but as long as she has such strong ties to her father, the force that represents sexuality must necessarily be beastly. "But then she realizes how much she loves the Beast," Bettelheim says, "a symbol of the loosening of ties to her father and transference of her love to the Beast. Only after Beauty decides to leave her father's house to be reunited with the Beast — that is, after she has resolved her Oedipal ties to her father — does sex, which before was repugnant, become beautiful."[24]

Like Beauty, Paulette is stuck in daughterhood, and in fact there is a rose painted on the pillar by the stairs leading up to her room. She is immature and dependent. At the party when she is asked her full name, she giggles and insists that it is "just Paulette!" When she fights with Lionel, she regresses into a child with stock responses such as "My brother's a U.S. Marine!" and "GET — OUT — OF MY — ROOM!" She asks if he loves her, and when he answers affirmatively, she replies, "Well, I don't love you!" Where Lionel uses the energy accumulated by their fights to paint, Paulette calls her parents, saying she wants to come home and go back to school because "I don't like it here!"—the standard plea of a child who wants to be taken home from camp. She uses her parents as a safety valve and, ironically, this is precisely what keeps her from developing into someone who can appreciate her own painting instead of helplessly pleading to Lionel for approval. The attention she needs so badly from him is basically that of a father figure.

It is interesting to compare her latest painting to the amateurish and childish ones we see on the floor of her studio, which we have to assume are her previous works. By contrast, her latest work is quite brilliant. It is simple and direct; it contains pain as well as a sense of humor, indicating that she has, in fact, been through a significant artistic process while living with Lionel. Only she does not realize this, and the upshot of Paulette's fairy tale is that she will never feel confident about her own work as long as she is dependent on having "Father" confirm and reassure her about its quality. As long as she is seeking the approval of the older man instead of painting and being an adult in her own right and not "just Paulette," the beast cannot be transformed into a prince, and Lionel will remain a monster.

Lionel's fairy tale corresponds to the songs he plays on his tape recorder, among them Bob Dylan's "Like a Rolling Stone" which begins "Once upon a time" and concerns a princess toward whom the singer is contemptuous. When Toro spends the night in Paulette's room, Lionel listens to the "Nessun Dorma" aria from *Turandot* while standing underneath her window. Like Puccini's prince, he cannot sleep because his life is in the hands of the heartless princess who neither understands nor deserves his valiant devotion. And symbolically the film is structured around three tribulations and temptations—all involving Paulette—that Lionel has to withstand in the course of the three weeks.

The first trial is Paulette's request that he evaluate her painting. He refuses to do so, telling her it is what *she* thinks that matters, then goes down and immerses himself in his work.[25] The second trial, the midpoint of the film, is Paulette's love scene with Reuben Toro. Lionel comes home from the party and sees and hears the lovers in the "tower room." His reaction to this provocation shows us the epitome of who he is: again he uses the energy of this incredible humiliation to paint, and only after he has finished working does he go to yearn underneath her window. Lionel fulfills his vocation before allowing himself to pine and is visually connected to Christ. As he stands looking up at Paulette's window, he looks stunned with agony. His face and torso are stained with blood-red paint that replicates the marks from the crown of thorns and the cuts of the whip. There are solid red marks on his hands from the nails and under his chest from the sword of the Roman soldier.

After Lionel triumphs over Toro the next morning, he is presented with the third trial, the most perilous one.[26] Paulette childishly demands that he prove his love for her by kissing a police officer in a squad car. If he does it, she will know that his "love is true" and if not, she will pack her things and leave. What makes this trial so dangerous is the fact that the two policemen—as the only ones in the entire film—do not recognize or even know who the famous painter is. He ends up blowing a kiss at the armed and apprehensive officer, which is as close as he can safely get. He turns around to see if that will satisfy the capricious princess, but realizes that she has already left, and shortly afterwards she moves out of his apartment and his life.

Lionel has chosen his vocation over domesticity a long time ago, but the three trials are temptations to see if he can be moved to renounce it. He passes the first two tests with flying colors. Giving in to Paulette's demand by telling her how good her painting is would pacify her and make her more dependent on him and thus flatter his ego, but refusing to do so means staying true to his artistic integrity (even at the risk of losing her) and forces her to stay true to hers. When faced with jealously over the rival, Lionel paints first and then pines. The third trial is always the hardest one, and this time Lionel, like Christ, actually succumbs to the temptation of the princess and lets himself be utterly degraded — we are even momentarily afraid that it might cost him his life, since he cannot hide behind the persona of his fame, and the police officer is pointing a loaded gun at him. In the first two temptations he unequivocally chose his vocation at the risk of losing Paulette, and paradoxically she stayed with him. When he finally gives in, that is precisely when he loses her for good. Symbolically, she does not even have to stay and see the outcome, because the point is made as soon as he submits and compromises his integrity.

In the opening scene Lionel tells his agent a mystifying anecdote: "I heard these two kids in a restaurant yesterday. One said, 'What's chocolate pudding?' The other said, 'It's good! It's a lot like chocolate mousse.'" This story seems to make no sense, but it turns out, like the parables of Christ, to contain latent significance. *Life Lessons* concerns two very different generations whose semantics and linguistics define their incompatible views of the world and make them virtually incapable of communicating. Lionel's parable expresses contempt for Paulette's entire generation; people whose youth and ignorance force them to resort to something fashionable and airy in order to define the basics that they ought to know.

In the final scene, an admirer walks up to Lionel and says out of the blue: "When I look at your stuff, I just wanna divorce my wife. I mean, like, thank you!" Like the chocolate mousse story, this remark seems totally absurd unless we see it in the context of the choice between vocation and domesticity. Jesus said that he would set family members against each other, and Paulette's namesake, St. Paul, wrote that whereas the unmarried man is free to follow the path of God, "The married man cares for worldly things; his aim is to please his wife; and he has a divided mind."[27] Here as in *The Last Temptation of Christ* and Michael Powell's *The Red Shoes*, vocation is incompatible with domesticity, and the lines spoken by the strange man — who, significantly, is played by Richard Price who wrote the screenplay for the film — make perfect sense. Even though Lionel's circle is about to start all over with yet another stunning young assistant — "I'm talking twenty *years* of this," his agent yells in frustration in the beginning — the words of this stranger remind us of Lionel's choice, and the pain, loneliness and sacrifice involved in his passion. As always, this is emphasized by Scorsese's trademark sound of the photographers' flash bulbs that sound like glass breaking.

6

To Be Without a Home

> Like all who have elected to follow, not the safely marked general highways of the day, but the adventure of the special, dimly audible call — she has known the dark night of the soul, Dante's "dark wood, midway in the journey of our life" and the sorrows of the pits of hell.[1]
>
> Joseph Campbell

No Direction Home: Bob Dylan (2005) is a 208-minute documentary based on hundreds of hours of footage accumulated by Dylan's manager, Jeff Rosen, which Scorsese helped shape into a film. It covers Dylan's career from its very beginning in 1961 until June 1966 when he retreated from touring following a motorcycle accident. While it does not warrant a full in-depth analysis, thematically it resonates deeply with Scorsese's fictional work.

Having been working consciously with shadow issues for the past two decades, I thought I had seen my share of shadow projection. But rarely have I seen it as overwhelmingly and as nauseatingly as in *No Direction Home*. Scorsese focuses on the excessive rage of the audience when Dylan, rather than catering to their wish for more folk music and protest songs, decided to continue to explore and develop his own artistic vision. Emotionally the film culminates during the *Manchester Free Trade Hall* concert on May 17, 1966, when a member of the audience shouted "Judas" at Dylan as he and The Hawks (the group that later became The Band) started performing "Like a Rolling Stone." Bob Dylan, as seen through Scorsese's vision, is an unbelievably admirable and committed artist, a man with a divine gift who stays with it and continues to express it in spite of the public response which is so angry and hateful that I repeatedly found myself feeling immense respect for the man for having the courage to even get out of bed in the morning, let alone continue year after year, decade after decade, to create some of the most astounding and insightful poetry in the history of rock music.

Like *The Last Temptation of Christ* and *Life Lessons*, the films discussed in this chapter all deal with people who feel compelled to follow an inner voice regardless of the price they have to pay. These films take place on the road, and their main characters are perpetual wanderers. Friedrich Nietzsche once suggested that we spend our lives searching for a family, a father; and Madonna refers to fame as a "substitute for love" in her song which deals with the painful lengths we can be willing to go to in order to get the attention and adulation of perfect strangers as a compensation for the real family that failed to provide it. Like Jesus Christ and Lionel Dobie — albeit on a smaller scale — several of these characters make the choice of achieving excellence within their chosen field and, in the process, implicitly give up the possibility of the loving comfort of a home.

Boxcar Bertha

In January of 1971, Martin Scorsese went to California in an attempt to get into the Hollywood mainstream after the release of his first feature film, *Who's That Knocking at My Door?* Among the people he met there were George Lucas, Francis Ford Coppola, Steven Spielberg, and Brian De Palma, who was already a friend. Together they came to form the nucleus of the generation of filmmakers that would be referred to as the Movie Brats.

During his first month in California, Scorsese managed to get a meeting with Roger Corman, who is best known for producing highly profitable B pictures and for launching the careers of a number of talented directors and actors. "The best post-graduate training you could get in America at that time," Scorsese says, "was to work for Roger Corman."[2] At their first meeting Corman asked if Scorsese would be interested in directing a film called *Boxcar Bertha,* which was to be a kind of sequel to *Bloody Mama,* drawing heavily on the success of *Bonnie and Clyde.* Scorsese did not believe that anything would ever come of it, but six months later Corman returned with a script and a $600,000 budget. Corman, Scorsese says, was "very open to letting you express yourself on film as long as it worked within the structure of what he needed," which meant constantly including a certain amount of sex and violence.[3] He told Scorsese to read and rewrite the script he wanted, "but remember, Marty, that you must have some nudity at least every fifteen minutes."[4]

Boxcar Bertha (1972) became Scorsese's debut as a Hollywood director. It is based on *Sister of the Road,* the autobiographical account of Bertha Thompson's life as a railroad hobo and outlaw during the Depression; it was shot in Arkansas on a disciplined schedule of 24 days. Scorsese had previously been fired from a project (in 1968) and was nervous about meeting the shooting schedule: "I was very much afraid that I would get fired again," he says. "So when I started on *Boxcar Bertha* I drew every scene, about 500 pictures altogether."[5]

At the time of its release, the film was criticized for being too violent and it was reviewed as "not much more than an excuse to slaughter a lot of people."[6] Barbara Hershey, who played the title character, sees the film less as a Scorsese picture than as a Roger Corman movie "embarrassingly so in some ways to me, but at the core of it are the wonderful characters that Marty helped us create."[7]

Boxcar Bertha starts with an extreme close-up of young Bertha's eyes as she is watching her father flying a crop duster. She comes across as rather simple-minded, lifting her dress to scratch the top of her thigh, oblivious to the gawking men who are working on the railroad tracks nearby, and her first words are, "Shit, here it comes again. Looky, Von!" The whole setup is so clichéd that it feels like a Mel Brooks sendup of John Steinbeck: an innocent country girl and her kind but hopelessly poor father, sweaty men working on the railroad tracks, a greedy capitalist boss who extorts Father back up into the rickety plane, and a black farmhand happily playing a harmonica at Bertha's feet.

Predictably, Bertha's father dies when the plane crashes minutes afterwards. She decides to hit the road and eventually teams up with Big Bill Shelley (David Carradine), a fervent union organizer who becomes her lover. They are joined by Bertha's harmonica-playing friend, Von (Bernie Casey) and Rake Brown (Barry Primus), a Yankee gambler whom Bertha sleeps with when she first leaves home. They are attacked by union-busters and start a life of crime, robbing money from railroad boss Sartoris (John Carradine). At the end Sartoris's hired guns shoot and kill Rake, crucify Bill, and finally Von slaughters them.

The narrator of *Sister of the Road,* the real Bertha Thompson, seems like an interesting woman who is spiritually enlightened by her suffering. In the film, she comes across as a borderline retard. She seems to have no will of her own or any depth of feeling. One might think that her father's brutal death would be what motivates her to go after the capitalist railroad magnate, but she seems to do it simply because the others do it, and because she takes childish pleasure in carrying a gun. When Bill first insists on making love to her, she goes from repulsion to rapture literally within two seconds and seems thrilled when he leaves money for services rendered. Later, when she is lured into a brothel to work, she makes a less than feeble attempt at leaving, then just acquiesces, staring vacantly into space between clients, so that we have no clue what is going on inside her mind. There is no indication that she evolves in the course of the film, and she seems as helpless and reactive at the end when she looks up at Bill, crucified on the train, as she did when her father was sacrificed in the crop duster. Slightly more interesting is Big Bill Shelley who at least has internal conflicts about what he is doing. "I am not a criminal," he keeps insisting, although his entire life testifies to the opposite. Bill is a man with a calling, dedicated to helping the Depression-era workers unite, yet ends up living like an outlaw.

Barbara Hershey, who had read Nikos Kazantzakis's *The Last Temptation* when she was 19, gave Scorsese a copy of the book. "You should make it into a film," she told him, "and if you do, I should play Mary Magdalene."[8] It is possible to see her role in *Boxcar Bertha* as a precursor for the character of Magdalene in *The Last Temptation of Christ*. Bill Shelley is vaguely compared to Christ, and his followers — a woman, a black man, and a Jew — seem to represent a cross-section of the population. Bertha is Magdalene to Bill's Christ, and Scorsese illuminates the point: when the gang seeks shelter in a church, he places them in front of a mural of Jesus and Mary Magdalene. Scorsese did not invent the scene in which Bill is crucified to the side of a boxcar, but reading it in the original script, he "thought it was a sign from God."[9] He did decide to make it more symbolically significant than it might otherwise have been, and he repeated elements of it in *The Last Temptation of Christ*. "I liked the way we shot it," he says, "the angles we used, and in particular the way you saw the nails coming through the wood, though they never were seen piercing flesh."[10] When Bertha runs alongside the moving train, she is filmed from above so that we look down on her from behind Shelley. Thus, Lawrence Friedman says, "The ascension effect is magnified. A close-up of the outstretched hand of the crucified Shelley and a final shot of the same hand protruding from the corner of the frame complete the allusion/illusion."[11]

Boxcar Bertha in no way measures up to Scorsese's other work. In fact, his mentor John Cassavetes reportedly told him upon first seeing the film, "Marty, you've just spent a whole year of your life making a piece of shit."[12] In typical Corman style, it unblushingly rips off contemporary hit movies from *Bonnie and Clyde* to *Butch Cassidy and the Sundance Kid*— culminating in the overwrought Peckinpahish shootout at the end — without having any of the depth or self-irony of the other films. It did, however, earn Scorsese a membership in the Directors' Guild which would allow him to make *Mean Streets* and *Alice Doesn't Live Here Anymore*. And as Scorsese himself says about the making of his first Hollywood movie: "It was a refreshing experience and I learned a lot from it."[13]

New York, New York

Despite the efforts of a talented creative team and a gigantic budget, *New York, New York* (1977) is generally considered Scorsese's greatest flop. It is an elaborate musical drama, set at the end of the big band era, and Scorsese has called it his valentine to Hollywood. He has been known throughout his career for carefully planning and preparing everything, laying out every shot in advance, even drawing entire films before shooting them, and for always finishing on schedule and within budget. On *New York, New York* he went completely overboard, finishing at a final cost that was $2 million over budget. He attributes this to his having gotten cocky over the tremendous success of his previous films.[14] After winning the Golden Palm in Cannes for *Taxi Driver*, Scorsese admits, "we got big heads and felt that no script was good enough."[15] As a result, he and the actors decided to improve on the script as they went along, and they started improvising. They spent weeks shooting the opening scene, until the original cut of that scene ran for an hour. "This was before *Heaven's Gate*," says Scorsese, "when it was a case of giving the director everything he wanted."[16] He adds, "In retrospect, I don't think we should have been given that free a hand. It was a mess, and it's a miracle that the film makes any kind of sense."[17]

On its deeper, darker levels, *New York, New York* is influenced by Michael Powell's and Emeric Pressburger's *The Red Shoes*, but it is made in the style of the classic Hollywood musicals of the 1940s and 1950s. Scorsese has said that every frame and every cut contains a reference to one of the great directors of the past. It alludes to films like *The Man I Love*, *A Star Is Born*, and innumerable MGM Technicolor musicals produced by Arthur Freed, often directed by Vincente Minnelli and starring Judy Garland.[18] Like so many of these, it was shot not in New York City, but on the backlots of Hollywood. The old sets turned out no longer to exist, so Scorsese had to have new ones made: In the classic MGM and Warner Bros. musicals he'd seen as a boy, New York City kerbs were always high and very clean. Even as a child, Scorsese says, he realized this wasn't right, but was part of a whole mythical city that they had created. Now I wanted to re-create that mythical city."[19] He wanted, he says, to combine different filmic styles, to recreate the artificiality of the Hollywood musical sets and then "approach the characters in the foreground like a documentary, combining the two techniques."[20] As so often before, Scorsese plays off two diametrically opposed concepts against each other: the unreal fantasy of the sets against the contemporary conflict of two creative people trying to live together. Critic Carrie Rickey perceptively referred to the film as a "wife-beating musical," and indeed it has a kind of Arthur Freed-meets-John Cassavetes feel to it.

The sentimental journey of *New York, New York* takes its start on Times Square on V-J Day, August 15, 1945. The streets are filled with cheering crowds, paper horns and confetti. Then the camera rests in close-up on a pair of shoes that turn out to belong to Jimmy Doyle (Robert De Niro). Jimmy stands out from the crowd, wearing a garish Hawaiian shirt with a New York pattern, and a big red neon arrows points him out to us. He makes his way to the Rainbow Room where, scored by Tommy Dorsey and his Orchestra, he frantically tries to find a girl for the night. He feels particularly challenged by a snubbing WAC, Francine Evans (Liza Minnelli), whom he tries tenaciously (and hilariously) to pick up for the entire eight-minute duration of "Opus One." Although he is unsuccessful and she finally leaves, she shows up at his hotel the following morning, and the battle/romance continues. The film tells the story of their courtship, marriage, and breakup, and their relationship — shaky to begin with — mirrors the decline of the big band business. The film opens and closes with Jimmy Doyle. At the beginning he is a silly kid making his way through the celebrating crowds. At the end he is poised, completely alone and the streets are deserted.

Jimmy has been described by critics as immature, self-centered, inconsiderate, aggressive and certifiably loony, and one might reasonably add embarrassing, annoying obnoxious, and antisocial to the list. Francine is consistently described as heroically patient and "a sweet kid," and the word "sweet" is used about her all the way through the film: "As sweet as she sings, that sweet she is," says her manager. However infuriating Jimmy may be, there has to be more to the story than what is so suspiciously obvious. For one thing I do not really buy Francine's virtuous martyr act, and for another, it would be very unlike Scorsese to present us with a character like Jimmy Doyle and expect us to only dislike him. If in the following it sounds as if I am exaggeratedly advocating Jimmy's case, it is partly because the opposite view — that Jimmy is offensive and Francine is adorable — has been taken by virtually every single critic on the planet, and partly because Scorsese's films usually do argue on behalf of the obnoxious ones.

Jimmy is connected with and reminiscent of many of Scorsese's other characters. From the beginning a kinship with Johnny Boy is implied. Jimmy's buddies ask about his Hawaiian shirt, and he says that he threw away his uniform when he won it in a poker game in which he had "three threes," a phrase that he repeats to the point where it becomes absurdly musical. Like Johnny, he seems to gain zest from confrontations and brawls. He is a gambler, a con man, and a swindler who stays at hotel after hotel under assumed names, running up gigantic bills and then sneaking out. He is also the only Scorsese character who comes close to being as embarrassing as Rupert Pupkin.

Less obvious, perhaps, is the affinity between Jimmy Doyle and Scorsese's Jesus Christ, Lionel Dobie and Howard Hughes. In addition to being unpleasant (which they all are), Jimmy is an artist with a divine gift; a tormented and driven man whose calling is as real and as painful as theirs. Doyle is frustrated in the big-band era, says Pauline Kael, because "he's already into the progressive bop that's not yet accepted."[21] Jimmy's dilemma is that he cannot seem to combine vocation and domesticity. In a key scene Francine complains that he has to work nights in a club in Harlem, and he offers to throw his sax "against the wall and smash it into a million pieces." Jimmy explains, pointing to his sax: "If I can't do this, then I'm no good for you and I'm no good for anyone, baby. You understand?" Significantly, Francine never answers, and nothing indicates that she does understand. As in *The Last Temptation of Christ* and *Life Lessons*, the happy relationship is only possible in a fantasy to which Jimmy can only a be spectator. One of the most enchanting moments in the film reflects his fundamental wish for romance and suggests a subconscious knowledge that it is unattainable. On his way home from the Rainbow Room on V-J night, Jimmy is standing on the stairs leading to the elevated train, wistfully watching a sailor and his girlfriend on the street below doing a silent, choreographed dance in the style of *On the Town* or *The Band Wagon*.

In a crucial early scene, on the way to Flatbush in a taxi, Jimmy describes to Francine his philosophy of "the major chord" — getting the three things he really wants out of life in a way that "everything works out perfectly. One is music. Number two is money, and number three is xxx," he says, making kissing noises. She asks him if they are always in that order, and he flirtingly says he might be willing to switch them around if he met the right woman. He is apparently willing to compromise his art, but during the following minutes, when he starts switching around the elements of the major chord, he cannot get the order straight. As it turns out, he is not actually capable of *having* a relationship, but much of his torment originates from his initial willingness to violate his authenticity in the attempt.

Whereas making concessions goes against the grain of who Jimmy is, Francine seems to thrive on it and at times to receive an almost sensual satisfaction from it. For her, music is just a living that she happens to be extremely good at, but she has no sense of a mission. Her one intention seems to be getting things to run as smoothly and with as little friction as possible. Where Jimmy is a natural born disrupter, Francine is a natural born diplomat. In that sense they mirror Johnny and Charlie in *Mean Streets*: Jimmy constantly comes across like the bastard and Francine like the saint. Where he overtly pushes people, she manipulates them, and in the final analysis she is a lot more successful at getting what she wants than he is.

Minutes after Jimmy has revealed his willingness to compromise his major chord for her sake, she starts cajoling him into doing exactly that. At the audition in Flatbush he plays one of his own numbers for the manager of the club. The manager seems mildly sympathetic, but explains that it is not commercial enough. Immediately, Francine pulls Jimmy aside and tells him to "play it just a little smoother," using the fact that he is interested in her (number 3) to get him to compromise the music (number 1) for the sake of the money (number 2). The manager suggests that Maurice Chevalier songs might be more acceptable to the general public, but Jimmy says that he would "rather get a job in a post office" than stoop that low. Now Francine bursts into a cute, jazzy version of "You Brought a New Kind of Love to Me," seducing Jimmy into playing along.

Her intentions may be good, and she may just want him to get the job, but the fact is that she interferes with what he has just told her means more to him than anything in the world. As a result, the two of them are hired together as a boy/girl act doing the Chevalier songs that Jimmy so abhors. The "sweet kid" creates an illusion of having solved the problem, but in reality she has undermined his self-expression, his autonomy and authority and made him dependent on her for his livelihood. To make matters even worse, a few hours later Francine gets a gig of her own and leaves Jimmy in the lurch to go on the road. She never shows up in Flatbush to tell him so, but she does plant a trail for him to follow by making her manager go out to deliver a note, knowing full well how incredibly persistent Jimmy is.

Jimmy is not really as good a con man as he thinks he is with his endless, weird stories. His real strength is his tremendous vigor. In fact, it is his persistence that defines him. Like other characters De Niro has played for Scorsese—Johnny Boy, Jake La Motta, Rupert Pupkin and Max Cady—Jimmy is driven by a frenetic, almost superhuman energy, and like them he keeps coming back until he drives everyone else crazy. He goes after Francine, and when he does not find her in Ashville, North Carolina, he follows her from town to town. At one point, his train pulls out of the station while he is on the phone trying to locate her, and hilariously he seems convinced that he can stop it by holding on to the door and pushing his feet against the ground. He finally catches up with her, and it becomes obvious that Francine has counted on this all along, having already arranged with her bandleader that he audition for a spot in the orchestra.[22] What follows is a power struggle in which Jimmy uses force and looks like a moron, and Francine uses passive manipulation and looks like an angel.

During the first hour of the film, Jimmy is obnoxious because of his *chutzpah* and energy; during the second hour he is obnoxious because he gradually becomes emasculated and, as a result, aggressive. At the end of the second hour, the importunate pest has been reduced to a pathetic whiner who blows his nose in Francine's sheets at the maternity hos-

Scorsese plays off the unreal fantasy of the sets against the very real conflict of two creative people — Jimmy Doyle (Robert De Niro) and Francine Evans (Liza Minnelli) — trying to live together in *New York, New York* (United Artists, 1977).

pital because he only has one clean handkerchief left. He leaves the hospital crying, not having the nerve to see his son whom she has already named without consulting him. The fact that she has named the child Jimmy only makes matters worse because he sees it as a deliberate reminder of his shortcomings.

The third player in this drama is Paul (Barry Primus), the pianist and rival. In the Rainbow Room scene it is clear that Francine has a crush on him. Paul is everything Jimmy is not, and Jimmy knows it: he is considerate, nice, civilized, slightly boring, and a decent musician without Jimmy's annoying and painful drive. When Jimmy first joins the orchestra, he gets up during Paul's solo and steals it. The next time we see them, the solo is officially Jimmy's. At the end of the first hour, when the bandleader decides to leave the orchestra, he leaves Jimmy, not Paul, in charge. Going into the second hour of the film, the power shifts away from Jimmy and over to Francine and Paul. Under Jimmy's leadership the orchestra gets a rave review in which Francine is singled out. Jimmy's ego is wounded by this, both because Francine gets better reviews than he does but primarily because he finds her sitting on the stairs with Paul, intimately and happily sharing the good news. Paul, Francine tells Jimmy, had this wonderful idea that they put the quote on their poster outside, and we cut to the poster on which Francine now has top billing: "Francine Evans and Jimmy Doyle and his orchestra."

It goes from bad to worse when Jimmy has an argument with the band in the following scene. He finally tries to relieve the tension in his own bizarre way, by throwing tables around. Everyone laughs nervously and seems relieved, but Francine redundantly starts mediating and ends up by kicking off the band. She humiliates him in public by invading his territory, and when he gets angry and slaps her butt, he looks like a lunatic. The more frightened he becomes as he loses territory, the more Francine revels in her martyrdom. Immediately afterwards she tells him she is pregnant (something they have obviously neither planned nor even discussed) and has decided to leave the orchestra. Because she is their main attraction, the audience disappears when she does, and three minutes of screen time later Jimmy is forced to sign over the orchestra to Paul.

Francine puts up with so many of Jimmy's shenanigans that "it's gotta be love," Roger Ebert says.[23] I could not disagree more. Francine marries Jimmy knowing full well exactly who he is — in fact, the wedding scene is his most tyrannical moment — and then she spends the entire rest of the film passive-aggressively trying to turn him into, for all practical purposes, Paul, and looking mortified and agonized when he cannot be that; an insidious form of abuse not unlike what Ace Rothstein exposes Ginger to in *Casino*.

The most painful scene takes place at the Up Club. Paul and the orchestra are playing, and Jimmy reluctantly agrees to go see them. Francine has invited her producer, Artie Kirks (Lenny Gaines), so Jimmy can meet him, because what Jimmy does for a living now — playing the music he truly loves with a black orchestra at the Harlem Club — is not acceptable to her. As they are about to enter this double-edged humiliation — recalling the bull being led to the slaughter in *Raging Bull*— Jimmy turns to her and says quietly and simply, "I can't do this!" Instead of listening, Francine is ready with an instant compromise: "So we'll just stay for one set!" Throughout the scene, Jimmy comes across like a complete bastard whereas Francine has everybody's undivided sympathy. Kirks is consistently patronizing to everyone and Jimmy objects: when Kirks orders him a Sloe Gin Fizz, Jimmy says that this is not what he wants to drink. Francine makes him look unreasonable by saying first that he should just have the drink, and then that *she* will have it. The more she insists on smoothening things out, the more unruly Jimmy becomes, until he is thrown out of the bar, kicking and screaming, looking like what he probably is: a drowning man fighting for his life.

The final blow to their relationship and Jimmy's self-esteem comes shortly afterwards when Francine (who is immensely pregnant) shows up at the Harlem Club with her agent and Kirks, who wants to sign her up for a big record contract. "Why'd you bring him here?" Jimmy asks sadly. She answers that she was unable to get Jimmy on the phone, but it is hard to believe that this big business deal came up suddenly and has to be decided immediately. The invasion reinforces Jimmy's sense of unworthiness: his wife, who is expecting their child, flaunts her success on his territory while he is doing drugs and obviously having a fling with a colleague.[24] When Jimmy has to go on stage, Francine — again, in her wide-eyed but ultimately transgressive manner — indicates that she wants to sing, which would undoubtedly mean stealing Jimmy's thunder in the single place he has left where he has any kind of autonomy and is taken seriously. He furiously changes into an aggressive number to prevent her from getting up onstage, and she rushes out, mortified. On the way home they have a fight in the car, Francine goes into labor, and the baby is born, concluding the second hour of the film.

As Jimmy walks out of the hospital room crying, leaving Francine and the baby, a jump cut takes us several years into the future. Except for a few minutes at the end, we spend the remainder of the film focusing on Francine's newfound independence and blossoming career. First she is in a recording studio, the small child sleeping on a couch. Then she lands a role in a movie and we see the famous "Happy Endings" sequence (which cost $350,000 to shoot). For a few moments we cut to Jimmy who is having modest success in a much less flamboyant way, then back to a concert performance of Francine doing the spectacular "New York, New York." During all this Paul is by Francine's side, suggesting that he has taken over Jimmy's personal life, too, and Jimmy is present only as a member of the audience, watching her thrive in his absence.

Although the musical numbers showcasing Liza Minnelli have been acclaimed by many critics, they always remind me of the romantic interludes in the Marx Brothers movies: you basically just want to fast-forward so you can get back to the film. "Trying to be subdued," said Pauline Kael, Minnelli comes across as "openmouthed and vacuous, and unpleasantly overripe."[25] I realize that this may be a matter of taste, but no matter how much one adores Minnelli and how beautifully produced these scenes are, it is virtually intolerable to be forced to sit through 30-odd minutes of hearing her sing while we are waiting to find out what happens to the main character of the film. By the time we get back to him, we have more or less stopped caring.

If we see *New York, New York* as a continual internecine power struggle which Jimmy gradually loses, however, these final scenes make perfect sense. In many of Scorsese's films an obnoxious and annoying man forces the main character through a necessary learning process. In this film the obnoxious and annoying man *is* the main character who is forced through a learning process. Often, the character with a vocation drains someone else of energy; in *New York, New York* the person with the vocation is the one who is drained and depleted. Francine squeezes Jimmy out his career, out of his life, and out of the entire film for almost 40 minutes, leaving *us* no choice but to sit and watch her if we want to find out what happens to him.

The use of the color red is fascinating in this connection. Red, as we have seen, is used to signify vocation and life energy in Scorsese's work. In *New York, New York*, it is used in the first hour as a background whenever Jimmy plays his music. During that part of the film, Francine, who does not have a sense of calling, is connected with red only through her lipstick. The very first time we see her after they are married, however, she is dressed all in red, suggesting that a transformation has taken place. Throughout the rest of the film she wears red to the point where it becomes mesmerizing, whereas Jimmy is associated with it less and less. In a sense, we see her draining him of his life's blood, his vocation. Despite her dramatic martyr act, she manages to get a big contract while they are still together, whereas Jimmy can only achieve professional success and satisfaction with the music that is his entire life (and which she tries to make him compromise) when he is away from her.

The main characters of *New York, New York* may illuminatingly be compared to Vickie and Julian in *The Red Shoes*. Like Vickie, Jimmy is shown as having a God-given calling from the start. It is clear throughout that his music is an extension of his soul and that the sax which emblemizes it is the equivalent of the words for Christ, the paint brush for Lionel Dobie, the glove for Jake La Motta, the pool cue for Eddie Felson, and the red shoes for Vickie. For Francine, on the other hand, music is a job like any other job. She has talent but no ambition and no sense of mission. She is quite happy to do demos and commercials, and she likes pleasing other people. When she is asked to sing like Peggy Lee, she needs a few seconds to collect herself after doing Jo Stafford, and then she just does it. This has got to seem like prostitution in the eyes of Jimmy, but for Francine it is fine because music is just work. No wonder the two older men — who agree that they're "gonna make money with her"— think she is "sweet." When she is dressed all red in the whole final section, it is not because she suddenly has a vocation — she says as much herself and admits that her film is garbage — but because, like Rupert Pupkin, she has drained it out of the true artist. One even has an uncanny suspicion that in her big climatic "New York, New York" number, she has simply been asked to "do" Judy Garland.

At the end, Jimmy and Francine have produced two things that contain the blood and essence of them both: a little boy and a song which, in two very different arrangements, becomes the yardstick of both their careers. Their egos, musical styles, and ambition levels may be incompatible, but the pain they have caused each other seems to have fueled a certain professional success and confidence. The major chord may not be possible for Jimmy in terms of having the three things he wants out of life, but true fulfillment through his vocation is, so he owns a club *called* the "Major Chord." At the end, Jimmy calls Francine and asks her out for dinner. She agrees, but as she comes to a door with a big EXIT sign, she hesitates and turns around with a dazed look on her face. Outside, Jimmy, too, seems to change his mind and walks away. A traditional happy ending is impossible except in the fantasy of Francine's awful film.

When the film was finished, Scorsese was disappointed with it, because it had been such a bad experience. "But over the years," he says, "I've been able to see that it has truth to it. I still don't really like it, yet in a way I love it."[26] As he told Mary Pat Kelly: "Eventually I understood the picture. Jean-Luc Godard came over for lunch one day and he was talking about how much he likes *New York, New York*. He said it was basically about the impossibility of two creative people in a relationship — the jealousies, the envy, the temperament. I began to realize that it was so close to home that I wasn't able to articulate it while I was making the film.... For a time after *New York, New York* I had really been thinking of going to live in Italy and making documentary pictures on the lives of the saints for the rest of my life. But *The Last Waltz* came along and that helped."[27]

The Last Waltz

On Thanksgiving Day 1976, The Band — Robbie Robertson, Levon Helm, Rick Danko, Garth Hudson and Richard Manuel — gave their farewell concert at the Winterland Arena in San Francisco.[28] On stage they were joined by some of the greatest performers in the history of twentieth century music, such as Joni Mitchell, Dr. John, Muddy Waters, Eric Clapton, Neil Young, Van Morrison, Neil Diamond, and Bob Dylan. It was decided that this legendary event be filmed for archival purposes, and Robertson sat down to make a list of directors who might understand what this was all about. He came up with only one name. "I had one man on my list, and a big long piece of paper," he remembers.[29] He felt that Scorsese had more knowledge of and feel for music than any other director, and that he would understand the deeper significance behind some of the choices that were made: "Everybody would say, 'Why is Neil Diamond in it?' And I would say, 'Tin Pan Alley.' Marty understood that."[30]

Originally the idea had been to use 16mm stock like they did at Woodstock, where Scorsese was assistant editor, but Scorsese decided that they might as well shoot it in 35mm with seven cameras, and they got some of the world's finest cinematographers, among them Michael Chapman, Laszlo Kovacs and Vilmos Zsigmond. After the concert, while Scorsese was editing *New York, New York*, Robertson came up with the idea of inserting a sound-stage sequence and some interviews. Thirty years later, Scorsese directed *Shine a Light* (2008), a film covering the Rolling Stones's *Beacon Theatre* performance in November of 2006. Whereas *Shine a Light* is merely documentation, a rock concert film that is better than other rock concert films, *The Last Waltz* (1978) became so much more than just archive material.[31] Artistically, aesthetically and thematically it deserves to be labeled "a Martin Scorsese picture," and it is arguably the greatest rock concert film ever made. What Scorsese created was a truly cinematic work that makes it possible to *feel* the overwhelming energy of what Robbie Robertson has called "a spiritual experience."[32] Now, decades later, it is as stunning and sensuous an experience as ever with its richly hued images and amazingly clear sound. In addition to being the farewell concert of The Band, it is a rare cultural document, a nostalgic portrait of an era in music that is ending, and it contains many of Scorsese's recurrent motifs. The symbolism of the structure, the lyrics, and the lighting is vintage Scorsese "with each color in some weird way meaning something," Scorsese says.[33] *The Last Waltz* is pure, scintillating cinema and rock music fused together in the most harmonious way one could imagine. Scorsese has called it "the most perfect thing I had made."[34]

As always, Scorsese planned meticulously. Things would be unbelievably hectic once the concert started, so he had all the lyrics to all the songs in front of him, broken down to match the camera movements he had planned. In the final film, the rhythm of the editing follows the songs, and the camerawork and shifting angles painstakingly mirror the number of bars of the music, as it did in the big band sequences of *New York, New York*. Scorsese had prepared 200 pages of script "so that when a camera ran out of film I could tell which other camera should pick up where."[35] He "planned the camera cues like a general," Pauline Kael says, and Mary Pat Kelly describes him as a "whirling dervish in headphones."[36] Set designer Boris Leven introduced the chandeliers and built the stage around a set from *La Traviata* that they got from the San Francisco Opera, but other than that they decided to keep it as simple as possible; to keep the full focus on the stage and the performers and to avoid all the hackneyed shots of the audience one sees in virtually all other concert films.

Scorsese called *The Last Waltz* (United Artists, 1978) "the most perfect thing I had made." *(From left to right)* Rick Danko, Robbie Robertson, and Levon Helm.

The structure is interesting in that *The Last Waltz* is not simply a chronological presentation of the concert—knowing Scorsese, of course, it would not be. It starts with a close-up of pool balls on a table as Rick Danko explains the game of Cutthroat. We then cut to the Winterland stage where Robbie Robertson surprisingly says: "You're still there, huh? We're gonna do one more song and that's it," and The Band plays "Don't Do It," the last song they ever played together before an audience. The seven hour concert is cut down to just under two hours, and the numbers are not presented in the order they were actually played. Instead, Scorsese structured the film so that adjoining songs add meaning to each other, and the snippets of interview give crucial information about the songs that surround them. The conversations with The Band give us an impression of who they are and of what living on the road for 16 years must have been like, but they also lend a richness to the music. "Each song," says Scorsese, "becomes like a rounded person. It's amazingly physical."[37]

The film falls into three distinct thematic sections, each corresponding to approximately one third of the film. The first section concerns surviving life on the road physically, mentally and spiritually. It gives us an introduction to The Band, how they started, how they got their name, how they sometimes had to steal food to survive. Between the lines, we can sense the enormous price they paid. During this section they play with Ronnie Hawkins who got them started, and Michael McClure reads the Prologue to Chaucer's *Canterbury Tales* about a motley group of pilgrims on the road to Canterbury "the holy blissful martyr for to seek." The songs played in this section deal with the strain and anguish of being on stage and living on the road. These appropriately include "Cripple Creek," "The Shape I'm In," "Helpless," and "Stagefright."

Connecting the first and second sections is the breathtaking rendition of "The Weight"—perhaps the most famous song The Band ever made. It intensifies the religious imagery that was hinted at in the first section which escalates throughout the rest of the film. Scorsese wanted (and eventually got) violet and yellow lights for the number, but it caused a lot of commotion: "There was this huge argument between Marty and Michael Chapman," says Robertson. "Marty was insisting that it was a very Catholic vision, it had to be. And Michael was saying 'No, this is a very Protestant story, it's Baptist, Marty.'"[38]

In the second section the symbolism becomes more profound. This section concerns the music itself: the mythology, the origins and expressions of rock music, and the vocation of being a musician as opposed to the hollow temptation of celebrity. How does one stay authentic and true to one's calling without making concessions to the worshipping crowd? Scorsese asks the members of The Band why they have always tried to keep out of the spotlight, and they answer that it is because they got more work done that way. "We'd be concerned," Garth Hudson says, "with fixing the tape recorder and fixing the screen door, you know, stuff like that. And getting the songs together." More irresistible has been the temptation of adoring women. One of the first things Hawkins told them, according to Robertson, was "You won't make much money, but you'll get more pussy than Frank Sinatra." When Scorsese asks them about this they become schoolboyishly lewd, as if to cover their discomfort over the subject, until the reticent Levon Helm indignantly insists that they stop talking about it.

Then we cut to Joni Mitchell singing "Coyote" which directly and poetically comments on the lifestyle the men have just been discussing. By cutting directly from the locker-room discussion about available women to this intelligent and poised female singer, Scorsese connects the two, placing Mitchell on a completely equal footing with her male colleagues. She is a woman of the road not in the sense of being a groupie, but in the sense that she has lived there exactly the way they have.

Finally, they talk about Memphis, Tennessee, where the primary industry, Levon Helm argues, is cotton, rice and music. People like Carl Perkins, Johnny Cash, Bo Didley, and Muddy Waters all came from that area. "If it comes down to that area, and if it mixes with the rhythm, and if it dances, then you've got a combination of all those different kinds of music: country, bluegrass, blues music, show music," Helm says. "What's it called then?" Scorsese asks. "Rock 'n 'roll," Helm says with a big, joyous smile.

Bridging the second and third sections is Eric Clapton's "Further on up the Road," a song about karmic destiny, and in the final section a deeper spiritual dimension is introduced. Robertson talks about how the music has had a significance beyond the immediate experience. It would take you where otherwise you would never go. "It took us to some strange places," he says. "Physically or spiritually?" Scorsese asks. "Physically, spiritually and psychotically," Robertson replies. Then Scorsese makes another stunning cut, giving the next song, the Emmylou Harris sound-stage segment, the quality of an epiphany. The isolated, floating stage has a dreamlike quality to it which is emphasized by the song about Evangeline who is standing in the moonlight on the banks of the Mississippi, watching her beloved drown. In contrast to the stories about stealing, spitting blood, whoring, drinking, and doing drugs, Emmylou Harris looks radiantly immaculate and ethereal with her floor-length dress and long black hair. Joni Mitchell's performance suggested a strong, thoroughly modern woman, equal with and sharing the same lifestyle as the men. Emmylou Harris becomes the antithesis to that, invoking both the eponymous Evangeline of bygone days who slips into madness, and being herself shown as a manifest and timeless Madonna whose light-blue dress is the same color as the one in which the Holy Virgin is traditionally depicted.

In the next interview the discussion of the spiritual nature of music is continued. We are told that when Garth Hudson joined The Band, they each had to pay him $10 a week so he could pretend to his parents that he was a music teacher rather than a rock musician. Where he came from certain kinds of music were considered evil, he says. "But actually the greatest priests on 52nd Street and on the streets in New York City were the musicians. They were doing the greatest healing work, and they knew how to punch through music which would cure, make people feel good." When Scorsese cuts to "Ophelia" at this point, he gives the song a slightly more mystical tone than it normally has. The runaway Ophelia becomes connected to Shakespeare's Ophelia by way of Evangeline who is slowly going insane.

Before the final part of the concert, Levon Helm talks about the traveling tent shows as the origin of modern rock. So when you would see "Elvis Presley or Jerry Lee Lewis or Chuck Berry or Bo Didley really shaking it up, you know, it didn't come out of nowhere," Robertson says. The tent shows were "the local entertainment everybody was going to see, so then *they* exposed it to the rest of the world, it was like this unknown beast that had come out of the grotesque of music with the devil inside."

Bob Dylan—for whom The Band played backup in the mid-sixties—was the last act at the concert after seven hours. He was worried that *The Last Waltz* would steal business from his own upcoming film *Renaldo and Clara*, so he would only allow Scorsese to film a few of his songs and the grand finale where all the performers are on stage singing "I Shall Be Released." This song completes a circle in that it was originally released on *Music from*

Big Pink, The Band's debut album, and the chorus resonates with the religious and spiritual significance that has been building up.

While the artists are leaving the stage, we cut to the last interview in which Scorsese, seen only in a mirror, lets Robertson have the final word: "The road was our school. It gave us a sense of survival, taught us all we know. There's not much left that we can take from the road," he says, "or maybe it's just superstitious."

"Superstitious in what way?" asks Scorsese.

"You can press your luck. The road has taken a lot of the great ones: Hank Williams, Buddy Holly, Otis Redding, Janis, Jimi Hendrix, Elvis. It's a goddamn impossible way of life."

"It is isn't it?" says Marty.

"No question about it," Robertson concludes.

We cut back to the sound-stage for the final section of "The Last Waltz Suite" which is every bit as haunting as the other two. The five members of The Band are alone on the stage with only a small light illuminating them from below. The camera starts slowly tracking backward, retiring through the theater, abandoning them there with their immense shadows on the back wall. An era in rock music has definitively ended.

The Color of Money

In September of 1984, after shooting *After Hours*, Scorsese was contacted by Paul Newman who wanted him to direct a film about Fast Eddie Felson, the character Newman played in Robert Rossen's *The Hustler* more than twenty years earlier. "Eddie Felson reminds me of the characters that you've dealt with in your pictures," Scorsese recounts Newman saying, "and I thought more ought to be heard from him."[39] At first Scorsese was reluctant to direct a film based on the script Newman had, because he felt it was too much of a direct sequel. In addition, he did not like the book *The Color of Money* by Walter Tevis (who also wrote the novel on which *The Hustler* was based). Eventually Scorsese brought in novelist and screenwriter Richard Price and the script was rewritten, keeping only Tevis's title. "It was the three of us," Scorsese says, "constantly reworking, constantly coming up with and battling ideas back and forth."[40] Initially, Scorsese wanted to shoot the film in black and white, but Touchstone Pictures begged him not to do so. He did not want too many allusions to *The Hustler* anyway, so he finally agreed to make it in color which makes it inherently much less dark than Rossen's film.

The Color of Money (1986) is often referred to as a sequel, but it is much closer to Scorsese's other work than it is to *The Hustler* (which Touchstone estimated that only ten percent of the audience would have seen anyway). Rather than continuing the narrative of the original film — Minnesota Fats, Bert Gordon and Sarah Packard are never so much as mentioned — Price and Scorsese use it primarily as a constant subtext. The basic story of *The Hustler* was Faustian in nature: like the young Faust, the young Fast Eddie strikes a bargain with the Devil and in the process sells his soul and loses the woman he loves. There is something unequivocally Mephisthelean about George C. Scott's dazzling portrayal of Bert Gordon. He is utterly repellent and at the same time magnetically attractive: this is a man who can buy a man's soul, who can whisper mysterious things into the ear of a woman and make her crumble, then moments later take her own life.

The Color of Money, like Scorsese's other films, is a mythological work about a journey of redemption. Richard Price took as his point of departure the psychological implications of Eddie's rebellion against Bert Gordon at the end of *The Hustler*: "I was interested in Bruno Bettelheim's notion of identification with the aggressor," Price says. "You become the thing that you're most terrified of and that makes you most powerless.... So Newman should become, when he reaches that age, George C. Scott — a cynic, a user of pool players, and hate himself and deny all the hunger and lust for this sport that he had when he was a young man."[41]

Eddie now makes a living hustling good, cheap whisky and Wild Turkey labels to bartenders, something at which he is extremely skilled. He is financially successful, but his only connection with the game he used to love with such passion is as a stake horse for a sleazy coke addict named Julian (John Turturro). In the first scene Julian loses to a wild kid named Vincent Lauria (Tom Cruise) who has a "sledgehammer break" and a divine gift for the game, and something inside Eddie wakes up which he would probably have preferred to leave dormant. There is a pained expression on his face the first time he lays eyes on Vincent, and although Vincent is "an incredible flake"— something Eddie never was— Eddie sees in him a younger, purer version of himself: "It's like watching a home movie," he tells his lady friend, Janelle (Helen Shaver).

Several things are involved in their journey together from the start: when Eddie takes on Vincent, he projects onto him the younger self that he has been repressing all these years, and in order to protect himself from the pain of that self, he feels compelled to corrupt

Eddie Felson (Paul Newman) instantly recognizes the greedy nature of Vincent's girlfriend, Carmen (Mary Elizabeth Mastrantonio), in ***The Color of Money*** (Touchstone Pictures, 1986).

Vincent's purity. In the process he masochistically re-corrupts the young Eddie Felson, this time playing the role of the aggressor. At the outset, Vincent is presented as totally innocent: he works at "Child World" and is more devoted to a computer game called "Stocker" than to pool. He is not interested in money at all: "I just want your best game," he says to Julian. "I think maybe the money's what's throwing you off." Thus Eddie has to approach him through his girlfriend, Carmen (Mary Elizabeth Mastrantonio), whose greedy nature he immediately recognizes. Eddie is as verbally agile as Bert Gordon was, and like him he uses his expensive car as a main argument in his seduction. When he buys Vincent and Carmen dinner, he rephrases (and misconstrues) Bert's speech about talent as opposed to character when he says that "pool excellence is not about excellent pool. It's about becoming someone." He tells them that he is a "student of human moves," but, as it turns out, his psychological insights are carefully planned parts of the con game, the hustle, to reel them in.

Although it is a story about corruption, *The Color of Money* is not Faustian the way *The Hustler* was, partly because Vincent is not aware that he is selling his soul, but mostly because Eddie is not conscious of having become the corrupter. When he behaves like Bert Gordon it is not out of conviction, or even consciously, and thus he does not have his Mephistophelean panache and quality of pure evil. Instead, this is a story in which the main character becomes the thing he represses; the shadow side takes over because he cannot bring himself to face it and endure the pain involved in doing so. It is a battle with the enemy inside, and like in *Raging Bull* it is played out symbolically through the sport.[42]

The basic mythology of *The Color of Money* is the story of the boy who has to walk the hero path, to go through a learning process with the help of a mentor in order to be able to finally reach out for and truly deserve the grail, the sword, or, in this case, the Balabushka pool cue. At first glance, Vincent would seem to be the hero, the young King Arthur or Luke Skywalker who has to learn to control his boyish impatience, his need to show off in order to become an expert hustler. Eddie would then be Merlin or Obi Wan Kenobi who presents him with the "light-saber" at the beginning of his journey and proceeds to teach him how to use the force, "to flake on and flake off," as Eddie tells Carmen, "to be himself but on purpose."

Eddie believes this scenario to be true, as do we during most of the movie, and as a result Vincent's shenanigans when he refuses to behave and learn seem as annoying as those of Johnny Boy in *Mean Streets*. Indeed, *The Color of Money*, like so many Scorsese films, is about two men, one of whom is an idiotic, unruly, and infuriating nemesis, constantly reminding the other of the things he has been trying to repress, in this case for half of his life. In a central scene Eddie tells Vincent that "you gotta have two things to win: you gotta have brains and you gotta have balls. Now, you've got too much of one and not enough of the other." This echoes the exchange between Sam and Nicky in *Casino*: "Where's your head?" says Sam. "Where's your balls?" Nicky replies. Eddie and Sam — representing the reluctantly struggling ego, the brains — are connected, as are Vincent and Nicky — representing the shadow nemesis, the balls.

The twist of *The Color of Money* is that the "boy" who has to go through a learning process in order to redeem the soul he lost 25 years ago is, in fact, 52-year-old Eddie Felson, whereas the unlikely mentor (who reminds him of the things about himself he has forgotten) is Vincent Lauria. If we view the film mythologically, in the first scene we see a subtle indication that Vincent may not be altogether unconscious of this: he swings his pool cue wildly at imagined enemies (the exact same way Johnny Boy does in *Mean Streets*) while he yells,

"Off with their heads!" The quote from Lewis Carroll's Queen of Hearts suggests that on some level he is aware that it is Eddie who, like Alice, has to go through the weird, educational journey in order to be able to face the majestic opponent. In the course of the film, as Paul Newman has pointed out, "Eddie Felson reeducates himself, and recaptures his excellence."[43]

When they go out on the road together, the constellation of Eddie, Carmen, and Vincent evokes Bert, Sarah, and Eddie going to Kentucky in *The Hustler*, and it underlines how crucial the difference is between Sarah and Carmen. Whereas Sarah fought for the soul of her lover and ended up paying for her rebellion against Bert with her life, Carmen gladly cooperates with Eddie in perverting Vincent's talent. Alcoholic, neurotic and lame, Sarah was a pathetic but insightful and poetic character. Carmen is tough as nails: there is nothing pitiable about her, but there is not a poetic bone in her body either. Sarah was smarter than Eddie — intellectually, morally and philosophically. Carmen is smarter than Vincent as far as survival and understanding the concept of the hustle are concerned. In terms of the hero's journey, however, the function of the two women is the same. Sarah, reflecting the feminine side of the young Eddie, was an intelligent but fragile conscience who died at the end, almost as if she deliberately sacrificed herself to wake him up. Carmen, reflecting the feminine side of the mature Eddie, is a jaded and greedy hustler who helps him contaminate the purity of Vincent whose transformation would neither be credible nor possible without her. Carmen, in a sense, helps Eddie become Bert Gordon, because only in this way will he ultimately see himself and be able to reclaim his lost soul.

When Eddie persuades Vincent to prostitute his talent, it recalls not only *The Hustler* but also *Raging Bull* and countless other films about sports, in which the main character is seduced into "taking a dive for the short-end money" (as Terry Malloy says), rather than playing his best game. These films, says Richard Pells, deal with "the failure of mentors, father-figures, older brothers, managers, people in authority who manipulate and corrupt the kid who believes in them. Mountain Rivera [in *Requiem for a Heavyweight*] may be proud of himself for having been ranked fifth and never having taken a dive. But there's always a John Friendly (whether it's Jackie Gleason in *Requiem* or George C. Scott in *The Hustler*), ready to subvert their talent and destroy their innocence, their chance to have class. They're not looked out for by the older, wiser, big brothers, as Brando complains to Steiger" at the end of *On the Waterfront*.[44] When Eddie is neither as dangerous nor as compelling as Bert Gordon or Johnny Friendly, it is simply because he is not a corruptor out of conviction but to cover over the pain of his past.

Eddie Felson tells Vincent to lose on purpose even though that clearly goes against the grain for Vincent. Repeatedly, Vincent tells him how painful this is for him, but Eddie just resorts to platitudes like: "Sometimes if you lose, you win." He assures Vincent that there is a higher goal, namely the money you can con out of the other guy by pretending not to be as good as you really are. The fact that Vincent is not only playing pool but participating in a bigger game of hustling may make it slightly less demeaning for him to lose on purpose than it was for Terry Malloy and Jake La Motta, but from Eddie's perspective there is no real difference between himself and Johnny Friendly and Tommy Como: he collects money from a moral compromise he has talked someone else into making against his better judgment. When Vincent has a chance to play against the champion Grady Seasons, Eddie rubs his nose in his having to "lay down" with a pleasure that ultimately is both sadistic and masochistic since he is doing it to a younger version of himself too: "You are gonna dump! You are gonna dump something fierce!"

The turning point comes when Eddie's own game is played against him. In front of Vincent and Carmen he is stung and humiliated by Amos (Forest Whitaker), a superb and merciless hustler. Eddie then makes Vincent and Carmen go on without him because there is nothing more he can teach them. The boy and the mentor customarily part ways on the mythological hero path: the mentor cannot come with the boy all the way, and the boy then has to go it alone. Invariably, we stay with the boy and follow *his* journey, and if we have not realized it before, this is the point where it becomes clear that Eddie Felson, the self-appointed mentor, is actually the hero of the story, while the boy is, in reality, the mentor.

When Eddie is alone he realizes that he has been blind, literally and metaphorically. Significantly, he confides this to Orvis (Bill Cobbs) who is the only character in the film who knew him in the old days. Blindness and the faculty of seeing is often used symbolically in Scorsese's films to reflect a character's ability to see psychologically or morally, and Eddie now gets new glasses and new eyes with which to view the world. We see him swimming, coming out of the water as a kind of cleansing ritual, and now he starts practicing his game with a new humility, as if he is reborn and starting all over. At the end of this sequence, he defeats the unbeatable Moselle and can move on to Atlantic City for the final test of the hero path, the dark night of the soul.

When Eddie enters the tournament room at Atlantic City, we hear organ music, and the lighting and solemnly devotional descending of the camera suggest that he enters a cathedral. When he sees Vincent and Carmen again, Vincent has gotten so good and so ruthless at the con game that even Carmen is perturbed. "You wouldn't believe Vincent now," she tells Eddie. "You wouldn't even recognize him."

Eddie defeats Vincent in the tournament and is sure that the battle is over. Only then does he realize the full extent of Carmen's words, however. Triumphantly, Vincent bursts into his hotel room with an envelope containing $8,000 and proudly tells him that he bet on Eddie winning and deliberately dumped the game. As Eddie did to him, Vincent continues to rub salt in the wound and gleefully describes the thrill when he "just missed the pocket by a hair."

Vincent does everything Eddie taught him with such skill, elegance, and decadence that he can outsmart even Eddie. At this moment Eddie realizes that he has created a Frankenstein's monster. "All of a sudden it's on its own! He's gone, he's wreaking havoc, he's a sorcerer's apprentice," Price says, and Eddie is forced to confront this "living testament to his own awfulness."[45] He might have thought, like Victor Frankenstein, that he can create a living being and forever control where it goes and what it does. But now it is an independent creature for which he is responsible, one that is created out of the repressed shadow of his past, and as Robert Johnson says, the repressed "shadow gone autonomous is a terrible monster in our psychic house."[46]

Moments later Eddie sees his own distorted reflection in a pool ball, and looking himself in the eye he decides to leave the tournament so he can face the corrupted boy and reclaim his life. First, he meets the women that represent two different kinds of female principle. Janelle, his lover, tries to console him by saying that she is "a real big fan of character in people," which suggests that she knows about Eddie's past. The game, Bert told him 25 years ago, is not about talent—"Everyone's got talent!"—but about character. The reason Minnesota Fats can beat Eddie while playing pool for 40 hours straight is that he has "got more character in one finger than you've got in your whole skinny body." If you do not have character, it is indicated, you might sell out, misuse your divine gift, and lose the sense

Who is the mentor and who is the boy who has to walk the hero path—Vincent Lauria (Tom Cruise, left) or the aging Eddie Felson (Paul Newman) in *The Color of Money* (Touchstone Pictures, 1986)?

of what it feels like to be functioning at the top of your craft when the punch or the saxophone or the pool cue is an extension of your soul. Young Eddie tried to explain this to Sarah, and it would seem that the mature Eddie has managed to explain it to Janelle.[47] Then Carmen shows up and Eddie repeats the words Vincent spoke to Julian at the beginning: "I want his best game!"

"So I gotta cover *your* ass now?" Carmen says.

"No," Eddie says, "you gotta *save* it!" Eddie is ready to go back to his purer self—the object of his journey—and a salvation is about to take place with help from the anima principle.

Some critics have expressed a hope that maybe in this last game Vincent can be saved, too, but I would suggest that there is no need for that. Many things bespeak that his behavior has been part of a symbolic act whose purpose is saving Eddie. In an early scene Vincent takes the Balabushka and goes out and ruins their chances at making money by revealing his skills. Eddie is furious and screams that Vincent does not deserve "this stick." Vincent yells back, "No—*you* don't deserve this stick!" This line makes absolutely no sense on a realistic level, but it makes all the sense in the world if we assume that Vincent is the mentor who is there to teach Eddie to walk the hero path and finally deserve and reach out for the legendary Balabushka, the most exquisite and precious of pool cues. Consequently, in the last scene Vincent bursts into the Green Room, looks Eddie straight in the eye and says, "Stings like a bitch, don't it?" as if throwing the game was a deliberate part of a bigger plan.

Eddie has been convinced that he can teach the flaky boy, when all the time the boy may have been there to teach *him*. For the longest time we were annoyed with the imbecilic Vincent for resisting Eddie's lessons, but in the end we realize that he was absolutely right to do so—after all they include relatively frightening concepts like: "The problem with mercy, it just ain't professional." Like Eddie we do not really see this, however, until Vincent has finally given in (or pretended to give in) and become exactly what Eddie wanted him to be.

Eddie says to Carmen that he will be waiting for Vincent "in the green room" for their final cathartic game. In addition to the practical function of a green room, the name itself is significant. The film is called *The Color of Money*, and the color of money is, of course, green, as is the color of pool tables. More importantly, however, to a film maven like Scorsese "The Green Room" is bound to call to mind the Truffaut film in which the green room represents holding on to and keeping alive a past that is dead and ought to be buried; and in the process robbing the living of life. "To come alive again," Scorsese says of Eddie, "he's got to face himself. He doesn't have to win, but he's got to play."[48] Fast Eddie Felson's last words—"I'm back!"—testify that the green room is a place of death and rebirth, a place where he can see things as they really are, withdraw the projection, face up to and reclaim the shadow, and finally be at peace with the pain of the past.

7

Paying Out the Shadow

> It is only when we have the courage to face things exactly as they are, without any sort of self-deception or illusion, that a light will develop out of events, by which the path to success may be recognized.[1]
>
> I Ching

All of Scorsese's films show us characters who have to go through the hero path and into the inmost cave where they must face death and their darkest fears. In the works discussed in this chapter, the journey is intensely spiritual, and the lives of the central characters are uprooted for extended periods of time, sometimes — as in the case of *The Age of Innocence* and *Kundun*— for decades. Whereas all of Scorsese's films concern mythological, psychological and spiritual issues, these films do so explicitly. The journey of these protagonists is catalyzed by an individual who appears, or reappears, to haunt the protagonist, and they all contain concepts of saving or liberating people. Max Cady says to Sam Bowden in *Cape Fear*, "You could say I'm here to save you," and Frank Pierce in *Bringing Out the Dead* suffers overwhelming agonies because he feels he failed to save Rose. At the end of each journey we hope that the main character sees that in the final analysis, "You cannot liberate me!" as the Dalai Lama says in *Kundun*. "I can only liberate myself!"

Kundun

Tibet had been autonomous since the overthrow of the Qing Dynasty in 1911 when in October of 1950 it was invaded by Communist forces from the People's Republic of China. The Tibetans were faced with a war that they could not possibly win, and during the following nine years the newly enthroned Dalai Lama tried to evade a military takeover of his country. Delegations sent to the rest of the world, urging them to intervene on Tibet's behalf, were all turned down. Reports of increasing savagery against the Tibetan people continued to pour in, culminating in 1959 when the Chinese Liberation Army besieged Lhasa, the capital city. Tens of thousands of Tibetans were killed, dismembered, crucified and buried alive. Eventually, in the winter of 1959, the Dalai Lama went into exile, having been promised asylum by the Indian government. To this day, he has not been able to return to his country, ruling instead from India with the Tibetan Government-in-Exile. Tibet is still an oppressed country under Chinese rule.

Kundun (1997) tells the story of the 14th Dalai Lama, the human incarnation of the Buddha of Compassion, the spiritual and secular leader of Tibet. The film spans the time he was recognized in 1937 at the age of two and a half, through the Chinese invasion in

1950, until he was forced to go into exile in 1959. The film project began in the early 1990s when screenwriter Melissa Mathison became fascinated by the subject, started doing research, and eventually submitted a treatment to the Dalai Lama in April of 1991. During the following years, she interviewed him on several occasions, as well as his family and various scholars and members of the Tibetan government. On a trip to Dharamsala in India (the seat of the exiled parliament) she spent six days with the Dalai Lama, correcting and expanding the manuscript. When she had finished the third draft, Mathison sent it to Martin Scorsese, whom she considered a very spiritual man and director, and he decided at once to direct the film. *Kundun*, as it says modestly at the end of the final title sequence, is "produced with the cooperation and contribution of His Holiness the Dalai Lama."

For obvious reasons it was not possible to shoot the film in Tibet, so Scorsese decided on Morocco where he had previously filmed *The Last Temptation of Christ*. The streets of Lhasa, The Norbulinka (the summer palace) and The Potala (the winter palace) look so real, so textural and saturated with color, that we can almost feel them, but the astoundingly beautiful images are actually images of the Sahara Desert and painstakingly precise recreations. More than a hundred Tibetan monks came from monasteries in India and Nepal to act in the film, as did hundreds of Tibetans used as extras. Many of them had lived in exile all of their lives, and when they stepped into the recreated Potala Palace they were awestruck, which is easy to imagine since one has that reaction just seeing it on the screen. Says Tenzin Lodoe who plays the Dalai Lama's oldest brother: "This will probably be the closest thing I'm ever going to see to the Tibet that my parents knew. It could be the closest thing to Tibet that I'll ever see in my life."[2] "Tibetan culture is on the verge of extinction," says Tenzin Trinley who plays Ling Rinpoche of whom he was once a student. "It's been very exciting to see this process of revival, of costumes and beautiful sets, to see it recorded for the younger generation, and all those people who don't know anything about Tibet, even if it's only for two hours."[3]

It has often been said that *Kundun* is very different from Scorsese's other work, but on its deeper symbolic and thematic levels it is, in fact, quite similar. It is the story of a journey involving tremendous hardship and the archetypal battle between good and evil, the gods and the devils. "What interested me about the story," says Scorsese, "was how a young man who lived in a society based on the spirit, found himself in conflict with a strongly anti-religious society, the Maoist government of the Chinese communists. How does a man of non-violence deal with these people."[4] The concerns of spirit versus matter, of whether it is possible to be a good man in a world that is ruled by violence, have imbued Scorsese's work since *Mean Streets* in the early 1970s.

The religious context of *Kundun* is Tibetan Buddhism, and on a superficial level the imagery may seem overwhelmingly new, but Scorsese stays faithful to the Tibetan tradition, even as he makes constant comparisons to his own Catholic tradition. Similarly, although the film is historically accurate to the point of hardly even being fiction, it is also the very essence of archetypal mythology. The main character holds a deeper, purer spiritual truth and is perceived as such a great threat to the rationally oriented society that he is eventually forced into exile, the exact same fate that befalls the Countess Olenska.

The first thing we see is the "Touchstone" logo which is not blue as it normally is, but red. Then water fills the screen and rippling circles form. The color, the water, and the circle, are significant symbols in the film. A title card informs us that in 1937 a holy man, disguised as a servant, found the reborn 14th Dalai Lama in a far corner of Tibet. We cut

7. Paying Out the Shadow

to a stunning image of The Himalayas and then to extreme close-ups of the Kalachakra Mandala.[5] Over these, we hear the spoken words of two-and-a-half-year-old Lhamo Dhondrup: "Tell me!" he says, and his mother tells the story of his miraculous birth.[6] After four years of bad crops and ill health for his father, the child was born at dawn, "and that day, your father got better. He named you Lhamo. The Protector."

This story has obviously been repeated endlessly for the boy, and it takes on the timeless quality of myth or even gospel. It calls to mind the story of the birth of Christ, and its divine nature is reinforced when Lhamo's mother remembers that a pair of crows was present when he was born, just as they were at the birth of Gedundrub, the first Dalai Lama. Like the infant Jesus was laid in a manger, so the infant Gedundrub was hidden in a cattle pen. The connection to The First Dalai Lama and to Christ is made again toward the end when the Dalai Lama, delirious from a fever, sleeps in a stable and thinks he sees himself as a baby, then looks again and sees a calf in a beautiful, ethereal light.

The Regent of Tibet had a vision that the Dalai Lama has been reincarnated in Lhamo, and so Keustang Rinpoche (Geshi Yeshi Gyatso), the Lama of Sera Monastery, comes to the Amdo province in North Eastern Tibet disguised as a servant. As soon as he sees him, the boy claims that the rosary around the holy man's neck is his, and when the Lama returns, the boy has to go through a test: pairs of objects are placed before him — walking sticks, drums, bells, and so on — to see if he knows which ones belong to him. Little Lhamo picks the right objects with very little hesitation, and the monks bow before him and reverently say, "Kundun," echoing the scene in *The Last Temptation of Christ* when the disciples call Jesus *Adonai*.

Two years later the monks take the child to Lhasa, and as they camp for the night he meets Reting Rinpoche (Sonam Phuntsok), the Regent of Tibet. As in all of Scorsese's films, the color red is used prominently and has double meaning. In *Kundun* it signifies the Dalai Lama's vocation and fervent commitment, as well as the invading Communist forces and the vast amount of Tibetan blood that is spilled. In this early scene, the frightened boy hides beneath the robes of the monk so that when Reting enters the tent, he sees him through a red filter. As he comes to trust Reting, the child walks over and sits under his red robe, enveloped by it as he is initiated into his vocation: "You are here to love all living things. Just love them. Care for them. Have compassion for them. As long as any living thing draws breath, wherever he shall be, there in compassion, shall the Buddha appear, incarnate."

Red is used again in the next scene at the ceremony when it is revealed to Tibet that four-year-old Lhamo Dhondrup, now renamed Tenzin Gyatso, is indeed the 14th Dalai Lama. The boy walks to the throne on a red carpet that we focus on as he looks down. When his family prostrate before him, the child starts giggling. Now he has to live at the Potala Palace without his parents, which is particularly frightening at night. The people he is surrounded by are Phala (the Lord Chamberlain), Taktra Rinpoche (a monk who will replace Reting as the Regent of Tibet), and two new friends, Norbu Thundrup (the sweeper who plays with him and teaches him the valuable lesson that "things change"), and the Master of the Kitchen (who watches over him and comforts him at night).[7] Over the child's bed hangs the mythical image of the Penden Lhamo. The Master of the Kitchen explains that, despite her frightening looks, she is actually the protectress of Tibet and the Dalai Lama. "Is she real or pretend?" the boy asks. "She is real," his friend assures him.

In 1944, the boy finds a room in the palace that is filled with wonderful treasures, gifts to the 13th Dalai Lama, among them a film projector and a telescope that he will end up

Martin Scorsese (left) directs Tulku Jamyang Kunga Tenzin who played the Dalai Lama at age five in *Kundun* (Touchstone Pictures, 1997).

cherishing. Both these objects have to do with the faculty of seeing, and they literally open up the world and allow him to see things he has never seen before. The telescope becomes his most treasured possession and, through it, he sees a Tibet he never knew existed. The film projector (obviously important since we are dealing with Scorsese, a true cinema enthusiast) lets the boy see the world outside Tibet and to understand the magic and the horrors of that world.

During this period his tutor, Ling Rinpoche, teaches him the important spiritual lesson of the "Four Noble Truths." They have to do with the concept of suffering, and the boy intelligently interprets them thus: "First, one understands that he causes much of his own suffering needlessly. Second, he looks for the reasons for this in his own life. To look is to have confidence in one's own ability to end the suffering. Finally, a wish arises to find a path to peace. For all beings desire happiness. All wish to find their purest selves."

He gains new knowledge of the world — the spiritual world through his studies, the outer world of Tibet through the telescope, and the rest of the world through the movie projector, a radio, *Life* magazine and an atlas. He learns of Hitler, Hiroshima and the Maoist movement in China. The Nechung Oracle warns him that there is danger both from within and without, and shortly afterwards the Maoists (the danger from without) try to convince the world that Tibet belongs to China. "I am no longer a child," the boy insists and assumes his first responsibilities as secular leader, initiating an attempt to get help from the rest of the world against the Chinese aggressors. His first spiritual responsibilities follow immediately afterwards: the boy's father dies, and he is asked to perform the burial ritual.

We cut to 1949 when Tenzin Gyatso is 15 years old and the Chinese invade Tibet. The obvious lack of spirituality of the invading forces — reflected in their clothes and demeanor and their harsh, jangling music — is a startling contrast to the sublimely beautiful world we have seen so far. The radio announces that the Chinese want to help rid this "feudal kingdom" of the "tyranny of the Dalai Lama." In reality, it is the wish of the Tibetan people that Tenzin Gyatso be enthroned immediately, even though he is not yet 18. Like Jesus in *The Last Temptation of Christ*, he expresses doubts about whether they found the right boy, whether he is, in fact, the reincarnated Buddha of Compassion. The Oracle pronounces that the time is right, and on November 17, 1950, the 14th Dalai Lama is enthroned.[8] He declares a general amnesty and has to leave Lhasa and go to the remote Dunkhar monastery so that he is safe while they wait for the world to recognize Tibet's independence. He dismantles his telescope while Norbu tells him not to get involved in politics, because he is a monk. "The gods will win. The devils will lose," Norbu says. Symbolically, the flashlight that he found with the other treasures does not work now, but Norbu fixes it for him so that he can see his way ahead and study in the dark times that are to follow. In his tent on the way to Dunkhar he reads the famous passage from the scriptures: "And at the time of midnight, the Bodhisathva saw clear light. Then he saw in a single instant the three states of existence: the past, the present, and the future, purified by the clear light and sitting at the tree of enlightenment, he conquered all the devils."

Great Britain, Nepal, America and India refuse to meet with the Tibetan representatives, and the United Nations vote not to hear their appeal. When the Chinese manage to produce an agreement that has been signed by the Local Government of Tibet (presumably a counterfeit), the Dalai Lama is forced to meet with the Chinese representative, General Chiang Chin-wu (Ben Wang), and offers the most interesting statement regarding the projection of shadow characteristics: "I thought he would be some kind of monster, even with horns growing out of his head," the young Dalai Lama says. "But, he is only a man, just an ordinary human being, like myself." Richard Gere once said, "The monster we *perceive* out there, is only there because it exists inside of us."[9] When we project our shadow onto things and people we fear and abhor, they will seem to be demons and monsters, but when we actually find the courage to look at them, they turn out to be just reflections of ourselves.

Directly connected with the theme of shadow projection is the theme of the hostile brothers, and in the next scene the Dalai Lama is back at the Potala and meets with his eldest brother who tells him that "the Chinese believe I've agreed to kill you," calling to mind Judas in *The Last Temptation of Christ*. The Dalai Lama is stunned that anyone would think that his own brother would consider killing him, but in the context of Scorsese's work it is not so surprising. When his prime ministers resign because they cannot bear the offensive Communist general with the gold Rolex, their resignation is accompanied by the constant reminder of the invasion, the Chinese music that is blaring from loudspeakers and virtually drowning Lhasa. "They have taken away our silence," says the Dalai Lama sadly.

Finally, he decides to go to Peking to see Chairman Mao (Robert Lin). At first, as his brother predicted, Mao seems friendly, but on their second meeting he reveals his true face: "Your attitude is good, you know. I understand you well," he says condescendingly. "But you need to learn this: religion is poison! Poison! Like a poison it weakens the race. Like a drug it retards the minds of the people and society. The opiate of the people. Tibet has been poisoned by religion and your people are poisoned and inferior." The Dalai Lama is palpably grieved that Mao's kindness so far has been deceptive, and that his trust has been betrayed.

On his way back, he visits his hometown in the Amdo Province. "Are you happy?" he asks an old woman who stands outside the house. "I am very happy and prosperous under the guidance of the Chinese Communist Party and chairman Mao Tse Tung," says the woman, repeating a line she has been fed, but unable to keep up the pretense she breaks down and cries. After this heartbreaking moment, the real terrors begin.

The following scene is appalling, and the fact that it is extremely simple aesthetically only adds to the unbelievable horror. The Dalai Lama is sitting in the serene forecourt of the Norbulinka looking at a newspaper photo of severed heads. The Lord Chamberlain tells him that towns are being bombed and the monastery of Lithang has been destroyed. "Nuns and monks are made to fornicate in the streets. They put their guns in the hands of our Khamba children and force the child to kill the parent." The Dalai Lama cries silently, and we cut to the fish pond where he used to play as a child. A thick, brightly red liquid is quickly spreading in the pond, covering all signs of life, signifying the Communist invasion as well as the unbelievable amounts of blood that are shed as a result of it. We then cut to an image of the Dalai Lama looking downward. As the camera starts pulling backwards and upwards, we realize that at his feet and surrounding him are dead monks in red robes, that he is standing at the center of a hideous circle of thousands and thousands of dead monks. As the camera pulls farther and farther away, the image assumes the appearance of a grotesque and gruesome mandala.

At his meeting with General Tan (Henry Yuk), the Dalai Lama is again assured that the Chinese want to heal and liberate Tibet. His simple and wise reply evokes what Jesus said to Judas and paraphrases the entire point of many of Martin Scorsese's films, notably those discussed in this chapter: "You can not liberate me, General Tan! I can only liberate myself!"

It becomes clear that the Chinese intend to kill him, and the Oracle is summoned to determine the impossible predicament of whether he should stay with his people and risk depriving them of their leader, or leave them and flee the country for safety. When the palace is bombed, it is decided that he should leave, and the Oracle draws a map to guide him safely out of Lhasa. Upon leaving the palace, camouflaged in a Chinese uniform, the Dalai Lama closes his eyes for a moment: "I see a safe journey. I see a safe return. Now I am ready." Then begins the stunning closing sequence of the film, intercutting two parallel and equally significant actions: the Dalai Lama's escape to India, and his ritual performing of the Kalachakra ceremony before leaving Tibet.

We see him sitting in bright sunlight on a platform above the monks, laymen, peasants and nomads who have come to attend the ceremony, moving closer to his face by means of dissolves. Then we cut to the Kyichu River at night, at which time he gets into a boat. The image of the boats gliding silently away on the river in the light of the full moon against a soft, ink-blue sky calls to mind the dead souls crossing the River Styx in Greek Mythology. A journey over water in art and in dreams is always suggestive and often involves tremendous change, and symbolic death and rebirth. We now focus on the Mandala that we saw in close-up at the beginning. It is made out of luminously colored sand particles (usually ground out of quartz or precious stones) and contains deeply symbolic geometric designs. Kalachakra teachings have been part of Tibetan Buddhism since the 11th century, and the mandala symbolizes the pure expression of the enlightened mind of the Buddha which nourishes the seed of enlightenment in the mind of each person attending the ceremony. It celebrates the impermanence of all things and is dismantled at the end. We see the hand of the Dalai Lama holding the *dorge*, the symbol for the thunderbolt, cutting across the circle, splitting it in half and destroying it. The blessed sand seems to become an emblem of him when it is collected and carried to the river. It is then poured into the water which is colored by it and carries it away so that it can live on in a new shape.

We cut to the Dalai Lama arriving at the Indian border. Although he is shivering and ill from a fever, he crosses ritually on foot rather than on horseback. The Indian soldier on guard is awestruck. "Are you the Lord Buddha?" he asks. "I think I am a reflection, like the moon on water," the Dalai Lama replies. "When you see me, and I try to be a good man, see yourself."

The film ends as it began with images of circles rippling through water, summing up several concepts that are essential in Scorsese's films. The circle represents the highest divinity, and the Dalai Lama is connected with the full moon, the water, and the rippling circles: he escapes over water by the light of the full moon, he is called the "Ocean of Compassion," and he describes himself as "a reflection" like "the moon on water." Reting Rinpoche had a vision of water and the first words he teaches the boy are: "May I be a bridge, a boat, a ship for all who wish to cross the water." The Dalai Lama is the water, the moon that is reflected in the water, as well as the bridge and the boat that will help others cross the water. Hence, the Oracle's enigmatic reply as to whether he should leave Tibet: "Where there is no crossing a big river, no fords, no shallows, where the only hope is a boat, and there is no boat, I will put a boat, Kundun. The Wish Fulfilling Jewel will shine from the West."

The archetypal battle between good and evil, light and shadow, is a recurring motif in Scorsese's work. We probably tend to automatically view the Chinese as the looming shadow that threatens the small light of the Tibetans, but perhaps it becomes more interesting if we turn the whole thing around. What if we regard the Dalai Lama himself—the man with the divine mission — as the shadow nemesis? He is inherently extremely dangerous to Maoist China, and at the end he is compelled to leave his country because the truths he holds are too unsettling for them. In *Kundun* it is the Chinese who feel compelled to project their repressed shadow energy unto the "tyranny" they perceive in him and in Tibetan Buddhism, not the other way around.[10] Quite early, we see Tenzin Gyatso withdraw his projection when he acknowledges that the general is not a monster with horns but an ordinary human.

The Dalai Lama represents a deeper, more luminous spiritual truth that neither China nor the rest of the world are ready to hear. The powers that be of the western world as well as the United Nations refuse to listen and turn their backs on Tibet's plea for help, something which lamentably holds true even to this day. At the end of *Kundun*— as at the end of *The Age of Innocence*— the character who knows and speaks the truth is forced into exile, swept away so that the surrounding world no longer has to look at him. The film closes with these simple but implicative words printed on a black background: "The Dalai Lama has not yet returned to Tibet. He hopes one day to make the journey."

Cape Fear

More overtly so than any of Martin Scorsese's other films until that point, *Cape Fear* (1991) concerns the embodied realization of the repressed shadow. It is based on J. Lee Thompson's film *Cape Fear* from 1962, which in turn was adapted from John D. MacDonald's novel *The Executioners* from 1957. The novel and Thompson's film both concern a morally upright and sympathetic man, Sam Bowden, who in the past was an eyewitness to a violent sexual crime and whose dutiful testimony in court helped put a brutal rapist behind bars. The plot begins when the psychopathic criminal is released from prison and wants revenge, and Sam's wholesome, all–American family is threatened.

Although often underestimated and misconceived, Scorsese's version of this story is a masterpiece. It is a complex metaphysical film with religious, philosophical, and spiritual implications that go far beyond the simple suspense plot offered in the first two versions. Rather than being just a story of revenge, Scorsese's *Cape Fear* is a modern morality play, an intensely captivating Gothic tale which — like the works of Hawthorne, Poe, and Hitchcock — is concerned with the sins of the past catching up with us; with retribution, responsibility, atonement, and the potential for redemption.

Like in the other two versions, Max Cady (Robert De Niro) was imprisoned for viciously raping and battering a very young girl, but in this version Sam Bowden (Nick Nolte) was his defense attorney, which immediately tells us that there has to be more to this story, because why would Cady be out to get revenge on the person who *defended* him unless that person did something to help get him convicted? Indeed, as Sam gradually admits, in order to get Cady behind bars he did decide not to uphold his sworn duty to zealously represent his client within the bounds of the law, and even buried a report which indicated that the girl Cady raped was promiscuous. What the film asks us to consider, however, is not so much the interesting but familiar concern of innumerable movies and TV shows of the frustrations involved for a defense attorney when he/she has to defend someone that he/she knows to be both guilty and dangerous. Rather, it is concerned with a deeper individual responsibility: it deals with commitment, authenticity and ethical and karmic concepts.

In the early versions the Bowdens were innocent victims of a madman, and in Thompson's film Cady is repeatedly described as a subhuman animal who is *so* disgusting that he "does not deserve civil rights."[11] Apart from Robert Mitchum's oversexed Cady, the characters are antiseptically asexual. Scorsese's characters, on the other hand, are neither virtuous nor innocent: Sam, his wife, Leigh (Jessica Lange), and their daughter, Danielle (Juliette Lewis), have deep, dark secrets that intensify as the film progresses, and sexuality figures prominently in those secrets. Sam Bowden is a complacent and shady character to whom his wife refers as "old slippery Sam." He constantly tries to rationalize his transgressions, and when he tells his boss about burying the report on Cady's victim he says that "there is no way *he* could know that," as if Cady's not knowing justifies and negates his conduct. On a personal level he is a self-righteous coward with a long history of promiscuity that has driven his wife to a nervous breakdown and has uprooted the family. Scorsese's Sam Bowden consistently refuses to acknowledge his responsibility and is an absolute master at repressing his shadow.

If we only take this film literally and see it as another thriller about a deranged lunatic out to get revenge, we cheat ourselves out of the substantial rewards that lie beneath the surface. On a deeper mythological and spiritual level, the issue is not whether Max Cady deserved to go to jail (which I am sure anyone would agree that he did), but the fact that his punishment was made possible by an injustice committed by Sam. In the past, Cady committed a vicious and horrible crime, and now he has paid for it both legally — he has spent fourteen years in prison — and karmically — he has suffered what he made the young girl suffer having been held down and gang-raped in jail. Max Cady's score is settled at this point and is, in fact, relatively uninteresting. Sam's offense, on the other hand, has never even been acknowledged. Like the report, his misdeed has been buried and purposely ignored. Even if the act itself — bending the law so as to put away a violent criminal — might be understandable to some, his transgression and his complacent attitude about it is not justifiable in the eyes of the higher morality which is now catching up with him.

In the two earlier versions, Cady wanted revenge over all those who let him down when he was convicted, and he comes after the Bowdens only after he has finished with his ex-wife and her new husband. In Scorsese's version, Sam is his *only* target, and Cady goes after him and his loved ones with enormous intensity and concentration, *not*, as it turns out, in order to kill or harm or rape them (which would have been easy enough), but to make Sam take responsibility for his actions.

At one point Cady reminds Sam that he, too, has a daughter Danielle's age who does not know he exists because her mother told her he was dead, "which in a sense I was," he says, introducing the concept of death and rebirth. The Max Cady who comes out of prison is not simply identical to the one who went away 14 years ago. In prison, he says, he was surrounded by people who were less than human, so he spent his time there totally committed to systematically building up his physical, mental and psychic powers. The Max Cady who went to jail was an illiterate "Pentecostal cracker," a piece of white trash from the hills. The reborn Max Cady, although still a coarse and offensive individual, has superhuman powers as well as being a quasi-educated man.

If Cady represents the forces that catch up with Sam Bowden, it is imperative to consider who and what Sam wronged when he buried the report in the past. Obviously he deprived the realistic Max Cady of his Sixth Amendment rights, and thereby he also violated the legal profession, the judicial system, and the moral concept of justice. Furthermore,

All the members of the Bowden family in *Cape Fear* (Universal Pictures, 1991) have dark secrets, which act as the rift through which the frightening Max Cady can get to them. *(Left to right)* Leigh (Jessica Lange), Sam (Nick Nolte), and Danielle (Juliette Lewis) on Independence Day.

taking the law into his own hands is an act of pride and an offence against God. Finally, sweeping his transgressions under the rug by leaving the public defender's office and closing the door and his eyes on the part of himself who did it, he committed a wrong against his own self. Symbolically, the reborn Cady—as his impressive tattoos attest—represents the sum total of all those Sam transgressed against and who now insist that he face the music: the cracker from the hills, the concept of justice, the judicial system, God, and his own repressed shadow self.

Rather than just regarding Cady as a dangerous psychopath—which he obviously is on the realistic level—it is possible to see him as someone who has come to force Sam through a spiritual learning process. He keeps insisting that his mission goes beyond just punishing Sam, and several times he claims he is there to *help* Sam, to *save* him, and to *teach* him about commitment and loss. This layer of symbolic meaning is suggested from the very beginning. During the title sequence, images of water fill the screen and under the surface we see human shapes.[12] The water gets more and more abstract, finally turning into blood, which indicates that rather than just being the literal, external landscape of the Cape Fear River in North Carolina, it is a psychological landscape that we are entering. Saul and Elaine Bass (who designed the sequence) have even said directly that what they and Scorsese were working towards visualizing was "a notion of the monsters of the deep."[13]

If the deep is the unconscious, then the monsters of the deep are, of course, the unacknowledged shadow. It is apposite to see Max as the personification of Sam's shadow, their names being virtually mirror images. Marie-Louise von Franz once said that, annoying as it might be when other people criticize us for our shadow faults, there is no way you can ignore it if "an inner judge in your own being" shows up to reproach you for them in your dreams.[14] *Cape Fear* has a distinct nightmarish feel to it, and it makes sense to see Max Cady as an inner judge who has come to execute justice for Sam's transgressions — an idea that lends credence to his claim (which at first sight seems so preposterous) that he is there to help him. Keeping in mind that the shadow becomes dangerous and aggressive if we ignore and repress it, it is little wonder that this shadow is mad as hell. Sam's shadow has been locked away for 14 years and has turned into a demon which now comes crashing out with a vengeance. Because Sam continues to fight it still, it becomes necessary for it to repeatedly invade his house in order to get through to him — one of the most common dream images of our shadow trying to get through to us, von Franz says.

Cady represents more than just Sam's shadow, however, and the very first image we see over the water is an eagle which — as opposed to the monsters of the deep — comes down from above. The name "Robert De Niro" is superimposed over it, instantly associating the eagle with Cady. In Christianity the eagle symbolizes a messenger from heaven, and Dante called it "the bird of God." Sam took the law into his own hands, and it is pertinent to assume that the eagle was sent by God to balance the scales of justice.

The Book of Job plays a notable role in the film. Max says to Sam, "You could say I'm here to save you," then looks directly into the camera, i.e., at us, and says, "Read the book between Esther and Psalms" as if that that would give substance to his assertion. In The Book of Job, Satan feels that Job needs to have his faith tested and persuades God to let him do it. It makes sense to see Cady as an emissary who is sent on behalf of God, a celestial prosecutor with a higher purpose. At the end of the title sequence the water turns into blood and the entire screen becomes red. Like so many of Scorsese's films, *Cape Fear* has a pervasive use of that color, and it is always connected with Cady, indicating that this apparently malevolent character has a vocation and is on a God-given mission. Indeed Scorsese has said that Cady is "on a religious quest," the purpose of which is "forcing this family through a redemption."[15]

Before he was relegated to the realm of darkness for leading the revolt against God, Lucifer (who is usually conflated with Satan in the Christian tradition) was an archangel whose name means "light-bringer." We might regard him as the religious and spiritual equivalent of the shadow, and in *The Seat of the Soul* Gary Zukav says that "temptation, the Luciferic principle, is that dynamic through which each soul is graciously offered the opportunity to challenge those parts of itself that resist light."[16] Max Cady may, in fact, be there to help Sam gain insight into himself, casting light on the things inside himself he has consistently refused to see. When red often becomes menacing in this film, it is because it reflects Sam's resistance and *unwillingness* to do this.

Emphasizing the Lucifer motif, the film is scored by Elmer Bernstein's subliminally disquieting rearrangement of Bernard Herrmann's music, which repeats four notes over and over: F-C-B-F.[17] The interval between B and F constitutes a tritone, i.e., it spans three whole tones. This is referred to as "the devil's interval" and in the Middle Ages was banned by the Catholic Church. It is notable that Scorsese chose to use Herrmann's original score in which the devil's interval is used so prominently, and throughout the film these four notes, spanning a full octave, are used as a leitmotif; always directly connected to Cady and constantly emphasizing that this is a conflict involving four people: Danielle, Leigh, Sam, Max.

At the end of the title sequence a red close-up of Danielle's eyes emerges. It dissolves into a negative image, then into a positive black-and-white image, then into a color image. "*My* reminiscence," she begins. Although the main conflict of the film is her father's, Dannie is the first character we see, and her narrative opens and closes the film: "I always thought that for such a lovely river the name was mystifying, Cape Fear, when the only thing to fear on those enchanted summer nights was that the magic would end and real life would come crashing in." She is standing in front of a huge pane of glass with water behind it, and when she says "come crashing in," we cut to Cady.

Hawthorne has described the shadow as a prisoner inside a dungeon, and the first time we see Cady, that is what he is. We focus on his awe-inspiring tattooed back as he pulls himself upward by the arms as if he is coming out of a hole in the floor. The camera moves over his belongings to reveal that one of his books is entitled *The Cell Within*, attesting that we are dealing not just with a literal cell, but with the prison cell inside the landscape of the human mind. When Cady walks out of jail after being locked up for 14 years, the sky is overcast and there is an electrical storm in the air. Nobody is there to pick him up and he is not taking anything with him. He is completely unencumbered, and he

"Born to raise hell," reads Cady's tattoo. In addition to being a 14-year-older version of the cracker from the hills whom Sam Bowden sent to jail, Max Cady (Robert De Niro) represents the concept of justice, the judicial system, God, and Sam's own repressed shadow self in *Cape Fear* (Universal Pictures, 1991).

walks straight into the camera and into us with frightening determination. Boundaries no longer exist for the shadow: he can walk in and out of places and people, moving freely between inner and outer spaces.

The film, as the title denotes, is concerned with the concept of fear — fear of the unknown, fear of intrusion, fear of one's own inner being. This is explicitly connected with the Southern setting. Private investigator Kersek (Joe Don Baker) points out that the South was born in fear, and Scorsese's use of Southern Gothic, of the sins of the past that are catching up, is almost Faulknerian. Fear is obviously related to the projection of shadow: we hate and fear those outside ourselves who remind us of the things inside that we do not want to look at and own. The film is even more interested in that very Catholic concept of guilt, however. Cady seems to be omniscient, and as he starts to infiltrate and disrupt all areas of the Bowdens's life, he knows the weak spots of all the characters — as the shadow and Lucifer invariably do; their feelings, their secret desires and longings, their sense of shame and guilt, and this is the crack through which he is able to get to them.

Thus, the reborn Cady first confronts Sam when he is getting into his car after playing a sexually loaded game of racquet ball with Lori (Illeana Douglas), a young clerk from the county courthouse, and Cady seems to appear almost as a result of it. Because of his past infidelities, Sam does not quite have an affair with Lori, but he takes it as far as he can. Adolescently, he keeps bumping into her, crushing her against the wall with all his strength which reveals that, like Cady, he has a propensity for associating sex with violence. Cady knows exactly what is going on between Sam and Lori. He removes Sam's possibility for escape, forcing him to listen, by snatching the keys out of the ignition of his car. He has not held a set of keys for 14 years, he says, but now the shadow seizes control of Sam's keys, saying that he will teach him about loss.[18] Even though Sam keeps trying to lock doors and windows to protect himself against the invader, he can no longer keep Cady locked inside his head or out of his house. "Is he out or is he in? I can't tell!" Sam laments to Kersek, as if he cannot decide which would be worse. Even when Kersek rigs up the house so that "the Holy Ghost" would not be able to come in, Cady manages to enter effortlessly and unnoticed.

The first time Cady shows up at the Bowden home, it is, likewise, in the aftermath of a sexual encounter. We see Sam and Leigh getting ready for bed, distortedly duplicated by the mirrors in their bathroom, discussing Dannie who has been caught smoking grass at school. The crooked Sam does not see what the big deal is, but Leigh replies that it is a taboo on a par with incest, necrophilia, bestiality, worship of idols, and cannibalism. Her ironic tone and expression seem to suggests that she considers these topics to be somehow relevant in their relationship. We cut to the two of them having sex, filmed in negative images, indicating that they have been catapulted into the dark side behind the mirror. Their lovemaking seems bleak and lonely which is emphasized by Leigh's enigmatic behavior after Sam has gone to sleep. She gets out of bed, sits down in front of the mirror and puts on lipstick.[19] Her mystifying, sensuous act testifies that she is not finished, that she is not satisfied. At this precise moment she looks out of the window and sees Max Cady sitting on the wall surrounding the grounds. She wakes up Sam and they go downstairs to chase away the intruder. She then remembers that she is wearing lipstick, and with the most exquisitely guilty look on her face wipes it off, manifesting that she put it on in the first place not for Sam, but in spite of him, and almost as if she senses that this is what summoned Cady.

Throughout the film Leigh seems brittle and on edge in the marriage. She obviously feels betrayed by Sam's habitual philandering and reacts violently to him on several occasions. At the same time she is an extremely attractive and sensuous woman who is unfulfilled. The morning after the encounter with Sam's darker self, and after being told that a violent criminal is out to get her husband, Leigh seems all aroused and blushing. She flirtatiously asks Sam if she can have a gun in case "things get exciting around here." Her name is one of the most interesting changes in Scorsese's version of *Cape Fear*. In both the earlier versions, Bowden's wife was named Carol, an ordinary American woman's name. Since Leigh is a more unusual name there must be a reason for this change. Like so many of Scorsese's films, this one contains parallels to Hitchcock: the title sequence was designed by Saul Bass and scored by Bernard Herrmann, instantly recalling the work both of them did on *Psycho*. Leigh is, of course, the last name of the actress who played the role of Marion Crane in that film, and Jessica Lange is made up to physically resemble Janet Leigh. Her hair is cut and dyed in a style similar to Marion's and we often focus on her bare neck and shoulders, as Hitchcock did on Janet Leigh's. Like Marion, Leigh has a seething, dark sexuality smoldering underneath her neat and well-tended exterior. Both look eminently respectable, but are aroused by the idea of crime and punishment, and both are involved with a rather bromidic man named Sam who cannot give himself to them fully and seems incapable of fulfilling their deepest needs.

Just like *Psycho*, *Cape Fear* is suffused with seemingly innocuous references to the relationship between parents and children, often containing some trace of parental brutality. From the moment Danielle opens the film, this theme runs parallel to and comments on the primary conflict between Sam and Max. Her narrative is prompted by a school assignment for which she is supposed to write something in a style similar to *Look Homeward, Angel*, a story of another troubled youngster from a destructive North Carolina family. Leigh wryly tells the dog that they switched babies on her at the hospital when Dannie was born. Sam's boss asks him to do something that is obviously not quite legitimate in connection with his daughter's divorce proceedings. "I thank you and my daughter thanks you," Sam's boss says, and we cut to an image of a man hollering "Heeeere's Daddy!" while crashing through the door to a nursery. We realize that the Bowdens are in a movie theater watching *Problem Child*, and although that film contains innumerable scenes during which the child acts up, Scorsese has chosen one in which it is the father who is totally out of control. Although *Problem Child* is a comedy, this father menacingly calls to mind Jack Torrance axing his way through the door in *The Shining*, and the image of a man forcing his way through a child's door yelling, "Heeeere's Daddy" may even hold faintly incestuous overtones. At this precise moment, the Bowdens first encounter Max Cady, who walks into the theatre. Significantly, we see him as a shadow projected onto the silver screen. He sits down in front of them, lighting an obscenely phallic cigar, and starts laughing uproariously.[20]

As in his relation with Lori, we see that Sam has a predilection for sexually tinged aggression disguised as jokiness when they go to have ice cream after the movie. Danielle teases him, saying that he should have taken on the annoying guy in the theatre. Sam then puts his entire arm around her neck, squeezes very hard, and says playfully, "I could take you, that's who I could take!"

If we consider Cady to be the manifested expression of Sam Bowden's unacknowledged shadow, it becomes interesting to examine precisely where his aggression is directed. After chasing Cady away when he first comes to the house, Leigh and Sam sit down in the kitchen and he gives her a partially true account of who Cady is and why he is there. Leigh's beloved dog keeps interrupting and wanting attention, which clearly annoys Sam no end. Shortly afterwards, the dog is mysteriously killed, even though it has not been outside the house which has been securely locked. Toward the end, after Kersek has completely safeguarded the house, Sam sits up in bed, half asleep in the middle of the night and thinks he sees Cady in the bedroom; first in negative, then in positive, then he is gone. "I know how the dog died," Sam tells Leigh with total conviction, as if he is finally realizing that Cady is able to move in and out freely because he materializes from the negative images where the lights and shades are reversed (as the Lean One said to Peer Gynt); that Max emerges from Sam's own unconscious.

Cady's next target is Lori. She is upset and frustrated over Sam's advances and retreats, and Cady effortlessly picks her up in a bar and takes her home. We are horrified that the inebriated woman roars with laughter as he handcuffs her and starts battering her to a pulp. Sam has been forced to sublimate his craving for Lori against his will, and now it expresses itself as near-cannibalistic oral sadism when Cady bites off her cheek. Although Lori is a minor character, her role is central. Through her, the sins of the past become the sins of the present. She is the rift through which Cady can get into Sam's marriage, and she becomes the link to the old case of 14 years earlier. Sam tries to reassure his enraged wife that she should not feel threatened by his sneaking around with Lori because "she's a baby!" This excuse is very revealing because it links Lori to the girl Cady raped as well as to Sam's own daughter and, thus, to the taboo of incest. Furthermore, when Sam asks Lori to testify against Cady, she is unwilling because she knows that, like the young girl, she will be accused of promiscuity and forced to explain under oath what she was wearing and why she was picking up a strange man in a bar. This is a subtle comment on how the absurd concept of promiscuity in rape victims has not changed over the last decades, and Sam cannot blame her for not wanting to expose herself in court, because essentially she is just making the exact same evaluation now that he did then. When she points out that questions might be asked about their covert relationship, too, he stops pressuring her which again shows his self-centeredness and hypocrisy.

There are two questions that one might reasonably ask: Why, if Sam is the main character, does Danielle's narrative open and close the film? And why was this precise moment in Sam's life chosen by Scorsese as the one in which Cady is released so he can go after him? The answers to these two questions are connected, I believe, and are directly related to what is hidden in Sam's shadow. Fourteen years earlier, he helped get Cady, an unacceptable part of himself, securely confined. All the way through, Sam is shown to be a self-serving coward, so one tends to think he somehow did this for his own sake as well as for society's. In effect he found it imperative to hermitically seal up his own darkest side shortly after his daughter was born. Cady, the shadow, has a daughter the same age as Sam's, and Danielle is now almost the same age as the girl whom Cady raped. Danielle and her budding sexuality are, in other words, pivotal in the conflict between the mask and the mirror.

Sam and Leigh are too caught up in their own problems to pay any attention to the needs of their pubescent daughter. Several times they just walk off after some traumatic encounter with Cady, leaving the girl behind, bewildered and frightened. They keep ordering her to go to her room whenever he is near, and, ironically, this is the reason she does not recognize him when she finally meets him. Their reluctance to let her grow up, and Sam's observable dread of her sexuality, is what makes possible the encounter between an adolescent girl and a dangerous rapist. Precisely because they treat her like a little girl and disregard her needs is she susceptible to Cady's flattery.

Her story is quite similar to the fairy tale in which a child leaves home, goes through some kind of shattering ordeal, and returns home transformed. This type of fairy tale concerns initiation, an essential step toward individuation and adulthood, and from Dannie's perspective, the experience with Max Cady is such a journey which she narrates to us from the vantage point of having returned home. Her opening words ("My reminiscence") are only a short step removed from the archetypal "Once upon a time..." and her introduction contains words like "mystifying," "enchanted," and "magic." The magic that would end is, of course, childhood, and the real life that would come crashing in is adulthood. Despite protests from her parents, Dannie is corrupted, i.e., she grows up, in the course of the film, and, significantly, this takes place around the celebration of Independence Day.

"Little Red Riding Hood" is explicitly referred to in the scene in which Danielle first encounters Max Cady who is pretending to be her new drama teacher. The scene fittingly takes place in the school theater in the basement, and the stage set is a small cabin in a forest with striped candy canes decorating the landscape. Danielle finds Cady on the stage smoking grass, the very thing she was recently punished for doing, and, apparently, he knows everything that goes on not only in her life, but also in her mind. He plays on her secret fears and longings, and when Danielle starts suspecting that maybe he is not her new teacher, she asks where he is from. His reply is that he is from "the Black Forest" and that maybe he is the big bad wolf. The morning after Cady first showed up at the house, Sam told Leigh that he would prefer it if Dannie didn't take any "soul-searching walks in the woods." But like Riding Hood, Marion Crane, and Leigh, Dannie is susceptible to the allure and danger of the forbidden.[21] When she enters the theater, she revealingly says twice that she is "here for drama," and so the wolf can easily tempt her away from the main road. According to Bruno Bettelheim, the story of Red Riding Hood concerns "a child already struggling with pubertal problems for which she is not yet ready emotionally because she has not mastered her Oedipal conflicts."[22] "In the title, as in the girl's name, the emphasis is on the color red, which she openly wears. Red is the color symbolizing violent emotions, very much including sexual ones.... It suggests that not only is the red cap little, but also the girl. She is too little, not for wearing the cap, but for managing what this red cap symbolizes and what her wearing it invites."[23] It is implied that Dannie has not mastered her Oedipal conflicts either, possibly because her father's shadow has been ignored since she was born. Whereas *she* may be old enough for an encounter with a wolf, in no way is she mature enough to handle *this* wolf.

Even after Dannie finds out who Cady is, she gigglingly (and terrifyingly) lets him embrace her, put his thumb into her mouth, and kiss her. When he suddenly walks away, she is left behind, all hot and bothered. Making this sexually charged meeting even more monstrous is the fact that Cady is inextricably connected with her father. When Sam questions her about the encounter later that day, Danielle is resting on her bed, wearing panties and a tank top. He walks into her room and snarls, "Put some clothes on, you're not a little girl anymore!" which is quite revealing because who is he afraid would be aroused by the sight of her? She is in her own room, and he is the only one present. Like the dangerous shadow psychopath, the father targets her mouth, but where Cady, ironically, was extremely tender (albeit with ulterior motives), asking her permission before he touched her, her father, in what amounts to a brutal assault, grabs her across the mouth and pushes her hard onto the bed.

"I think we're alone now!" Max Cady (Robert De Niro) plays the part of the big bad wolf in the Black Forest to seduce Danielle's Red Riding Hood in *Cape Fear* (Universal Pictures, 1991).

In the two earlier versions of *Cape Fear*, Sam was nice and morally upright; in this one he is neither. The fact that Cady has gotten through to Dannie prompts Sam to take the law into his own hands again. He hires three thugs to attack Cady with lead pipes and bicycle chains in a parking lot, while he himself crouches behind a dumpster, watching. This seems so cowardly and offensive that when Cady suddenly gets the upper hand, we might catch ourselves feeling slightly relieved, momentarily rooting for him in spite of ourselves. Sam's resorting to vigilante justice certainly shows us beyond a doubt that he has not changed since 14 years earlier, and it leads directly to the final act, Max Cady's apocalyptic trial of Sam Bowden.

The Bowdens barricade themselves with the private investigator in their house, so that Sam will have a legally justifiable excuse for killing Cady if he invades it. During the night Kersek is talking to Graciella (Zully Montero), the maid, who is standing at the kitchen table with her back turned. Suddenly, she swivels around and she is not Graciella anymore, but Cady, who proceeds to garrote Kersek with the piano wire that was missing earlier. A horrible symbiosis has taken place. Cady has not simply killed Graciella and donned her clothes: it was *definitely* Graciella's voice we heard and much slimmer shape we saw, but a split second later she has turned into Cady. The sight of him swiveling around wearing a dress and a wig manifestly calls to mind the climactic scene in *Psycho* when we see that Norman and Mrs. Bates are one and the same. Afterwards, on the houseboat, Danielle tells her mother that Graciella "has a brother." While I do not mean to propose in any literal sense that Cady is her brother, at the very beginning an uncanny connection *is* established between them: we see Cady walking out of prison and into the camera, and then we continue on to a strange camera angle of Graciella's foot emerging from a car, logically continuing and inverting Cady's movement. The two of them do look like each other and both carry dirty laundry into the Bowden house, Graciella literally and Max Cady figuratively.

The Bowdens discover the dead bodies of Kersek and Graciella and flee to their houseboat, just as Cady wants them to. If what he wanted was to kill or hurt them, that would obviously have been the easiest thing in the world in the house, but he wants them alone in the middle of the river for his climactic trial of Sam. Throughout the film, and always in connection with Sam's cheating, various seemingly innocuous legal metaphors are used. He says to Lori that maybe they should stop seeing each other for a while, and she replies, "I like hanging out with you, so sue me!" Lori tells Cady that Sam is the only married man she has ever been involved with, and Cady answers, "Tell it to the judge!" Leigh catches Sam in their bedroom whispering to Lori on the phone and throws a fit. Sam accuses her of overreacting and she screams, "*I'm* not on fucking trial here!" the emphasis suggesting: but you *are*! These metaphors pave the way for the trial at the end, and they imply that it is necessitated by Sam's questionable morality. What Cady wants, he says repeatedly, is to teach Sam about loss and about making a commitment. He wants him to own up to everything he has done in the past, because only then can he truly take responsibility for his life in the future.

Sam has brought this repressed demon, this monster of the deep on his family, but all through the last sequence he remains frighteningly passive. Except for a very subdued attempt of one sentence to persuade Cady to keep it between the two of them and leave the women alone, he says nothing — not a single word! When Cady threatens to rape Dannie, Leigh reacts promptly, begging him to take her instead and spare her child. She utterly humiliates herself to make him think that the two of them are kindred spirits, hoping that this will save her daughter. Morally, Leigh thus expiates herself: she is authentically willing to sacrifice her own life for the sake of someone she loves. When Cady pauses and lights a cigar, Danielle squirts gasoline on him so that he catches fire. The child sums up immense courage to save her parents and herself. Like her mother, she takes action and shows what she is truly made of when push comes to shove. Because Cady is not a realistic, human opponent, however, he cannot be destroyed physically. He jumps into the river to extinguish the fire, and within minutes, he is back on the boat. Mother and daughter have both redeemed themselves, but Sam still tries to keep as low a profile as possible, and Cady begins the trial against him.

"The People call Samuel G. Bowden," Cady says, and assigns the women as jurors. He repeatedly looks into the camera, addressing it as "Your Honor," suggesting that either God is the judge at this trial (he is looking upward) or that we are (he is looking at us). He interrogates Sam, and it becomes clear that a lot more is at stake here than revenge, that this prosecutor signifies more than just the "Pentecostal cracker" who went to jail 14 years earlier. Cady says that he is Virgil who has come to lead Sam through the gates of Hell, a reference to Dante's *The Divine Comedy* in which the author journeys through Purgatory and Hell, guided by the Roman poet Virgil. They are now in the Ninth Circle of Hell, Cady says, the circle of traitors, "traitors to country, traitors to fellow man, traitors to God. You, sir, are charged with betraying the principles of all three." He reminds Sam of the Bar Association Rules of Professional Conduct which he betrayed when he buried the prior sexual history report, and at the end he finds Sam "guilty of betraying your fellow man, guilty of betraying your country, guilty of abrogating your oath, guilty of judging me and selling me out. And with the power vested in me by the Kingdom of God, I send you to the Ninth Circle of Hell."

Through it all, Sam continues to justify himself, glossing over his unethical behavior, never really listening or taking it in. He is not even close to owning up to the transgressions he has committed against his family, the law, his country, his own Self, or God. As if to give him one last chance to protect and defend his family and thereby redeem himself, Cady orders Leigh and Dannie to take their clothes off and get down on their knees. While they scream in terror, Cady keeps repeating his demand to them for almost a full minute, looking all the while not at them but intently at Sam.

For me this is without comparison the most frightening moment in the film, not because I think Cady will harm the women (which he could easily have done all along), but because Sam remains incapable, even now, of yielding his colossal narcissism. A frenzied psychopath threatening to rape and kill may be frightening, but it is nothing compared to the horror of the complete passivity and silence of a father whose little girl is threatened with rape. Sam never attempts to defend his wife and daughter, physically or verbally. He does not bat an eyelid, and one might even suspect that he is slightly relieved that the pressure is off him for a while. As in the story of Red Riding Hood, the wolf only does what you would expect a wolf to do, but this man, the protagonist with whom we are supposed to identify, behaves atrociously.

Finally God intervenes and a storm tips the boat. Dannie and Leigh manage to escape while Sam and Cady still struggle. In the last scene they are all on the shore. Cady is lying on the bank, handcuffed to the wreck of the boat. Sam, still just trying to get rid of the shadow, picks up a gigantic rock and brings it down with tremendous force toward his head, only to realize that he has been taken out by a wave. As he is being pulled down into the river, Cady starts speaking in tongues — a remnant of his Pentecostal background and/or suggesting the presence of the Holy Spirit — then stops for the longest time with his eyes at the surface line and looks Sam (and us) directly in the eye.[24] With his foot he clanks the iron bar to which he is chained, as if giving a sign to someone that now they can drag him down. All through the end titles we hear the sounds of the river and every now and then sounds of breathing, suggesting that Cady is, in fact, not dead but has merely gone back into the deep from whence he came. At the very end, after the titles have stopped, there is a faint sound resembling the flapping of wings, as if the eagle, too, has taken flight and gone back from where *it* came.

The question is whether Sam has learned or will continue to live in denial. After Cady is gone, he reaches into the water to wash the blood off his hands, and when he takes them out he sees clear stigmatization marks in his palms. Startled, he puts his hands back into the water, and the marks disappear. The concept of washing the blood off one's hands and thus evading responsibility is, of course, associated with Pontius Pilate, which would seem to indicate that Sam has learned nothing about commitment and responsibility. Even if we accept the stigmatization marks as signs of a potential salvation, he chooses to put his hands back into the water so that they disappear, attesting he has not deserved them.

If we examine what Cady has, in fact, done to this family, an interesting pattern forms. Remarkably, he never actually inflicts bodily harm on the Bowdens. Rather he makes them harm him, always knowing exactly what buttons to push to make them do so. Manipulating them into harming him is a lot more insidious, because they cannot walk away from what they did after it is all over. It forces them to look their own shadow in the eye, acknowledging what they are capable of. Those he does harm are Benjamin (the dog), Lori (the mistress), Graciella (the maid) and Kersek (the male protector). Leigh treats Benjamin, her dog, almost like a child, telling it that they must have switched babies on her at the hospital when Dannie was born.[25] Bruno Bettelheim says that fairy tales frequently split up Mother into two separate entities: the fairy godmother (the purely benevolent and good mother) and the wicked stepmother (the purely threatening and evil mother). This "not only preserves the good mother intact," he says, "it also prevents having to feel guilty about one's angry thoughts and wishes about her — a guilt which would seriously interfere with the good relation to Mother."[26] In *Cape Fear* it is the mother who splits the child into two: Benjamin (symbolically the youngest child), her darling, the purely good "child" toward whom her daughter and husband feel jealous; and Danielle, the troublesome and naughty child. Conversely, Graciella is like a second mother. She is the fairy godmother in whom Dannie can confide, who accepts and truly listens to her.

When Cady kills the dog and the maid, on a symbolic level he removes the false child and the false mother, and thereby clears the path for unity, harmony and a deeper, more authentic relationship between mother and daughter. At the end of the film, Danielle and Leigh have both redeemed themselves, each risking her life to save the other, and we see them in a symbiotic embrace in a strange, primeval landscape. When Cady takes Lori and Kersek out of the game, he removes even more serious impediments to the family's happiness. Lori evidences Sam's continued betrayal, and with Kersek gone he would presumably have to take over the role as protector of the family himself. The hope of future harmony is short-lived, however: Lori is still alive, symbolizing that Sam has no intention of making amends or changing his ways. At the end he walks over to his wife and his daughter who are embracing. He reaches out and touches Leigh, but she turns and looks at him with unutterable contempt. He clearly does not deserve to be included in their unity.

The most potent sign that Sam has learned nothing from the grueling enforced shadow process, I think, is the fact that it is Danielle who tells the story, indicating that she is the only one who has learned enough to be capable of doing so. Unlike her father, she is receptive to the shadow, and unlike Lori she is not completely blind to its danger. Interesting in that connection is a character who was invented specifically for this version, namely Dannie's best friend, Nadine, whom (significantly) we never see. In the 1962 film, Bowden's daughter was named Nancy; in Scorsese's version her name is changed to Danielle. And just as "Max" is a slightly distorted mirror image of "Sam," so "Nadine" is an anagram of "Dannie." Whereas her father constantly refuses to have anything to do with his darker side, Dannie is in continuous contact with hers. Twice Dannie calls out for Nadine — once on the phone and once in the school theater. In both cases the one who answers her summons is Max Cady.

Danielle's closing words are a far cry from the familiar fairy tale ending about living happily ever after: "We never spoke about what happened — at least not to each other. Fear, I suppose, that to remember his name and what he did would mean letting him into our dreams. And me, I hardly dream about him anymore. Still, things won't ever be the way they were before he came, but that's all right, because if you hang onto the past, you die a little every day. And, as for myself, I know I'd rather live."

It seems horrific that the Bowdens never spoke about this experience to each other, but Danielle is implicitly saying that she *has* spoken about it with others. She *has* let Cady into her dreams and, thus, has let go. In the final analysis, she says, the change he brought about was necessary. It forced her not to hang on to the past which equals dying a little every day. Because she has embraced her shadow, it no longer invades her dreams. Because of Cady, she is now able to live.

When the shadow finally gets through to us, von Franz says, "The painful and lengthy work of self-education begins."[27] *Cape Fear* provides the means for significant growth not just for the Bowdens, but also for us, the audience. Even before the title sequence begins, we hear the sound of waves over the familiar Universal Studios logo, the globe with the word "Universal" written over it. The logo starts swaying as if water is pouring over it, indicating that what we are about to see is not simply the story of one man, but — as the image says loud and clear — *universal*. Max Cady is the quintessential embodiment of the shadow and he speaks directly to the parts of us we all hide somewhere deep inside. The fact that Sam learns nothing from his experience leaves us high and dry at the end of the film, and one might hope that this is so provoking that it incites *us* to learn, to pay attention to our dark side *before* it starts wreaking havoc on us and our families. One might hope that, instead of pushing away this harrowing experience, we can be inspired by Danielle and let the shadow get through to us so that we, too, are able to live, so that we, too, can "earn the freedom to choose what we do in this world." Because, as Debbie Ford says: "As long as we keep hiding, masquerading, and projecting what is inside us, we have no freedom to be and no freedom to choose."[28]

The Age of Innocence

The Age of Innocence (1993) is dedicated to Charlie Luciano Scorsese, who died on August 23, 1993, shortly after his cameo in this film. In the scene in which Newland greets Madame Olenska at the railway station, we see an enchanting close-up of Charles and

Catherine Scorsese in 19th century costumes. It was during the filming of that shot that they first realized something was wrong with Charles; the next day he had a heart attack.

Superficially, Edith Wharton's Pulitzer Prize–winning novel from 1920 may seem an unlikely project for Martin Scorsese to undertake. Where most of his New York films deal with the contemporary underside of that city, Wharton's book concerns the morals of New York high society in the late-nineteenth and early–twentieth century. In some ways the film looks quite different from Scorsese's other work, and its lavish scenery has led people to compare it to the work of James Ivory. This comparison only holds water on the most superficial, aesthetic level, however. As soon as we look just a little bit closer, we realize that in this, as in all Scorsese's pictures, there are foreboding undertones of pathways that lead into the dungeon inside the human mind. From the very first shot we are actually in familiar Scorsese territory, and as Roger Ebert said in his review: "Through some miracle it is all Wharton, and all Scorsese."[29]

Wharton's novel is, in fact, a perfectly logical choice for Scorsese, and there are innumerable reasons it would appeal to him. Underneath the polished surface, the central themes of the book are similar to the recurring concerns in Scorsese's films, and like so many of these, it states explicitly and repeatedly that it deals with "the inner devils."[30] Scorsese was fascinated by Wharton's use of language, much of which is preserved in the film, spoken by a slightly ironic, omniscient voice-over narrator (Joanne Woodward). According to Jay Cocks, Scorsese was so intent on keeping Wharton's wit and "sculpted perfection" that he "timed camera moves to the narration with hairsbreadth accuracy," thus making language and voice-over narration exquisitely filmic, and attributing to Wharton's cadences the same all-important rhythmic function that he has always attributed to music.[31]

Resonating with Scorsese's metaphorical use of architectural elements, Edith Wharton once described the mind of a woman as a "great house full of rooms." There are the rooms, Wharton says, where family and other people come and go on a daily basis, "But beyond that, far beyond, are other rooms, the handles of whose doors are never turned; no one knows the way to them, no one knows whither they lead; and in the innermost room, the holy of holies, the soul sits alone and waits for a footstep that never comes."[32] The fact that Scorsese and screenwriter Jay Cocks chose to quote this intensely sad passage at the beginning of their book on the making of *The Age of Innocence* indicates that they, too, see it as an important connection between the works of Edith Wharton and those of Martin Scorsese. I cannot think of a fictional character who better fits Wharton's description of the lonely inner space that nobody ever visits than the Countess Olenska, and she is indeed one of the central links between this and Scorsese's other films.

Preposterous though it may sound, *The Age of Innocence* is closely connected with *Mean Streets*, *GoodFellas*, *Casino* and especially *Cape Fear*. Like Scorsese's films on organized crime, *The Age of Innocence* concerns a "tribe" that lives by its own rules and rituals, an extended unit that calls itself a family. Through obscure conventions, unwritten rules and "arbitrary signs," this family controls and terrorizes entire neighborhoods of New York, and like a live organism, it expels or kills off any foreign body: When collectively everyone decides to snub the Countess Olenska (Michelle Pfeiffer), it is referred to by the narrator as an "eradication." "The savagery of this ritual," says Thelma Schoonmaker, is "perhaps more savage than the ritual [Scorsese] grew up in."[33] Scorsese himself has said that over the years he has created a lot of violent and brutal characters, but that those in *The Age of Innocence* are the most brutal of them all.

Despite the obvious difference in class, these families correspond precisely to the mobsters in *Mean Streets*, *GoodFellas* and *Casino* and the Zealots in *The Last Temptation of Christ*. They have their own laws which invalidate those of society, and they leave both central and peripheral members in terror of the repercussions and subtle retributions any false move or transgression would invoke. Ellen Olenska comes to America because here she can divorce the Count, but the law of the family overrides the law of the country, and it says she cannot. When someone steps out of line, one goes to the head of the tribe, Henry van der Luyden (Michael Gough), whose position of power is exactly the same as that of the mob bosses in Scorsese's work: Uncle Giovanni in *Mean Streets*, Tommy Como in *Raging Bull*, Paul Cicero in *GoodFellas*, Remo Gaggi in *Casino*, and Frank Costello in *The Departed*. Phrases like: "It's a family matter—maybe it's best settled by the family" seem to take on slightly more sinister overtones here than in Wharton's universe, and when Newland (Daniel Day Lewis) appeals to the van der Luydens on Ellen's behalf, he is told that "if a member of a well-known family is backed by that family, it should be considered final!"

Producer Barbara De Fina has pointed out that Wharton's book is about missed opportunity which is "a perfect subject for Marty," and in that sense Newland is related to Charlie in *Mean Streets*.[34] At the heart of both films is the struggle inside the protagonist of deciding whether to stay in the neighborhood and conform to the stifling but safe rules of the group or to join his lover and move away, thus taking on the wrath of the tribe as well as the frightening responsibility of his own individuation. Both Charlie and Newland ultimately prove to be incapable of making an active choice to leave.

Likewise significant are the similarities between *The Age of Innocence* and *Cape Fear*. Newland Archer is closely related to Sam Bowden, and—however outrageous it sounds—Ellen Olenska has a number of things in common with Max Cady. Both films concern family members who appear happy together until a disreputable and embarrassing stranger, whom they would prefer to leave locked up and forgotten in the dungeon of the past, suddenly turns up out of nowhere. Like Cady, Ellen brings disruption. With her mere presence this outsider draws attention to their flaws and weak spots, and thus makes the group feel threatened and invaded. Their surface starts cracking up until they manage to oust the intruder.

The Age of Innocence opens with a stunning title sequence designed by Saul and Elaine Bass, again, as in *Cape Fear*, consisting of intricate layers. The main images are red and yellow flowers—seen through pages from a book on etiquette and a veil of lace—that open into full bloom. The fact that the images are layered indicates that so, too, is the reality the film is going to depict. The book on etiquette reflects the rules and arbitrary signs of the tribe while the flowers connote a natural sensuality which forms a marked contrast to these rules. Depending on our point of view, the flowers that open up to display their innermost core as a contrast to the rigidity of the book, point toward either a shameless, vulgar exhibitionism or an honest, beautiful authenticity.

We cut from the abstract space of the titles to the Academy of Music. The first thing we see is a strangely artificial love scene between a man and a woman, and gradually we realize that they are part of the opera that the main characters of the film attend. The fact that the film opens on the stage suggests that the story will be about violent and passionate emotions that are acted out in a ritual way. The title sequence was scored by the introduction to Charles François Gounod's *Faust*, and that classic story of a man's mythical struggle with Lucifer, with his own shadow, is indeed what the characters of our film are watching. By implication then, *The Age of Innocence* picks up exactly where *Cape Fear* left off.

"They never knew what it meant to be tempted. But you did. You understood," Countess Olenska (Michelle Pfeiffer) says to Newland Archer (Daniel Day-Lewis) in *The Age of Innocence* (Columbia Pictures, 1993).

At the center of the film is Newland Archer's reluctant learning process, and Ellen Olenska's function is quite similar to Cady's function for Sam Bowden. Although Cady is horrifying and Ellen is one of Scorsese's few completely sympathetic characters, both of them have been "beyond" and seen things other people have not. "I'm sure I'm dead and buried and this dear old place is heaven," Ellen says the first time we see her, implying a metaphorical death and rebirth similar to the one Cady underwent in prison. They are both unwanted by people who do not want to hear the truth. Ellen's presence seems to threaten the "smooth hypocrisies" and causes as much fear and agitation as that of Cady. They both act as a kind of Jiminy Cricket to the protagonist (and to anyone else who dares to pay attention) whispering his moral shortcomings into his ear, and reminding him that there are sides of himself he has been ignoring which he should perhaps listen to and learn from.

From the beginning there are strong indications that the perfect surface is nothing but a defense against the fascinating but frightening things that are going on underneath it. As in all of Scorsese's works, it soon becomes obvious that the "lights and music and revelry above" cannot completely hide the dungeon, and that the ones who break the rigid rules are well acquainted with the road that leads to it.[35]

When we enter the Beaufort house for the annual ball right after the opera scene, we do so through long, mysterious hallways that turn out to lead to something forbidden, namely the crimson drawing room where Julius Beaufort (Stuart Wilson) has had "the audacity to hang in plain sight" William-Adolphe Bouguereau's scandalous erotic painting "Return of Spring." In the same scene we are told that old Mr. Sillerton Jackson (Alec McGowan) carries "a register of the scandals and mysteries that had smoldered under the unruffled surface of society for the last fifty years." The things that were carefully locked away, and which are flaunted by the unwelcome intruder, clearly have to do with sexuality and passion. This world is "precariously balanced," we are told, and from the start Madame Olenska, like Max Cady, is associated with the disruptive and uncontrollable "prisoners or buried ones" that may come out of the dungeon at any moment to stir up the surface.[36]

The Countess is explicitly associated with tombs and dungeons no less than five times within the first few minutes. In the opening scene, she says she feels as though she has been "dead and buried." A few minutes later we are told that her secret is a "buried treasure" which old Mr. Sillerton Jackson "hastened to excavate." The Count has "kept her practically a prisoner" and her existence in New York is referred to with the word "entombment." Newland asks Sillerton Jackson during their first conversation about her, "Why should we bury a woman alive?" It is thus suggested from the beginning that on a symbolic level Ellen Olenska, like Max Cady, is on a mission to disrupt the precarious balance and in the process educate one or more of the other characters. This is emphasized by the fact that all through the film she is associated with the color red which, as usual, signifies vocation and passion but also pain and potential danger.

From the very first she provokes Newland. She says in the theater that she can still picture all the people she used to know when she was a young girl "the same way, dressed in knickerbockers and pantalettes." She brings them down to size as well as pointing out that even then they were hiding behind a persona of conformity while she — in her unusual clothes that we are told about later — was the only one who stood out from the crowd. She is introduced as a nemesis who remembers things about which they are embarrassed and who is not afraid to say them out loud. She moves on from the general deflation and singles out Newland's carefully concealed secrets: once when they played together, she says, he kissed her *behind a door*.

Madame Olenska consistently breaks the unwritten rules of this society. At first we have the impression that maybe she does so out of ignorance. When Henry van der Luyden invites her to the dinner party for the Duke so as to reprimand those who have snubbed her, she arrives late, signaling, says the narrator, a "carelessness of which she was entirely *unaware.*" The narrator laughs a little when saying the last word, however, as if it is not necessarily true, and since Ellen is neither ignorant nor frivolous there has to be some other reason for this provocation. After dinner the Countess transgresses again: she leaves the company of one man and walks across the room to talk to another, Newland — and now the narrator leaves little room for doubt about the conscious intention behind this act: "The countess did not *observe* this rule," she says. Immediately afterwards Louisa van der Luyden sends over her husband to "rescue" Newland from Ellen. When Newland gets up, Ellen looks him straight in the eye with unmistakable impertinence: "Tomorrow, then. After five. I'll expect you!"

In *After Hours* and *Alice Doesn't Live Here Anymore* the protagonist falls into a dark hole, is faced with a number of strange characters and forced to grow and change. *Cape Fear* and *The Age of Innocence* show the reverse picture: a strange character crawls out from inside that rabbit hole in order to bring about growth and change, primarily for Sam and Newland, but also collectively. Toward the end of *Cape Fear*, Cady said he was Virgil who had come to lead Sam through Hell. As Dante is getting ready to move on from Purgatory and the Inferno to Paradise in *The Divine Comedy*, Virgil takes leave of him in order to let someone greater than himself be Dante's guide for the rest of his journey. That someone turns out to be Dante's beloved Beatrice, one of the great anima figures in Western literature. Similarly, Cady disappears at the end of *Cape Fear* to leave room for the Countess Olenska at the beginning of *The Age of Innocence*. Both are a guide for the protagonist through his reluctant individuation, and like Virgil and Beatrice, they signify different aspects of Sam and Newland and their societies.

Usually in art and in dreams the shadow is manifested as being of the same sex as the protagonist or dreamer. Although Ellen Olenska comes from the shadow, she represents Newland Archer's anima, his feminine side. Where Cady was best explained by scrutinizing Sam's inner dungeon, Ellen is best explained by contrasting her not with Newland but with the women of the tribe and particularly Newland's fiancée May Welland (Winona Ryder).

Like many of Scorsese's films, *The Age of Innocence* is about the use and abuse of power. The subgroup this film concerns is to a great extent defined and controlled by women. Their hands, an ancient symbol of power and authority, are modeled in clay and immortalized by a sculptor in Paris, we are told more than once. This recalls the modeled hands in the bedroom of Mrs. Bates which manipulate and wield power long after she herself is gone. Although May appears innocent, she rules her world and Newland with an iron hand. Our attention is drawn to the fact that she is a master at archery. It is a game of which she is in complete control, which is interesting since Newland's last name is Archer. This girl-woman may seem fragile and delicate, but like the lily of the valley with which she and her betrothal to Newland are associated, she is actually poisonous and potentially deadly.

Because Newland's tribe is defined by women, it makes sense psychologically, mythologically and spiritually that the counter-energy and potential antidote needs to be a woman, too. Newland's is not merely a choice between two different women, May Welland and Ellen Olenska, but between what each woman represents inside himself: the conformity of the group whose rules leave the individual free from making choices on the one hand, and personal responsibility, wholeness, authenticity, and true freedom on the other.

Throughout the film, the differences between May and Ellen are illustrated by means of colors, landscapes and the elements. In Wharton's book the two women and the differences between them are described with fairy-tale–like simplicity: One is a pure, untouched *girl*

The innocent-looking girl-woman, May Welland (Winona Ryder), with her lethally poisonous lilies of the valley, sent to her every day by her fiancée, Newland Archer (Daniel Day-Lewis), in *The Age of Innocence* (Columbia Pictures, 1993).

with blonde hair, the other is a *lady*, pale and dark, who has mysterious secrets and tempts the protagonist away from innocence. The fact that the color of their hair has been switched around in Scorsese's film adds complexity. Ellen is associated with red, fire, ice, and the ocean — all signifying violent and deep emotions as well as potential danger. Often when Newland is with her, or imagines a future with her, he is standing in front of a fireplace, and at one point she lights her own cigarette and then Newland's, literally offering him fire. She exists in a universe of overwhelming and forceful natural landscapes.

May's landscapes are superficial, restrained, and man-made. When Newland goes to see Ellen at the van der Luyden cottage, she is standing in an open, snow-covered landscape, wearing a blood-red velvet coat. When in the next scene he goes to Florida to see May, it is still mid-winter, but she is in an artificial and unnaturally spring-like garden, wearing a white dress, which suggests a purity and innocence that turns out to be as deceptive and false as the landscape, and therefore much more dangerous than what Ellen openly represents. Perhaps May's niceness, Newland thinks was just "a curtain dropped in front of an emptiness." Ellen is authentic to herself and her beliefs and on a deeper level possesses a purity that goes far beyond May's manipulative innocence which is based on repressing the truth.

Newland Archer has many things in common with Sam Bowden, and the process he reluctantly goes through likewise has to do with his inability to accept responsibility for his life. Already in the second scene we are told that he enjoys people who challenge conformity, but that he himself upholds traditions because it is easier. This split predicts his becoming torn between Ellen — the rebellious outsider who cries and speaks the truth freely, who is creative and unconventional and dark — and May — the ultimate representative of the safe but silently manipulative and restrictive world. Like Sam, Newland is a lawyer and has a tendency toward fence-sitting rather than making firm commitments. The fact that he finds rebellion so thrilling and yet sticks with the conventions out of convenience makes him somewhat of a hypocrite, even compared with May who actually believes in the rules of this rigid society. Newland offers the shocking opinion to Mr. Sillerton Jackson that perhaps women should have the same rights as men, yet at the same time he chooses May, the girl who "hadn't the dimmest notion that she was not free" over Ellen, the woman who believes that her freedom is more important than the scandal her divorce might cause.

Behind his facile opinions Newland's view of women is quite similar to that of Scorsese's other male characters. There was, says the narrator in the novel, an "abysmal distinction between the woman one loved and respected and those one enjoyed — and pitied."[37] In the film, May tells Newland that maybe he should reconsider their wedding plans if there is someone else he ought to marry instead. He tells Ellen that that is ridiculous. "Why?" Ellen asks. "Because there is no other woman?" "No," he answers, "because I don't mean to *marry* anyone else." This leaves one wondering what, in fact, he does intend with her.

The lilies of the valley that Newland sends to May every day comment on their relationship, as do the yellow roses he sends to Ellen. Like Sam Bowden who *almost* has an affair, Newland has neither the courage to leave Ellen alone nor to make the unequivocal statement of sending red roses (the way Beaufort does). Even more cowardly, he removes his card and sends them anonymously. Where the lilies of the valley become the emblem of May's lethally false innocence, the yellow roses signify Newland's hypocrisy and cowardice.

Newland's choice between the two women and what each represents in himself is not completely unlike the choice Christ and Dobie have to make. May represents the restrictive femininity of domesticity and manipulates him into making the choices *she* wants. The Countess represents the wild and strong, but also tortured and isolated, femininity of vocation, and she insists that he make his *own* choices. When Madame Olenska appears into his life he is forced to choose between the expectations and conformity of the tribe and his individual identity and freedom, the point being that the responsibility for this is his and his alone. Ellen cannot go through the individuation process and become an authentic individual for him, nor will he automatically do so just by choosing her over May.

Symbolically, Ellen's primary mission is to bring about change in Newland's life on the individual level, but she has the same potential as an anima for all the men in this society. However rigidly the women observe the rules and arbitrary signs, the men are shown to be even more uniform. In the scene at the opera, they are all wearing white gardenias in their lapels, a conformity which is confirmed moments later at the Beaufort ball when Newland leaves his gloves on a table with rows upon rows of identical white gloves. The provocative Beaufort is presumably the only one whose gloves are not on the table since he lives there.

The narrator says that Newland felt as if he was being "buried alive under his future," and on his honeymoon he realizes that gradually May will wear down all the rough edges, the parts of himself "he most wanted to keep." At the heart of both novel and film is the idea of men who used to have dreams and visions and who have more or less willingly acquiesced to having their individuality removed in the name of holy matrimony. In Wharton's book Newland wonders if his father-in-law, too, had visions that were wonderful and frightening in his youth and maybe he "conjured up all the hosts of domesticity to defend himself against them."[38]

Ellen is unforgivably shocking to this society because she does not conform, she has kept her rough edges, and she offers the men a glimpse of what they are losing or have lost. The discrepancy between faceless conformity and passionate dreams is crystallized toward the end in a beautiful and painful scene. Newland takes leave of Ellen in Boston and we dissolve to a group of anonymous men, Newland being one of them, walking down a windy street in slow motion, holding onto completely identical bowler hats. Contrapuntally, and overlapping from the previous scene, we hear Enya singing "Marble Halls," a song filled with passionate, archetypal dream images belonging in the past.

Madame Olenska is constantly connected with the past — not just the recent past in which the others would prefer to leave her buried and forgotten, but the distant, mythological and archetypical past of the collective unconscious. The objects and unusually shaped paintings of desert landscapes in her mysterious, dark house — "little pieces of wreckage," as she calls them — bespeak a forceful, dramatic, ancient femininity. She associates with dramatic artists, and the only people who really appreciate her company and what she has to offer are the Blenkers, a family whose male head is an archeologist. This connection between the Countess and the timeless and unavoidable archetypal elements culminates in the lighthouse scene in which Newland sees her again for the first time after his marriage. Mrs. Manson Mingott (Miriam Margolyes), the formidable and rebellious matriarch, sends him down to the beach to find Ellen. As he approaches, he sees the breathtaking vision of her staring out over the ocean as the sun is setting. Instead of taking responsibility, he makes a deal with himself and leaves his future up to fate: if she turns around before a boat has passed the lighthouse, he will go to her; if not, he will go back and say he could not find her. On his way down to the beach, seeing Ellen again reminds him that some children have found ancient paintings in a cave in Tuscany. He compares Ellen to those ancient images, buried in the past and yet always there staring down at us. Their faces cannot be ignored, they will pop up and stare us in the eye no matter how much we try to repress, ignore or bury them.

This eternal, haunting past is contrasted with the superficial era of May Welland and her tribe. They are the members of a dying breed which, as May's name connotes, *may well end*. The difference is illustrated in the scene in which Newland and Ellen meet at the museum. As we enter we see in the foreground an artifact that is labeled "Use unknown." Like the perfect, fashionable surface of May's society, it had no real lasting value, and some day soon the mores of this society, too, will be extinct and their meaning forgotten. In the background, however, there are mummies, again suggesting burial and something timeless and perhaps a bit frightening, which will last and cannot be ignored and forgotten in the long run.

In the course of the film, Newland becomes interested in mysterious and exotic things that represent the same values as Ellen. His personal process can be measured by paying attention to his study, the one room in the house which is his more than May's. Like Ellen's home, it is dark and mysterious. He has pictures of pyramids on the walls and starts reading about Japan, something that leaves May totally mystified. At one point he feels stifled when May is in his room, and he opens a window and leans out into the snow. Since snow is connected with Ellen (and something May travels to get away from), he essentially leans into and lets in Ellen's power and energy. May gently but commandingly tells him to close it or he will catch his death. He obeys and then realizes that he is already dead and has been for some time.

When Ellen Olenska arrives at the beginning, Newland, like Sam Bowden, is given a chance to break out of the hypocrisy of his life and work toward authenticity. When she leaves at the end (after May lies to her about a pregnancy), the last thing Ellen does, significantly, is to return the *key* that Newland has given her, metaphorically leaving him alone with the responsibility for his life. The question at the end, as at the end of *Cape Fear*, is whether the protagonist has been able to accept the gift the intruder has given him, and has learned and developed. Certainly at the point halfway through the film when he decides to go to Ellen only if she turns around before the boat has passed the lighthouse, he has not learned very much about assuming responsibility, and repeatedly after that he chooses to let May manipulate him as opposed to making his own choices and being true to himself. "The worst of doing one's duty," Wharton has Newland think, "was that it apparently unfitted one for doing anything else."[39]

Toward the end, the narrator sums up Newland's life from the time Ellen was finally eradicated by the tribe until the present day. It is now the dawn of the 20th century and May has been dead for some time. He is looking back at his choices, and even now, it seems, he is still vacillating. Even though he has sincerely loved May, he has never really been able to actively choose his life with her, and Ellen has become the "complete vision of all that he had missed." He has put the Countess on a pedestal, reducing her to a life-long fantasy, so that he can endure his self-deceptive life. He has been incapable of dealing with her as the authentic and admirable person she is, and by projecting his anima as well as the gold of his shadow onto her, he has prevented himself from embracing and assimilating these valuable elements in his own unconscious.

The final scene is ambiguous. A new century with less rigid moral standards has begun. May is dead and Newland, as he thinks to himself at the Louvre, is only 57. At the end he is sitting in front of Madame Olenska's apartment building in Paris, after his adult son (Robert Sean Leonard) has gone upstairs to visit her. He still seems frozen in resignation and passivity. He looks up at her window as a servant with white gloves closes it. In the brief flash of the setting sun reflected in the window pane, Newland once again sees the haunting image of Ellen in front of the lighthouse. This time she turns around and smiles at him, and he gets up from the bench and leaves the little square.

This ending indicates two diametrically opposite things. Maybe Newland decides that he would still rather keep the projection, the immaculate vision of Ellen, than have to deal with the real woman (who has aged), and so he gets up and leaves, in which case he has still learned absolutely nothing. Or maybe he is finally ready to take on the arduous task of his own individuation, and what we see is his release as he withdraws his projection, gives up Ellen as a love object, and instead embraces the sides of himself that she represents, the gold in his shadow and his glorious anima who turns around to greet him.

The Countess Olenska is one of Scorsese's few genuinely sympathetic and admirable characters, and she synthesizes several of his characters as well as reflect himself as a director. Like Max Cady she is on a mission to teach the protagonist things about himself that he has been refusing to see. Like the Dalai Lama she is sent into exile because the truths she holds are too unsettling. Like the uncontrollable nemeses in Scorsese's work, from Johnny Boy in *Mean Streets* to Nicky in *Casino*, she refuses to be subdued regardless of the price she has to pay. Interestingly, in connection with *The Last Temptation of Christ* and *Life Lessons*, Ellen is the temptress as well as the very embodiment of vocation. As in those two films, the only union between the lovers that is harmonious and free from torture, takes place in a dream sequence as Newland imagines Ellen embracing him in the van der Luyden cottage. She is connected with Scorsese's Magdalene when Newland bends down and kisses her foot, while on the soundtrack we hear her voice: "They never knew what it meant to

Martin Scorsese with Michelle Pfeiffer as Ellen Olenska in *The Age of Innocence* (Columbia Pictures, 1993), one of Scorsese's many alter egos. Ellen's words to Newland perfectly capture the essence of Scorsese's work and our resistance to it: "Does no one here want to know the truth?"

be tempted. But you did. You understood." In effect what Ellen Olenska tries to do is to tempt Newland *away from* domesticity and toward more exciting, creative and authentic parts of himself.

During the coach ride back from the railway station in Edith Wharton's novel, Newland commends the Countess: "I think you're the most honest woman I ever met!... You look at things as they are." She explains that she has paid an exorbitant price for that, describing the frightening inner country "beyond" that she has been to and lived in: "I've had to look at the Gorgon," she says. "She opened my eyes, too; it's a delusion to say that she blinds people. What she does is just the contrary — she fastens their eyelids open, so that they're never again in the blessed darkness. Isn't there a Chinese torture like that? There ought to be."[40]

The notion of someone who forces us to open our eyes to things we may not want to acknowledge and thus excludes us permanently from the darkness of innocent self-deception is so familiar in Scorsese's work that the lines do not have to be spoken explicitly in his adaptation of the novel. All through his career he has invented characters who have done just that, so in a sense Scorsese, too, is a kind of Gorgon, albeit of a more well-intentioned and constructive variety. Like several of Scorsese's characters, Ellen does not fit in with her surroundings. She is condemned to the unenviable and painful position of being "on the outside looking in," as Scorsese once said about himself.[41] Like Scorsese, Ellen Olenska refuses to give up her authenticity, even though the people around her may not want to hear what she has to say. That courageous position is one she pays for dearly, and Michelle Pfeiffer's profound portrayal of the Countess is suffused with passion and suffering, the price she has had to pay for her chosen path. Her question to Newland when he wants her to stop crying is a fitting question to all those who resist Scorsese's works: "Does no one here want to know the truth?"

Bringing Out the Dead

Bringing Out the Dead (1999) is the story of Frank Pierce (Nicolas Cage), a paramedic for the New York Emergency Medical Service who works the graveyard shift. It is based on a novel by Joe Connelly (who acted as technical advisor on the film), and it takes place in the early 1990s, before Mayor Giuliani cleaned up the city. From the beginning it is clear that the horror and misery Frank witnesses on a daily basis is beginning to take its toll and he is on the verge of a breakdown. Lots of people can handle the job as a paramedic, says Connelly, who was one himself for a decade. What he wanted, however, was to describe what happens when you "have somebody like Frank, who has absolutely no walls between him and the suffering — who feels everything."[42] Interestingly, this sounds very similar to what United Artists executive David Field said of Scorsese, with whom he worked on *Raging Bull*: "Suddenly I had this clear vision of Marty as a man born without enough skin. Everything came in at him at incredibly full strength, at a level of reality most of us screen out. I wanted to weep for who he was, and the courage it took for him to simply live any given day, given the fact that's how the universe hit him. And I just thought I was in the presence of this extraordinarily heroic man."[43] Frank Pierce may not look it, but he, too, is heroic, and he is certainly the kindest of all Scorsese's fictional protagonists.

The script for *Bringing Out the Dead* was written by Paul Schrader, with whom Scorsese had collaborated on *Taxi Driver*, *Raging Bull*, and *The Last Temptation of Christ*. Schrader's work, he himself has said, often uses occupational metaphors. During most of *Bringing Out the Dead* we drive through the streets of New York at night with a man who cannot sleep and is on the edge of physical and mental burnout induced by his experiences on those streets. This has led many critics to compare the film to *Taxi Driver* and Frank Pierce to Travis Bickle, but on deeper levels he is much closer to the central characters of the other two Scorsese/Schrader collaborations. He may be on the brink of psychosis, but his basic personality is extremely different from Travis's. Travis is sure that God has entrusted him with a mission; Frank feels that God has taken His hand off him. Where Travis "perpetuates his own loneliness," Frank wants "to be with somebody," says Schrader.[44] Travis's anger is directed outwards and makes him explode in violence against his surroundings; Frank implodes because of his harrowing sense of guilt and responsibility over the suffering and deaths of others. His anguish, like Jake La Motta's, is masochistically turned inwards.

Some critics have seen the film as a social and political critique, but the fact that it is set almost a decade before it was made speaks against that. Even though the fictional Our Lady of Perpetual Mercy Hospital (nicknamed "Perpetual Misery") looks so real that people kept coming in for treatment during the shooting of the film, the squalor and hideousness of Hell's Kitchen are used for purposes other than mainly realistic and political ones. "The hospital is just a base," says Scorsese, "the story is really outside on the street, and in Frank's head — *the journey that he takes*."[45]

Like most of Scorsese's work, *Bringing Out the Dead* is a mythological and spiritual story. When Frank drives through the city, he calls to mind Dante on the voyage through the levels of the Inferno in *The Divine Comedy*, and the streets of Manhattan can once again be likened to the River Styx that leads to Hades. Frank has to endure the dark night of the soul, and "there is an element of grace," says Scorsese, when "he has to come through to the other side of the night."[46] During 56 hours — a "weekend of full moons"— we share Frank's pain and disintegration. This time span corresponds to the Easter Triduum — the three days of the Passion, Crucifixion and Resurrection of Christ — as well as to the period during which Dante traveled through the realms of the dead on *his* journey to the other side of the night, symbolized by the sun behind the mountain.

The first thing we see as the film begins is a car on which is written the word "ecnalubma." On a realistic level this is, of course, so that drivers can read the word "ambulance" in their rearview mirror, but like the legendary "mooreeffoc" it instantly evokes the other side of the mirror. "Mooreeffoc" is merely "coffee-room" as viewed from the inside of a glass door by Dickens on a dark day in London's St. Martin's Lane. Later G.K. Chesterton used the word "to denote the queerness of things that have become trite, when they are seen suddenly from a new angle," as J.R.R. Tolkien explains, and it serves to remind us to be humble about the world that lies beyond our automatic, immediate perception.[47] This linguistic distortion immediately propels us into Frank's warped mind and escalating physical, mental and spiritual fatigue, and (as in *Taxi Driver*) we cut from the car to an extreme close-up of his burned-out eyes.

"I was good at my job: there were periods where my hands moved with a speed and skill beyond me," Frank says in voice-over. He also compares saving lives to the work of God: "You wonder if you've become immortal, as if you saved your own life as well. What was once criminal and happenstance suddenly makes sense. God has passed through you, why deny it, that for a moment there, God was you." But things have changed because "in the last year I had started to lose that control. Things had turned bad. I hadn't saved anyone in months." Resentful spirits have started haunting him, not even waiting for him to go to sleep anymore, and "it was impossible to pass a building that didn't hold the ghost of something." More than anything, it is the memory of Rose, an 18-year-old, asthmatic, homeless girl he failed to save six months ago, that torments Frank. As the film progresses, her face gradually takes over, erasing the faces of the living. She has become the composite image of all the people he has lost; an emblem of the intense guilt that is eating him up, and increasingly Frank looks as ghostly and tormented as the people he believes have come back to accuse him.

The film is pervaded with religious imagery. Frank's face is lit so that he resembles a Christian medieval icon. At the beginning of his journey through the night he resurrects Patrick Burke, an elderly man who has been dead for ten minutes, the way that Jesus resurrected Lazarus. The hospital is called Our Lady of Perpetual Mercy. Frank went to a school called Holy Cross, Patrick's daughter, Mary Burke (Patricia Arquette), went to Sacred Heart, and at their childhood pizzeria they would get plastic figurines of the Madonna or St. Anthony on top of their pizza. Many of the names have religious significance: Frank invokes St. Francis of Assisi; Noel means Christmas; Mary and the Puerto Rican girl Maria (who gives birth to immaculately conceived twins) recall the Holy Virgin — a powerful anima figure. So, symbolically, does Rose, since the rose signifies virginity, and the Holy Virgin is often depicted in the branches of a rose bush.

The number three is repeated throughout the film, especially in connection with time. Mary has not spoken to her father for three years; the crazy, homeless Noel (Marc Anthony) spent three months in a coma after he was shot, and Frank's journey into darkness takes place over three consecutive nights, each markedly different from the others. Three is always significant in connection with the hero path: there are three thresholds to cross, *The Divine Comedy* consists of three canticas containing 33 cantos each, and three invokes the Holy Triduum of the Passion. In a Catholic context the number represents "all that there is, or at least enough," which is why, says one scholar, "Christ was three days in the tomb: he was there enough time."[48]

On each of the three nights, Frank has a different co-driver whose personality — along with the increasingly frenetic aesthetics — reflects Frank's state of mind and the stages of his decomposition. The first night he drives with the detached and lethargic Larry (John Goodman) who copes with their stressful occupation by means of denial and overeating. On the second night his co-driver is Marcus (Ving Rhames), a flamboyant, fatalistic gospel-style Christian who seems to understand what Frank is going through and to have been there himself. He tries to convince Frank that his guilt serves no purpose and to convey a spiritual message similar to the one Jesus tried to convey to Judas in *The Last Temptation of Christ*: "You can't change what's out there, only where you're coming from. So you gotta let the Lord — thank you, Jesus — take over, in here," he says pointing to his heart. On the third night Frank is beginning to grin like a man possessed and things are getting even more frenzied, paralleling the fury of his partner, the totally unhinged Tom Walls (Tom Sizemore). Time-lapse photography streaks the colors, and the ambulance is shot in fast-motion with wild tilts that turn the image upside down. Walls uses violence and abuse to cope with the stress, and he confides to Frank that he has often tried to exterminate the ambulance: "This old bus is a warrior, Frank, just like us. I have tried to kill him many times and he will not die. I have a great respect for that."[49]

7. *Paying Out the Shadow*   173

During a weekend of full moons, Mary Burke (Patricia Arquette) accompanies Frank Pierce (Nicholas Cage) on several steps of his voyage through the dark night of the soul in *Bringing Out the Dead* (Touchstone Pictures, 1999).

In *The Last Temptation of Christ*, Jesus gave in to the temptation of Satan and stepped down from the cross in order to assuage the excruciating torment of his vocation. Frank similarly tries to evade the pain of his voyage through the darkness. He repeatedly attempts to persuade his co-drivers to abort their trips and go back to the hospital, and twice he pleads with his captain to fire him. During the second night, Marcus urges him on, assuring him that quitting will not stop the ghosts and the agony.

At the beginning of the third night Frank is getting desperate and injects himself with a "vitamin B cocktail, followed by an amp of glucose and a drop of adrenaline." A few minutes later when Tom says, "Our mission: to save lives!" Frank is already in need of further stimulants: "Our mission is coffee, Tom!" he responds. "El Toro de Oro," Tom says triumphantly, as if somehow those words hold the key to the mystery of life itself. "El Toro de Oro" turns out to be the place where they get their coffee, but additional significance is suggested by the name. Considering the multitude of religious symbols in the film, it seems appropriate to assume that "the golden bull" might allude to the false idol in Exodus, a sacrificial calf made out of gold which Aaron fashioned for the Israelites and which they worshiped until Moses returned from Mount Sinai with the Ten Commandments and found them in a drunken orgy.

The film is pervaded by substance abuse, and the receiving nurse at the hospital keeps reprehending the patients: "You say you've been snorting cocaine for three days and now you feel as if your heart is beating too fast and you would like us to help you. Well, to tell you the truth, I don't see why I should.... Did we sell you the cocaine? Did we push it up your nose?" Under other circumstances addiction to coffee would probably not be considered a big deal, but in *Bringing Out the Dead* this stimulant is referred to with the words: "It's time to just say no!" which traditionally is associated with hard drugs. The word "coffee" is used again and again, and never just in passing. "We like our coffee *bloody*," Tom says, and Frank can hardly wait to get to El Toro de Oro so he can have his fix. So intense is his need for caffeine that he uses it as his excuse for screaming at an old homeless man who has just tried to commit suicide: "I told you to stop for coffee," he says to Walls. He tells Larry he cannot eat until he has had coffee, i.e., he is incapable of taking in nourishment until his craving has been satisfied. "Whiskey and coffee," Larry replies. "Lucky you ain't dead with that diet." When they arrive to rescue drug dealer Cy Coates (Cliff Curtis) who is impaled on a railing, he asks what took them so long, and Frank answers, "I was tired. I needed a coffee."

The Golden Calf and false idol in *Bringing Out the Dead* is indeed the abuse of addictive drugs, each one of which is addressed explicitly, repeatedly, and at length: caffeine, nicotine, alcohol, marihuana, pills, cocaine, heroin, and Cy Coates's new designer drugs, Red Lion and Red Death.[50] We have seen repeatedly in Scorsese's work how counterproductive and even dangerous it is to give in to Satan's temptation: the easy quick fix that alleviates the torment of the journey through the dark night of the soul. Once you have started down the transformational hero path of change, you cannot cheat your way out of the inmost cave, and worshipping whatever will get you through the night comfortably numb will only make the voyage longer and more agonizing. In the final analysis, the only thing that will appease the shadow — the monsters and the ghosts that haunt you — is completing the entire journey one step at a time, finally facing them, acknowledging that they are a part of you, and listening to what they are trying to tell you.

Frank's attempt to ease the pain and the motif of the false god of drugs, culminates between the second and the third night when he visits The Oasis, the apartment and outlet of Cy Coates. The illness and impending death of her father becomes too overwhelming for Mary, so she goes back to the dealer from her past. Frank follows her and is welcomed by the smoothly suave Cy, a Mephisthophelean man who is simultaneously revolting and seductive. He instinctively knows Frank's every thought, particularly his intense need for relief and sleep, and seems genuinely interested in helping him. All he wants, he says, is to relieve suffering, and Frank falls for the temptation and takes the pill he is offered. Rather than making him relax, however, the drug induces frightening hallucinations: Frank sees himself pulling out dead people who are trapped underneath the pavement, and he and Larry helplessly watch Rose die all over again.

Cy's lethal street drug, Red Death, is presumably a reference to Poe's horrifying story "The Masque of the Red Death." The pill Frank is given at The Oasis, on the other hand, is the more exclusive Red Lion. Red Lion is one of the many esoteric names for the philosopher's stone, and so the connotations of this pill — immediate as well as implicit — are much more appealing than those of Red Death. The allure is illusory, however. Coates's business is named Sunrise Enterprises, and what he offers is, in effect, an artificial way of skipping through the dark night so you can reach out for the reward of the sunrise instantly and effortlessly. But in most mythologies if you reach out for the reward, the philosopher's stone or the Holy Grail, before you have faced the monsters of the inmost cave, it will invariably harm and potentially destroy you. Cy Coates pronounces his name "psycho-tssss," and when Frank tries to cheat his way out of the pain of the night, he is catapulted into a psychotic state. As in *The Last Temptation of Christ*, the temptation of instant alleviation for the pain involved in the passion backfires.

When they leave The Oasis, Mary points out that Cy's professed benevolence and empathy is indeed as illusory as Satan's: "You and Cy have a nice talk? He tell you about Sunrise Enterprises, helping people? Well, I've seen him hurt people." So has Frank if he could only remember: on his shift with Larry they picked up a young man who had been shot by Cy's strong-arm man, Tiger, and died on the way to the hospital. Mary also tells Frank the truth about the deranged Noel. We have assumed that he is crazy because of some drug or disease, but actually, Mary says, he was her brother's best friend until Cy put a bullet through his head.

Whereas the slick and handsome Cy represents temptation, depravation and evil incarnate, Noel, the filthy, homeless basket case, may well represent innocence, purity and potential redemption for Frank. Noel is constantly thirsty because, he insists, he just came out of the desert: "For days I've eaten nothing but sand," he laments, "O Lord, I've waited so long." This weirdly dressed outcast calls to mind both Christ and John the Baptist whom St. Matthew describes as wearing "camel's hair and a leathern girdle about his loins" and living off "locusts and wild honey."[51] Noel keeps asking for water but, like Christ on the cross, he is denied. It is, in fact, Noel who marks the turning point and makes Frank's redemption possible.

At the beginning of the film, Frank resurrected Patrick Burke, Mary's father. Like Lazarus in Kazantzakis's *The Last Temptation*, however, Burke is less than enthusiastic over having been brought back from the dead. Toward the end, Frank saves another life when Cy Coates has been impaled on a railing; a vampire motif that again likens Coates to the anti–Christ. As they are cutting him loose, Cy watches the sparks from the acetylene torch which look like fireworks against the night sky and frighteningly he starts chanting: "When the fire starts to fall, then the strongest rule it all." "You saved my life," he says when they get him to the hospital. "I know," Frank tonelessly replies, looking more dejected than ever.

He now feels the need to destroy something, he says, and Tom Walls proposes that they beat up Noel with a baseball bat. In the nick of time Frank comes to his senses and prevents Noel from being battered to a pulp, saving a life *for the third time*. As if this balances the score of having saved Cy, evil incarnate, Frank is ready for his final act of atonement. Although his savior complex is considerably kinder and more benevolent than Travis Bickle's, he has gradually realized that in his obsession with rescuing people, he has been holding on to them more for his own sake than for theirs. During the night Mary's father has died and been resuscitated 14 times, and tried to pull out the tubes whenever he was conscious enough to do so. Now Frank hears the voice of the old man's spirit telling him he has had enough, begging Frank to let him go. Finally, Frank releases Patrick Burke and allows him to die, releasing and redeeming himself in the process.

Frank now goes to Mary's apartment in the early dawn — the real sunrise after the dark night — to tell her that her father is dead. As his reward and final step of coming through the dark night, he is allowed to come to peace with the dead girl, Rose. Mary opens her door, and as Frank is talking to her she has her own voice but Rose's face. Frank asks Mary/Rose to forgive him, and her simple but powerful reply sets him free: "Nobody asked you to suffer," she says, "that was *your* idea." All through the film, Frank has been haunted by these women, Rose and Mary. When the two of them — the dead girl who is haunting him from the inside and the living woman who is stirring him from the outside — fuse into one, the miracle happens. She invites him in and the last thing we see is Mary holding Frank in her arms in the most beautiful Pietà, an image that contains the ultimate surrender as well as the promise of resurrection.[52]

Bringing Out the Dead marks the end of an era in Scorsese's production, and it is probably no coincidence that he felt the need to make this overwhelming film about death and dying shortly after both his parents passed away. Whereas the previous Scorsese characters who stand on the brink of psychosis fall hopelessly into the abyss at the end, Frank does not. He faces his ghosts and ultimately comes to terms with them. Mary Burke seems to be his equal, and the words of wisdom she speaks at the end seem to be addressed not only to Frank, but to most of Scorsese's protagonists, and possibly to Scorsese himself and to many of us, and they help him take the final step and come through to the end of the night.

One of the most important spiritual lessons the young Dalai Lama learns in *Kundun* are the "Four Noble Truths" which likewise propose that a path can be found out of the pain: if we understand that we cause much of our own suffering needlessly, we can have confidence in our ability to end the torment. These simple insights — Mary/Rose's as well as those of the Lord Buddha — argue that by looking deep within ourselves, we can replace our feelings of guilt and suffering with authentic spiritual responsibility for our own life, with peace and with grace. Most of Scorsese's characters might have been better off if someone had told them these words during their grueling resistance toward and struggle with the darkest sides of themselves: "Nobody asked you to suffer. That was *your* idea."

8

To Beat the Devil

> To own one's own shadow is to reach a holy place—an inner center—not attainable in any other way. To fail this is to fail one's own sainthood and to miss the purpose of life.[1]
>
> Robert A. Johnson

Marking the beginning of the New Millennium, Martin Scorsese started a new epoch in his career. Initially his collaboration with actor Leonardo DiCaprio, the superstar teen idol of *Titanic*, may have been frowned upon by many, myself included. But as it turns out their films together have proved to add a surprising depth to Scorsese's work psychologically and mythologically, in no small part thanks to the roles played so passionately by DiCaprio. Their collaboration has given DiCaprio a chance to break out of the restricting public persona induced by his role as Jack Dawson in *Titanic*—being worshiped by billions of pubescent girls all over the world—and instead to prove his astounding range as an actor. For Scorsese it has meant going into new thematic territory and inventing a brand new alter ego. Where *Bringing Out the Dead* marked the end of an era, the DiCaprio films mark the beginning of a new one.

Their three films together in the period from 2002 to 2006 concern coming to terms with the loss of Father. They all start with a significant scene from a male character's childhood; a scene where an encounter with a parental figure leaves a lasting impression on the mind of the child. In *Gangs of New York*, we have a meeting with Father whereas Mother is blatantly missing. In *The Aviator*, Mother instigates the defining moment, and Father is missing. In *The Departed*, a young boy is seduced by a dangerous father figure because both his real parents are missing. Conversely, *Shutter Island* from 2010 concerns the protagonist's having to come to terms with his own failure as a father.

Gangs of New York

In the course of his career, Martin Scorsese has been examining the surfaces and undersurfaces of New York City. In 1970 he discovered Herbert Asbury's classic book *The Gangs of New York* and decided almost instantly that he wanted to make a film based on its accounts of a little known period in the history of lower Manhattan. It would take almost 30 years before he found the backing for the project, and in September 2000 he walked through the gates of Cinecittà—Italy's famous film production complex—and into an astoundingly faithful recreation of the neighborhood of the Five Points of the 1860s which would be the set for his film.

Like so many of Scorsese's films, *Gangs of New York* (2002) is a painstakingly researched historical document as well as a universal, archetypal tale. Many of the characters in the film are based on (or composites of) real people, and many of the events are factual, although occasionally the chronology is changed for the sake of the dramatic and psychological impact of the story. Asbury's book is used as the basis for Scorsese's fictional tale of Amsterdam Vallon (Leonardo DiCaprio), and the account of the 19th century gangs and their territorial battles over the Lower East Side is set against the historical backdrop of the corrupted Boss Tweed of Tammany Hall, the American Civil War and the first Conscription Act, culminating in the Draft Riots in July of 1863.

Gangs of New York traces the origins of the neighborhood in which Martin Scorsese grew up. It shows us the primordial mean streets out of which Little Italy sprang, and it tells a story of organized crime, decades before that term was even invented.[2] The themes are familiar: like so many of Scorsese's films it concerns the codes of the streets, the struggle for territory, male camaraderie, trust and betrayal, and the restrictive safety of the clan versus the necessity of following one's own path. The gangs of the Five Points are the prototype for Scorsese's subcultural groups: they have their own laws that differ from the established laws of the land, some have their own language which no one else understands, and in a precise parallel to the "mook" scene in *Mean Streets*, Amsterdam gets into a fight when someone calls him a "fidlam ben" even though he is not sure precisely what that means.

This film contains interesting allusions to various classical works, and most consistently it echoes Charles Dickens's *Oliver Twist*.[3] Both works concern an orphaned boy (Oliver/Amsterdam) who grows up in the poorhouse, then goes to the big city where he falls in with a gang of thieves led by a mesmerizing potentate and criminal (Fagin/Bill the Butcher). The boy has to learn to resist the temptation of evil and the allure of the brotherhood, and he is aided and defended by the protégée of the despot, a feisty demimondaine (Nancy/Jenny) who saves his life. Both Charles Dickens and Martin Scorsese examine the brutish underbelly of society and the squalor of the 19th century city slums, and both draw parallels between the public evil of society and the private evil in human beings, as personified by Bumble/Tweed on the one hand and Fagin/Bill on the other. Held up against the vast array of fascinating and grotesque secondary characters, Amsterdam Vallon, like the typical Dickensian protagonist, is not necessarily the most interesting person on the canvas, as Roger Ebert has pointed out.

In addition, *Gangs of New York* bears a close resemblance to the tragedies of Aeschylus and Shakespeare. This is the archetypal story of a young man who, like Orestes and Hamlet, feels compelled to avenge the brutal murder of his father. Like Orestes (and Disney's Lion King, Simba) Amsterdam is forced into exile after the death of his father, and for years he gathers strength so that he can go back and settle the score. Like Hamlet, Amsterdam is vague and irresolute, which makes him hesitate and fail when he is close to achieving his goal. The mythological territory he has to venture into is pervaded by the concept of father and masculinity, and on his hero's journey through the realms of Hades, Amsterdam, like Simba and Luke Skywalker, has to face not only his own shadow, but also the dark side that annihilated his father.[4]

On its deepest levels, *Gangs of New York* is a modern myth which addresses one of the most painful traumata of the western world during the past century and a half, namely the loss of Father and the gradual disintegration of the masculine principle. Amsterdam's journey is set in motion by an excruciating Fisher King wound — watching the brutal slaying of his father—which is never healed. Because he is incapable of addressing his pain, he projects it onto the world around him. Consequently, he makes a number of fatal choices during his hero's journey so that he is forced to undertake it not once but twice, as we shall see.

Amsterdam's ordinary world is introduced in the haunting opening scene. We hear a scraping sound over the dark screen, then cut to an extreme close-up of a pair of eyes. A stately man, Priest Vallon (Liam Neeson), is shaving in an underground cavern lit by a single candle. As his son comes out of the shadows to watch him apprehensively, Vallon cuts his cheek determinedly then hands the boy the knife. "No son, never," he says, when Amsterdam wants to wipe it on his jacket. "The blood stays on the blade. One day you'll understand."

This opening has double significance. The sound of shaving is the ultimate sound of father, and because we experience it in extreme close-up—visually and aurally—it makes Amsterdam's bereavement in the following scene acutely palpable. Secondly, the process of shaving obviously has a deeply ritual significance for Priest Vallon that goes far beyond the practical act of beard removal.[5] He is preparing himself for battle, and the razor and the act of cutting himself assumes a sacramental quality on par with putting on his vestments immediately afterwards. We cut to Amsterdam standing on a table. Vallon hangs a medal around the boy's neck depicting the expulsion of Lucifer and prays: "Saint Michael, the

The neighborhood of the Five Points of the 1860s was recreated in Cinecittà in Italy for *Gangs of New York* (Miramax Films, 2002).

Archangel, defend us in battle! Be our protector against the snares and the wickedness of the devil!"[6] He drills the boy, implicating him in the rite: "Now, son, who's that?"

The boy answers: "St. Michael!"

"And what did he do?" Vallon asks.

"He cast Satan out of Paradise!" the boy replies fervently.

A central symbolic structure is introduced here, namely the dichotomy and potential discord involved in the number two. The fact that Amsterdam's journey starts in the underground emphasizes Scorsese's recurring concern with the battle between ego and shadow, and throughout the film we keep returning to images of dark landscapes, basements, sub-basements and catacombs. We encounter numerous antagonistic, irreconcilable pairs. The opposition of Saint Michael and Lucifer foreshadow Priest Vallon and Bill the Butcher (and later Amsterdam and the Butcher) and the constantly fluctuating antipathies between Amsterdam and Johnny, Amsterdam and Jenny, Bill and Boss Tweed, and Bill and Monk. The concept of internecine hostility is further emphasized by the battles between natives and immigrants, North and South, rich and poor.

At the end of the ritual the boy blows out the candle, leaving the cavern in pitch darkness, at which exact moment fifes and drums start playing vigorously. As if carried on the crest of the music, Priest Vallon starts marching up through dark tunnels, holding a Celtic cross in his left hand and his son's hand in his right. The two of them seem to ascend from the pits of Hell, passing people getting ready for combat.

"What's the battle?" asks Johnny, a boy Amsterdam's age.

"Natives against the Dead Rabbits," Amsterdam replies.

"Which are you?" Johnny asks.

"Which do you think?" Amsterdam quips, pointing to the eponymous carcass carried by one of the warriors.

At the gate that leads out of the Old Brewery, Vallon's army encounters Monk (Brendan Gleeson), an imposing man holding a club of mythological proportions whom Vallon is clearly anxious to have on his side. He asks Monk whether he is with them or not, and Monk replies: "For the last time, Vallon, I'm with you if the money is right." After agreeing on a price, Monk rams open the gate with his foot, affecting a transformation that betokens his powerful status in the story: instantly the music stops, and whereas the inferno they came from was dark, dingy, noisy and claustrophobically crowded, Paradise Square outside the door is blindingly bright, snowy, soundless and empty.

Monk takes on several archetypal functions in the course of the film. At this stage he is obviously threshold guardian and warrior. What distinguishes him from everyone else, however, is the fact that — like the wanderer — he is not involved on either side. Like Han Solo at the beginning of *Star Wars* and Aragorn/Strider at the beginning of *The Lord of the Rings*, he keeps a mercenary and apparently selfish distance from the cause. This impression of Monk appears to be reaffirmed when, in the next scene, he bends down over Vallon's dead body, taking what we think is his payment. Only much later does his most significant function become clear when he shapeshifts into the mentor, revealing that what he took from Vallon was not money, but the razor, the magical object that is crucial for Amsterdam's mythological journey.

We pan counterclockwise to the opposite end of Paradise Square and, within moments, the Natives appear under the leadership of William Cutting, a.k.a. Bill the Butcher (Daniel Day-Lewis), armed with axes, knives, and meat cleavers.[7] Historically, the territorial battle

All through *Gangs of New York* (Miramax Films, 2002), Jenny (Cameron Diaz) is shown as the symbolic feminine counterpart of Amsterdam Vallon (Leonardo DiCaprio). At the Mission Ball she picks her king from inside a looking glass.

over the Five Points is ethnic and religious in nature: the Natives, who are of Anglo Dutch Protestant origins, are enraged that "foreign hordes," the more recent Irish Catholic immigrants, are "defiling" the country to which they feel "rightwise born." In an archetypal sense, however, this is a battle between two kings — a dark king and a luminous king — and the battle is not over until one king dies.

It is apposite to see the flamboyant and brazen Butcher as complementary to the pensive and enigmatic Priest. Indeed, they are presented as mirror images. Both are lean, majestic, and considerably taller than the members of their clans. Both wear ankle-length coats; Vallon his cassock and Bill a threadbare but sartorially elegant overcoat. Vallon looks dignified and immaculate; Bill has an animalistic and dilapidated quality. And it now becomes clear that the very first shots we saw of Vallon shaving were, in fact, not Vallon, but his mirror image. We *saw* him cutting his *right* cheek, holding the razor in his left hand, but now we realize that the cut is actually on his *left* cheek. This assumes importance because Bill has a similar cut on his *right* cheek, which we learn later that Vallon inflicted, too. Bill is thus indisputably the embodiment of Vallon's dark mirror image.

The first picture we see of the Butcher is an extreme close-up of his booted feet. He scrapes them and stomps the ground like a bull marking its territory. Where Vallon invoked St. Michael, Bill's feet call to mind the hooves of the Devil. From a wide-shot of Bill, we cut closer three times, ending in an extreme close-up of his left eye which is made out of glass and adorned with the American eagle. If we consider this as a symbolic battle between a man and his mirror image, then in effect the ego/priest/rabbit/luminous king is up against the shadow/butcher/eagle/dark king. In this constellation the dark mirror image, the sides of himself that Vallon has refused to look at, incontrovertibly has the upper hand.[8]

A number of smaller gangs join the Dead Rabbits and the savage battle over the Five Points begins. The boy looks expectant and excited at first, but gradually his expression changes to one of horror and incredulity as he sees his father killing men and finally perishing at the Butcher's hand. He runs to his dying father who urgently whispers the words that will turn out to be the object of Amsterdam's hero's journey: "Oh, my son, don't never look away!"

With the utmost tenderness the Butcher caresses the dying Vallon's head, and in his final moments the good king turns away from his son to face his dark alter ego. Bill takes the knife with which he delivered the coup de grace and puts it on the chest of his slain enemy. "You may need this across the river," he says respectfully, then pronounces his victory and outlaws the Dead Rabbits. "No hand shall touch *him*," he says, pointing to Vallon, when he permits his gang to take bodily trophies from the dead. "He'll cross over whole, in honor."

Amsterdam snatches the Butcher's knife from his father's chest, fends off the Natives, then runs to the underground cavern and buries it along with the medal. This is portentous for various reasons. Bill has just made a mythological assumption that Vallon might need this knife across the river, so when Amsterdam swipes it and buries it, the innocent boy (rather than the Butcher) seems responsible for the ensuing strife since it is he who prevents his father from crossing over in peace. Furthermore, by taking possession of an object that belongs to the Butcher — the weapon that killed his father no less — Amsterdam unconsciously assumes a part of the identity of the dark king. The knife is undoubtedly the magical object this orphan prince needs for his journey, but he takes the dark knife and thus the dark path, rather than Vallon's razor — the true magical knife — which Monk takes into safekeeping.

The camera pulls back to show us the Five Points, then the Lower East Side, then, superimposed over the image: "New York City, 1846." We dissolve and see an adult Amsterdam being released from Hellgate, the House of Reform, on the equally ominously named Blackwell's Island, where he has spent the intervening period.[9] The fact that 16 years have passed in a single dissolve suggests that Amsterdam has grown up instantly and been catapulted into premature adulthood like Scorsese's Alice. The Calvinist minister admonishes him to "forgive," but he angrily tosses the Bible into the river—an act of rebellion which again points to an unconscious rejection of his father, Priest Vallon.

Amsterdam returns to the Five Points, where everything has changed: a civil war is raging and vast hordes of Irish immigrants are flocking into the country. Bill the Butcher is the sovereign ruler, rather than merely a gang leader, and has been invited into an alliance with Tammany Hall. Now Amsterdam has to learn the rules of the extraordinary world and encounter various friends and enemies. He goes to the Old Brewery (now a mission house) and climbs down into the cave to unearth the knife and medal he buried there. Significantly, he *looks into his father's mirror*, asking St. Michael for strength, and instantly his childhood friend Johnny (Henry Thomas) shows up. Just as Johnny appeared when Charlie talked to God in *Mean Streets*, so his namesake here manifests as if in answer to Amsterdam's request. Johnny asks the existential question of Alice's caterpillar—"Who are you?"—and he becomes Amsterdam's most important ally during the first part of the journey. He teaches Amsterdam the new rules, tells him about the annual commemoration of the victory over Priest Vallon, and enables him to make plans for avenging his father.

The approach to the inmost cave begins, but before long Amsterdam's objective is obscured by obstacles. With Johnny's help he is able to enter into the very core of the Butcher's existence, his appositely named lair, Satan's Circus. He manages to impress Bill with bravado and enterprise, and the Butcher—not knowing Amsterdam's true identity—quickly warms to the personable youth and makes him his "young associate" and apprentice. The closer Amsterdam gets to the Butcher, however, the more jealous Johnny becomes. The reticent and compliant Johnny is hurt by "Father's" preference for the returned "prodigal son," and it only adds insult to injury when Amsterdam and Jenny (Cameron Diaz) become attracted to each other. Johnny is obviously head over heels in love with the charming and insolent pickpocket and even risks his life to pilfer a music box for her from at burning house. He confides his feelings to Amsterdam, but Amsterdam heedlessly allows Jenny to make a move on him.

By now it is evident that we are in familiar Scorsese territory. In addition to a troubled relationship between symbolic brothers and a father figure, we have a beautiful blonde who becomes the catalyst for the animosity between two men. The conflicts between irreconcilable pairs are taken over by more complex and opaque triangles as 3 replaces 2 as the central symbolic number, and Amsterdam's helper and ally becomes his foe.

Amsterdam's internal ambivalence makes matters worse. Not only is Bill taken with *him*, he gradually becomes drawn to Father's dark counterpart as well. The Butcher has made a shrine to Priest Vallon and still speaks reverently of his enemy and mirrored twin. "I killed the last honorable man 15 years ago," he says to Amsterdam. "The Priest and me lived by the same principles. It was only faith that divided us." In a pivotal scene, the Butcher teaches Amsterdam how to kill with a knife, illustrating on a pig's carcass. We cut to flashback shots as Amsterdam remembers how his father once performed a ritual with a knife which he then handed him. When Amsterdam accepts the knife the Butcher offers him he allows himself, symbolically, to be adopted, and Father's shadow becomes his new father. "Funny feeling being took under the wing of a dragon," he muses. "It is warmer than you might think." By passively allowing this to happen, he takes a wrong turn in the maze of the hero's journey, leaving himself stuck between wanting revenge on the one hand and craving the love of the dark father on the other. Hubristically, he tries to travel both roads and fails miserably.

His Hamlet-like confusion culminates at the midpoint of the film when an assassin attempts to kill the Butcher during a performance of *Uncle Tom's Cabin* at the Bowery Theatre. With lightning-speed reflex, Amsterdam jumps forward and averts the murder. Bill is understandably thrilled and proud of his apprentice, but the boy is panic-stricken and leaves to be alone with his conflicting emotions: Did he instinctively save the life of his sworn enemy so that he himself can kill him at the commemoration of Priest Vallon's death, or was his reaction motivated by actual feelings for the dark father? At this exact moment, Monk steps out of the darkness and sneers contemptuously, "That was bloody Shakespearean out there!" His comment is cloaked in humor (apparently he thinks Shakespeare is "the guy who wrote the King James Bible"), but it gives us a first glimpse that he is Amsterdam's mentor.

In effect, he warns the youngster that he is on the wrong path: if you follow Hamlet's example, Monk seems to say, not only will the dark king be dead at the end, so will you and everyone else. Amsterdam is only a few steps away from the inmost cave, and his continued apathy and lack of focus at this dangerous stage of the journey become fatal. Later that night during a drunken celebration in Satan's Circus, he lets himself be provoked when Jenny defiantly and flirtatiously nurses the Butcher's wounds. As soon as they are alone

"Funny feeling being took under the wing of a dragon. It is warmer than you might think," says Amsterdam Vallon (Leonardo DiCaprio), who battles with the shadow of his dead father, Bill the Butcher (Daniel Day-Lewis), in *Gangs of New York* (Miramax Films, 2002).

Amsterdam lashes out at her, and from their fighting erupts the passion they have been suppressing. A crushed Johnny is watching their lovemaking from outside the door, and consumed with jealousy, he reveals Amsterdam's true identity to Bill the Butcher.

Shortly afterwards, on February 3, 1863, the Natives are celebrating the 16th anniversary of the death of Priest Vallon at Sparrow's Chinese Pagoda. The Butcher starts the evening by demonstrating his famous knife-throwing skills. He asks Jenny, his former apprentice, to come up on the stage with him, and his malevolence toward her and Amsterdam is blatant. Although Amsterdam reacts to it, astoundingly he does not really *see* it. He has crossed into the dark territory where he is supposed to look his deepest fears in the eyes, but his attitude is dangerously flippant, and he is heedless of his father's admonition to never look away.

Amsterdam has reached the moment he has been waiting for most of his life, and when Bill the Butcher salutes Priest Vallon, "this great and noble man," Amsterdam throws the knife to kill him. Being forewarned, Bill easily wards it off, however. At the outset of his journey, Amsterdam proclaimed in voice-over: "When you kill a king, you don't stab him in the dark! You kill him where the whole court can watch him die!" Although he does attempt to assassinate Bill in front of the whole court, he does it clandestinely. He thinks he can sneak up on Bill and kill him when he is off his guard, thus cheating the forces of darkness. It goes without saying that you cannot get through the inmost cave in this cowardly fashion. Amsterdam cavalierly expects his opponent to be an easy target, but the forces inside the cave, always dangerous by the very nature of things, have been made even more frightening and deadly by Amsterdam's own perfidy. At the point where the hero's true character is shown, Amsterdam proves to be undeserving, and instead of grabbing the magical reward, he is nearly beaten to death, and Bill brands his cheek because he wants him to "walk amongst you marked with shame!"

The hero often symbolically dies and is reborn toward the end of the journey, connoting that he is ready to let go of his old identity and deserves to be called a hero. In this case, however, there is still an hour left of the film, and Amsterdam now has to start all over and begin the hero's journey again. Thus the following scene serves as a new opening which contains a new call to adventure, and it becomes necessary to redefine helpers and enemies, most importantly Jenny and Monk. We are in the dark catacombs beneath the basement of the Old Brewery. Surrounded by graves and skeletons, Jenny nurses Amsterdam back to life, telling him about her mother, her dreams for the future, and her buried treasure. Since she was a girl she has been saving ten cents out of every dollar she has made, so she can get away from the slums and go to San Francisco, a land of milk and honey where they dig gold out of the river.[10]

At this point it becomes pertinent to regard Jenny as something more than just a beautiful woman who has come between two friends. From the beginning she has been shown as Amsterdam's feminine counterpart, his symbolic sister and mirror image, the anima with which he is on hostile terms during the first half of the film. Jenny's role is crucial since there is an acute denial of femininity in this animalistic male world.[11] We never hear about Amsterdam's mother, Jenny's mother is dead, and when Jenny herself was pregnant, her baby was cut out of her — a horrifying image of mutilated womanhood and motherhood. Their childhoods reflect each other: Amsterdam's mother was gone, then his father died; Jenny's father was gone, then her mother died. Both were left with Bill the Butcher as a dubious substitute parent, both have matured under the wing of the dragon, and both have been the Butcher's Apprentice.

At the Mission Ball Jenny is chosen to be queen and is told to pick her king. She gazes into a *looking glass* and chooses Amsterdam, implying that they are two sides of the same psyche. Accordingly, the very first time they encounter each other alone and Jenny bumps into him, their movements are perfectly mirrored as they both suspiciously search their clothes to see if anything is missing, and they speak the same sentence in unison. Amsterdam realizes that Jenny has stolen his precious medal and follows her uptown on a trolley. In effect, she takes away St. Michael, then leads him out of the confines of the neighborhood and into a world of plenty he never knew existed.

Keeping this in mind, her entreating him to go to San Francisco with her now that the second hero's journey begins can be understood on two levels. Like Teresa in *Mean Streets* and the Countess Olenska in *The Age of Innocence*, Jenny can be seen as an anima force who offers the protagonist an opportunity to leave the neighborhood and live in authenticity and abundance. On this level, her call to adventure corresponds to the famous real-life advice of Horace Greeley (who all through this film represents the voice of reason): "Go West, young man!" When she removes his medallion, she metaphorically impels Amsterdam to leave behind his father's conflicts and start his own individuation. She asks him to follow a hero path of his own rather than staying stuck in the archaic, one-track male world.

It is possible, however, that her removal of the medal and promise of San Francisco have even more profound symbolic significance, since that city was named after Francis of Assisi, a favorite saint in Scorsese's work. On a deeper level, Jenny seems to propose that Amsterdam relinquish the battle against Satan/Bill as symbolized by St. Michael's sword, and instead choose the path of St. Francis who renounced the inheritance from his father in order to follow his own inner voice, giving up a selfish existence to help the poor and downtrodden. Although Amsterdam does not literally follow Jenny's call to adventure (like Charlie and Newland, he never finds the courage to actually leave the neighborhood), one *could* argue that he does follow it symbolically, as we shall see shortly.

When Amsterdam wakes up after his deathlike coma, Monk shows up in the catacombs, finally revealing himself as the mentor when he hands the young man Priest Vallon's razor. A new hero path is about to begin, so the mentor gives the boy a magical object in this scene, a precise parallel to the scene in *Star Wars* in which Obi Wan Kenobi presents Luke Skywalker with Anakin's light saber. The constellation of characters is very similar: the boy (Amsterdam/Luke), the good father (Vallon/Anakin), the dark father (Bill the Butcher/Darth Vader) and the mentor/father's successor (Monk/Obi Wan). Monk logically takes the place of Vallon whom we associate with shaving: he has been safeguarding the razor and owns a barbershop, and there is a powerful animosity between Monk and the Butcher, just as there is between Obi Wan and Darth Vader.

Monk intimates that Vallon, like Anakin, may have had unacknowledged dark sides: "I often wondered if he'd lived a bit longer, would he have wanted a bit more." It is explicitly proposed that Vallon is akin to Bill and might in time have turned into him. The concepts of good father/dark father are, of course, relative, but for Amsterdam the division is unequivocal, so that the good father is purely benevolent and the dark father is purely evil. If the unassimilated shadow of a parent is transferred onto a child, it "splits the personality of the child and sets the ego-shadow warfare into motion," Robert A. Johnson says, and "when that child grows up, he will have a large shadow to cope with."[12] As long as he will not allow Father to be a whole person with good *and* bad sides, Amsterdam will exist in painful denial, and as long as he projects all his hatred onto Father's ghastly shadow, he will be incapable of living his own life and integrating his *own* shadow.

"This war is a thousand years old," Monk declares, referring to the persecution of the Irish Catholics which has followed them to The New World. "Your father tried to scratch out a corner in this country for his tribe!" he says, suggesting, like Jenny, that Amsterdam give up the futile and basically self-indulgent battle against the dark father and embark on a more altruistic path. With the mark of Cain on his cheek, Amsterdam begins his second hero's journey to shape a new future for himself and for his people.[13] He ventures out of the catacombs to hang a dead rabbit in Paradise Square, and with this provocation begins the second approach to the inmost cave. Where the first journey was clandestine and solitary, Amsterdam now openly sets himself up as a leader of men, his new goal being to create hope for the oppressed Irish immigrants, and, consequently, squeezing out the Butcher by showing him as a "relic of an ancient law."

In the following scenes Amsterdam's role as redeemer takes on religious overtones. The new Dead Rabbits congregate in a church that is under construction, calling to mind the San Damiano church that St. Francis restored at the beginning of his journey as he was joined by more and more of *his* little brothers. The tableau-like scenes inside the church are composed and lit so that they recall Jesus and the disciples at the Last Supper, Jenny taking on the role of Magdalene (by way of Boxcar Bertha). When Johnny shows up and admits that it was he who betrayed Amsterdam and is banished, the reference to Judas is obvious.

"We ain't got a gang, we've got an army," Amsterdam says, and before long he has the attention of the ever-greedy Tweed (Jim Broadbent) who offers him the protection of Tammany Hall in exchange for Irish votes. Amsterdam agrees on the condition that Monk be the first Irish candidate for sheriff. By making a pact with Tweed, however, Amsterdam again strays fatally from the hero path. He steps on the Butcher's toes as well as into his shoes, since *he* has been Tweed's alliance in the Five Points so far. The unhealed wounds are ripped open, and the past is doomed to be repeated. Thus, as soon as Monk is elected for office, Bill butchers him, symbolically killing Father a second time, and once more Amsterdam is stuck on the old path. At Monk's funeral he challenges Bill to a battle, and we are back to square one.

Amsterdam is even more blinded by his hatred of Father's shadow. The city around him is in a state of emergency because of the draft riots, but he is in complete denial: "The earth was shaking, but I was about my father's business."[14] While rioters run amok, Amsterdam imitates his father's shaving ritual. As he is looking into the mirror, Jenny, the anima, emerges, offering him one last chance to abandon his reactive and regressive pattern and reclaim his own path. Again he tries to travel both roads: he asks Jenny to wait one more day, assuring her that by then it will all be over, but the whole point is, of course, that he *must* choose one path or the other.

Like his father he marches to war through the underground tunnels of the Old Brewery, but just as he barely nicks his cheek while shaving, his approach to the gate does not have the grace and momentum that Vallon's did. For one thing we are seriously distracted from it because we constantly cut to the mayhem outside, and for another, he simply does not possess the majestic force of his father. He appears like a child imitating a resolute adult, a brat playing at being king. As he and the Irish gangs emerge to face the Natives, the city is a powder keg, and soon Paradise Square is covered by an impenetrable smoke from mortar fire. Amsterdam's revenge is amputated by the confrontation between government soldiers and rioters, and his big showdown ends up as a gigantic anti-climax. Again his blindness has led him to a dead end, and even at this late point there are still significant things that he cannot or refuses to see. He tries to be his father and repeat his battle, and that fact alone is bound to result in tragedy. In addition, the world that surrounds him has changed significantly since the last battle took place, as has the view of masculinity and warfare.

Priest Vallon and Bill the Butcher were kings in a world where battles were fought between equals and according to the "ancient laws of combat." Now we are approaching the modernity of the 20th century. Seventeen years earlier, the Five Points was dominated by mysterious male rituals and passionately held beliefs. However barbaric and animalistic the opening battle seemed, it was fought on the basis of human emotions and according to a code of honor that was agreed upon by all. Now we are at that crucial point in history where the western world moves definitively away from the powerful ancient archetype of the warrior toward the modern, disempowered concept of the conscripted soldier. We are entering a supposedly more civilized era, but Bill's savagery is merely giving way to the officially legitimized faceless mass killings of the government. The soldiers are shown as underprivileged hired guns who are conned or forced into war. They are killing (or being killed) from a distance, and have little or no idea for what they are fighting. Scorsese juxtaposes the chaos of the rioters with the inhumanly well-ordered ranks of the government soldiers by means of an Eisensteinian montage. We see people slaughtered by the thousands from a safe distance by soldiers who do not hate them or even know them. According to Bill's ancient laws of combat, physical contact was necessary in order to kill anyone, and the bloodiness itself put a limit to how many people one could actually kill. For the efficient war-machine there is no such limit, and entire neighborhoods are wiped out in a matter of hours.

When Amsterdam and the Butcher are finally face to face, they are surrounded by smoke, and they are both on their knees. Bill pulls a large piece of shrapnel from his side, which means that in effect "progress" has already killed him. Although Amsterdam gets to deliver the coup de grace, he does so with Bill's blessing, and there is no sense of victory or glory or even relief in this moment for which he has been waiting for 17 years.

At the exact second when Bill the Butcher dies, we dissolve from an extreme close-up of his eye that closes to a long shot God's-eye view of Jenny returning across Paradise Square while the fog is lifting. Since we see her from the perspective of the Almighty, and since the image of Bill dying melts into the image of Jenny returning, it makes sense to assume that the two are connected. The anima had to leave when Amsterdam insisted on remaining stuck in the past, but now Father's heavy shadow is gone and he is free to build a future of his own, so she must return.

The streets of the Five Points are lined with a horrific number of corpses. While Tweed is trying to attract new voters to make up for all the lost ones, Amsterdam and Jenny go out to Potter's Field to conclude the hero's journey. Normally, after looking death in the face in the inmost cave, the hero can seize the magical object that will heal him and the nation. What Amsterdam must do is the exact opposite; his task is not to reach out for something but to let go of something. Like Frodo Baggins in *The Lord of the Rings*, he must surrender the powerful symbol that otherwise might devour him and his entire world, and almost has. Frodo must get rid of the ring, Amsterdam must get rid of Father's razor and the past it signifies.

At the outset, Amsterdam's father twice gave him crucial information about the nature of his journey, corresponding to the call to adventure and the advice of the mentor. Priest Vallon looked his mirror image straight in the eye, cut his cheek, and insisted that "the blood stays on the blade. One day you'll understand." Later with his dying breath he implored the child: "Oh, my son, don't never look away!" The lessons to be learned from this advice have to do with the razor, with blood, and with seeing.

Vallon's shaving rite forms a part of his preparation for battle and possible death. The razor emblemizes manhood and masculinity, and symbolically blood is held to be the medium of life in virtually all cultures. When Vallon looks at his reflection and draws blood, he is thus connecting to his own innermost masculine force. He includes his son in the ritual and hands him the knife with the blood on it, making a sacred covenant with the child. Because "the blood stays on the blade," this pact reaches beyond death, and its essence — Amsterdam's original call to adventure — is that he must seek his own inner core, the true masculine power inside himself. He must strive to know and own all sides of himself, positive as well as negative, so that he can look himself in the eye and recognize his mirror image and shadow side. If Amsterdam is to learn to truly see himself, so that he does not spend his life projecting the sides he does not want to embrace, it is imperative that he "never look away!" Vallon's dying words are a warning of how lethal and insidious the unintegrated shadow is, and the only way to balance it, so that one can benefit from its strength and not spend one's entire life battling it, is to build up the courage to face it and to never look away.

The symbolic use of eyes and seeing that goes through so much of Scorsese's work culminates in *Gangs of New York* in that the entire film revolves around these concepts. Amsterdam says he wants to kill the Butcher where the whole court can watch him die, but symptomatically he ends up killing him in a thick fog where we, the only audience, can hardly make it out. In the past Bill cut out his left eye and gave it to Priest Vallon, his enemy, as a constant reminder that he could not look him in the eye when Vallon once could have killed him in battle. The butcher has replaced the eye with a glass eye adorned with the eagle, so rather than symbolically having a blind eye he is, in fact, eagle-eyed. Despite the fact that his dying father implores him to never look away, Amsterdam does little else throughout the film. The terrible trauma of watching his father killed catapults him prematurely into adulthood, and this makes him constantly go astray in the maze of the hero path. Instead of acknowledging all sides of himself, he has spent his life trying to deny and destroy his father's shadow, without ever truly *seeing* him.

"If you hang on to the past, you die a little every day," Danielle says at the end of *Cape Fear*. In his final spiritual act of surrender — letting go of the razor and of the past — Amsterdam allows Father to cross over and thus makes room for his own future. Despite the tragic and cataclysmic historical context, the ending contains harmony, and a measure of redemption and closure. Priest Vallon and Bill the Butcher are buried side by side, both aspects of Father are laid to rest, the ego and the shadow form a balanced whole. When Amsterdam takes Jenny's hand, allowing himself to merge with the anima, the masculine and feminine principles likewise form a balanced whole.

Amsterdam's real calling was not to avenge Father's death, but to become a whole person and the best man he can be, and his journey is a reflection of the universal journey we all have to make. As always, Scorsese admonishes *us* too to "never look away" from the enlightening and valuable shadow sides of ourselves that we might find unpleasant and objectionable. Hopefully, Amsterdam is finally able to embrace the true meaning of the covenant his father made with him: to find his own inner power, to know and own all sides of himself without looking away, to start the process of facing and integrating his *own* dark mirror image.[15]

The Aviator

The Aviator (2004) tells the story of Howard Hughes during the period from 1927 when at the age of 22 he started directing *Hell's Angels*, until 1947 when he bested Senator Owen Brewster at a Senate hearing and managed to get his gigantic flying boat, the *Hercules*, airborne. The project was initiated by Leonardo DiCaprio, who passionately wanted to make a film about Hughes. He contacted director Michael Mann, and they brought in John Logan to write the screenplay and, eventually, Martin Scorsese to direct the film.

Most accounts of Hughes have focused on the excessive womanizing of his Hollywood youth or the pathological nature of the escalating eccentricity of the billionaire in his old age. As the title suggests, Scorsese and DiCaprio have chosen instead to focus on a hitherto largely forgotten aspect of Hughes's life: his amazing and very considerable achievements and visionary technological breakthroughs in aviation.

"Howard Hughes, the aviator, performed feats of incredible bravery in his life," says Scorsese. "Here was a nineteenth century–type figure who was a pioneer in two of the greatest phenomena of the twentieth century: aviation, with his innovative designs and speed records, and filmmaking."[16] Although the film concerns the most prolific period of Hughes's life, Scorsese has never been one to shy away from the dark side, and from beginning to end we can sense how Hughes's ghastly demons gradually creep in and eventually take over his entire life in the years after the film itself has ended.

The Aviator is an extravaganza of aesthetic and cinematic craftsmanship, glamorous art deco set design, and, unusually for Scorsese, special effects and digital technology. Not only, as Perry Seibert said, does it feel "like the most fun Martin Scorsese has had behind a camera in over a decade," it is also easily and without comparison the best film he has made in many years.[17] Visually, it perfectly reflects the progress of the film industry at the time it takes place, the most astounding effect being the use of color. During the first part — taking place from 1927 to 1938 — Scorsese employs a color scheme that seeks to emulate the process of making multi-chromatic film at the time before color film stock had been invented. This method, referred to as two-color Technicolor, exposed two strips of black-and-white film through a red and a green filter, and they were then cemented together to create a primitive type of color film. Because this process could not reproduce true blue, these early films tended to have a brilliant bluish green tint, so that in *The Aviator* both the sky, the sea, the peas on Hughes's plate, and the lawns seem surrealistically turquoise. The color scheme changes 53 minutes into the film, to emulate three-strip Technicolor in which black-and-white film was exposed through red, green and blue filters to create the familiar saturated color of the films of the 1940s.[18]

Like so many of Scorsese's pictures, *The Aviator* is truthful on historical as well as deeply psychological and mythological levels. Marty and Leo "were committed to understanding the character in the depth of his soul," says screenwriter John Logan. "What was important to each of us was to maintain a high level of honesty as we adapted the details of Hughes's story."¹⁹ That being said, various facts *have* been changed for the sake of the psychological truth of the story: chronological accuracy in the period from 1938 to 1942 has been sacrificed; details have been altered in his relationships with Katharine Hepburn and Ava Gardner; DiCaprio's eyes are blue whereas Hughes's were brown; and Hughes's marriages, racism, anti–Semitism, and syphilis have wisely been ignored to keep the dramatic conflict as simple as possible. Needless to say, one can never capture the entire life of a person as complex as Hughes in a 170-minute film. "Howard Hughes is probably one of the 20th century's most iconic and mysterious figures — and in some ways the more you learn about him the more mysterious he becomes," Leonardo DiCaprio says. "Just when you think you have him figured out, there's another layer to the story."²⁰ Indeed, he and Scorsese have focused on carefully chosen aspects in order to tell us a coherent *version* of the story.

Many have responded to *The Aviator* as if it were a biography, and reactions have ranged from the article on the World Socialist Web Site with the unintentionally hilarious title, "Why This Dishonest Portrait of a Despicable Figure?" to history professor Cathy Schultz's wish that "perhaps with this film, Martin Scorsese will rehabilitate Hughes's image" so that "we'll think of Howard Hughes as he would have wanted to be remembered, as the Aviator."²¹ Some have accused it of being a whitewash: others have proclaimed that "it is the clear-eyed empathy Scorsese brings to *The Aviator* that makes it one of the most emotionally rewarding films of his career."²² In the final analysis, however, this film is not a biography nor even a biopic. The film's verisimilitude is mythic rather than literal: what is recreated visually is not Hollywood or America the way they looked from the late 1920s to the late 1940s, but an approximation of how they would have looked in two-color and three-strip Technicolor. The accuracy is not to history but to film history and to a grander, more deeply mythological history. To paraphrase novelist E.L. Doctorow, *The Aviator* does not concern what *really* happened, but what *truly* happened.

The brilliance of Scorsese's film is that it gives a tender picture of this driven and tormented man, at the same time that he becomes the embodiment of things that go beyond an individual level. "Our favorite people and our favorite stories become so not by any inherent value, but because they illustrate something deep in the grain, something unadmitted," wrote Joan Didion in her 1967 essay on Hughes. "That we have made a hero of Howard Hughes tells us something interesting *about ourselves*, something only dimly remembered," she continues. "In a nation which increasingly appears to prize social virtues, Howard Hughes remains not only antisocial but grandly, brilliantly, surpassingly asocial. He is the last private man, *the dream we no longer admit*."²³

In its essence *The Aviator* is not primarily related to the multitude of biographical books and documentaries on the life of Howard Hughes, the reclusive billionaire — and after all, how accurate are they *really*? Rather, it belongs with grandly iconic works like F. Scott Fitzgerald's *The Great Gatsby* and Orson Welles's *Citizen Kane*. Hughes's complex story can only be told in kaleidoscopic versions that shift according to who is narrating them. Like Kane's "Rosebud," the opening story of Hughes's childhood explains everything and nothing. Like Fitzgerald's novel, Scorsese's film is interested in what preyed on this man — "what foul dust floated in the wake of his dreams." Hughes's lawn, like Gatsby's, is mysteriously blue, and although, as Nick says about Gatsby, he may have "represented everything for which I have an unaffected scorn," we may have to admit that he "turned out all right at the end."²⁴ Like Jay Gatsby and Charles Foster Kane, Howard Hughes typifies

America in the first decades of the 20th century. He is an immensely rich, powerful, self-invented man who ends up alone, losing everything that matters to him.

The opening scene of *The Aviator* is a companion piece to that of *Gangs of New York*: it takes place in a mysterious, ceremoniously lit room and is an encounter between a child and a parent. To the left stands a naked boy of about ten in a bathtub, immovable, almost like a statue. In from the right of the room walks a young woman. What we are about to witness is obviously not simply an incident from the life of this boy. It is a ritual act, a defining moment. We cut to a close-up of the woman's hands, exquisitely beautiful and tender hands, the hands of Mother. They reach out for a tin, take out a cake of lye soap, and gently dip it in the water. We expect a loving ceremony of a mother bathing her child, but instead she performs what amounts to a horrifying, corrosive assault on the mind, body and spirit of the vulnerable and trusting boy.

"QU-AR-ANT-INE," she spells, as she sensually and lingeringly caresses the boy's thighs with the lye. "Quarantine," the boy concludes. He obligingly starts spelling the difficult, portentous word, and Mother's dubious reward for his playing along is visually suggested: the camera is placed behind the boy's right shoulder, viewing Mother in a downward tilt as she kneels in front of him. Her eyes determinedly gaze downward toward his genitals, and her hand reaches out. Then we hear a gasp and cut to a slightly startled momentary reaction on the boy's face, and Mother's hand moves up to his shoulder.

As the seductive lathering continues, so does the assault on the naked child. "You know the cholera?" Mother asks. "You've seen the signs on the houses where the coloreds live?" The boy affirms. "You know the typhus?" she proceeds. "You know what they can do to you?" The undefined "they" might equally well refer to the colored people, the bacteria, and to women, I suppose, since sexuality is quite explicit in the scene. This beautiful young woman now delivers the crushing blow. She reaches up and holds the head of the child between her hands, gazing earnestly into his eyes, and concludes: "You are *not* safe!"

Howard Hughes (Leonardo DiCaprio) in Scorsese's *The Aviator* (Miramax Films, 2004) is much more than a historical figure. He is a mythological giant on par with F. Scott Fitzgerald's Jay Gatsby and Orson Welles's Charles Foster Kane.

Like in *Gangs of New York* what we witness is a ceremonial moment in the life of this child. Through the ritual Amsterdam's loving father enabled his son, who was soon to become an orphan, to take care of himself. Through an equally powerful ritual Howard's mother mutilates the boy for life.

Throughout the film, much of Hughes's torment seems to stem from this horrifying experience. Mother's words — "You are *not* safe!"—uttered as a statement of fact rather than merely a warning becomes a self-fulfilling prophecy. The notion of "QUARANTINE" with its implications of detention and isolation due to suspicion of contagious disease becomes central in the film; in fact, it turns out to be the inmost cave where Hughes has to face his darkest fears. The main conflict of the film is an innovative variation on the classic Scorsese concern of spirit as opposed to flesh, which for Hughes is the battle between his dreams and his demons. Certainly his inner torment, masochism, obsessive-compulsive behavior and self-imposed exile is in perfect tune with that of Scorsese's other protagonists.

At the very end, Howard Hughes (Leonardo DiCaprio) is standing in front of a mirror in which he sees not only the reflection of his own tormented face, but also, in the background, the boy in the bathtub whose mother again assures him that he is not safe. The prepubescent boy then makes a solemn pledge: "When I grow up, I'm gonna fly the fastest planes ever built, make the biggest movies ever, and be the richest man in the world!" The child is clearly not speaking to Mother, who does not seem to even hear him, but looks resolutely at the older Hughes on the other side of the mirror. This indicates that his pledge is meant as a three-pronged incantation to protect the two of them—little Howard and the adult Hughes—against Mother's curse, recalling Wordsworth's famous statement that "the child is father of the man."[25]

The two thus should be viewed as antitheses; Mother's allegation of contagion and infectious disease on the one hand, and little Howard's dreams of flying machines, movie-making and affluence on the other. These conflicting elements and their symbolic significance form the basic structure of the mythological journey Howard Hughes has to undertake in the course of the film. Occasionally the boy's safeguards against Mother's curse appear to work and almost seem able to deliver Hughes from destruction. What ultimately brings him down, however, is the fact that like Parsifal he has made an underlying, unconscious commitment to Mother's fears so that he carries them around with him for the rest of his life in the shape of her emblematic soap tin. This talisman against the evil of germs reveals that far from having transcended the curse, he is indeed as stuck in it as ever. Whenever we see Hughes fall into the pit of his obsessive-compulsive patterns, it is a sign that Mother triumphs over little Howard's triple charm.

"I'm gonna fly the fastest planes ever built," is Howard's first vow, and the love of Hughes's life is clearly aviation. When Katharine Hepburn (Cate Blanchett) becomes increasingly jealous over the multitude of other women in his life and finally leaves him, she fails to see that her only real rivals for his attention are the *Hercules*, the XF11, and the Constellation fleet. This is illustrated in the scene where during a screening of rushes of *The Outlaw*, Hughes hands Glenn "Odie" Odekirk (Matt Ross), his right-hand man, a folded picture of his dream for the future. Odie unfolds it and sees a photo of Jane Russell and her much-debated breasts. "No," Hughes gruffly corrects him, "other side," at which point Odie turns over the paper and finds a drawing of Hughes's true love: the *Hercules*.

Marking the high points of the film are thus the scenes where Hughes changes aviation history: His first major triumph when, on September 13, 1935, he breaks the air speed record with 352 mph in the H1 racer plane and goes home to celebrate with Kate Hepburn. Setting a new round-the-world speed record of 3 days, 19 hours, 14 minutes, and 28 seconds in July 1938 in a twin-engine Lockheed plane, which made him the most famous flyer since Charles Lindbergh. His near-fatal crash with the XF-11 reconnaissance plane in a Beverly Hills neighborhood on July 7, 1946. His prolonged battle with nemesis Juan Trippe (Alec

Baldwin), owner of Pan American Airlines, when Hughes opposed the Pan Am monopoly on transatlantic flights and thus changed the future of the civil aviation industry. And finally his invention of the flying boat the *Hercules*, to this day the largest aircraft ever built, culminating in the maiden flight in 1947 at the end of the film.

Symbolically, Hughes's love of aviation, freeing himself from the force of gravity, can be seen as the urge to rise above the physical level, the frailty of the body and the fear of contagion. Little Howard's vow that he will fly the fastest planes ever made expresses a wish to transcend the flesh which Mother says is not safe, to transcend the dangers of the entire human experience. The word "flight"—deriving from either "fly" or "flee"—can, of course, mean both (a) lifting off from the ground and moving through the air by means of wings and (b) running away, escaping. The image of human beings flying has indeed connoted escape from imprisonment since the time of the very first aviator, Daedalus. In Greek mythology, Daedalus was, like Hughes, one of the greatest inventors and artisans of his time, and he built the labyrinth to save the Cretans from the dangerous minotaur. When King Minos imprisoned him and his son Icarus, they could not escape the island by land or by sea, so Daedalus fashioned a pair of artificial wings for each of them. He warned the boy against flying too close to the sea lest the wings get wet, or too close to the sun which would melt the wax that held them in place. Icarus did not heed his father's advice. He flew too close to the sun, destroyed his wings, fell into the ocean and drowned.

In virtually all mythical traditions, one has to earn and deserve wings. The Old Testament states: "Oh that I had the wings of a dove to fly away and be at rest!"[26] To have wings, then, says the Penguin Dictionary of Symbols, is "to leave earthly things behind and to attain to the heavenly."[27] Flying involves leaving the human plane and approaching the realm of the gods, thus it stands to reason that it could easily lead to hubris and pride. The Icarus myth involves mastering all four elements: leaving the earth, going into the air, taking care not to fly too close to the water or to the fire of the sun. Although Icarus was warned against flying too close to the sea as well as too close to the sun, the only real temptation was in flying too high. Indeed he has often been associated with hubris, with reaching too far. "His waxen wings did mount above his reach, and melting, heavens conspired his overthrow," says the chorus of Marlowe's "Dr. Faustus," comparing him to the ill-fated boy.[28]

Since Hughes is the one who designs the wings as well as the one who flies too close to the sun, he takes on the role of both Daedalus and Icarus. He is the aviator, Inventor Father, as well as the plumed, high-spirited son who endangers his own life. Interestingly, we never see Howard's father in the film, whereas in the final scene Hughes is represented as both man and child in the same image: the tormented man in front of the mirror and the naked boy in the bathtub. Throughout, he is the Daedalian visionary and creator as well as the youngster whose Icarean inability to heed advice against flying too far, too high, too fast, makes him crash more than once. When he goes up in the H1 racer in 1935, Odie admonishes him: "Keep your eye on the fuel. She's got a minimum to keep her weight down. Two runs. That's it! After that, you're flying on vapors." Nevertheless, Hughes takes three runs, breaks the air speed record on the third run, but crashes the plane in a beet field. At the XF11 test flight in 1946, Hughes takes the plane up to 292 mph. "Take her back to 200," Odie implores him on the radio.

"No damn way!" is Howard's response.

"We gotta bring her home," Odie says when the scheduled one hour and 45 minutes have elapsed.

"Ten more minutes," says Hughes hubristically, and instantly suffers the crash that permanently impaired him, physically and mentally, and nearly cost him his life.

The plot of the film starts with the second of little Howard's vows, to "make the biggest movies ever." It is 1927, the first year of production on *Hell's Angels*. Hughes's obsessive perfectionism is already obvious since he owns and is directing "the largest private air force in the world." He will not have his crew tell him that things cannot be done, he feels a desperate need for two more cameras in addition to the 24 he already has, and two years later during the wrap party of the film (which has already cost a record $2 million out of his own pocket), Hughes decides to reshoot the entire movie for sound. Even during the 20-minute standing ovation at the 1930 premiere, his only comment is: "Reel four played too long. Too many coughs. Get the team out of the party and to the office. I wanna cut a few shots."

Making the biggest movies ever signifies for Hughes the ability to create a world all of his own, again entering the domain of God. It is a slightly infantile desire for a world over which he and he alone has complete control; a perfected, immaculate, germfree world made out of shadows and light. Additionally, Hollywood means the accessibility of an infinite supply of women who are there for the taking. Apart from being an eccentric recluse in his later years, Hughes is probably most famous for his notorious womanizing. *The Aviator* abounds with references to the hundreds of women he seduced: floozies and aspiring starlets as well as major stars, but "lots of evidence suggests that Hughes's libido was never as strong as he pretended," says Cathy Schultz. "His obsession seemed more in collecting women than loving them."[29] That he sees women mainly as commodities is revealed when Ava Gardner (Kate Beckinsale) amiably turns down his impromptu proposal of marriage right before his 15-year-old mistress rams them with her car. "Look, you got girls stashed all over town. You got a damn harem just at the Bel-Air. Marry one of your bungalow girls," she says, to which Hughes responds: "Those are employees. I won't marry an employee. How would that look?" Or as he says to Kate Hepburn when she is leaving him: "You wanna go? Go on! Actresses are cheap in this town, darling, and I got a lot of money."

The Don Juan figure was associated with Oedipal dynamics by Otto Rank as early as 1924, and there is reason to believe that Hughes's womanizing was related to his mother's abuse. This becomes significant when we see his first conquest in the film, the seduction of the cigarette girl, Thelma. This scene is shot from an angle that approximates the angle in the opening scene. Where Mother was filmed in a downward tilt over Howard's right shoulder, Hughes is now filmed in a downward tilt over Thelma's left shoulder, and his actions are virtually identical to Mother's. He cajoles the girl, then reaches out his hands and touches her genital area: "I mean, say, you're just standing there, right? And I just touch you. Just — Just like this. With my fingertips. Do you — Do you like that? Do you?" Although this is a scene between adults, Hughes violates the girl's boundaries in that he is in a position of power, and it takes place in public at her place of work in full view of the other Cocoanut Grove patrons. Indeed, her ambivalent, befuddled, but ultimately obedient response precisely echoes that of little Howard in the bathtub.

If the trauma of children who have been abused — emotionally, physically or sexually — is not addressed, there is a tendency that when they grow up they will respond to emotional situations on the basis of the childhood trauma, identifying with and emulating the behavior in the original situation of either the abuser (the one who did this to them) or the abused (themselves). The most thought-provoking thing about this first, and presumably prototypical, seduction in *The Aviator* is that it shows Howard emulating the abuser, i.e., Mother. His excessive philandering is thus incontestably linked with her. Psychiatrist Jeffrey Schwartz, who in real life studied Hughes for ten years, believes that when his mother "compulsively checked and rechecked Howard's body, his temperature, his every move, she was actually making love to her beautiful son. And Howard grew dependent on that intense form of love. So, for the rest of his life, he went from lover to lover trying to recapture the all-encompassing passion."[30]

It has to be significant that Scorsese chose to downplay Hughes's prolonged struggle with the Hollywood censors over the use of violence in *Scarface* which delayed the film's release for two years, and instead focuses on his battle over *The Outlaw*, which in essence is a battle over breasts. "Howard, do you really think they're gonna let you put out a whole movie just about tits?" asks Odie. "Sure," Hughes answers naively. "Who doesn't like tits?" One of the very first things we see Hughes do in the film is to hire two paternal men—one, Noah Dietrich (John C. Reilly), to handle the money he has inherited from his father, and another, Professor Fitz (Ian Holm), to provide him with "clouds like big breasts filled with milk" to provide perspective as the backdrop for the planes in *Hell's Angels*. During the meeting with the Breen Office, Fitz is again supposed to deal with the breast situation: Hughes introduces him as Dr. Branson, provides him with calipers, and places him in front of seven gigantic enlarged close-up of the breasts of various major stars: "Jean Harlow, Ann Sheridan, Irene Dunne, Claudette Colbert, Rita Hayworth, Betty Grable, and the lovely Miss Jane Russell."

The scene takes on Oedipal overtones because Hughes is standing in front of a committee of much older men who reprimand his interest in denuding the female breast. Throughout the scene, the attributes of the leading ladies are referred to as mammaries. The adjective "mammary" is defined as "of or relating to a breast or mamma" and the mammary gland, is of course, characterized by the one fact that it is milk producing.[31] Repeatedly in the film, we see Hughes drinking milk from the bottle "with the cap still on," and while it may be less than ingenious to point out that breasts and milk are inherently connected with Mother, this does make Hughes's obsession and processes of association abundantly clear: Hollywood = women = breasts = milk = mother. Again everything comes back to Mother, filmmaking as well as the women he beds.

Two women stand out and play a markedly different role in Hughes's mythical journey. One is Katharine Hepburn, who during this period was considered box-office poison; the other is Ava Gardner who was a struggling starlet. Hepburn is the only woman in the film Hughes ever really connects with emotionally. She is presented as his feminine counterpart and soul mate, and together they form a perfect whole. This is clear from their first scene together, the golf course scene which is virtually a recreation of the one Hepburn plays opposite Cary Grant at the beginning of *Bringing Up Baby*. Hepburn is as famously loquacious as Hughes is taciturn. Where his private thoughts revolve primarily around himself, her nonstop babbling expresses her firm conviction of what everybody else ought to do, and she strikes out at Hughes's golf game, his profession, his opinions, his tastes, and his entire gender.

The exultant scene in which they escape from the insufferable Errol Flynn (Jude Law) at the Cocoanut Grove and Hughes takes her flying is among the most magical and erotic in Scorsese's production, and it illustrates why Hepburn is generally considered the greatest love of Hughes's life. He lets her take the yoke and gently teaches her how to take control of the plane: "That's too hard. Relax your hand. Relax your hand. You see, you gotta feel the vibration of the engine through your fingertips. Do you feel that?" "Yes," sighs Hepburn who for once is rendered speechless. Moments later, she is conclusively manifested as his symbolic anima sister when Hughes takes a bottle of milk and pours the white liquid into her mouth. Then he hesitates for a second, worried about germs, and in the most intimate gesture of the entire film decides to drink from it anyway.

Unfortunately the two of them are connected and alike in ways that reinforce Hughes's darkest sides. Kate mirrors his obsession with germs: she proudly states that she takes seven showers a day and perceives this as evidence that "I keep healthy!" Howard's mother forced her beliefs on the child, and Kate turns out to come from an entire family that endlessly and indiscriminately violate others with their opinions. "You're a fine bunch of bullies, aren't you?" Kate scolds them, and then continues doing it herself.

The dark kinship between them culminates in what is also the last truly close moment they have together in the film. Hughes comes rushing home to tell her that he has broken the speed record. Kate is joyously proud of him, but the crash has injured him, so she takes him into the bathroom to bathe his foot. Then she realizes that Howard's achievement will be all over the news, and she freezes and gravely admonishes him against fame: "Howard, we're — We're not like everyone else," she says. "Too many acute angles. Too many eccentricities." Kate is then directly connected to Mother: while bathing him, the kneeling woman strikes right at the heart of his darkest fear: "We have to be very careful not to let people in, or they'll make us into freaks," Hepburn says.

"Kate, they can't get in here. We're *safe*," Hughes surprisingly replies.

"They can always get in," she continues, paraphrasing Mother's warning: "You are *not* safe!"

Her well-meant warning reinforces the madness that will eventually consume Hughes: "You know, sometimes I, I get these feelings, Katie. I get these ideas, these crazy ideas about things that may not — Things that may not really be there.... Sometimes I truly fear that I'm losing my mind." Although she kindly assures him that if that happens, she will take the wheel, it would obviously be preferable not to push him over that edge to begin with. Visually, the saving grace in this scene is the fact that it recalls the woman with the alabaster box, generally interpreted as Mary Magdalene, who washes the feet of Jesus in her tears and then kisses and anoints them.[32]

Eventually, Kate gets tired of his womanizing, and just before the midpoint of the film, she leaves him for Spencer Tracy. From then on, things start going downhill and the approach to the inmost cave escalates. Hughes burns his clothes and starts wearing his cheap suits from Sears and trademark white sneakers. Then he takes up with 15-year-old Faith Domergue and, although he does not suffer any of the torment over statutory rape that Jake does in *Raging Bull*, the appearance of the child-woman is often presageful in Scorsese's films. At exactly the same time, Juan Trippe brings Senator Brewster (Alan Alda) into their battle of wills.

The climactic moment of symbolic death and rebirth comes when Hughes crashes with the XF11. Although miraculously he survives the crash, he is barely alive: "He has burns to 78 percent of his body," the doctor tells Noah Dietrich. "Nine ribs are shattered. Not broken, shattered. As are his nose, his chin, his cheek, his left knee, his left elbow. He has 60 lacerations on his face, to the bone. His chest was crushed, so his left lung collapsed, and his heart has shifted to the right side of his chest cavity." When Noah protests that Hughes is not going to like the fact that they have given him a blood transfusion, the doctor virtually declares him dead: "Mr. Dietrich, I doubt he's ever gonna like or dislike anything again."

What brings Hughes back to life, it is indicated, are the flowers that Juan Trippe sends him at the hospital. While on a realistic level Trippe's way of handling the threat Hughes posed to Pan Am may have been questionable, his function on Hughes's mythical journey, if we regard him as the dark shadow brother and nemesis, turns out in the final analysis to be beneficial and empowering. Hughes had all the other flowers taken out of the room to avoid aphids, but he has kept Trippe's because the gesture annoys him so much that it makes him virtually rise from the dead.

Just how important Trippe is to Hughes's journey is shown in subtle ways. The first time we see him, 53 minutes into the film, is the precise moment when Scorsese chooses to go from the abstraction of two-color to the heightened reality of three-strip Technicolor. We cut from black-and-white footage of Hughes's ticker-tape parade after his round-the-world flight to a black-and-white close-up of the top of the Chrysler Building, to an identical color close-up of the top of the Chrysler Building, to a medium shot of Juan Trippe sitting at his desk with his back to us. It feels almost like coming out of a somnambulant, hypnagogic state, waking up to another level of reality. Stunning art deco settings capture the glamour and energy of Hollywood all through the film, but Trippe's office — the first time we see true blue and green as distinguishable colors — comes across as an astounding, magical space with stars exploding across the clear blue ceiling.

The first time we see Hughes and Trippe in the same space is at the Cocoanut Grove, a few minutes of screen time after Hepburn walks out on Hughes. His vulnerability is shown by the fact that he relies for emotional support on a wide-eyed 15-year-old child, so when the ugly battle over the airways begins for real, Hughes responds to Trippe's provocation by going to the men's room and taking out Mother's soap tin in one of the most amazing moments of the film. We first realized that he is still carrying around the soap tin in a similar scene in the Pantages Theatre restroom where he was incapacitated by his obsessive hand washing to the extent that he dared not hand a crippled man a towel — his mental handicap overriding the other man's physical handicap. Now, Mother's legacy imprisons him: After he has ritually scrubbed his hands until they are bleeding (images of *The Big Shave* come to mind), he realizes that he has used up all the clean towels, and since he cannot touch the doorknob, he is stuck in the men's room until someone else opens the door.

Concurrent with his rivalry with Trippe, Hughes's descent into madness begins. In a haunting scene which foreshadows his imminent confinement inside the inmost cave as well as the ending of the film, he feels threatened by an ancient janitor with long, dirty fingernails whose diabolic appearance is emphasized by the fact that his name is Nick, so that in actual fact he is "Old Nick," i.e., the devil.[33] At this point, Hughes gets trapped inside one of his sentences for the first time — "Show me all the blueprints!" Moments later, when he cracks up in his car, he is framed so that we see his reflection in the car window, indicating that the dark mirror image might swallow him up at any time, and he starts spelling Mother's word: "Q-U-A-R-A-N-T-I-N-E."

After his crash and resurrection, Hughes loses everything: the Air Force cancels the contract on the *Hercules*, the *Constellation* fleet is grounded, Ava Gardner finds out he has been bugging her and throws him out, and Trippe ups the ante and sets the FBI and Senator Brewster on him. Brewster threatens Hughes with the double-edged humiliation of public hearings unless he supports the C.A.B. Bill, and this sends him over the edge.

"In a real dark night of the soul, it is always 3 o'clock in the morning, day after day," wrote F. Scott Fitzgerald.[34] Hughes now has to face his inner demons inside the darkened projection room at 7000 Romaine. His descent into madness amounts to nothing less than self-imposed QUARANTINE, as Mother's horrifying prophecy is fulfilled. Despite his determination to fly the fastest planes, make the greatest movies, and be the richest man, he has always carried around the objective correlative for Mother's obsession, her soap tin. Increasingly inside the inmost cave, his thoughts revolve around two repeated sentences, one that focuses on the other symbol of Mother—"come in with the milk"—and one that emblemizes the endless loop he is stuck in "repeated from the beginning." In his darkest hour he is naked and alone, trapped by his own mind in a dark, red room which evokes the womb. He has been driven into Hell by his own darkest fears, and his excruciating torment and the disintegration of his soul are brilliantly visualized by the images of saguaro cactuses from his film *The Outlaw* that are projected onto his body as he stands in front of the movie screen. Eventually, all logic breaks down: The milk is gone from the neat row of bottles which are now filled with Howard's urine, and Mother's word has been decomposed into: "Q-R-N-T-Q-U-E-I-T-I-N-E-N-E-E-I."

Kate Hepburn, the symbolic sister, fails to make him emerge from the inmost cave; that is a job for the nemesis brother. Juan Trippe arrives and sits down comfortably on the other side of the door until Howard breaks down, surrenders his control completely, and

Howard Hughes (Leonardo DiCaprio) and Ava Gardner (Kate Beckinsale) in *The Aviator* (Miramax Films, 2004). Where Katharine Hepburn unwittingly reinforces Mother's curse—"You are not safe!"—Ava Gardner becomes the antidote. She is also the first one to see him as he emerges from the inmost cave, as Mary Magdalene was the first to see the resurrected Jesus.

is finally able to come out into the light. It was the dark brother and his flowers that recalled Hughes to life after his crash; it was the dark brother that drove him into the belly of the whale where he has to face his darkest fears, and it is the dark brother that brings him out of that room for the final showdown.

Whereas in real life Ava Gardner apparently brought turmoil and disorder into Hughes's life for almost two decades, in the film she has a positive, almost mystical role. She turns up at important moments of his journey, and her sassy lines always carry a deeper significance, much like those of the chorus in an ancient Greek tragedy. When Hughes comes out of the cave, Ava is the first one who sees him, as Magdalene was the first to see the resurrected Jesus. Where Mother bathed his whole body, and Kate bathed his foot, Ava now shaves him. Shaving has always symbolized the civilization process, and in a mythological sense Ava frees him from the ropes of the cave. She removes the residue of the realm of the shadows and gets him ready for the battle with Senator Brewster.

Where Kate unwittingly reinforced Mother, Ava is the antidote to her. She is the only woman in the film who repeatedly challenges Hughes, the great collector of women: "You can't buy me, Howard, so stop trying. Don't buy me any more diamonds or sapphires or any other damn thing. You can buy me dinner. How about that?" Her boundaries are so crystal clear that she leaves no room for power struggles. Now, before his reemergence into the light, she tells him to put his hands into the shaving water and rinse off his face. "Does that look clean to you?" the obsessive-compulsive asks. Ava's gentle, matter-of-fact reply dispels the darkness of Mother's original curse: "Nothing's clean, Howard. But we do our best, right?"

Little Howard's first pledge — to fly the fastest planes — is a typical boyhood wish. His third pledge — to be the richest man in the world — has to do with the concept of Father. Money in *The Aviator* is always, and quite logically, connected with Father. The money that enables young Hughes to make *Hell's Angels* and carry on the way he does is inherited from Father. Whereas Hughes desires the authority, influence and power that comes with having money, he wants nothing to do with the adult responsibility for it, so he hires Noah Dietrich to manage his fortune. Dietrich is a kind, benevolent father figure who genuinely has the boy's best interests at heart and who admonishes and reproves him when he spends too much.

There is little doubt that in real life Hughes owed a significant amount of his success to Dietrich, and that without him, he would never have been able to manifest his visionary talents. Psychologically and mythologically, however, Dietrich's paternal support and assistance allows Hughes to remain in the rebellious and self-destructive mode of Icarus, to stay regressively stuck in adolescence without taking responsibility, and as long as he does that Mother's curse will control him, and he will not be safe. The object of his journey might well be gaining the courage to leave Mother's little boy behind and truly embrace the Daedalus side of his nature. This is why his rivalry with nemesis Juan Trippe ultimately is beneficial. There are two sets of sons and fathers in this film: Howard Hughes and Noah Dietrich on the one hand, and Juan Trippe and Owen Brewster on the other. Noah Dietrich, in his kindness and tender feelings for the boy, allows him to remain irresponsible and, therefore, the encounter with the dark father of the dark brother becomes necessary.

Howard's original dreams of aviation constitute an infantile desire to transcend and compensate for the powerlessness he feels upon Earth due to Mother's assertion that he is not safe. It is a dream of flying higher, faster, and farther than the other boys. His rivalry with Juan Trippe, however, is not a puerile question of performing aviation feats. It is a mature, territorial battle over domination of the airways. The C.A.B. Bill proposes that Pan Am get a monopoly on international passenger flights. Hughes opposes the bill, and this time his contrariety is not an attempt to provoke and annoy "Father" like the mammary fight with Joseph Breen (Edward Herrmann). This time, he is changing the future of the entire concept of commercial air travel in a decidedly adult manner. Trippe is sometimes called "the father of the tourist class" and it is by way of Trippe's incitement that Hughes's dream of aviation develops beyond the narcissistic and Oedipal level into something more selfless and altruistic, using it to the benefit of ordinary people everywhere. This is a battle between men, and so the climactic showdown has to be with the dark and crooked side of *Father*, Senator Owen Brewster.

It is quite obvious that in the guise of a public senate hearing, Brewster is out on a deeply personal crusade. When Hughes walks into the caucus room we feel his vulnerability and discomfort over being among hundreds of spectators, reporters and photographers. The room is so brightly lit that many wear dark glasses, and the cameras and lights are filmed and edited so that the psychological threat they pose to Hughes is palpable. Throughout the film the flashbulbs of the inescapable photographers have had Scorsese's agonizing trademark sound of glass breaking. Since *Raging Bull* this sound has signified the imminent slaughter of the sacrificial animal, and they seem to be the materialization of the germs against which Mother warned Howard: "You know what they can do to you?" she asked, and when Kate reiterates that they are not safe, she is referring specifically to the press and the public who are now waiting to witness Hughes's televised crucifixion. He manages to turn the tables on Brewster, however, and to gradually expose his hypocrisy and venality.

The role Noah Dietrich plays in the course of the hearings is significant. At the opening, he interrupts the senator to declare that Hughes has a statement. The kind father takes the reins, but Hughes, despite his discomfort, puts aside the statement that was prepared for him and instead speaks passionately from the heart, using his own words. All through these scenes, the image is framed so that Noah Dietrich is constantly seen sitting behind Hughes to his right. To begin with, Dietrich looks worried as Hughes points out that Brewster is essentially abusing his position, and throws the accusation of bribery right back in Brewster's face: "I suppose you could consider them bribes," Hughes acknowledges. "I don't know whether it's a good system. I just know it's not illegal. You, Senator, you are the lawmaker. If you pass a law that states no one can entertain Air Force officers, well, hell, I'd be happy to abide by it." As Hughes gains composure, strength and momentum, and begins to handle himself with the confidence of an adult, rather than as a child accused of stealing and lying, Dietrich's relief is written all over his face, and he begins to relax and even enjoy himself.

At the heart of Brewster's vendetta is Hughes's invasion of Juan Trippe's territory. Hughes now reveals that the C.A.B. Bill which Brewster has been "flogging ... all around the world" was actually "written by Pan Am executives and designed to give that airline a monopoly on international travel." Hughes continues: "On February 12th, at the Mayflower Hotel, did you or did you not tell me that if I were to sell TWA to Pan Am that this entire investigation would be called off?" The last confrontation is intercut with the scene of the maiden voyage of the *Hercules*. We crosscut between a close-up of Brewster and a two-shot of Hughes with Noah Dietrich, as Hughes illustrates how he has put millions of his own money into the planes that Brewster has accused him of profiteering from during the war. "See, the thing is, I care very much about aviation." He continues. "It has been the great joy of my life. That's why I put my own money into these planes. And I've lost millions, Senator, and I'll go on losing millions. It's just what I do." Then at the very end, we cut closer to Hughes, alone in the tight frame now, as he delivers his final lines: "Now, Senator Brewster, you can subpoena me, you can arrest me, you can even claim I've folded up and taken a run-out powder, but, well, I've had just about enough of this nonsense. Good afternoon." Howard Hughes has established that he is more than a match for the crooked father, that he can handle himself as a man, and thus the kind father, Noah Dietrich, is no longer needed in the image: Hughes can stand on his own!

We cut to Juan Trippe who turns off the TV, realizing that the battle is lost, then back to Hughes getting the gigantic *Hercules* airborne. The levitation of this plane which "is over five stories tall" and which Brewster lambasted as "the Spruce Goose" on national television seems to be Hughes's ultimate triumph over the dark father. However, as we find out minutes later, his struggle with his inner demons is far from over. At the celebration party inside the hangar, Hughes is surrounded by his symbolic family: Ava Gardner, the antidote against Mother; Noah Dietrich, the kind father who has just granted him independence; and Glenn Odekirk, the symbolic light brother. One would think that we are approaching a glorious ending as Hughes is planning the next giant step in the history of aviation: jet airplanes. As in the beginning, however, things turn out less harmonious than they appear. Howard sees an eerie troika of men in white gloves and bluish black suits who are staring at him from a distance. "Noah, who are those guys? They work for me?" he asks. "Everyone works for you, Howard," replies Dietrich, not really answering the question and not indicating whether he sees the three men or whether they are a figment of Hughes's plagued imagination.

Hughes assures his friends that jet engines are "the way of the future," and the three ghostly men start walking menacingly toward him. Now Hughes's triumphant finale crumbles, and, helplessly, he starts repeating "the way of the future" over and over. As Noah and Odie steer him away from the party, we cut back, and the phantasmic trinity is nowhere to be seen, now that Hughes's gaze is no longer on it. Just as he invented three vows against Mother's curse, so now three demons have come to get him.

At the very end, Howard Hughes is alone in a bathroom that manifests his darkest fear, in that it is in reality filthy and disgusting. He is standing in front of a mirror in which he sees not only his reflection, but also himself as a boy being bathed by Mother. Little Howard makes his three pledges while looking at Hughes, and as the childhood image fades away, Hughes is able to look at his adult face with a kindness and acceptance that resembles Jake La Motta's at the end of *Raging Bull*. Then—

"The way of the future!" In *The Aviator* (Miramax Films, 2004), Hughes (Leonardo DiCaprio) is finally able to look at his mirror image with kindness, compassion and acceptance. The resemblance between DiCaprio and the real Howard Huges in this image is breathtaking, as is the look on DiCaprio's face.

this time intentionally and resolutely—he resumes the incantation of the words "the way of the future" as he looks himself straight in the eye. He repeats the sentence over and over until the image fades to black, as if, willfully and peacefully, he surrenders to the abyss, letting the mirror image devour him. In real life, of course, the darkness on the other side of the mirror did, in fact, become "the way of the future" for Howard Hughes.

The Departed

With a domestic gross of more than $132 million and a total worldwide gross of close to $290 million, *The Departed* (2006) became by far the most commercially successful film of Martin Scorsese's career up until that point. The screenplay, written by William Monahan, is based on the 2002 Hong Kong action film *Infernal Affairs*. Thelma Schoonmaker vows that neither she nor Scorsese had seen the original when they made *The Departed*, and that Scorsese did not even know that it was a remake when he decided to take on the project. Apparently, he simply read Monahan's screenplay and was fascinated by its themes, which is small wonder since most of them are lifted right out of his own works to the extent that it almost feels like a paint-by-number kit.

It is extremely ironic that *The Departed* finally won Scorsese the Oscar he has coveted for so many years, because it is fairly obvious that it is not nearly as close to his heart as either *Gangs of New York* or *The Aviator* and that, for him, it was meant primarily as a pot-

Martin Scorsese joking with cast and crew of *The Departed* (Warner Bros., 2006). *(In the foreground, from left to right)* Leonardo DiCaprio, Martin Scorsese, Michael Ballhaus, and Jack Nicholson.

boiler. Scorsese is a famously modest man, but his own assessment of his Academy Award is probably heartfelt: "We wanted to make a nice genre movie, you know, and look what happened," he quipped as he arrived at the red carpet. The critical acclaim and many accolades notwithstanding, *The Departed* is an extremely flawed work which contains a confounding amount of errors, inconsistencies, and dramaturgical illogicalities that are quite uncharacteristic for Scorsese who has always been famous for painstakingly overseeing and controlling every single detail of his work.[35]

On the positive side, *The Departed* marks the third time that Scorsese uses Leonardo DiCaprio to play his central character and new persona, and DiCaprio's acting is so convincing, passionate and earnest that it almost saves the film. In fact, the three main things the film has going for it are the complex character of Billy Costigan, the fast-paced, captivating plot of doubling and inversion that makes one wish it was possible to overlook the many annoying goofs, and the scintillating use of the Dropkick Murphys song, "I'm Shipping Up to Boston."

The Departed takes place mainly in South Boston where — according to actor Mark Wahlberg who grew up in the area — you either become a crook or a cop. Like so much of Scorsese's work it is set in a world that is virtually all male, it deals with organized crime, and it is a story of trust, betrayal, duplicity and deception. The characters and themes are likewise familiar: we focus on a battle between two men who are inextricably connected. The story involves a questionable father figure, a blonde trophy woman to whom both men are attracted, the territorial rules of the streets, and the lethal battle with the unacknowledged shadow.

In an attempt to overthrow omnipotent, but slightly decrepit mob boss Frank Costello (Jack Nicholson), Captain Queenan (Martin Sheen) of the Massachusetts State Police convinces Billy Costigan (Leonardo DiCaprio), a young cadet, to go undercover and gain Costello's trust in order to bring him down from the inside.[36] As such, the basic premise is similar to that of *Gangs of New York*, but this story has an added twist: while they are infiltrating the mob, Costello has planted a mole inside the State Police in the shape of his eminently respectable-looking young protégé Colin Sullivan (Matt Damon) who has recently graduated from the Police Academy. The main theme of *The Departed* is identity, and as each of the two young men — Billy Costigan and Colin Sullivan — assumes his new persona and starts lying about who he is, he begins to lose sense of himself until the persona consumes him and he *becomes* the mask.

We first meet Colin at the beginning of the film as a young boy of approximately 12. He is sitting in a luncheonette when Costello comes in to collect his payment. The owner of the lunch counter seems intimidated by Costello but at the same time slightly annoyed by his autocratic manner. Colin, on the other hand, is awestruck, and his admiration visibly increases when Costello orders the owner to give the boy a huge brown paper bag filled with bread and cold cuts to take home to his grandmother with whom he apparently lives. The image of a child being sent off to his aging grandmother with a bag filled with goodies calls to mind the Red Riding Hood motif that is prevalent in other Scorsese films, and it is accentuated when Costello demonstratively stuffs a *Wolverine* comic book into the bag for the boy.[37] Their first encounter establishes Costello as the wolf and gives his advances to the boy a suggestion of seduction. Just moments earlier we saw Costello making passes at an adolescent girl by asking her if she had gotten her period yet, so undertones of sexual depravity are implied from the start, introducing Costello as a corrupter of children.

Gangs of New York begins with a boy who has a father but no mother. In the opening of *The Aviator*, Mother is the dominant figure whereas Father is missing. *The Departed* introduces a boy who has neither a father nor a mother, which leaves him particularly vulnerable to the advances of the wolf. Colin is clearly starving for fatherly attention, and Costello knows intuitively that the best way to tempt him is by appealing to his hunger and greed: "If you ever want to make extra money come see me on L Street."

In the following scenes Costello takes on the role of mentor and father figure (and throughout Colin calls him "Dad" on the phone to obfuscate who he is talking to). Costello teaches him a whole new set of mesmerizing but twisted life philosophies which the child swallows hook, line and sinker. This culminates when Costello replaces the authority of the church with his own: "Non Serviam!—I will not serve!" he says. Colin precociously recognizes the reference to James Joyce, but actually the implications are darker and much more ominous since the words refer to Satan swearing off God: it is "better to reign in Hell, than serve in Heav'n," says Milton's Lucifer.[38] This scene is the perfect mirror opposite to the opening of *Gangs of New York*. Amsterdam's father, Priest Vallon, invoked Michael the Archangel to protect them, whereas Colin's new father gleefully steps into the role of Satan whom St. Michael cast out of Paradise. When Costello proudly pronounces, "That's my boy" seconds later, it implies that Colin, the altar boy, has given in to the Devil, and the seduction and adoption is complete.

Colin Sullivan is easily corrupted through his hunger—Costello tempts him with attention, food, money, and expensive gifts—and all through the film, he is defined by his insatiable selfish ambition. He needs the adoration of every woman he meets, yet also wants the trophy blonde; he is going to law school at night, yet also craves praise and promotions within the State Police. He is yearning for social advancement and covets the luxurious and expensive Beacon Hill apartment with a view of the State House which seems to be the ultimate object of his desire. At the root of it all seems to be his father hunger, and as long as that is left unacknowledged, it can never really be assuaged.

One might wonder whether Colin's self-aggrandizing ruthlessness was born out of Costello's pernicious influence, or whether Costello picked him to begin with because he could sense it in the boy, as Scorsese himself has suggested. Throughout, Colin's only instinct seems to be for self-preservation, for holding onto his newfound prestige and prosperity and keeping the mask of respectability intact. In the screenplay, it is stated that he is supposed to feel guilty over Captain Queenan's death, but in the film his only response is regret that "now I got no access" which more than suggests a psychopathic personality.

Colin is a callous, merciless man, brought up by a callous, merciless father figure. Thus he has no qualms whatsoever about sacrificing even Costello the moment he becomes a threat, real or perceived. Their final exchange before Colin executes him is revealing in that Colin's only interest is whether Costello has given him up to the FBI. "You know I'd never give you up. You're like—" says Costello. Colin derisively interrupts him: "A son—to you? Is that what it is about, all that murderin' and fuckin' and no sons?" In the end, however, the concept of father and son no longer means anything to either of them, and Colin feels only scorn for the old man.

Five minutes into the film, Colin has already been won over by the dark side. He crosses over almost instantly and never looks back. He has been consumed by the mask of respectability that the Devil has placed upon him and he is thoroughly enjoying himself every step of the way. There is never any question of the film being a spiritual journey Colin has to go through to redeem himself, and if he budges at all it is only to sink deeper and deeper into his arrogance and insensitivity. So, although Colin is presented first, the real protagonist of *The Departed* is Billy Costigan, whom we see six minutes into the film when, as a young adult, he is taking a multiple-choice test during his traineeship. Billy, too, has known the temptation of power and wealth from an early age: he has spent his entire life withstanding the lure of the old money of his mother's shallow WASP family on the one hand, and the easy money of his father's mob-connected family on the other. The multiple-choice test is a perfect way of presenting Billy, because all his life mutually exclusive choices have been lined up for him. His Uncle Jackie was part of the innermost circle of Costello's crew, whereas his father was a morally upright man who preferred being a baggage handler at the airport to a life of crime. Billy has chosen the life of his father against all odds, and it is clear that he feels an unutterable contempt for both sides of his family. Whereas it is indicated that Colin joins the State Police because Costello wants it that way, one has a feeling that Billy does it partly because it is the perfect way to provoke and annoy both sides of his family.

Costigan's call to adventure comes when he is called in for a meeting with the sympathetic Captain Queenan and his obnoxious right-hand man, Sergeant Dignam (Mark Wahlberg). A new choice is now presented to him: he has a history of aggressive behavior, and so Queenan wants to have him convicted on a trumped-up charge of assault and battery, expelled from the Academy, sent to jail, and put on probation, so he can let himself be

In *The Departed* (Warner Bros., 2006), Billy Costigan (Leonardo DiCaprio, left) is sent into the darkness, disguised as everything he most abhors. His task is to let himself be recruited into the ranks of mob boss Frank Costello so he can bring him down from the inside. Here making the first moves with Fitzy (David O'Hara).

recruited into Costello's ranks. At first Billy hesitates, but then he accepts the challenge and is thrown head-first into a situation in which he has to pretend to be everything he most abhors. Billy Costigan's voyage is the classic mythological journey into the realm of darkness, but he descends into Hades as an impostor in order to overthrow the Lord of the Darkness at the very real risk of losing himself, because, as Nietzsche said, "Anyone who fights with monsters should take care that he does not in the process become a monster."[39]

It makes sense that we meet Colin first, because his story presents us with the worst-case scenario of what might happen to Billy when he ventures into the abyss. Colin has already been through his ordeal and succumbed completely, and Billy's conflict is a perfect repetition of it: One fatherless boy was sitting on a stool at a lunch counter in 1982 at the age 12 and was taken "under the wing of the dragon," as Amsterdam Vallon put it. Now, 29 minutes into the film, another fatherless boy is sitting in the same place at the same lunch counter a couple of decades later in order to attract the same dragon. The main question becomes whether Billy, too, will lose his identity. Will he sell his soul to the Devil to assuage the pain of the lost father, sign away his humanity, get lost in the mask he has to wear, and sink into oblivion?

It is crucial for Billy's journey that the one who sends him into the darkness is Captain Queenan, the herald and mentor. Queenan has chosen Billy because he has been playing double roles all his life, and the magical words that convince Billy to take on the call to adventure are Queenan's plea: "Do it again! For me!" Just as Costello's adage: "Non Serviam" marked Colin's giving in to the wolf, Queenan's words: "For me!" convince Billy. Later, when he is on the verge of giving up, all Queenan has to say to keep him going is, "Hang tight *for me*, kid!" As in the previous Scorsese/DiCaprio collaborations, the concept of father is central in *The Departed*. Billy has inherited the shadow of his father, and so he cannot resist the behest of the kind, paternal Queenan to go undercover to bring down the dark father, posing as the very thing he has vowed to himself (and presumably to the memory of his father) that he would never become.

The letter X is used innumerable times in the film. Explicitly this is an allusion to Howard Hawks's and Howard Hughes's *Scarface* from 1932 in which X denotes death. In *The Departed* it has a more profound significance which has to do with the deepest and most interesting structures and themes. In a mythological sense, the story concerns the good and decent father who sends his son into the realms of darkness to beat the Devil. At the same time, the Devil sends his corrupted son into the light, the very heart of human civilization, to corrupt and derange it. Costigan and Sullivan are mirror images, but rather than being simply parallel reflections of each other, the two cross over, and like in Hitchcock's *Strangers on a Train*, the X comes to signify that crisscross principle.

This basic philosophical idea was hinted at by Lewis Carroll in his books about Alice, and it has been fascinatingly developed by David Lynch: if you go through the looking glass and venture onto the other side, where does your mirror image go in the meantime? Does he perhaps go into your ordinary world to wreak havoc? Billy Costigan ventures into the darkness, while Colin Sullivan, his shadow counterpart and doppelganger steps out, ready to take his place.

Everything in *The Departed* is now doubled, inverted, reflected, and re-reflected, and images of doubling and duplicity are pervasive. The two characters constantly echo each other and they both have double identities. Colin has a sidekick at the Academy named Barrigan who turns up in the climactic scene; Billy has a sidekick at the Academy named

Brown who turns up in the climactic scene. They are both fatherless: Colin's father was a janitor; Billy's father was a baggage handler. Their names—William Costigan and Colin Sullivan—are virtually anagrams. Billy's birthday is 7-11, Colin lives in apartment 711.

A superhero motif was introduced in the beginning when Costello gave young Colin a *Wolverine* comic book, and it seems reasonable to assume that this connection between Costigan and Sullivan—the number 711—might be a reference to the Quality Comics 1940s superhero. The story of *#711* echoes many of the main themes of *The Departed*: Daniel Dyce, a District Attorney, is a dead ringer for his friend, Jacob Horn, a convicted criminal. Wanting to see his newborn son, Jacob convinces Daniel to trade places with him for a short while. On the way to the hospital, however, Jacob is killed in a car crash, and Daniel is declared dead and stuck in jail. Assuming the number of his jail cell, #711, Daniel leaves the prison every night to fight crime and returns before morning.[40] The concept of two men representing two sides of the same psyche, of trading places at the risk of being stuck inside the dark side of the masquerade, is contained within the oblique reference to *#711* as well as in Scorsese's use of the letter X.

Like so many of Scorsese's characters, Costigan and Sullivan become involved with the same woman (although in *The Departed* there is no real rivalry over her since neither man knows of the existence of the other until the very end). Madolyn Madden (Vera Farmiga) is one of the weakest elements in the film, and her character is utterly unbelievable as a medical doctor and psychiatrist. Even if the film intends us to see her as an unimaginably bad one, it is more than incredible that a trained professional who is working mainly with hardened criminals and traumatized police officers would have no experience in dealing with aggressive patients. Billy Costigan gets agitated when she refuses to give him a prescription, and this—we are supposed to believe—unsettles her to the point that she runs off in pursuit of him, virtually begging him to take a prescription as well as her card.

If we can manage to see beyond this, however, certain patterns emerge. Twice, attention is drawn to her business card—first she presents it to Colin and later to Billy—and thus to her name and credentials: Madolyn Madden, MD, PhD. Her last name, presumably, contains a filmic reference. At the midpoint of the film, Scorsese has a minor character watch John Ford's 1935 classic *The Informer* on TV. Katie Madden is the name of the girlfriend of the main character in *The Informer* who is haunted by a nightly vision of her standing, pure and virginal, underneath a lamppost. Then a man approaches her and she takes off her shawl to reveal herself as a prostitute. This suggests a Madonna/whore motif in *The Departed* which is underscored because Madolyn's first name is a variation of Magdalene, and her full name is a near-anagram of Mary Magdalene.

She and Billy seem attracted primarily to the emotional comfort they can provide for each other, and the song played over their sexual encounter is, very appropriately, "Comfortably Numb." Billy's journey goes from the light and into the darkness, and most of their meetings take place at night and/or underground. She and Colin, on the other hand, are more interested in each other as trophies. They each came from modest or poor backgrounds, and Colin's Beacon Hill home is quite literally a giant step up from Madolyn's basement apartment. He is embarrassed by her childhood photo (i.e., the very foundation of who she is) and will not let her display it in his home, whereas he is extremely proud of her diploma and credentials (i.e., her assumed persona). Colin is sent from the darkness and into the light, and his encounters with Madolyn take place in elevators going up, in fancy restaurants, in daylight, and in the bright apartment high above the ground.

Madolyn serves to illuminate the mirroring effects and parallels between Billy and Colin, and the film is structured so that whenever one character has an encounter with her, it is echoed and put into perspective by an encounter the other character has with her. First she meets Colin Sullivan, hands him her card, and goes out to dinner with him. Shortly afterwards she meets Billy Costigan, hands him her card, and meets him privately for coffee. When we next see her with Colin after their date, she is in his expensive, sunlit apartment in the morning, trying to convince him that what happened the previous night is quite common. This indication of impotence more than suggests that Colin does not satisfy her in bed. When we next see her with Billy after *their* date, Billy comes to her crummy, dark apartment late at night. They end up in bed together, and Billy seems to have no problems satisfying her. Colin flirts with her and tries to impress and flatter her. Billy constantly confronts her and challenges her professional and personal ethics, as do we: despite her professional pretext, her handing him the card can only be understood as a come-on, since she says in the same breath that she is transferring him to another counselor. While Colin woos her immaculate persona and insists on seeing only that part of her, Billy pulls off her clothes and her mask, revealing that she, too, is prone to lying and deception.

It is vital to keep in mind that Billy is seeing Madolyn in the first place as part of his trumped-up probation for assault and battery, i.e., his dark mask. She is the court-ordered shrink that Queenan was planning with from the very beginning, and so she knows absolutely nothing about Billy being a courageous undercover cop. In other words, she allows herself to be professionally manipulated by and then becomes sexually and emotionally involved with a patient whom she believes to be a violent offender. Simultaneously, she is moving in with a psychopathic undercover criminal whom she does not see through despite her repeatedly flaunted credentials and all the telltale signs. If we ignore the fact that this is implausible, it presents to us a woman who is not only incompetent, but also neurotic and highly self-destructive underneath her cool exterior.

As Billy goes to bed with Madolyn, we have just entered the second half of the film, and things become dizzyingly complicated. At the midpoint Billy found out that, unbeknownst to the State Police, mob boss Costello is actually a protected FBI informant which blurs the lines even further. Meanwhile, the search for the traitor — the one within Costello's ranks as well as the one within the State Police — intensifies. Everyone in Costello's crew is ordered to give out his citizens' data so that Colin can search through the police computer and hopefully expose the rat among them, and Billy has to endanger himself even further by refusing to give out his data. He reports back to Captain Queenan that an envelope marked "CITIZENS" is to be taken to Costello's man inside the police. Ironically, Colin is placed in command of a new police sub-unit whose job it is to find that same mole inside the department, i.e., himself. He overhears Queenan telling Billy that if he follows Costello, he will find his mole, and deduces that conversely, if he follows Queenan, he will find *his* mole, i.e., Billy. Each of them is now directly involved in smoking out himself as well as tracking down the other one. Each has to pretend that he is corroborating in uncovering the identity of one infiltrator, i.e., himself, while at the same time he is under tremendous pressure to find the other one before he himself is exposed.

Billy Costigan is rapidly approaching the inmost cave. In this story the hero goes into the heart of darkness not simply to *face* what he most abhors in himself, but actually *disguised* as everything he has tried his whole life not to be. If we wear the shadow as our outer persona and mask, or if we inhabit it extendedly, it may become stuck on our face. When

Billy makes love to Madolyn — his most intimate act in the film — he is wearing the false persona of the violent offender which is what she knows him as and for which she apparently hungers. Presumably this is the point when it begins to take over his life, since Madolyn is part of the very definition of that mask, being part of the conditions of his probation and thus of the disguise that allowed him to enter Costello's ranks in the first place.

An hour into the film, Dignam provokingly threatens to erase Billy's file. Dignam reminds Billy that he and Queenan are the only two people in the entire world who know that he is actually a cop. As far as everyone else is concerned, he is a criminal who gave in to his true nature and joined forces with Frank Costello. If Dignam were to erase his file, Billy's true identity would disappear and only the paradoxical shadow mask would remain. One of our most basic fears, says Bruno Bettelheim, is the fear of being devoured. Billy now realizes that not only could either side — the mob or the police — take him out at any time, but his identity could be swallowed up at the single push of a button. The threat of complete obliteration — logistically, physically, psychologically, and spiritually — becomes real, imminent and very frightening.

During the second half, Billy's identity and sense of self begin to deteriorate. Images of disintegration become pervasive, testifying that as Billy is losing strength, Colin is gaining ground. The two of them have switched places: Colin, who originally came out of the shadow, now represents the airtight persona incarnate, whereas Billy, the ego, is reduced to

Who is the ego and who is the shadow? During the second half of *The Departed* (Warner Bros., 2006), Billy Costigan's (Leonardo DiCaprio, right) identity and sense of self begin to deteriorate as the shadow, Colin Sullivan (Matt Damon) takes over his life. It becomes increasingly difficult to tell the two apart.

living in the shadows. He follows Colin around Chinatown like a shadow, he sleeps with Colin's girlfriend behind his back, and he becomes the one who points out people's pretenses. Billy has no home but is living in the dark, empty house of his dead mother. In and of itself a shocking image of the state of the psyche, this becomes even more alarming when we consider that Colin, the shadow, is living in an exquisite, bright apartment. Colin is, in fact, gloriously and triumphantly living the affluent lifestyle of Billy's family that Billy has tried to resist, while he himself is withering away.

The most exquisite objective correlative for Billy's psychological and spiritual disintegration comes when he follows Colin through Chinatown, and his face is reflected in a pendant made out of crystal and mirror rectangles. This astounding image is the equivalent of the one in *The Aviator* in which cactuses are projected onto Hughes's body during his self-imposed quarantine. We actually see Billy's face cut into fragments, some of which are real, some of which are distorted through crystal, and some of which are reflected in mirrors. We also glimpse the reflected back of Colin Sullivan as he walks away. Billy Costigan is truly on the verge of extinction, and moments later it is affirmed that the two of them have changed places when a surveillance camera captures them both. If Billy had access to that tape, the rat he is chasing would be exposed instantly, but he no longer has access to anything — only Colin does. Colin, on the other hand, sees only his own face on the tape, because Billy can no longer be identified — he has no face. It is as if Abraham Van Helsing and Count Dracula have traded places, and now it is Van Helsing who has no mirror image.

The parts of himself Billy has been trying to deny, have taken over his life. Colin is living a lifestyle of which Billy's mother's wealthy family would be proud, and has connections to the very core of the Boston mob of which Billy's father's family would be proud. Captain Queenan, for whose sake Billy is doing this in the first place, is dead, and Sergeant Dignam, the only living person who knows who Billy truly is, has disappeared. When Billy enters the inmost cave, he has all but ceased to exist. "I want my identity back," he says to Colin four times during the last 20 minutes of the film, implying that Colin is the only one who can give it back to him. "You want to be a cop again?" Colin asks, revealing that ironically he has no clue what Billy means. "Being a cop is not an identity," Billy has to tell him. Colin has become so swallowed up by the mask that he is no longer capable of knowing what an identity is.[41]

In numerous classical works dealing with the relationship between the ego and the shadow, the ego is forced to accept defeat and stand by while the doppelganger takes over his life. In Dostoyevsky's *The Double*, the main character has no choice but to retreat into oblivion. In David Lynch's *Twin Peaks*, Agent Dale Cooper's shadow self emerges from the Black Lodge while he himself is stuck there. In Hans Christian Andersen's *The Shadow*, the protagonist is forced to let the shadow usurp his life and is finally executed by it. In *The Departed*, just as Colin is on the verge of giving Billy back his identity, he realizes that Billy has seen the "CITIZENS" envelope on his desk and thus knows that he, Colin Sullivan, is Costello's inside man. Dignam threatened to erase Billy; Colin actually does it. Billy is standing in the inmost cave, ready to reach out for the grail that is the reward for his journey through the dark realms — in this case reclaiming his true identity — but, instead, he is obliterated. He no longer exists as an individual, he has been abolished by the paradoxical shadow persona whose sole instinct is self-preservation.

Billy Costigan's journey through the dark regions ends up costing him first his *sense* of identity, then his actual identity, then his place as a citizen and human being, and, finally, his life. In the climactic scene, he summons Colin to meet him on the roof from which Queenan, the good father, was thrown to his death. Billy has more than enough evidence to blow Colin's cover and threatens to expose him unless he helps him. "I want my identity back," he insists for the fourth time. He manages to get Colin into the elevator, so that he can finally, and literally, bring him down. Surprisingly, the shadow crumples and surrenders, accepts impending exposure and defeat, and begs Billy to kill him. At the exact moment of Billy's apparent triumph, however, when the shadow is willing to give him back his life, the elevator doors open, and Billy (who is inattentive) is shot by Barrigan, Colin's sidekick from the Academy. In *Gangs of New York*, Priest Vallon's final words to his son were about being persistently mindful of the shadow: "Don't never look away!" It is Billy's hubris that destroys him at the end. Instead of looking at the door, he is overconfident, lets go of his caution, looks away, and loses his life.

Barrigan reveals that all along he, too, has been an informant for Costello inside the State Police, and since no one else is still alive who knows his secret, the unscrupulous Sullivan naturally kills him instantly. He now officially lets the dead Barrigan take the rap as Costello's rat, while recommending Costigan for the Medal of Merit.

In the final scene, Colin Sullivan returns smugly to his glorious apartment with a bag full of expensive groceries. We have come full circle: the little boy who was once dependent on and grateful for a paper bag with food given to him by the wolf, is now able to afford his own more luxurious groceries. Every single person who knows that he is really an impostor is dead, he believes. Colin's victory seems complete, but if we consider Billy Costigan to be the ego and Colin Sullivan his shadow self, he is living on borrowed time, now that Billy is dead. As he enters his apartment, Sergeant Dignam is standing by the window against the backdrop of the coveted State House with a loaded gun. Dignam shoots and kills Colin Sullivan, and then simply leaves.

At the beginning of the film Dignam provoked Billy who paraphrased Hawthorne: "Don't you know any Shakespeare?" Now, like the conclusion of *Hamlet*, all the male players are dead. Only Dignam, like Horatio, is left standing. There is no basis for comparing each character and event in *The Departed* with those in *Hamlet*, but there are a number of interesting similarities. Hamlet, like Billy, is a torn young man whose father's death and mother's remarriage forms the basis of his torment. His surroundings are entangled in a web of information and misinformation, espionage and counterespionage, trust and betrayal and lies, and the perfidy of Rosencrantz and Guildenstern might be compared to Brown and Barrigan. While Dignam is hardly Billy's most trusted friend — the way Horatio was Hamlet's — in the final analysis it seems that he is the only one Billy could really depend on. When Dignam kills Colin it only makes sense to see it as revenge for Captain Queenan and Billy Costigan, and if any kind of balance is to be restored in this tragedy, we need Dignam to go out and tell the true story. Hamlet's dying words to Horatio thus seem exceedingly appropriate as an epitaph for Billy Costigan: "If thou didst ever hold me in thy heart, absent thee from felicity a while, and in this harsh world *draw thy breath in pain to tell my story*."[42]

Shutter Island

Shutter Island (2010) opened on February 19, 2010, having been moved back from its original release date in October of 2009. When it finally hit the theatres it grossed an astounding $40.2 million on the first weekend, beating the $26.9 million of even *The Departed* by a mile. Some of this success may be explained by the expectations created by the long wait, but it is my guess that this film will strike a deep chord with audiences worldwide who hopefully will have the courage to recognize dark sides of themselves in the hapless protagonist.

This fourth collaboration between Martin Scorsese and Leonardo DiCaprio is based on Dennis Lehane's bestselling novel. It takes place in 1954 in the wake of World War II and the Korean War, and it gives Cold War paranoia whole new depths of meaning. It concerns a U.S. marshal who is sent to Ashecliffe, a treatment facility for the criminally insane on Shutter Island, to find a missing patient during a storm that turns into a hurricane. Over the next several days he undergoes a dramatic change and has to face haunting truths about himself and his own life. Like the previous Scorsese/DiCaprio collaborations, the concept of Father is at the heart of his struggle, but this time because of his intense guilt over his own abysmal failure as a father.

The film was inspired by the stories of Edgar Allan Poe as well as a number of Hollywood noir and horror films. Explicitly it calls to mind the sublime works of Val Lewton, and most poignantly it evokes *The Ghost Ship*. Also, of course, it refers back to classic feverish films about insane asylums, notably Robert Wiene's German expressionistic silent film *The Cabinet of Dr. Caligari* (1919) and Samuel Fuller's *Shock Corridor* (1963). Finally, it calls to mind *the* masterwork about Cold War brainwashing experiments, John Frankenheimer's *The Manchurian Candidate* (1962).

Shutter Island is an overwhelming cinematic tour de force. With his use of light, color, image, sound and music, Scorsese pulls and seduces us into this eerie, nightmarish, gothic world of madness and terror. The "Passacaglia" from Krzysztof Penderecki's *Symphony #3* becomes one of the most haunting pieces of film music since Bernard Herrmann. And the sadness of Max Richter's post-classical "On the Nature of Daylight" is almost unbearable when added to Teddy/Laeddis's trauma — particularly when it is played over the end credits, superimposed over Dinah Washington's "This Bitter Earth."[43] And Leonardo DiCaprio makes Teddy Daniels's anguish so palpable that it is physically transferred to the audience. By the end of the film we feel a profound sense of compassion, grief and loss for him and his loved ones.

I consider myself unbelievably lucky that I get to finish my long journey through the works of Martin Scorsese by delving into a film that so exquisitely sums up the arguments I have presented throughout this book. *Shutter Island* is an excruciating hero's journey in which a reluctant protagonist is taken through a highly symbolic landscape. It is *the* most devastating battle between ego and shadow in Scorsese's entire career. At the end of *Shutter Island*, Andrew Laeddis and Teddy Daniels (Leonardo DiCaprio) are both destroyed by the battle. Like the journey of Billy Costigan in *The Departed*, Teddy's journey turns out to revolve around the concept of getting his identity back. The elusive grail that he has the opportunity to seize after facing the forces of darkness inside the inmost cave is his own total self. Astonishingly, he rejects it and chooses instead to hand them both over for symbolic crucifixion.

Many of Scorsese's main characters struggle with an unrelenting nemesis, an alter ego who is the embodiment of the demons inside himself. *Shutter Island* presents us with a perturbing twist, however, when at the very end Teddy Daniels turns out to *be* the alter ego, the shadow, the demon inside, whereas Andrew Laeddis, the professed monster, turns out to be the real person. Not only has the shadow gone autonomous, it has taken over the psyche and locked up the ego inside the inner dungeon. Furthermore, it manages to convince us, the audience, that the ego is a terrible fiend — an "ugly looking son of a bitch" with a "huge scar from right temple to left lip" — and if we take Teddy's very last words at face value, that it's better to die as a good man than to live as a monster, then we must realize that he still has *us* locked up inside his twisted logic. In the final analysis there is nothing to suggest that Laeddis is a monster, that he is anything other than an extremely traumatized individual.

At the heart of the film is the intense inner torment of a man who has sealed off the majority of his own psyche. Inherently and inexorably, his hero's journey must thus move toward a supreme ordeal during which he uncovers and realizes the truth about his own identity and existence. From the very first moments, it becomes clear that this journey will take us into the very darkest recesses of the human mind. Mythologically, trips across water always involve major upheaval, and islands often symbolize the conscious mind as opposed to the unconscious of the surrounding water. As we enter the film, Teddy Daniels is on the ferry on his way to an insular treatment facility that only takes "the most dangerous, damaged" criminals. The conscious that this particular island represents is thus shown to be extremely warped, and, within minutes, it will be completely cut off from "the other side" (i.e., the normal, everyday world) due to a storm.

Like the main character of *What's a Nice Girl Like You Doing in a Place Like This?*, Teddy has an intense fear of water, and as he is throwing up he tries to console himself: "Pull yourself together, Teddy. It's just water," he says. "It's a lot of water." Since water is symbolically linked to the unconscious, his dread of it perfectly echoes his fear of the identity that he has hermetically sealed off to cover up his grief and guilt over the death by drowning of his children.[44]

One of the very first images we see is Teddy Daniels looking at his own face in the mirror, and thus it is established from the beginning that there are two of him: the real man and the twisted reflection. Since we end up realizing that Teddy is Laeddis's dark alter ego and not vice versa, one might argue that the entire journey takes place inside the mind, on the other side of the mirror. Like in *Taxi Driver*, we are experiencing this hero's journey filtered through a sick mind, and we stay so close to Teddy's perception that at times it is virtually impossible to orient ourselves. Things and people are often drenched in water, and many of the interior walls are made out of dark red brick. It almost feels as if we are inside Teddy's head, moving deeper and deeper. In Lehane's novel we are given clues and might be able to figure out the anagrams for ourselves, but in the film we are so close to his experience that we have absolutely no way of solving the mystery until *he* is forced to do so.[45]

Like Teddy's journey, the film falls into two distinct and very different sections. During the first half he arrives on Shutter Island with a certain authority, accompanied by his new partner, Chuck Aule (Mark Ruffalo), wearing his U.S. marshal's clothes, with the objective of finding the missing patient, Rachel Solando. During the second half he is wearing clothes that belong to the institution. Rachel has been found, his partner disappears, all control is taken away from him, and the real purpose for his visit becomes clearer and clearer as step by step we approach the inmost cave.

There is something slightly stilted and artificial about the arrival at Ashecliffe, which in retrospect makes all the sense in the world since it all turns out to be a construct of which

U.S. Marshall Teddy Daniels (Leonardo DiCaprio, center) and his new partner, Chuck Aule (Mark Ruffalo, left) arrive at Ashecliffe, a treatment facility for the criminally insane in *Shutter Island* (Paramount Pictures, 2010).

everyone is conscious (and self-conscious) except Teddy and the viewer; a "radical, cutting edge role play," as Dr. Cawley (Ben Kingsley) eventually admits, specifically designed to reflect Teddy's delusion. Most of the film thus consists of pieces which we need in order to understand the jigsaw puzzle that is the mind of Teddy/Laeddis.

The visit to Dr. Cawley's house on the first evening is meant to trigger Teddy's memories of the liberation of Dachau, which are partly truth and partly fiction. The record Cawley has chosen to put on the turntable is Gustav Mahler's piano quartet, the exact same piece that was played when the commandant at Dachau botched his suicide. As we enter Teddy's memory of this event, we see an interesting streak of sadism in his character: when the wounded commandant reaches for the gun on the floor to finish the job, Teddy moves it further away with his foot; and so it could well be Teddy's doing that it "took him an hour to die." Cawley's guest and colleague, the austere Teutonic Dr. Jeremiah Naehring (Max von Sydow) purposefully provokes Teddy and fuels his aggression so that Teddy ends up shouting at him in German. Naehring alludes to his being a recovering alcoholic, compliments him for his "impressive defense mechanisms" and refers to Teddy and Chuck as "men of violence." For them, Naehring says, retreat from a physical conflict "isn't something you consider an option."

Following this provocation, Teddy's dead wife, Dolores (Michelle Williams), comes to him that night in a haunting dream. Although we are outside of Dr. Cawley's construct, she obviously still represents a part of the subconscious of the main character. She tells him not to leave the island because Rachel is still there, and adds a significant new piece to the puzzle as we move into the second act: "And so is he.... Laeddis."

The next day Teddy keeps alluding to "a patient named Andrew Laeddis" until finally Chuck insists on being told who Laeddis is. In the cemetery mausoleum, where they seek shelter as the storm turns into a hurricane, Teddy reveals that the missing patient, Rachel, is not his real reason for being on Shutter Island. Andrew Laeddis is that man who "lit the match that caused the fire that killed my wife," he says, and he has every reason to believe that Laeddis is now a patient at Ashecliffe. He is not here to kill Laeddis, he says. At the liberation of Dachau he helped kill innumerable guards, and he does not want to kill again. He is really here to unravel the very fabric of Ashecliffe, to expose that it is funded by HUAC and that they are conducting gruesome experiments on human beings.[46]

At this point Chuck, who eventually turns out to be Dr. Sheehan and thus part of Dr. Cawley's passion play, activates Teddy's paranoia which will escalate throughout the rest of the film. "What if they wanted you here," he asks. What if "while you were looking into them, they were looking into you" and they invented the whole story of Rachel Solando as a ploy? When Deputy Warden McPherson comes to their rescue, Teddy marvels that "they found us." "It's an island, boss," Chuck persists. "They're always gonna find us."

As we approach the midpoint of the film, Teddy and Chuck are taken back to Ashecliffe, and their clothes, which have been drenched in the storm, are removed. This constitutes a major turning point. On a symbolic level, the protagonist has been wearing the protective persona of Teddy Daniels as a shield against his true identity. That persona now is stripped off, and he gradually loses all outer control until he finally remembers who he is. Thus, seconds later, he suffers an even more significant loss of power. Teddy figures out what the mysterious note they found in Rachel Solando's cell means: "Who is 67?" There are 42 patients in wards A and B and 24 patients in ward C. Teddy deduces that there must be a 67th patient, and that presumably that patient is the horrific Andrew Laeddis. At the exact moment he cracks this code, his official U.S. marshal authority is removed completely when he is told that Rachel has been found.

Rachel Solando (Emily Mortimer) clearly reflects Dolores in that she has drowned her children, but she also reflects Laeddis (her creator), in that she has completely repressed the memory of the event and has formed an "elaborate fictional structure" to protect herself from it. "How is it possible that the truth never gets through to her?" Teddy asks incredulously. "Sanity is not a choice," Dr. Cawley answers, and later adds that the greatest obstacle to her recovery was "her refusal to face what she had done."

Teddy's meeting with Rachel is a mirror image of his dream of Dolores. In the dream, Teddy expressed a deep longing for his wife who assured him, "I'm bones in a box." Rachel "buried an empty casket" and likewise aches for her lost love: "You're dead. I cry every night," she says. Rachel is a part of Laeddis's scenario of repression and represents a part of himself, but interestingly so, too, does Jim, as Rachel believes that Teddy is him. Laeddis's original trauma was clearly acquired during the war, and Jim Solando becomes a part of him that died and never made it back. Appropriately, the encounter with Rachel ends up being a question of identity. Suddenly she shouts: "My Jim's dead. Who the fuck are you?" rephrasing the caterpillar's question to Alice, and repeating verbatim the mystery man's question to Fred Madison (who also hermetically sealed off the memory of killing his wife) in David Lynch's *Lost Highway*.

This aggravation triggers a paralyzing migraine which sends Teddy into his most terrifying nightmare. A little girl at Dachau looks at him sadly: "You should have saved me," she says. "You should have saved us all." We then cut from the concentration camp to Andrew Laeddis (Elias Koteas) who is sitting in Dr. Nahring's chair in Dr. Cawley's living room. The most interesting thing about this scene is that even in his dreams the denial and repression are so airtight that what we see are still screen memories: we are led to believe that the little girl is referring to the concentration camp victims (only at the very end do we realize that she is directly related to his deepest grief and guilt), and Laeddis is a horrific atrocity of a man (only at the very end do we realize that Laeddis is Teddy).

Although he no longer has any authority, Teddy escalates his frenetic search for the hideous monsters that he believes exist outside of himself—the 67th prisoner and the ghastly scientific experiments—and the approach to the inmost cave, the dark night of the soul, begins.

First, he and Chuck go to Ward C, the ward where the most dangerous and damaged inmates are kept. This is the most gothic and frightening-looking place in the film—due to the storm some of the prisoners may not even be contained in their cells—and we have an acute sense that we are moving ever deeper into the recesses of a warped mind. The first person they encounter here is a deranged patient who insists on telling them about the hydrogen bomb, in the process presenting a perfect description of Teddy's mental state: unlike other bombs, the hydrogen bomb implodes, it falls in on itself "and the fury of its own self-destruction creates an entirely new monster" so that "it implodes with an explosion of the thousandth, the millionth degree."

Teddy now ventures deeper into this inferno alone, and in the heart of Ward C he finds George Noyce (Jackie Earle Haley), the man who originally told him that Laeddis was an inmate on Shutter Island. Like the helpers in fairy tales, Noyce presents him with valuable information, all of which points to the real truth of Teddy's identity: "This is a game. All of this ... is for you!" he says, although Teddy does not really hear him. "You can't dig out the truth and kill Laeddis at the same time. You gotta make a choice," he continues. And finally he says about Dolores that if "you wanna uncover the truth, you gotta let her go" or "you'll never leave this island."

Teddy must take the final steps into the heart of darkness alone, so as he leaves Ward C, Noyce feeds his paranoia by reminding him that he does not really know his new partner and maybe cannot trust him. "I'm going on alone," Teddy tells Chuck, and magically Chuck disappears for good. Thinking that he has fallen or been pushed over the edge of a cliff, Teddy climbs down to look for him, and this leads him to a cave in the rocks where he meets "Rachel Solando. The real one."

This is one of the most crucial and brilliant scenes in the film. Although this Rachel Solando (Patricia Clarkson) is a good ten years older than the other one, she too looks exactly like the photograph Teddy was shown when he first arrived. The first Rachel was Dr. Cawley's staged version of Teddy's fictional invention. The second one, we are told at the end, is not there at all; she is pure hallucination and part of the symptoms of his withdrawal from antipsychotic drugs. "It's this ritualistic encounter almost like an old myth," Scorsese says. "She is like the Oracle of Delphi."[47] To begin with, she is a figment of his imagination—there is no Rachel Solando except in his mind—and so, in that sense, Teddy is absolutely right: this is the real Rachel Solando. This means, of course, that she is pure anima, a perfect projection and reflection of the deepest parts of his soul.

Throughout the scene, the framing confirms this. The two of them sit across from each other in the cave as she tells her alarming story, and she is framed so that we see her on the right side of the screen with the fire in front of and to the left of her. When we cut to Teddy, he is framed so that we see him on the left side of the screen with the fire in front of and to the right of him. The two of them thus become perfect mirror images of each other, and the fire is the objective correlative for the inflamed mind in which this conversation takes place.

Her story becomes the ultimate nightmare that affirms and even surpasses Teddy's own paranoia and worst fears. She used to be a brilliant doctor who worked at Ashecliffe, and she came from a prominent family, but when she started questioning the other doctors and their use of psychotropic drugs and experimental surgery, they managed to convince the outside world that she had gone insane. "You understand that they can't let you leave," she tells Teddy, and assures him that with his history, it will be a small matter to convince everyone that he cracked and to keep him locked up forever.

Like the Oracle of Delphi, Dr. Solando makes utterances that turn out to be cryptic, so that much depends on our own translation and interpretation of them: "The brain controls pain, the brain controls fear, empathy, sleep, hunger, anger, everything. What if you could control it?" she says. The dubious experiments that were carried out in North Korea, on the Jews in the concentration camps, and in the Soviet Gulags are now continued right here at Shutter Island, she warns him, and affirms what Noyce told him, that the lighthouse is "where they create the ghosts."

In the climactic scene, Teddy forces his way into the inaccessible lighthouse, and waiting for him there is Dr. Cawley, the godhead and puppet master, the man who cares enough about him to stage this elaborate play in a final attempt to save him.[48] Traditionally, lighthouses are beacons of safety that enable sailors to navigate in the dark. Symbolically they represent the ability to travel safely through the stormy seas of the unconscious. When Teddy Daniels finally makes it to the mysterious lighthouse, the inmost cave, he is given an opportunity to venture into the dark night of his own soul, to uncover the real truth.

Dr. Cawley now proceeds to unravel the truth for him, step by step. Teddy Daniels is really Andrew Laeddis, the 67th patient. Everything that has happened in the past several days has been part of an elaborate stage play constructed by Dr. Cawley to reflect Teddy/Laeddis's delusions, in the hope that it would finally make him see the truth. He has been on Shutter Island for the past 24 months, replaying the same scenario of finding a missing patient, searching for the horrific Laeddis, and unraveling a conspiracy over and over. He has blocked out his own identity to protect himself from a truth that is too harrowing for him to face. Teddy Daniels, a persona created out of the shadow of his past, has taken over, but neither he nor Rachel Solando exist other than in Laeddis's fevered mind. The name Edward Daniels is constructed out of the letters of his name, Andrew Laeddis, just as Rachel Solando is an anagram for Dolores Chanal, the name of his dead wife. Showing him Laeddis's intake form, Dr. Cawley attests that the horrendous monster he has been chasing is himself.

The real truth that Laeddis has been protecting himself from and now has to face inside the inmost cave is his excruciating guilt over the death of his children and his wife. A U.S. marshal with an untreated war trauma and a drinking problem, he refused to see that his wife, Dolores, was mentally ill and needed help. One day he came home to find that she had drowned their three children. When she begged him to set her free from the "insect" that was "living inside her brain," he shot her.

At this point we may realize that "Shutter Island" is a homophone for "shot 'er island." And — exquisitely — just as Edward Daniels and Rachel Solando are anagrams for Andrew Laeddis and Dolores Chanal, so "Shutter Island" is an anagram for "truths and lies."[49] Ordinarily, islands represent the conscious in dreams and mythology, as opposed to the unconscious of the surrounding water, but in this case the name *Shutter* Island indicates from the start that this is a heavily secured and boarded-up conscious, a shuttered island. Throughout the film, Teddy/Laeddis employs what Freud called screen memories — i.e., false memories that are constructed by the mind to keep the real memories at bay. Screen memories are defined as the compromise between the elements that are repressed and the defense against them.

When Dr. Cawley asks him if he is going to deny that his beloved daughter, Rachel, ever lived, Teddy Daniels finally relinquishes his control, the screens and shutters give way, and Andrew Laeddis breaks through to remember finding his three children in the lake behind their house. This heartbreaking scene echoes the opening of Nicolas Roeg's amazing *Don't Look Now*.[50] When we see Laeddis standing in the lake holding his dead children and screaming his pain out, we can palpably feel his torment and understand why it has been necessary for him to block out this memory.

Like Roeg's John Baxter, Laeddis responds to the trauma by refusing to see the real truth until it threatens to annihilate him: Dr. Cawley has been permitted to carry out this radical experiment as a last resort before the other doctors have Laeddis lobotomized. He

Andrew Laeddis (Leonardo DiCaprio) finally remembers the horrible truth about his identity in *Shutter Island* (Paramount Pictures, 2010). The memory that has caused him to forget is coming home to find that his wife, Dolores (Michelle Williams), has drowned their three children.

is the most violent and dangerous patient at Ashecliffe, Cawley tells him, and the others have had enough of having this self-proclaimed, trained U.S. marshal running around questioning and beating patients and orderlies to a pulp when they get in the way of his investigations or point out that he is Laeddis.

In Teddy Daniels's mind, Andrew Laeddis is a horrific monstrosity of a man. In everyone else's perception, Teddy is the violent and dangerous 67th patient. In his fight against the perceived monster, he has himself become one. Where Teddy has clear memories of having participated in the killing of hundreds of guards at the liberation of Dachau, there is no evidence that Andrew Laeddis did that: "You were at Dachau, but you may not have killed any guards," Dr. Cawley tells him. And Teddy does, in fact, shoot and kill Dr. Cawley: only because the gun is not real does Cawley not die.[51]

We repeatedly see streaks of a sadism in Teddy's character, and it is always directed at aggressors who have been guilty of causing suffering in others (i.e., at himself). When he first arrives, Cawley tells him how he works at trying to install in the patients a sense of calm. "These are all violent offenders, right?" Teddy asks contemptuously. "They've hurt people, murdered them in some cases?" And, when Cawley confirms, "Then personally doctor, I'd have to say screw their sense of calm." Teddy consistently acts aggressively on behalf of helpless, innocent victims—his children—while ensuring that the aggressor—he himself—has no peace of mind.

Like Amsterdam Vallon in *Gangs of New York*, Teddy/Laeddis is incapable of addressing his own wound and his harrowing guilt, and so he continues to project them onto his surroundings. Like Eddie Felson in *The Color of Money*, he becomes the very thing that he represses, and the shadow side takes over because he cannot bring himself to face it and endure the pain involved in doing so.

In the attempt to seal off the identity that was so excruciating, Teddy has become much more abhorrent than Andrew Laeddis ever was. Ironically, the only way he can now save himself is by accepting and embracing that he *is* Andrew Laeddis.

It seems appropriate that in Teddy's nightmare, Andrew Laeddis looks like Robert De Niro's version of the Frankenstein creature.[52] People tend to think that Frankenstein is the name of the monster, but actually it is the name of the man who created the monster. In *Shutter Island*, the creature is roaming around at large, an independent person created out of the repressed shadow, while the real man is locked up in the dungeon inside. But in the final analysis, it *was* Andrew Laeddis's mind which *created* poor Teddy Daniels, just as Victor Frankenstein created the creature.

Dr. Solando, the oracle, Anima Mother in the cave, told him that there were two sides to the horrors of Shutter Island: the purely personal one and the larger political conspiracy of scientific experiments. The great thing about paranoia as far as the conspiracy is concerned, Solando told him, is that "once you're declared insane, then anything you do is called part of that insanity." Now Dr. Cawley, the godhead, puppet master father in the inmost cave, presents the reverse side of the same picture: The great thing about a conspiracy as far as the paranoiac is concerned, is that you can blame everything on the conspiracy and "everything we tell you can be seen as lies."

Solando and Cawley are thus shown as reflections of each other, and they turn out to represent virtually the same thing in terms of the larger ramifications of the Teddy/Laeddis experiment. Dr. Cawley's reason for putting him through an enforced hero's journey is not simply a question of him regaining his sanity and avoiding a lobotomy. There are much larger things at stake in this passion play than Andrew Laeddis's personal redemption, as Dr. Cawley and Dr. Sheehan — who played the part of Teddy's partner, Chuck — proceed to explain.

Dr. Solando told Teddy a gruesome tale of radical experiments to control the human brain that were being conducted on Shutter Island — a tale which was a part of his own paranoid schizophrenia. But we have only to remove the feverish, delusional overtones to see that it is not really all that far-fetched, according to what Dr. Cawley tells him. When Teddy arrived, Cawley told him that there is a war going on inside the psychiatric community: "The old school believes in surgical intervention, psychosurgery," which makes the patients "reasonable" and "docile." The new school wants instead to tame the patients with psychopharmacology. Dr. Cawley offers a third approach which is much more humane: "I have this radical idea that if you treat a patient with respect, listen to him, try and understand, you just might reach him." "These patients?" Teddy asks scornfully when someone starts screaming further down the hall. And Cawley makes his ultimate point: "What should be a last resort is becoming a first response."

This process of zombification — whether by surgery or the seemingly less barbaric (and much more financially profitable) medicating — is for the time being restricted to the criminally insane on Shutter Island, but it is more than implied that it will eventually be used on any individual who has given in to the dark side of his or her own mind. The goal — whichever method is used — is to make the inner wolf permanently submissive and compliant. This is the real horror vision of the future of psychiatry. "Someday, Marshall," says

Martin Scorsese directing a scene in *Shutter Island* (Paramount Pictures, 2010). *(From left to right)* Ben Kingsley, Leonardo DiCaprio, Martin Scorsese, and Mark Ruffalo.

Dr. Cawley in Lehane's novel, "we'll medicate the human experience right out of the human experience."[53]

My initial encounter with Shutter Island — before I had read the book — was when I saw the original trailer for the planned October 2009 release of the film. In that trailer was one image that I responded to passionately and that continued to haunt me. It was an image of Teddy Daniels's hand holding the note which reads: "Who is 67?"[54] My gut response to the image was that the digit sum of 67 is 13, and that 13 is a number that is symbolically connected with Jesus (there were 13 people present at the Last Supper; the 12 disciples and Jesus) or occasionally with Judas (the outsider of the 13). By the end of Shutter Island, we know for sure that Teddy Daniels is really Andrew Laeddis, and we know for sure that Andrew Laeddis is patient number 67. Thus we could make an argument that Teddy Daniels = Andrew Laeddis = 67 = 13 = Christ (Judas).

Fighting against both sides of the war at Ashecliffe, Doctors Cawley and Sheehan are on a mission to redeem, if not the entire human race, then at the very least *the dark side* of the entire human mind. Where the other two fractions want to eradicate the wolf completely, Cawley and Sheehan want to see, understand, and find a way to live with it. At this point, they tell him, it is completely up to Andrew Laeddis whether they fail or still have a fighting chance. "If we fail with you, then everything we've tried to do here will be discredited. Everything," Sheehan says. "We're on the frontline of a war here, old boy," Cawley confirms. "And right now, it all comes down to you."

In addition to being an archetypal story about the personal struggle with the shadow, *Shutter Island* is a deeply political story about how we deal with the dark sides of the human mind, the inner wolf, on a collective scale. It is also a Passion Play, a twisted, inverted version of the first part of Passion Week. The final scene, in which Teddy is sitting on the stairs with Chuck waiting for the doctors to come get him, calls to mind a number of Renaissance paintings of Christ waiting in Gethsemane in the early morning for the soldiers to come and arrest him; one of the most stunning of these being Andrea Mantegna's "Agony in the Garden." The crucifixion that awaits Teddy/Laeddis is, of course, the transorbital lobotomy.

At the beginning of the film, Teddy questioned how Rachel could completely shut out the truth, and Andrew Laeddis kept hoping that Dolores would eventually pull herself together and snap out of her mental illness. But Dr. Cawley repeatedly reminds both of them that "sanity is not a choice." Nevertheless, at the end Cawley himself ironically expects Teddy/Laeddis to be able to *choose* to reclaim his real identity. In effect he asks him to perform a miracle, all but promising him eventual liberty if he does, the exact same way that Herod Antipas did with Christ. Where Herod wanted the miracle for his own amusement, however, Cawley wants it for a larger altruistic purpose. When Christ would not show him a miracle, Herod turned Him over to Pontius Pilate for crucifixion. Similarly Cawley is forced to turn Teddy/Laeddis over to Jeremiah Naehring for a transorbital lobotomy.

"Which would be worse?" Teddy asks Chuck at the very end while waiting to be apprehended. "To live as a monster or to die as a good man?" Initially, these famous last words may sound seductively sympathetic, but on closer inspection they turn out to be nonsensical, even horrifying, in this context. If Teddy were to let Laeddis take over, the conflict would be solved, and no one would have to "die." So he must mean that he would rather die as Teddy Daniels than go on living as Andrew Laeddis whom Teddy has always regarded as a monster. In the penultimate scene we see Laeddis in his cell, and there is no way this man qualifies as a monster except in his own unforgiving mind. Andrew Laeddis may be fallible, alcoholic, traumatized, shell shocked, prideful, and arrogant. He may even have been a bad and negligent husband and father. But a monster he is not. For him to have felt compassion for and embraced his own human weakness, his pain, shame and guilt, to have chosen to be Andrew Laeddis again and to have let go of poor, aggressive Teddy Daniels who has been forced to shutter him, cannot possibly be regarded as living as a monster.

Interestingly, the last person Teddy talks to before entering the inmost cave was Dr. Naehring, the Teutonic proponent of psychosurgery. "Did you know that the word trauma comes from the Greek for wound?" he asks and reminds Teddy that the German word for dream is traum. "You are wounded, marshal," he says, and lest we confuse this conclusion with sympathy, he immediately delivers the final blow: "Wouldn't you agree? When you see a monster, you must stop it!" Dr. Naehring, like Teddy Daniels, considers Andrew Laeddis, the 67th patient, a monster that must be eradicated at all costs, and Teddy readily agrees with him.

The savage battle that takes place both inside and outside of Laeddis's mind has two opposing sides. Dr. Sheehan, Dr. Cawley and Dr. Solando (the anima side of himself) are fighting with all their might to prevent the onslaught of zombification by psychosurgery or psychotropic drugs. They are advocates for a dialogue with the wolf, the dark side of the human mind. Dr. Naehring, the warden and probably Teddy Daniels represent violence, brute force against what they deem monsters.

Sitting on the stairs at the end, Teddy Daniels still believes that Andrew Laeddis is a monster, and that he would rather "die" than feel compassion for him. Naehring's subtle manipulation of Teddy as he was about to enter the inmost cave worked: "When you see a monster, you must stop it!" Thus the Naehring/warden/Teddy side wins that battle, and Doctors Cawley, Sheehan and Solando lose. The image of the lighthouse at the very end may suggest that even if the stormy night is over and the sun is out, the nightmare vision of creating ghosts out of human beings is not that far off.

When Teddy talks about it being a choice whether he is to live as a monster or die as a good man, he reveals that he has at least some remnant of a memory that Laeddis is, in fact, himself. Thus, like Howard Hughes at the end of *The Aviator*, he consciously and purposefully surrenders to the abyss. The final twist to the comparison with Passion Week is the fact that the one who delivers the Judas kiss — the kiss of betrayal — is Teddy Daniels. He becomes Judas Iscariot to Andrew Laeddis's Christ when he voluntarily surrenders Laeddis to the soldiers and Pharisees. And again we have the equation: Teddy Daniels = Andrew Laeddis = 67 = 13 = Christ (Judas).

In *Raging Bull*, Jake La Motta makes his redemption possible when he steps up and lets himself be crucified. In *The Last Temptation of Christ* and *Bringing Out the Dead*, the main character temporarily prevents the redemption when he tries to alleviate the pain of his journey through the night. This would suggest that what Teddy does at the end when he surrenders to the doctors is a good and noble thing, but, in the final analysis, I do not believe that it is. The real question inside the inmost cave is whether you can accept and embrace all sides of yourself and live out your true purpose, whether you have the courage to face the darkness and the pain; or whether you try to ease the pain by making yourself comfortably numb. By letting Himself be crucified, Christ redeemed mankind. If Teddy Daniels had embraced his whole self, the part that he is unable to live with and to forgive, if he had given way to Andrew Laeddis, he could have ensured Dr. Cawley's project to redeem the dark side of mankind, to prevent the eradication of the wolf whether by surgery or medication. By surrendering to Dr. Naehring, he does the opposite, and he condemns himself and Laeddis to a future in which they will be comfortably numb for all eternity.

Priest Vallon admonished his son to "never look away." Andrew Laeddis is not some terrible monster, but simply a tormented man whose looking away has cost his children and his wife their lives, and he cannot forgive himself for that. His sin — looking away, turning a blind eye to the suffering of his loved ones — is one that most of us have probably been guilty of, although, fortunately for us, with less severe consequences. Laeddis ignored the "insect" that was "clicking across her skull" and "crossing the wires" and now he feels so responsible for the death of his family that he refuses to let himself have a life. Clearly Andrew Laeddis had been through harrowing traumas during the war, and presumably he, too, could have used help, which means that society also looked away. We might end up agreeing with Teddy's statement that it is better to die as a good man than to live as a monster, instead of extending to Andrew Laeddis the compassion he cannot give himself. But if we do, we too look away and condemn the tormented, self-immolating, unforgiving part of us that he represents.

Martin Scorsese: The Devil's Advocate

When someone is proposed for beatification or canonization within the Roman Catholic Church, an official is chosen for the vital function of being the Devil's Advocate. It is the duty of this person to critically examine the evidence, to oppose and offer reasons why the canonization should *not* take place. Only when the Devil's Advocate, also known as the Promoter of the Faith, has had his say, can the conclave finally decide.[55]

As an artist Martin Scorsese has taken on a very similar function, always pointing out the necessary opposite and presenting the unaccepted, unpopular point of view. "I deal with aspects that people would rather not see," he says. "They'd rather keep it underground. And I'll put it up there. I don't give a damn."[56] The same could be said of his work that was said of the Gothic and the grotesque: "It is not ashamed to wade through sewage and frog spit to find poetry."[57]

In his song "To Beat the Devil" Kris Kristofferson says that the Devil haunts a hungry man and that unless you want to join him, you've got to beat him."[58] Scorsese consistently presents the perspective of the dungeon, the dark side, the shadow, the wolf inside, because only when we have taken those sides of ourselves into consideration, are we in a position to see ourselves and the world clearly and to make authentic choices. I truly believe that if you don't run with the wolf, the wolf *will* run with you, and once the wolf starts running with you, the Devil is well on his way to beating you.

The way in which Martin Scorsese has explored the sides of us that we feel compelled to amputate and hide, and the filmic style he has developed to do so, is his main contribution, not just to world cinema but to our potential spiritual evolution. As a ritual way of acknowledging and paying out the shadow so that we can make peace with all that we are, Scorsese's films are an equivalent in our modern secularized world of the Catholic Mass. Certainly, his childhood notion that he wanted to become a priest, that film is something that is being done in front of an altar, is exceptionally appropriate.

Scorsese's characters remind us of traits within ourselves that the conventions of our culture have taught us are unacceptable, sides of us that we have relegated to the shadow, the dungeon within our own unconscious. Whether we like and admit it or not, we have to relate Scorsese's dungeons to our own. The dark sides that are explored and exposed in his films concern and belong with all of us, as does the responsibility — and the substantial rewards — for acknowledging that fact.

At the end of this long journey, I passionately encourage you to keep looking at Scorsese's films and characters until you really see them; to keep looking without self-deception or illusion, without glossing them over, without pushing them away. And see if you can find it in yourself to truly feel kindness, compassion, and forgiveness for your own wounded, imperfect Andrew Laeddis. As long as Martin Scorsese has the courage to hold up the mirror so that we have to see ourselves, have the courage to keep looking. In the words of Priest Vallon: Don't never look away!

Filmography

1963

What's a Nice Girl Like You Doing in a Place Like This?

Director: Martin Scorsese
Producer: New York University Department of Television, Motion Picture and Radio Presentations, Summer Motion Picture Workshop
Screenplay: Martin Scorsese
Still Photography (B/W): Frank Truglio
Editor: Robert Hunsicker
Music: Richard H. Coll
9 minutes
Leading Cast: Zeph Michaelis (Harry), Mimi Stark (wife), Sarah Braveman (analyst), Fred Sica (friend), Robert Uricola (singer)

1964

It's Not Just You, Murray!

Director: Martin Scorsese
Producer: New York University Department of Television, Motion Picture and Radio Presentations
Screenplay: Martin Scorsese, Mardik Martin
Cinematography (B/W): Richard H. Coll
Editor: Eli F. Bleich
Music: Richard H. Coll
15 minutes
Leading Cast: Ira Rubin (Murray), Andrea Martin (wife), Sam De Fazio (Joe), Robert Uricola (singer), Catherine Scorsese (Mother)

1967

The Big Shave

Director: Martin Scorsese
Producer: Martin Scorsese
Screenplay: Martin Scorsese
Cinematography (Color): Ares Demertzis
Editor: Martin Scorsese
Song: "I Can't Get Started with You" (Bunny Berrigan)
Production company: A Scorsese Films Inc. Release
6 minutes
Cast: Peter Bernuth (young man)

1969

Who's That Knocking at My Door?

Director: Martin Scorsese
Producers: Joseph Weill, Betzi Manoogian, Haig Manoogian
Screenplay: Martin Scorsese
Cinematography (B/W): Michael Wadleigh, Richard H. Coll
Editor: Thelma Schoonmaker
Art director: Victor Magnotta
Selected Songs: "Jenny Take a Ride" (Mitch Ryder and the Detroit Wheels); "The Closer You Are" (The Channels); "I've Had It" (The Bellnotes); "El Watusi" (Ray Baretto); "Don't Ask Me" (The Dubbs); "Shotgun" (Jr. Walker and the All Stars); "The End" (The Doors); "Ain't That Just Like Me" (The Searchers); "Who's That Knocking at My Door" (The Genies); "The Plea" (The Chantels)
Production company: A Joseph Brenner Associates Inc. Release of a Trimod Films Production
90 minutes

Leading Cast: Harvey Keitel (J.R.), Zina Bethune (the girl), Lennard Kuras (Joey), Michael Scala (Sally GaGa), Catherine Scorsese (J.R.'s mother), Anne Colette (young girl in dream), Harry Northrup (Harry, the rapist), Robert Uricola (young man at party), Phil Carlson (guide on the mountain), Martin Scorsese (gangster)

1970

Street Scenes 1970

Producer: New York Cinetracts Collective
Production Supervisor and Postproduction Director: Martin Scorsese
Cinematography (B/W and color): Don Lenzer, Harry Bolles, Danny Schneider, Peter Rea, Bob Pitts, Bill Etra, Tiger Graham, Fred Hadley, Ed Summer, Nat Trapp
Editors: Peter Rea, Maggie Koven, Angela Kirby, Larry Tisdall, Gerry Pallor, Thelma Schoonmaker
75 minutes
Cast: William Kunstler, Dave Dellinger, Alan W. Carter, David Z. Robinson, Harvey Keitel, Verna Bloom, Jay Cocks, Martin Scorsese

1972

Boxcar Bertha

Director: Martin Scorsese
Producer: Roger Corman
Screenplay: Joyce H. Corrington and John William Corrington, based on *Sister of the Road* by Bertha Thompson, as told to Ben L. Reitman
Cinematography (Color): John Stephens
Editors: Buzz Feitshans and Martin Scorsese
Visual consultant: David Nichols
Music: Gib Guilbeau and Thad Maxwell
Production company: American International Pictures
88 minutes
Leading Cast: Barbara Hershey (Bertha), David Carradine (Bill Shelley), Barry Primus (Rake Brown), Bernie Casey (Von Morton), John Carradine (H. Buckram Sartoris)

1973

Mean Streets

Director: Martin Scorsese
Producer: Jonathan T. Taplin
Screenplay: Martin Scorsese, Mardik Martin
Cinematography (Color): Kent Wakeford
Editor: Sid Levin
Visual consultant: David Nichols
Selected Songs: "Jumping Jack Flash," "Tell Me (The Rolling Stones); "I Love You So" (The Chantels); "Please Mr. Postman" (The Marvelettes); "Rubber Bisquit" (The Chips); "Pledging My Love" (Johnny Ace); "Be My Baby" (The Ronettes); "Mickey's Monkey" (The Miracles)
Production company: Warner Bros.
110 minutes
Leading Cast: Harvey Keitel (Charlie), Robert De Niro (Johnny Boy), David Proval (Tony), Amy Robinson (Teresa), Richard Romanus (Michael), Cesare Danova (Giovanni), Victor Argo (Mario), David Carradine (drunk), Robert Carradine (assassin), Jeannie Bell (Diane), Barbara Weintraub (Heather Weintraub), Catherine Scorsese (woman on landing), Martin Scorsese (Shorty, Michael's hired killer)

1974

Alice Doesn't Live Here Anymore

Director: Martin Scorsese
Producer: David Susskind, Audrey Maas
Screenplay: Robert Getchell
Cinematography (Color): Kent Wakeford
Editor: Marcia Lucas
Production designer: Toby Rafelson
Music: Richard LaSalle
Selected Songs: "All the Way from Memphis" (Mott the Hoople); "Roll Away the Stone" (Leon Russell); "Daniel" (Elton John): "Jeepster" (T.Rex); "You'll Never Know" (Alice Faye); "I'm So Lonesome I Could Cry" (Kris Kristofferson); "Where or When," "When Your Lover Has Gone," "Gone with the Wind," "I've Got a Crush on You" (Ellen Burstyn)
Production company: Warner Bros.
112 minutes
Leading Cast: Ellen Burstyn (Alice Hyatt), Kris Kristofferson (David), Alfred Lutter (Tommy), Diane Ladd (Flo), Billy Green Bush (Donald), Vic Tayback (Mel), Jodie Foster (Audrey), Harvey Keitel (Ben), Lelia Goldoni

(Bea), Lane Bradbury (Rita), Valerie Curtin (Vera), Mardik Martin (customer in club), Martin Scorsese and Larry Cohen (patrons at diner)

Italianamerican

Director: Martin Scorsese
Producers: Saul Rubin, Elaine Attias
Treatment: Martin Scorsese, Mardik Martin, Larry Cohen
Cinematography (Color): Alex Hirshfield
Editor: Bertram Lovitt
Production company: National Communications Foundation
45 minutes
Cast: Charles Scorsese, Catherine Scorsese, Martin Scorsese

1976

Taxi Driver

Director: Martin Scorsese
Producers: Michael Phillips, Julia Phillips
Screenplay: Paul Schrader
Cinematography (Color): Michael Chapman
Editors: Marcia Lucas, Tom Rolf, Melvin Shapiro
Music: Bernard Herrmann
Production company: Columbia Pictures
113 minutes
Leading Cast: Robert De Niro (Travis Bickle), Jodie Foster (Iris), Cybill Shepherd (Betsy), Harvey Keitel (Sport/Matthew), Steven Prince (Andy, the gun salesman), Albert Brooks (Tom), Peter Boyle (Wizard), Leonard Harris (Charles Palantine), Diahnne Abbott (woman at concession stand), Joe Spinell (personnel officer), Martin Scorsese (man watching silhouette)

1977

New York, New York

Director: Martin Scorsese
Producers: Irwin Winkler, Robert Chartoff
Screenplay: Earl Mac Rauch, Mardik Martin
Cinematography (Color): Laszlo Kovacs
Editors: Irving Lerner, Marcia Lucas
Production designer: Boris Leven
Musical supervisor: Ralph Burns
Original Songs: (by John Kander, Fred Ebb): "Theme from New York, New York," "There Goes the Ball Game," "But the World Goes Round," "Happy Endings" (Liza Minnelli)
Other Selected Songs: "You Brought a New Kind of Love to Me," "Once in a While," "You Are My Lucky Star," "The Man I Love," "Taking a Chance on Love" (Liza Minnelli); "Blue Moon" (Mary Kay Place); "Honeysuckle Rose" (Diahnne Abbott)
Music: "Opus One," "Song of India," "I'm Getting Sentimental Over You," "Don't Blame Me," "It's a Wonderful World," "For All We Know," "South America Take It Away," "Just You, Just Me," "Billets Doux" (Hot Club of France Quintet)
Production company: United Artists
Original release version, 136 minutes; re-release version, 163 minutes
Leading Cast: Robert De Niro (Jimmy Doyle), Liza Minnelli (Francine Evans), Lionel Stander (Tony Harwell), Barry Primus (Paul Wilson), Mary Kay Place (Bernice), Georgie Auld (Frankie Harte), Lenny Gaines (Artie Kirks), Clarence Clemons (Cecil Powell), Diahnne Abbott (Harlem Club singer), Steven Prince (record producer)

1978

The Last Waltz

Director: Martin Scorsese
Producer: Robbie Robertson
Cinematography (Color): Michael Chapman, Laszlo Kovacs, Vilmos Zsigmond, David Myers, Bobby Byrne, Michael Watkins, Hiro Narita
Editors: Yeu-Bun Yee, Jan Roblee
Production designer: Boris Leven
Songs: "Don't Do It," "Theme from the Last Waltz," "Up On Cripple Creek," "Shape I'm In," "It Makes No Difference," "Stagefright," "The Night They Drove Old Dixie Down," "Chest Fever," "Ophelia," "Ole Time Religion," "Genetic Method," "Sip the Wine" (The Band); with The Band "The Weight" (The Staples); "Evangeline" (Emmylou Harris); "Who Do You Love" (Ronnie Hawkins); "Such a Night" (Dr. John); "Helpless" (Neil Young); "Dry Your Eyes" (Neil Diamond); "Mystery Train" (Paul Butterfield); "Coyote" (Joni Mitchell); "Mannish Boy" (Muddy Waters); "Further On Up the Road" (Eric Clapton); "Caravan" (Van Morrison); "Forever Young," "Baby Let Me Follow You Down" (Bob Dylan); "I Shall Be Released" (Bob Dylan, Ringo Starr, Ron Wood et al.)

Poems: Introduction to Chaucer's *The Canterbury Tales* read by Michael McClure; "Loud Prayer" read by Lawrence Ferlinghetti
Production company: United Artists
117 minutes
Cast: The Band (Robbie Robertson, Rick Danko, Levon Helm, Garth Hudson, Richard Manuel), Paul Butterfield, Eric Clapton, Neil Diamond, Bob Dylan, Emmylou Harris, Ronnie Hawkins, Dr. John, Joni Mitchell, Van Morrison, The Staples, Ringo Starr, Muddy Waters, Ron Wood, Neil Young, Martin Scorsese, Michael McClure, Lawrence Ferlinghetti

American Boy: A Profile of Steven Prince

Director: Martin Scorsese
Producer: Bertram Lovitt
Treatment: Mardik Martin, Julia Cameron
Cinematography (Color): Michael Chapman
Editors: Amy Jones, Bertram Lovitt
Song: "Time Fades Away" (Neil Young)
Production company: New Empire Films/Scorsese Films
55 minutes
Cast: Steven Prince, Martin Scorsese, George Memmoli, Mardik Martin, Julia Cameron, Kathy McGinnis

1980

Raging Bull

Director: Martin Scorsese
Producers: Irwin Winkler, Robert Chartoff (in association with Peter Savage)
Screenplay: Paul Schrader, Mardik Martin, from the book *Raging Bull* by Jake La Motta with Joseph Carter and Peter Savage
Cinematography (B/W, color): Michael Chapman
Editor: Thelma Schoonmaker
Production designer: Gene Rudolf
Selected Songs: "Cow Cow Boogie" (Ella Fitzgerald and the Ink Spots); "Whispering Grass," "Do I Worry" (The Ink Spots); "Big Noise from Winnetka" (Bob Crosby and The Bobcats); "Blue Velvet" (Tony Bennett); "Flash," "Two O'Clock Jump," "All or Nothing at All" (Harry James); "Drum Boogie" (Gene Krupa); "Jersey Bounce" (Benny Goodman); "Come Fly With Me," "Mona Lisa" (Nat King Cole); "I Ain't Got Nobody" (Louis Prima, Keely Smith)
Production company: United Artists
129 minutes
Leading Cast: Robert De Niro (Jake La Motta), Cathy Moriarty (Vickie La Motta), Joe Pesci (Joey La Motta), Frank Vincent (Salvy), Nicholas Colasanto (Tommy Como), Theresa Saldana (Lenore), Mario Gallo (Mario), Johnny Barnes (Sugar Ray Robinson), Floyd Anderson (Jimmy Reeves), Eddie Mustafa Muhammad (Billy Fox), Louis Raftis (Marcel Cerdan), Johnny Turner (Laurent Dauthuille), Charles Scorsese (Charlie, man with Como), Mardik Martin (Copa waiter), Martin Scorsese (Barbizon stagehand)

1983

The King of Comedy

Director: Martin Scorsese
Producer: Arnon Milchan
Screenplay: Paul Zimmerman
Cinematography (Color): Fred Schuler
Editor: Thelma Schoonmaker
Production designer: Boris Leven
Music production: Robbie Robertson
Selected Songs: "Jerry Langford Theme," "Rupert's Theme" (Bob James); "Come Rain or Come Shine," "Sweet Sixteen Bars" (Ray Charles); "Fly Me to the Moon," (Frank Sinatra); "Between Trains" (Robbie Robertson); "T'Ain't Nobody's Bizness If I Do" (B.B. King); "Wonderful Remark" (Van Morrison)
Production company: Twentieth Century–Fox
108 minutes
Leading Cast: Robert De Niro (Rupert Pupkin), Jerry Lewis (Jerry Langford), Diahnne Abbott (Rita), Sandra Bernhard (Masha), Ed Herlihy (himself), Shelley Hack (Cathy Long), Fred de Cordova (Bert Thomas), Kim Chan (Jonno), Victor Borge, Tony Randall (themselves), Harry Ufland (Langford's agent), Martin Scorsese (television director), Charles Scorsese (first man at bar), Mardik Martin (second man at bar), Catherine Scorsese (Rupert's mom), Cathy Scorsese (Dolores)

1985

After Hours

Director: Martin Scorsese
Producers: Amy Robinson, Griffin Dunne, Robert Colesberry

Screenplay: Joseph Minion
Cinematography (Color): Michael Ballhaus
Editor: Thelma Schoonmaker
Production designer: Jeffrey Townsend
Music: Howard Shore
Other Music: Symphony in D Major, K 73n by Wolfgang Amadeus Mozart; "Air" from *Suite no. 3* by Johann Sebastian Bach.
Selected Songs: "You're Mine," "We Belong Together" (Robert and Johnnie); "Last Train to Clarksville" (The Monkees); "Chelsea Morning," "I Don't Know Where I Stand" (Joni Mitchell) "Over the Mountain and Across the Sea" (Johnnie and Joe); "Is That All There Is?" (Peggy Lee)
Production company: Warner Bros., Double Play/The Geffen Company
97 minutes
Leading Cast: Griffin Dunne (Paul Hackett), Rosanna Arquette (Marcy), Verna Bloom (June), Linda Fiorentino (Kiki), Teri Garr (Julie), John Heard (Tom, the bardender), Thomas Chong (Pepe), Cheech Marin (Neil), Catherine O'Hara (Gail), Will Patton (Horst), Larry Block (taxi driver), Victor Argo (diner cashier), Clarence Felder (bouncer), Martin Scorsese (man with spotlight)

Mirror, Mirror

(episode in "Amazing Stories" TV series)
Director: Martin Scorsese
Producer: David E. Vogel
Screenplay: Joseph Minion, from a story by Steven Spielberg
Cinematography (Color): Robert Stevens
Editor: Joe Ann Fogle
Production designer: Rick Carter
Music: Michael Kamen
Production company: Amblin
24 minutes
Leading Cast: Sam Waterston (Jordan), Helen Shaver (Karen), Dick Cavett (himself), Tim Robbins (Jordan's phantom)

1986

The Color of Money

Director: Martin Scorsese
Producers: Irving Axelrad, Barbara De Fina
Screenplay: Richard Price, based on the novel by Walter Tevis
Cinematography (Color): Michael Ballhaus
Editor: Thelma Schoonmaker
Production designer: Boris Leven
Music: Robbie Robertson
Selected Songs: "One More Night" (Phil Collins); "Werewolves of London" (Warren Zevon); "Out of Left Field" (Percy Sledge); "Two Brothers and a Stranger" (Mark Knopfler) "Who Owns This Place?" (Don Henley)
Production company: Touchstone Pictures
119 minutes,
Leading Cast: Paul Newman (Fast Eddie Felson), Tom Cruise (Vincent Lauria), Mary Elizabeth Mastrantonio (Carmen), Helen Shaver (Janelle), John Turturro (Julian), Bill Cobbs (Orvis), Keith McCready (Grady Seasons), Forest Whitaker (Amos), Bruce A. Young (Moselle), Richard Price (guy who calls Dud), Charles Scorsese (first high roller)

1988

The Last Temptation of Christ

Director: Martin Scorsese
Producer: Barbara De Fina
Screenplay: Paul Schrader, based on the novel by Nikos Kazantzakis
Cinematography (Color): Michael Ballhaus
Editor: Thelma Schoonmaker
Production designer: John Beard
Music: Peter Gabriel
Production company: Universal Pictures
163 minutes
Leading Cast: Willem Dafoe (Jesus), Harvey Keitel (Judas), Verna Bloom (Mary, Mother of Jesus), Barbara Hershey (Mary Magdalene), Barry Miller (Jeroboam), André Gregory (John the Baptist), Harry Dean Stanton (Saul/Paul), David Bowie (Pontius Pilate), Juliette Caton (girl angel), Peggy Gormley (Martha, sister of Lazarus), Randy Danson (Mary, sister of Lazarus), Thomas Arana (Lazarus), Nehemiah Persoff (Rabbi), Gary Basaraba (Andrew Apostle), Irvin Kershner (Zebedee), Victor Argo (Peter Apostle), Michael Been (John Apostle), Paul Herman (Philip Apostle), John Lurie (James Apostle), Leo Burmeister (Nathaniel Apostle), Alan Rosenberg (Thomas Apostle)

1989

New York Stories: Life Lessons

(segment of a three-part film)
Director: Martin Scorsese

Producers: Barbara De Fina, Robert Greenhut
Screenplay: Richard Price
Cinematography (Color): Nestor Almendros
Editor: Thelma Schoonmaker
Production designer: Kristi Zea
Music: "Nessun Dorma" from *Turandot* by Giacomo Puccini
Selected Songs: "Whiter Shade of Pale," "Conquistador" (Procul Harum); "Politician" (Cream) "The Right Time" (Ray Charles); "Like a Rolling Stone" (Bob Dylan and The Band)
Production company: Touchstone Pictures
44 minutes
Leading Cast: Nick Nolte (Lionel Dobie), Rosanna Arquette (Paulette), Patrick O'Neal (Philip Fowler), Jesse Borego (Reuben Toro), Steve Buscemi (Gregory Stark), Illeana Douglas (Paulette's friend), Brigitte Bako (Young woman), Deborah Harry, Peter Gabriel (themselves), Richard Price, Michael Powell (gallery patrons)

1990

GoodFellas

Director: Martin Scorsese
Producer: Irwin Winkler
Screenplay: Nicholas Pileggi, Martin Scorsese, based on the book *Wise Guy* by Pileggi
Cinematography (Color): Michael Ballhaus
Editor: Thelma Schoonmaker
Production designer: Kristi Zea
Selected Songs: "Rags to Riches," "The Boulevard of Broken Dreams," (Tony Bennett) "Can't We Be Sweethearts" (The Cleftones); "I Will Follow Him" (Betty Curtis); "Then He Kissed Me," "He's Sure the Boy I Love" (The Crystals); "Look in My Eyes" (The Chantels); "Roses Are Red" (Bobby Vinton); "Atlantis" (Donovan); "Pretend You Don't See Her" (Jerry Vale); "Baby I Love You" (Aretha Franklin); "Beyond the Sea" (Bobby Darin); "Gimme Shelter," "Monkey Man," "Memo from Turner" (The Rolling Stones); "Frosty the Snowman" (The Ronettes); "Christmas (Baby Please Come Home)" (Darlene Love); "The Bells of St. Mary's" (The Drifters); "Layla" (Derek and the Dominos); "What is Life?" (George Harrison); "Mannish Boy" (Muddy Waters); "My Way" (Sid Vicious)
Production company: Warner Bros.
146 minutes
Leading Cast: Ray Liotta (Henry Hill), Lorraine Bracco (Karen Hill), Robert De Niro (James Conway), Joe Pesci (Tommy De Vito), Paul Sorvino (Paul Cicero), Frank Sivero (Frankie Carbone), Frank Vincent (Billy Batts), Frank Dileo (Tuddy Cicero), Gina Mastrogiacomo (Janice Rossi), Debi Mazar (Sandy), Margo Winkler (Belle Kessler), Julie Garfield (Mickey Conway), Christopher Serrone (young Henry), Ealine Kagan (Henry's mother), Beau Starr (Henry's father), Kevin Corrigan (Michael Hill), Catherine Scorsese (Tommy's mother), Charles Scorsese (Vinnie)

1991

Cape Fear

Director: Martin Scorsese
Producer: Barbara De Fina
Screenplay: Wesley Strick, based on James R. Webb's screenplay and John D. Macdonald's novel *The Executioners*
Cinematography (Color): Freddie Francis
Editor: Thelma Schoonmaker
Production designer: Henry Bumstead
Music: Bernard Herrmann, adapted by Elmer Bernstein
Selected Songs: "Do Right Woman — Do Right Man" (Aretha Franklin); "Been Caught Stealing" (Jane's Addiction); "The Creature From the Black Leather Lagoon" (The Cramps)
Production company: Universal Pictures
128 minutes
Leading Cast: Robert De Niro (Max Cady), Nick Nolte (Sam Bowden), Jessica Lange (Leigh Bowden), Juliette Lewis (Danielle Bowden), Joe Don Baker (Claude Kersek), Robert Mitchum (Lt. Elgart), Gregory Peck (Lee Heller), Martin Balsam (Judge), Illeana Douglas (Lori Davies), Fred Dalton Thompson (Tom Broadbent), Zully Montero (Graciella), Domenica Scorsese (Dannie's friend)

1993

The Age of Innocence

Director: Martin Scorsese
Producer: Barbara De Fina
Screenplay: Martin Scorsese, Jay Cocks, based on the novel by Edith Wharton
Cinematography (Color): Michael Ballhaus
Editor: Thelma Schoonmaker
Production designer: Dante Ferretti

Music: Elmer Bernstein
Other Music: Scene from Act III of *Faust* by Charles Gounod; "Radetzky March" by Johann Strauss I
Song: "Marble Halls" (Enya)
Production company: Columbia Pictures
136 minutes
Leading Cast: Daniel Day-Lewis (Newland Archer), Michelle Pfeiffer (Ellen Olenska), Winona Ryder (May Welland), Miriam Margolys (Mrs. Mingott), Richard E. Grant (Larry Lefferts), Alec McCowen (Sillerton Jackson), Geraldine Chaplin (Mrs. Welland), Mary Beth Hurt (Regina Beaufort), Stuart Wilson (Julius Beaufort), Sian Phillips (Mrs. Archer), Michael Gough (Henry van der Luyden), Alexis Smith (Louisa van der Luyden), Jonathan Pryce (Riviere), Robert Sean Leonard (Ted Archer), Joanne Woodward (narrator), Domenica Scorsese (Katie Blenker)

1995

A Personal Journey with Martin Scorsese through American Movies

(three-part documentary on the history of American cinema)
Part One: The Director's Dilemma; The Director as Storyteller; The Western; The Gangster Film, The Musical
Part Two: The Director as Illusionist, The Director as Smuggler
Part Three: The Director as Smuggler, The Director as Iconoclast
Director: Martin Scorsese
Producer: Florence Dauman
Script: Martin Scorsese, Michael Henry Wilson
Cinematography (Color): Jean Yves Escoffier
Supervising Editor: Thelma Schoonmaker
Music: Elmer Bernstein
Production company: British Film Institute TV
Part One: 73 minutes; Part Two: 80 minutes; Part Three: 74 minutes
With: Martin Scorsese, Billy Wilder, Gregory Peck, André De Toth, Sam Fuller, Arthur Penn, Clint Eastwood, George Lucas, Francis Coppola, Brian De Palma, Fritz Lang, Howard Hawks, King Vidor, Douglas Sirk, Nicholas Ray, Orson Welles, Elia Kazan, John Cassavetes, Frank Capra, John Ford

Casino

Director: Martin Scorsese
Producer: Barbara De Fina
Screenplay: Nicholas Pilleggi, Martin Scorsese, based on the book *Casino* by Pilleggi
Cinematography (Color): Robert Richardson
Editor: Thelma Schoonmaker
Production designer: Dante Ferretti
Music: Final Chorus from *St. Matthew Passion* by J. S. Bach; Prelude from *Also Sprach Zarathustra* by Richard Strauss; *Flight of the Bumblebee* by Nicolai Rimsky-Korsakov; "Theme de Camille" from *Le Mepris* by Georges Delerue
Selected Songs: "Angelina," "Zooma Zooma" (Louis Prima); "(I Can't Get No) Satisfaction," "Gimme Shelter" (The Rolling Stones); "Love Is Strange" (Mickey & Sylvia); "Love Is a Drug" (Roxy Music); "What a Difference a Day Makes" (Dinah Washington); "Nights in White Satin" (The Moody Blues); "(I Can't Get No) Satisfaction" (Devo); "The Thrill Is Gone" (B. B. King); "The House of the Rising Sun" (The Animals); "Stardust" (Hoagy Carmichael); "Ain't Got No Home" (Clarence "Frogman" Henry)
Production company: Universal Pictures
178 minutes
Leading Cast: Robert De Niro (Sam "Ace" Rothstein), Joe Pesci (Nicky Santoro), Sharon Stone (Ginger McKenna), Don Rickles (Billy Sherbert), Kevin Pollack (Phillip Green), James Woods (Lester Diamond), Frank Vincent (Frank Marino), Alan King (Andy Stone), Pasquale Cajano (Remo Gaggi), L. Q. Jones (Pat Webb), Vinny Vella (Artie Piscano), Dick Smothers (Senator), Melissa Prophet (Jennifer Santoro), Oscar Goodman (himself), Phillip Suriano (Dominick Santoro), Frankie Avalon, Steve Allen, Jayne Meadows, Jerry Vale (themselves), Catherine Scorsese (Piscano's mother), Cathy Scorsese (Piscano's daughter)

1997

Kundun

Director: Martin Scorsese
Producer: Barbara De Fina
Screenplay: Melissa Mathison
Cinematography (Color): Roger Deakins
Editor: Thelma Schoonmaker
Production designer: Dante Ferretti
Music: Philip Glass
Production company: Touchstone Pictures

134 minutes
Leading Cast: Tenzin Thuthob Tsarong (Dalai Lama, adult); Gyurme Tethong (Dalai Lama, age 12); Tulku Jamyang Kunga Tenzin (Dalai Lama, age five); Tenzin Yeshi Paichang (Dalai Lama, age two); Tencho Gyalpo (Mother); Tsewang Migyur Khangsar (Father); Sonam Phunstok (Reting Rinpoche); Gyatso Lukhang (Lord Chamberlain); Robert Lin (Chairman Mao)

1999

Bringing Out the Dead
Director: Martin Scorsese
Producer: Barbara De Fina, Scott Rudin
Screenplay: Paul Schrader, based on the novel by Joe Connelly
Cinematography (Color): Robert Richardson
Editor: Thelma Schoonmaker
Production designer: Dante Ferretti
Music: Elmer Bernstein
Selected Songs: "TB Sheets" (Van Morrison); "What's the Frequency, Kenneth?" (R.E.M.); "Nowhere to Run" (Martha Reeves and the Vandellas); "Janie Jones," "I'm So Bored with the U.S.A. (The Clash); "Red Red Wine" (UB40); "Too Many Fish in the Sea" (The Marvelettes); "Rang Tang Ding Dong (I'm a Japanese Sandman)" (The Cellos); "Rivers of Babylon" (The Melodians); "Bell Boy" (The Who)
Production company: Touchstone Pictures
121 minutes
Leading Cast: Nicolas Cage (Frank Pierce), Patricia Arquette (Mary Burke), John Goodman (Larry), Ving Rhames (Marcus), Tom Sizemore (Tom Walls), Marc Anthony (Noel), Mary Beth Hurt (Nurse Constance), Cliff Curtis (Cy Coates), Cynthia Roman (Rose), Cullen O. Johnson (Mr. Burke), Martin Scorsese (dispatcher), Queen Latifah (Dispather Love, voice)

2001

My Voyage to Italy (Il mio viaggio in Italia)
Director: Martin Scorsese
Producer: Barbara De Fina, Giuliana Del Punta, Bruno Restuccia
Script: Suso Cecchi d'Amico, Raffaele Donato, Kent Jones, Martin Scorsese
Cinematography (Color): Phil Abraham, William Rexer
Editor: Thelma Schoonmaker
Production company: Miramax Films
246 minutes

2002

Gangs of New York
Director: Martin Scorsese
Producer: Alberto Grimaldi, Harvey Weinstein
Screenplay: Jay Cocks, Steven Zaillian, Kenneth Lonergan
Cinematography (Color): Michael Ballhaus
Editor: Thelma Schoonmaker
Production designer: Dante Ferreti
Music: Howard Shore
Selected Songs: "Shimmy She Wobble" (Othar Turner); "The Hands that Built America" (U2); "Signal to Noise" (Peter Gabriel); Vows (Jeff Johnson and Brian Dunning)
Production company: Miramax Films
138 minutes
Leading Cast: Leonardo DiCaprio (Amsterdam Vallon), Daniel Day-Lewis (Bill "the Butcher" Cutting), Cameron Dias (Jenny Everdeane), Jim Broadbent ("Boss" William Tweed), John C. Reilly (Happy Jack), Henry Thomas (Johnny Sirocco), Liam Neeson ("Priest" Vallon), Brendan Gleeson (Walter "Monk" McGinn), Gary Lewis (McGloin), Cara Seymour (Hell-Cat Maggie), Cian McCormack (young Amsterdam), Michael Byrne (Horace Greeley), Martin Scorsese (wealthy homeowner)

2004

The Aviator
Director: Martin Scorsese
Producer: Michael Mann, Sandy Climan, Graham King, Charles Evans, Jr.,
Screenplay: John Logan
Cinematography (Color): Robert Richardson
Editor: Thelma Schoonmaker
Production designer: Dante Ferretti
Music: Howard Shore
Selected Songs: "I'll Build a Stairway to Paradise" (Rufus Wainwright); "Happy Feet" (Manhattan Rhythm Kings); "Moonglow" (Benny Goodman); "Thanks" (Bing Crosby with Jimmy

Grier and his Orchestra); "I Can't Give You Anything But Love" (Django Reinhardt); "Howard Hughes" (Leadbelly); "Nightmare" (Artie Shaw & His Orchestra)
Production company: Miramax Films, Warner Bros.
170 minutes
Leading Cast: Leonardo DiCaprio (Howard Hughes), Cate Blanchett (Katharine Hepburn), Kate Beckinsale (Ava Gardner), John C. Reilly (Noah Dietrich), Alec Baldwin (Juan Trippe), Alan Alda (Senator Owen Brewster), Ian Holm (Professor Fitz), Gwen Stefani (Jean Harlow), Jude Law (Errol Flynn), Matt Ross (Glenn Odekirk), Kelli Garner (Faith Domergue), Frances Conroy (Mrs. Hepburn), Edward Herrmann (Joseph Breen), Stanley DeSantis (Louis B. Mayer), Jacob Davich (Howard Hughes — nine years old), Amy Sloan (Howard's mother), Willem Dafoe (Roland Sweet), Josie Maran (Thelma, the cigarette girl), Martin Scorsese (*Hell's Angels* projectionist), Franceska Scorsese (little girl)

2005

No Direction Home: Bob Dylan

Director: Martin Scorsese
Producer: Jeff Rosen, Susan Lacy, Nigel Sinclair, Anthony Wall, Martin Scorsese
Cinematography (B/W, Color): Mustapha Barat, et al.
Editor: David Tedeschi
Music: Bob Dylan, et al.
Production company: Paramount Pictures
208 minutes

2006

The Departed

Director: Martin Scorsese
Producer: Brad Pitt, Brad Grey, Gianni Nunnari, Graham King
Screenplay: William Monahan
Cinematography (Color): Michael Ballhaus
Editor: Thelma Schoonmaker
Production designer: Kristi Zea
Music: Howard Shore
Selected Songs: "I'm Shipping Up to Boston" (Dropkick Murphys); "Gimme Shelter," "Let It Loose" (The Rolling Stones); "Comfortably Numb" (Roger Waters, feat. Van Morrison and The Band); "Sweet Dreams (of You)" (Patsy Cline); "Sweet Dreams" (Roy Buchanan);
Production company: Warner Brothers
138 minutes
Leading Cast: Leonardo DiCaprio (Billy Costigan), Matt Damon (Colin Sullivan), Jack Nicholson (Frank Costello), Vera Farmiga (Madolyn Madden), Mark Wahlberg (Staff Sgt. Dignam), Alec Baldwin (Cpt. Ellerby), Martin Sheen (Cpt. Queenan), Ray Winstone (Mr. French), Anthony Anderson (Brown), James Badge Dale (Barrigan), David O'Hara Fitzy), Kevin Corrigan (Cousin Sean), Mark Rolson (Timothy Delahunt), Kristen Dalton (Gwen), Conor Donovan (young Colin), Emma Tillinger (woman with dog), Franceska Scorsese (little girl at airport)

2008

Shine a Light

Director: Martin Scorsese
Producer: Steve Bing, Michael Cohl, Zane Weiner
Cinematography (Color): Robert Richardson
Editor: David Tedeschi
Music: The Rolling Stones
Production company: Paramount Classics
122 minutes
Leading Cast: Mick Jagger, Keith Richards, Ron Wood, Charlie Watts

2010

Shutter Island

Director: Martin Scorsese
Producer: Martin Scorsese, Mike Medavoy, Arnold W. Messer, Bradley J. Fischer
Screenplay: Laeta Kalogridis
Cinematography (Color): Robert Richardson
Editor: Thelma Schoonmaker
Production designer: Dante Ferretti
Music supervisor: Robbie Robertson
Selected Music: Fog Tropes by Ingram Marshall; "Passacaglia" from *Symphony No. 3* by Krzysztof Penderecki; *On the Nature of Daylight* by Max Richter; *Quartet for Stings and Piano in A Minor* by Gustav Mahler; *Lizard Point* by Brian Eno; *Root of an Unfocus* by John Cage

Selected Songs: "Cry" (Johnnie Ray); "Wheel of Fortune" (Kay Starr); "This Bitter Earth"/*On the Nature of Daylight* (Dinah Washington/Max Richter)

Production company: Paramount Pictures
138 minutes

Leading Cast: Leonardo DiCaprio (Teddy Daniels), Mark Ruffalo (Chuck Aule), Ben Kingsley (Dr. Cawley), Max von Sydow (Dr. Jeremiah Naehring), Michelle Williams (Dolores), Emily Mortimer (Rachel 1), Patricia Clarkson (Rachel 2), Jackie Earle Haley (George Noyce), Ted Levine (warden), John Caroll Lynch (Deputy Warden McPherson), Elias Koteas (Andrew Laeddis), Robin Bartlett (Bridget Kearns), Christopher Denham (Peter Breene), Nellie Sciutto (Nurse Marino); Curtiss Cook (Trey Washington), Ruby Jerins (Little Girl)

Notes

Preface

1. Jung, *Letters, Vol. 1: 1906–1950*.
2. As opposed to other art forms, films are always collaborative efforts, and a number of remarkably gifted people have put their creative talent into Scorsese's works and contributed to their outstanding quality. Nevertheless, his films — whether genuine auteur projects or made from screenplays he did not write or even co-write, adaptations of books, remakes, or biographical accounts — are always manifestly Scorsese films. They bear the mark of his creative thumbprint, his idiosyncratic cinematic style. The themes, the exhilarating use of the film medium and aesthetics, the way all the bits and pieces are put together, tell us clearly and unmistakably that we are watching a Scorsese film. Whatever type of project I will be dealing with in the following, it is thus pertinent, I believe, to treat all of Scorsese's films equally as works of art by one single artist and to discuss them as a cohesive body of works.
3. Campbell, *The Hero with a Thousand Faces*, 29.

Chapter 1

1. Osbon, *A Joseph Campbell Companion*, 24.
2. Campbell, *The Hero with a Thousand Faces*, 25.
3. Vogler, *The Writer's Journey*, 13.
4. Hawthorne, "The Haunted Mind" in *Selected Tales and Sketches*, 106.
5. Johnson, *Owning Your Own Shadow*, 5.
6. Ibid., 10.
7. Kazantzakis, *The Last Temptation*, 7.
8. For a thorough, step-by-step guide to the history, structure, and symbolism of the Catholic Mass, see Johnson, *Why Do Catholics Do That?*, 57–68.
9. Campbell, *The Hero with a Thousand Faces*, 19.
10. On a daily basis, we habitually and casually watch people die in movies and on the news without batting an eyelid, but we have to ask ourselves if violence shouldn't be sickening to watch, if that isn't, in fact, the only morally defensible way of depicting violence.
11. Kelly, *Martin Scorsese: The First Decade*, 3. In addition to being Scorsese's friend and mentor, Powell was married to editor Thelma Schoonmaker from 1984 until his death in 1990.
12. Campbell, *The Hero with a Thousand Faces*, 29.
13. Ford, *The Dark Side of the Light Chasers*, 2.
14. Johnson, *She*, xi.
15. Since most of Scorsese's protagonists are male, I will be generically referring to the mythical hero as "he" rather than "he or she" from now on.
16. Among the most common archetypal figures the hero encounters along the way are the mentor, the gatekeeper, the shapeshifter, and the shadow. In the following we shall look at all four of them.
17. Richardson, *The Unmistakable Touch of Grace*, 2.
18. Campbell, *The Hero with a Thousand Faces*, 16–17.
19. At the beginning of *Life Lessons*, Lionel's agent yells at him in frustration that he has been repeating the same pattern ad infinitum: "I'm talking twenty years of this!"
20. Rowe, *Beyond Fear*, 47.
21. Thompson and Christie, *Scorsese on Scorsese*, 60.
22. This scene alludes to the subtextual connection between Marlon Brando and Robert De Niro: De Niro was considered Brando's anointed successor as a method actor when he played the young Vito Corleone to Brando's aging Vito Corleone in *The Godfather II*, and now we witness De Niro repeating one of Brando's most famous roles. In effect, Robert De Niro plays Jake La Motta who emulates Marlon Brando who played Terry Malloy who was talking to his brother Charley in the back of the car. All of this is, of course, doubled because the scene takes place in front of a mirror.
23. Jung, *The Archetypes and the Collective Unconscious*, CW 9, Part I, 43.
24. Jung, *Man and His Symbols*, 168.
25. Jung, "The Psychology of the Unconscious," *Two Essays on Analytical Psychology*, 38.
26. The hostile brothers appear in the Bible stories of Cain and Abel (Gen. 4:1–16), Moses and Aaron (Exod.), and the parable of the Prodigal Son (Luke 15:11–32.), as well as in John Steinbeck's novel *East of Eden*, Sam Shepard's play *True West*, Bruce Springsteen's song "Highway Patrolman," Bob Dylan's song "Where Are You Tonight?" and Kris Kristofferson's song "The Silver Tongued Devil and I."
27. Thompson and Christie, *Scorsese on Scorsese*, 48.
28. Reber, *The Penguin Dictionary of Psychology*, 26.
29. With the obvious exception of his minor roles,

Ben in *Alice Doesn't Live Here Anymore* and Matthew in *Taxi Driver*.
30. Sucher and Fischler, *All This Filming, Is It Healthy?*
31. Agan, *Robert De Niro: The Man, the Myth, and the Movies*, 23.
32. Reber, *The Penguin Dictionary of Psychology*, 694.
33. Ibsen, *Peer Gynt*, 192.
34. Sucher and Fischler, *All This Filming, Is It Healthy?*
35. Jung, *Man and His Symbols*, 31.
36. Ibid., 178.
37. Whitmont, *The Symbolic Quest*, 195.
38. Ibid., 188.
39. Holly Millea, "My Father, Myself," *Premiere*, March 1994, 35.
40. Hilariously, in *GoodFellas* Scorsese has his father play the role of Vinnie, a mobster who cooks wonderful meals for the main characters in jail.
41. Holly Millea, "My Father, Myself," *Premiere*, March 1994, 34.
42. Ehrenstein, *The Scorsese Picture*, 33.
43. Thompson and Christie, *Scorsese on Scorsese*, 3.
44. Ibid., xxv.
45. Sucher and Fischler, *All This Filming, Is It Healthy?*
46. Thompson and Christie, *Scorsese on Scorsese*, 9.
47. Ibid., 14.
48. Pye and Myles, *The Movie Brats*, 192.
49. Ibid., 192.
50. Ibid., 193.
51. Ibid., 191.
52. Thompson and Christie, *Scorsese on Scorsese*, 14.
53. This prolific period ended with a bang in 1980 with the collapse of United Artists following Michael Cimino's notoriously irresponsible behavior while making *Heaven's Gate*. For a detailed account, see Steven Bach's excellent book, *Final Cut*.
54. Kelly, *Martin Scorsese: The First Decade*, 96–7.
55. Thompson and Christie, *Scorsese on Scorsese*, 118. In Charles Scorsese's childhood home the first radio they had was shaped like a church.
56. Paul Schrader, "Paul Schrader on Martin Scorsese," *The New Yorker*, March 21, 1994, 124.
57. Hayden, *Movies Are My Life*.
58. Ehrenstein, *The Scorsese Picture*, 35.
59. Scorsese, *A Personal Journey*, 166.

Chapter 2

1. Jung, *The Archetypes and the Collective Unconscious*, CW 9, Part I, 43.
2. The motif of the pale, blonde woman that is seen in many of Scorsese's films apparently has its roots in his own life: "When I went to the university," he says, "I met girls who were blonde. As a kid, I had literally only known dark-haired girls. But the girls of N.Y.U. were blonde, sweet-looking, intelligent, wore pleated skirts, and spoke proper English. And they were very rich." He married Laraine Brennan in 1964 at the age of 21, and she is the mother of his eldest daughter, Catherine Scorsese. According to Les Keyser, in whose book the above is quoted, Scorsese's first marriage was his own trial over the blonde woman: "Scorsese has been reticent about discussing his marriage to Laraine Brennan," Keyser says; "It led him to face crises in his life, raising questions about religion, about career versus domesticity, and about severing connections to his past." Keyser, *Martin Scorsese*, 19.
3. Johnson, *Inner Work*, 166.
4. This is probably also a reference to the scene in Michael Powell's *The Red Shoes*, in which Boris Lermontov disgustedly hammers his fist into his own mirror image.
5. The idea of cameras as lethal weapons may have been inspired by Michael Powell's *Peeping Tom*.
6. The protagonists of *Public Enemy* (William A. Wellman, 1931), *Little Caesar* (Mervyn LeRoy, 1930), and *Scarface* (Howard Hawks, 1932), respectively.
7. Sally Gaga, an early version of Johnny Boy, is named after an actual neighborhood character Scorsese once knew.
8. This scene found its way into the film through inverted censorship in the frantically liberated climate of the late 1960s. Scorsese was told that he could only get the film distributed if he added a scene with nudity.
9. Thompson and Christie, *Scorsese on Scorsese*, 28.
10. Revelation 3:19–21.
11. One of the most stunning of these paintings is William Holman Hunt's *The Light of the World*, which hangs in the north transept of St. Paul's Cathedral in London.
12. Kelly, *Martin Scorsese: A Journey*, 68.
13. Most of the interior scenes were actually filmed in Los Angeles. Traditionally, the phrase "mean streets" is attributed to Raymond Chandler, who used it in a famous essay that first appeared in the *Atlantic Monthly* in 1945. However, Jack London used it in *The People of the Abyss* in 1902 after a visit to Whitechapel in London's East End, and as early as 1838 Charles Dickens in *Oliver Twist* described Fagin getting lost in Whitechapel's "maze of the mean and dirty streets." Dickens, *Oliver Twist*, 168.
14. Thompson and Christie, *Scorsese on Scorsese*, 47.
15. Kathleen Murphy, "Made Men," *Film Comment*, September/October 1990, 29.
16. Thompson and Christie, *Scorsese on Scorsese*, 28.
17. Ibid., 48.
18. They form the same constellation as in *Who's That Knocking at My Door?* Charlie, like J.R., is more intelligent than his friends. Johnny Boy is an extension of Sally Gaga, the idiot who owes everybody money. Joey, the club owner and smart aleck has been split into two characters: Tony, the club owner, and Michael, the smart aleck.
19. Scorsese says of various neighborhood types that they would think nothing of stealing and cheating for a living, but they would disapprove of drugs "not for moral reasons, but because it draws attention to them." Thompson and Christie, *Scorsese on Scorsese*, 48–9.
20. Patrick Agan recounts that before auditioning for the role, De Niro went into his extensive collection of second-hand clothes and came out with the porkpie hat. "When I saw that crazy hat," Scorsese says, "I knew

he'd be perfect." Agan, *Robert De Niro: The Man, the Myth, and the Movies*, 44.

21. So closely are the two characters connected that Charlie's grandmother, like J.R.'s, lives on Staten Island. This becomes even more significant when one considers that Scorsese's own grandmother lived there, too.

22. Mick Jagger was famously likened to the Devil in Don McLean's song "American Pie" shortly before the film was released.

23. Kolker, *A Cinema of Loneliness*, 213. Ian Penman, "Jukebox and Johnny Boy," *Sight and Sound*, 10–11.

24. Thompson and Christie, *Scorsese on Scorsese*, 48.

25. *World's Greatest Classic Books*.

26. Kelly, *Martin Scorsese: A Journey*, 71.

27. Johnson, *He*, 48–9.

28. Ibid., 49.

29. Kelly, *Martin Scorsese: A Journey*, 72.

30. Peter Biskind, "Slouching Toward Hollywood," *Premiere*, November, 1991, 68. Following the immense success of *Taxi Driver*, Scorsese and his second wife, Julia Cameron (mother of his daughter Domenica), had unlimited access to excess, resulting in substance abuse, Scorsese's affair with Liza Minnelli while making *New York, New York*, and eventually his divorce from Cameron. Much has been written about this period of Scorsese's life. I have no interest in delving into sensationalism by discussing it further, but see, for instance, Julia Cameron's *Floor Sample: A Creative Memoir*.

31. Sucher and Fischler, *All This Filming, Is It Healthy?*

32. Kelly, *Martin Scorsese: A Journey*, 118.

33. Kael, *5001 Nights at the Movies*, 612.

34. Cinebooks' Motion Picture Guide Reviews, "The Harder They Fall," *Cinemania 97*.

35. In his 106 professional fights, La Motta had 83 wins (30 by knockout), 19 losses, and four draws.

36. Kelly, *Martin Scorsese: A Journey*, 140–1.

37. The seven Instruments of the Passion are the column to which Christ was tied and whipped, the crown of thorns, the cross, the nails, the sponge from which he drank vinegar, the lance with which the Roman soldier pierced him, and the cup in which his blood was caught. The number of this round — thirteen — also calls to mind the crucifixion as it was the number of people present at the Last Supper.

38. In his entire career, his opponents never succeeded in knocking down La Motta.

39. Kelly, *Martin Scorsese: A Journey*, 119.

40. John 9:24–26 NEB.

41. Thompson and Christie, *Scorsese on Scorsese*, 76.

42. Kelly, *Martin Scorsese: A Journey*, 259.

43. Ibid., 273.

44. Ibid., 264.

45. This is perhaps the most interesting point in which the film differs from the book in which we have no reason to doubt what Henry Hill tells us.

46. Young Henry is played by Christopher Serrone.

47. Douglas, *Journey Into Darkness*, 9.

48. Rhythmic framing is used self-evidently in the Scorsese films that have music as their main subject matter — such as *New York, New York* and *The Last Waltz* — but they are also used in *Raging Bull* where we move and cut to the punches of the fights, and in *The Color of Money* where we follow the strokes of the pool game.

49. Ebert, Roger, *Awake in the Dark*, 170.

50. Navasky, *Naming Names*, xi, xii.

51. Friedman, *The Cinema of Martin Scorsese*, 175.

52. Hawthorne, *The Scarlet Letter*, 154.

53. In both Hitchcock's *Marnie* and Truffaut's *La Sirene du Mississipi*, a man falls in love with a beautiful, blonde woman *because* she is a thief and impostor.

54. Charles Scorsese, who was very much concerned with behaving in a morally responsible manner, wore glasses very much like them.

Chapter 3

1. Carroll, *Alice's Adventures in Wonderland & Through the Looking Glass*, 25.

2. Esther B. Fein, "Martin Scorsese: The Film Director As a Local Alien," *New York Times*, September 29, 1985.

3. Ibid.

4. Campbell, *The Hero with a Thousand Faces*, 23.

5. "McGuffin" is a term coined by Alfred Hitchcock to describe a device or plot element that catches the viewer's attention and/or drives the logic of the plot, but does not have the deeper significance we assume.

6. Additionally, it could be a *carpe diem* reminder to Paul not to waste his life by resisting it.

7. Freud, *The Interpretation of Dreams*, 83–91.

8. Dreams involving loss of hair are often expressions of castration anxiety.

9. In *It's Not Just You, Murray!* Murray smashes his own mirror image; in *The Big Shave* the main character mutilates himself in front of a mirror; in *Taxi Driver* we have Travis's famous duel with his mirror image; and in *Raging Bull* Jake smashes his head into his shadow on the wall.

10. In the documentary *All This Filming, Is It Healthy?*, Catherine Scorsese tells a haunting story about Marty's childhood. When he was about two years old, they took him to the hospital for a tonsillectomy. He was terrified to be left there alone, so his mother told him that a lady (i.e., the nurse) was going to come and take him to the circus and then went home. When they came to pick him up the next day, he was so "bitter" that he refused to talk to them. Subsequently his parents forgot all about this devastating incident, but, predictably, it stayed with Marty all his life.

11. The actual fare for a single boarding on the New York subway in 1985 was 90 cents.

12. I am indebted to Henrik Frederiksen for this point about Tom's name.

13. Dougan, *Martin Scorsese: The Making of His Movies*, 126.

14. Whitmont, *The Symbolic Quest*, 189.

15. *The American Heritage Dictionary of the English Language, Third Edition*.

16. Campbell, *The Hero with a Thousand Faces*, 16–17.

17. Chopra, *The Path to Love*, 156.

18. Odysseus's description of Persephone in *The Odyssey*.
19. Haskell, *From Reverence to Rape*, 323.
20. Ibid., 327–8.
21. Ibid., 323.
22. Kelly, *Martin Scorsese: A Journey*, 83–4.
23. Friedman, *The Cinema of Martin Scorsese*, 55.
24. Williams, *Road Movies*, 19.
25. Vadmand, *On the Road to Somewhere: The Feminist Road Movie*, 20.
26. According to Les Keyser, Scorsese was passionately in love with Wendy when he was a child. Keyser, *Martin Scorsese*, 5.
27 Vadmand, *On the Road to Somewhere: The Feminist Road Movie*, 45.
28. Roger Ebert, "Alice Doesn't Live Here Anymore," http://rogerebert.suntimes.com.
29. Ehrenstein, *The Scorsese Picture*, 215.
30. Blanche McCreary Boyd, "The Natural" *American Film*, October 1984, 25.
31. Kelly, *Martin Scorsese: A Journey*, 84–5.

Chapter 4

1. Carroll, *Alice's Adventures in Wonderland & Through the Looking Glass*, 136.
2. Nietzsche, *Beyond Good and Evil*, 68.
3. Dougan, *Martin Scorsese: The Making of His Movies*, 24.
4. Kristofferson, "The Pilgrim (Chapter 33)" from *The Silver Tongued Devil and I*.
5. Stephen Whitty, "Driven to Greatness," *Austin American-Statesman*, March 28, 1996, 52.
6. Kolker, *A Cinema of Loneliness*, 248.
7. Kelly, *Martin Scorsese: A Journey*, 92–3.
8. Friedman, *The Cinema of Martin Scorsese*, 64.
9. Thompson and Christie, *Scorsese on Scorsese*, 62.
10. Friedman, *The Cinema of Martin Scorsese*, 65.
11. Ressler, *Whoever Fights Monsters*, 137–8.
12. Kolker, *A Cinema of Loneliness*, 238.
13. Vickie does the exact same thing in the equivalent scene in *Raging Bull* when Jake first takes her to his father's apartment, which emphasizes that she is not as innocent as he prefers to think.
14. Friedman, *The Cinema of Martin Scorsese*, 79.
15. This, of course, is the preferred weapon of "Dirty Harry" Callahan, and, as Lawrence Friedman has pointed out, all the guns Travis buys are signature weapons of famous popular culture gunslingers. Although this may not mean much to Travis, who seems oblivious to popular culture, for the viewer it adds perspective to his vigilantism.
16. Robert Penn Warren's 1946 Pulitzer Prize winning novel, *All the King's Men*, portrays brutally ambitious demagogue Willie Stark, who was inspired by Louisiana governor and senator Huey Long, who was assassinated in 1935. In 1949 *All the King's Men* was made into a film directed by Robert Rossen, and its title later lent itself to the title for *All the President's Men*. Originally, the words were from the nursery rhyme about Humpty Dumpty.

17. For further implications concerning the knight in shining armor, the dragon and damsel, see the discussion of *The King of Comedy* in the next section of this chapter.
18. Patricia Patterson and Manny Farber, "The Power and the Gory: Taxi Driver," *Film Comment*, May/June 1998, 30.
19. Thompson and Christie, *Scorsese on Scorsese*, 48.
20. Friedman, *The Cinema of Martin Scorsese*, 70–71.
21. In real life, John Hinckley left a similar note for Jodie Foster when he went out to assassinate Ronald Reagan. Additionally, the words are the opening words of one of Scorsese's favorite films, Max Ophuls's *Letter From an Unknown Woman*, which begins, "By the time you read this letter, I may be dead."
22. Ressler, *Whoever Fights Monsters*, 131.
23. Kelly, *Martin Scorsese: A Journey*, 89.
24. Ibid., 98.
25. Dougan, *Martin Scorsese: The Making of His Movies*, 69.
26. Thompson and Christie, *Scorsese on Scorsese*, 92.
27. The voice of Rupert's mother's is actually that of Catherine Scorsese.
28. The parallel with *Psycho* is emphasized because, when Rupert turns around to answer her, he yells in the direction of a wide open door to an empty bathroom which Scorsese had built specifically for this set, Thelma Schoonmaker told me.
29. Similarly, on Wednesday morning Mother yells at him: "Rupert, hurry up, the bus is here. Try to be on time for once." If Mother is actually yelling that sentence in the present to the adult Rupert, it makes no sense, since, if the bus is already there, he cannot possibly make it no matter how much he hurries. Only if the bus is a school bus (that *would* wait for him) and Mother's voice belongs in the past and exists only in Rupert's mind, does her admonition make sense.
30. Bettelheim, *The Uses of Enchantment* 111.
31. Ibid., 112.
32. Thompson and Christie, *Scorsese on Scorsese*, 88.
33. Bettelheim, *The Uses of Enchantment*, 163.
34. Wood, *Hollywood from Vietnam to Reagan* 265.
35. For further information, see Robert A. Johnson, *He*.
36. Like in *Taxi Driver* this last scene may take place inside the main character's head. Similarly, it is possible that the monster Rupert is catapulted into at the end is his own psychosis.
37. Johnson, *He*, 25.
38. Kelly, *Martin Scorsese: A Journey*, 152.
39. Jean Callahan, "Ordinary People," *American Film*, October 1983, 63–4.
40. Boorstin, *The Image*, 57.
41. Ibid., 46–48.
42. Ibid.

Chapter 5

1. Gilchrist, *The Life of William Blake*, 175.
2. Jung, *The Development of Personality*, CW 17, par. 299.

3. 1 Cor. 7:25–38 NEB.
4. Campbell, *The Hero with a Thousand Faces*, 249.
5. Johnson, *Why Do Catholics Do That?*, 43.
6. Thompson and Christie, *Scorsese on Scorsese*, 99–100.
7. Wattis, Nigel. *A South Bank Show Special: Scorsese—The Last Temptation of Christ*.
8. Kazantzakis, *The Last Temptation*, 7.
9. Ibid., 119.
10. Jung, *Memories, Dreams, Reflections*, 107–8.
11. 1 Cor. 7:25–38 NEB.
12. The Hebrew name for God.
13. Matt. 3:10–12 NEB.
14. Ibid., 7:15–20.
15. Ibid., 10:34–39.
16. In Kazantzakis's book, the guardian angel that turns out to be Satan comes in the shape of a young man. When Scorsese instead chose a blonde girl for the part, he was possibly inspired by *Toby Dammit*, Fellini's 50-minute interpretation of Edgar Allan Poe's "Never Bet the Devil Your Head." Fellini substituted Poe's little old man as the Devil with a blonde girl. This choice on Fellini's part was in turn inspired by the homicidal ghost girl in Mario Bava's *Operazione Paura*.
17. Gilchrist, *The Life of William Blake*, 175.
18. Played by Randy Danson and Peggy Gormley.
19. *Life Lessons* forms the first third of the film *New York Stories*. The other two thirds, *Life without Zoe* and *Oedipus Wrecks*, were directed by Francis Ford Coppola and Woody Allen, respectively.
20. Friedman, *The Cinema of Martin Scorsese*, 155.
21. In real life this work was painted by Chuck Connelly and is entitled *Bridge to Nowhere*, whereas Paulette's painting was created in the early 1980s by Susan Hambleton.
22. The scene echoes the one in Michael Powell's *The Red Shoes*, in which late at night Vickie determinedly goes to tell Julian that she needs to start dancing again, but as she hears him composing, she caves in and sinks down beside the piano at his feet.
23. Poe, *Tales of Mystery and Imagination*, 320–321.
24. Bettelheim, *The Uses of Enchantment*, 303–9.
25. Lionel's refusal to endorse Paulette's work can be regarded from different perspectives. He obviously takes artistic integrity very seriously and accordingly tells her that it is what *she* thinks that is important. She cannot lean on him for approval, but has to take herself seriously. It is significant that what he promises her, and later his new assistant, as payment for services rendered, are not art lessons, but life lessons. At the same time he is a fallible and vain human involved in a relationship that is falling apart. He knows her intentions with the painting, and he just may not want to give her the satisfaction of telling her how good she has become. One of the few instances in the film in which Lionel is caught off guard and gives her a spontaneous, emotional reaction is when she considers staying home to work in order to avoid an encounter with Gregory Stark. "Don't use work as an excuse," Lionel says entreatingly, grabbing her by the arm; "your work is sacred!" Implicitly, he gives her the approval she so desperately wants, but Paulette does not hear it, and immediately afterwards he slips back into his usual manipulative role-playing.
26. The idea for this was taken from Dostoyevsky's *The Gambler*.
27. Matt. 10:34–39. 1 Cor. 7:25–38 NEB.

Chapter 6

1. Campbell, *The Hero with a Thousand Faces*, 21.
2. Thompson and Christie, *Scorsese on Scorsese*, 30.
3. Kelly, *Martin Scorsese: A Journey*, 67.
4. Thompson and Christie, *Scorsese on Scorsese*, 34. Toward the end of *Mean Streets* Charlie and Johnny Boy go into a movie theater to hide from Michael, and the film that is playing is Roger Corman's *The Tomb of Ligeia*, based on Edgar Allan Poe's story.
5. Ibid.
6. Dougan, *Martin Scorsese: The Making of His Movies*, 113.
7. Kelly, *Martin Scorsese: A Journey*, 66–7.
8. Ibid., 67.
9. Thompson and Christie, *Scorsese on Scorsese*, 36.
10. Ibid. Also interesting is the fact that Bill Shelley is played by David Carradine, whereas the railroad boss that has him crucified is played by his real-life father, John Carradine. In Scorsese's next film, *Mean Streets*, David Carradine is shot by his real-life brother, Robert Carradine.
11. Friedman, *The Cinema of Martin Scorsese*, 49.
12. Thompson and Christie, *Scorsese on Scorsese*, 38.
13. Ibid., 36.
14. *Mean Streets* got excellent reviews, *Alice Doesn't Live Here Anymore* won Ellen Burstyn an Academy Award, and *Taxi Driver* won the Golden Palm at Cannes.
15. Thompson and Christie, *Scorsese on Scorsese*, 68.
16. Ibid.
17. Ibid., 72. It does not make things any easier that the film exists in numerous different versions. Originally, it was reduced from four-and-a-half hours to 153 minutes and the "Happy Endings" sequence was cut out. For the European release it was cut back further to 136 minutes. In 1981 the film was re-released at 163 minutes and the "Happy Endings" sequence was put back in. I am basing my analysis on the 163-minute MGM Special Edition DVD that was released in February of 2005.
18. Scorsese even got Minnelli's and Garland's daughter, Liza Minnelli, to play the female lead.
19. Thompson and Christie, *Scorsese on Scorsese*, 69.
20. Ibid., 68.
21. Kael, *5001 Nights at the Movies*, 520.
22. Bandleader Frankie Harte is played by Georgie Auld, who also plays all De Niro's saxophone solos in the film.
23. Roger Ebert, "New York, New York," http://rogerebert.suntimes.com.
24. It is hard not to see this as a *mea culpa* from Scorsese who had an affair with Minnelli while making the film even though his wife, Julia Cameron, was pregnant.
25. Kael, *5001 Nights at the Movies*, 521.
26. Thompson and Christie, *Scorsese on Scorsese*, 72.

27. Kelly, *Martin Scorsese: A Journey*, 111–12.
28. The group was reformed with three of the five original members in 1983. Because Scorsese had problems both in his personal life and with the postproduction work on *New York, New York*, it took two years before *The Last Waltz* was released.
29. Kelly, *Martin Scorsese: A Journey*, 114.
30. Ibid., 117.
31. In the introduction to *Shine a Light*, Scorsese all but disavows the work by indicating a frustrating battle of wills between the creators of the film (himself and cinematographer Robert Richardson included) and Mick Jagger. Jagger comes across as narcissistic and insolent, as someone who neither understands nor cares one whit about the film. He keeps childishly kvetching about the cameras that "whittle around," "annoying" the audience and the band (he even does this in front of President Clinton), so that Scorsese — who is more frustrated and annoyed than I have ever seen him — has to justify himself that "it would be good to have a camera that moves." At the same time, Jagger refuses to let Scorsese know what the final set list is going to be: "I really would like to *know* what the first song is gonna be," Scorsese says.
32. Kelly, *Martin Scorsese: A Journey*, 117.
33. Ibid., 115.
34. Ibid., 117.
35. Thompson and Christie, *Scorsese on Scorsese*, 73.
36. Kael, *5001 Nights at the Movies*, 411. Kelly, *Martin Scorsese: A Journey*, 112.
37. Kelly, *Martin Scorsese: A Journey*, 116.
38. Ibid.
39. Peter Biskind and Susan Linfield, "Chalk Talk," *American Film*, November 1986, 31.
40. Ibid., 32.
41. Ibid. Terrence Rafferty, "High Stakes," *Sight and Sound*, Autumn 1986, 264.
42. Incidentally, Jake La Motta has a cameo role as a bartender in *The Hustler*.
43. Kelly, *Martin Scorsese: A Journey*, 193.
44. Richard Pells in a letter to the author.
45. Kelly, *Martin Scorsese: A Journey*, 196.
46. Johnson, *Owning Your Own Shadow*, 5.
47. I am indebted to Richard Pells for some of these points.
48. Kelly, *Martin Scorsese: A Journey*, 193.

Chapter 7

1. *The I Ching*, Hexagram 5.
2. *Kundun: Production Information*, Touchstone Pictures, 8.
3. Ibid., 10.
4. Ibid., 6.
5. The Kalachakra Mandala is a circle made out of sand that symbolizes the enlightened mind of the Buddha.
6. Tencho Gyalpo who plays the mother is really playing her own grandmother. The Dalai Lama is played at age two by Tenzin Yeshi Paichang, at age five by Tulku Jamyang Kunga Tenzin, at age 12 by Guyrme Tethong, and as an adult by Tenzin Thuthob Tsarong.
7. Lord Chamberlain is played by Gyatso Lukhang, Taktra Rinpoche by Tsewang Jigme Tsarong, Norbu Thundrup by Jamyang Tenzin, and the Master of the Kitchen by Lobsang Samten.
8. It is an interesting coincidence that he was enthroned on Martin Scorsese's birthday.
9. Extra material on the Region 2 DVD of *The Mothman Prophesies* by Warner Home Video.
10. In fact, according to Scorsese, the Dalai Lama's only objection to the finished film was, "You were a little too tough on the Chinese." Jan Stuart, "Scorsese Gets Spiritual," *Otago Daily Times*, 29.
11. Quite a frightening notion if you start thinking about it, that people others find disgusting do not deserve civil rights.
12. The first images we see underneath the water are extreme close-ups of an eye, and then teeth. Customarily, it is assumed that the expression "an eye for an eye and a tooth for a tooth" signifies revenge, punishing whatever wrongs others do to one by equal measure. Another theory about the meaning of that expression, however, is karmic by nature: whatever you do to others will eventually come back to you; your own wrongs will eventually show up at your own doorstep.
13. Pat Kirkham, "Looking for the Simple Idea," *Sight and Sound*, February 1984, 20.
14. Jung et al., *Man and His Symbols*, 168.
15. *MTV at the Movies*, 1991.
16. Zukav, *The Seat of the Soul*, 144.
17. Bernard Herrmann originally wrote this score for Thompson's 1962 film.
18. At their next meeting Cady is sitting in a car, and Sam is standing on the sidewalk, indicating that their positions of power have been inverted.
19. This is probably also an allusion to Michael Powell's *Black Narcissus*.
20. As we focus on Cady, the mayhem on the screen stops and a voice-over says: "He liked me, all this time, he actually liked me!" emphasizing that Cady is here for something more than just revenge.
21. Hitchcock said that *Psycho* is simply his version of "Little Red Riding Hood."
22. Bettelheim, *The Uses of Enchantment*, 171.
23. Ibid., 173. Interestingly, the girl Danielle talks to just before going down to Cady in the basement is played by Scorsese's daughter, Domenica.
24. Pentecostalism is a fundamentalist Protestant movement whose members practice speaking in tongues, baptism with the Holy Ghost, and faith healing; they also believe in the impending second coming of Jesus Christ. The practice refers back to Acts 2:4, wherein the Apostles spoke in tongues at Pentecost when the Holy Spirit descended upon them.
25. In the other versions of *Cape Fear*, the dog does not have a name and is the *family* dog. In Scorsese's film it is specified repeatedly that it is Leigh's dog.
26. Bettelheim, *The Uses of Enchantment*, 68–9.
27. Jung et al., *Man and His Symbols*, 168.
28. Ford, *The Dark Side of the Light Chasers*, 2.
29. Roger Ebert, "The Age of Innocence," http://rogerebert.suntimes.com.
30. Wharton, *The Age of Innocence*, 283, 286.

31. Martin Scorsese, Jay Cocks, and Robin Standefer, ed., *The Age of Innocence: A Portrait of the Film Based on the Novel by Edith Wharton*, xv.
32. Ibid.,vii.
33. Thelma Schoonmaker during a two-day seminar at the Danish Film School in February 2003.
34. Rachel Abramowitz, "In the Works," *Premiere*, December 1991, 22. De Fina was Scorsese's producer and fourth wife.
35. Hawthorne, "The Haunted Mind" in *Selected Tales and Sketches*, 106.
36. Ibid.
37. Wharton, *The Age of Innocence*, 83.
38. Ibid., 244.
39. Ibid., 293.
40. Ibid., 240, 242–3.
41. "When I lost for *Raging Bull*," Scorsese says about the Academy Awards, "I realized what my place in the system would be, if I did survive at all: on the outside looking in." Peter Biskind, "Slouching Toward Hollywood," *Premiere*, November 1991, 71.
42. *Handbook of Production Information*, Buena Vista International, 8.
43. Kelly, *Martin Scorsese: A Journey*, 159.
44. *Handbook of Production Information*, Buena Vista International, 5.
45. Ibid., 4. My emphasis.
46. Ibid., 4.
47. Tolkien, "On Fairy Stories" in *Tree and Leaf*, 54.
48. Although the Bible does not say specifically how many Wise Men were at the manger, three are always shown, because "then all civilized persons will understand that enough Magi came." Johnson, *Why Do Catholics Do That?*, 216.
49. Right before the final scene, Frank walks past Tom, who seems to be attempting to kill the car.
50. When Mary talks about her past, she makes a connection between substance abuse (the false god) and religion and true spirituality. "You must get a lot of overdoses," she says to Frank. "I bet you picked me up a couple of times." She ran away from home to a convent at the age of thirteen, but "Sister Mary or Mary the Junkie—it didn't really matter to me."
51. Matt. 3:4. K.J.
52. Frank's redemption is marked by the fusing of Mary and Rose. Incidentally, *Mary Rose* was the name of one of Hitchcock's pet projects, a film that was to be based on J.M. Barrie's play, whose deepest theme was if the dead were to come back, what would we do with them?

Chapter 8

1. Johnson, *Owning Your Own Shadow*, 17.
2. The term "organized crime" was first used during Prohibition, in the 1920s. Chronologically, *Gangs of New York* marks the beginning of Scorsese's ongoing portrayal of New York City over the centuries: *Gangs of New York* (the 1860s), *The Age of Innocence* (the 1890s to the early 1900s), *Italianamerican* (turn of the century and onwards), *New York, New York* (August 15, 1945 and onwards), *Raging Bull* (1941–1964), *GoodFellas* (1955–1980), *Who's That Knocking at My Door?* (late 1960s), *Mean Streets* (early 1970s), *Taxi Driver* (mid-1970s), *The King of Comedy* (early 1980s), *After Hours* (mid-1980s), *Life Lessons* (late 1980s), *Bringing Out the Dead* (early 1990s).
3. Dickens actually visited the Five Points in 1842 and described the appalling conditions he witnessed there, in *American Notes*.
4. Darth Vader is a near-anagram of dead father.
5. The same way that it did in Scorsese's *The Big Shave*.
6. Pope Leo XIII's "Prayer to Saint Michael" was, in fact, written several decades *after* 1846 when the scene takes place, thus marking one of the instances wherein history is sacrificed for the sake of the poetry of the narrative.
7. Daniel Day-Lewis's performance in this film is absolutely amazing, and his range as an actor can be measured simply by comparing the two roles he has played for Scorsese: Newland Archer in *The Age of Innocence* and Bill the Butcher in *Gangs of New York*.
8. The original meaning of the slang term "dead rabbit" was a man who is greatly to be feared, but it makes sense to read the gang name literally, too, since a deceased, furry, long-eared mammal—an actual dead rabbit—is used as their emblem.
9. Blackwell's Island is the present-day Roosevelt Island.
10. As romantically glorified as this sounds, it was, of course, literally true at the time of the Gold Rush.
11. The only other significant female character is the savage Hell-Cat Maggie whose near-cannibalistic slayings are even more brutal than those of the male gang members.
12. Johnson, *Owning Your Own Shadow*, 34. At one point, Bill the Butcher mentions that *his* father was killed fighting Britain in the War of 1812. This means that Bill's fierce Americanism was passed down from his father and is a result of his brutal death in battle, too.
13. Also known as the curse of Cain.
14. On July 13–16, 1863, rioters protested against the fact that you could pay your way out of conscription, which meant that only the sons of the poor were forced to go to war. "I was about my father's business" is a reference to Luke 2:49.
15. Unfortunately, while we are trying to grasp this profound and touching moment, we are blasted out of our seats by the U2 song that ends the film. Just like Amsterdam cannot learn the lessons he is supposed to because he is traumatized by being hurtled 16 years into the future at the beginning, it might be difficult for the audience to assimilate the potent lessons this film could teach us when we are suddenly hurtled 140 years into the future for no reason at all. One is wondering why Scorsese—who usually has impeccable timing when it comes to using music—did not wait just a few seconds longer before introducing the song.
16. *Production Notes*, Miramax Films, 3.
17. Seibert, *All Movie Guide*, http://allmovie.com.
18. Rather than trying to recreate the Technicolor process with real cameras, the visual effects team used modern color stock combined with digital technology.

19. *Production Notes*, Miramax Films, 5.
20. Ibid.
21. www.wsws.org, www.stfrancis.edu/historyinthemovies.com.
22. Seibert, *All Movie Guide*, http://allmovie.com.
23. Didion, *Slouching Towards Bethlehem*, 81–82. My emphasis.
24. Fitzgerald, *The Great Gatsby*, 8.
25. Wordsworth, "My Heart Leaps Up When I Behold" in *The Major Works*.
26. Psalms 55:6 NEB.
27. Chevalier, *The Penguin Dictionary of Symbols*, 1117.
28. Marlowe, *Dr. Faustus*, 4.
29. www.stfrancis.edu/historyinthemovies.com.
30. Brown and Broeske, *Howard Hughes: The Untold Story*, 273.
31. *The American Heritage Dictionary of the English Language*.
32. Luke 7:37–38.
33. This becomes even more poignant because the name of this character was changed for the film. He was called Josh in John Logan's screenplay.
34. Fitzgerald, *The Crack-Up*, 75.
35. In all fairness, most of these mistakes were in Monahan's original screenplay, but one wonders why Scorsese did not catch them. The internet abounds with long lists of these, but for me the gravest, most annoying problem is the chronology: The film opens in "Boston — Some years ago," or — to be specific — during the busing riots of 1974. The screenplay points out that the historical montage is a background for Costello's voice-over, but since the race question has *absolutely* nothing to do with the rest of the film on any level, introducing it during the first few intense minutes serves only to inexcusably confuse the viewer. The film then cuts about ten years, but since it does not inform us of this, we naturally assume that the pubescent Colin, whom Costello now befriends, was approximately 12 in 1974 (whereas this is actually supposed to be the early 1980s). When we next see Colin graduating from the Police Academy, he is intercut with Billy who is a cadet and thus, presumably, a year or two younger. Judging by the cell phones used and the mention of the Patriot Act, the main action takes place during the present time, i.e., 2005–2006. All this would mean that Colin at his graduation is fast approaching middle age: he would be either 44 (if he was 12 in 1974) or 36 (if he was 12 in 1982, see footnote 37 below). Things become even more perplexing at the end when we learn that Billy is *decades* younger than that: in his confidential file on the computer screen it says that Billy was born 11/7/1984, then a few seconds later it says 11/7/1980. This tremendous goof aside, that would mean that until November of 2006, Billy is either 21 or 25. In other words, during the main action of the film, Colin Sullivan would be either in his mid-40s or mid-30s, whereas Billy Costigan would be in his early- or mid-20s, depending on which pieces of information we choose to take seriously. I am sorry if it seems like nitpicking to point this out at length, but how can one take seriously the internal logic of a film that cannot be bothered to have one? It feels as if Scorsese considered this film merely a potboiler, which makes it extremely ironic that *The Departed* would be the film that finally won him the Academy Award.
36. Although there was a real-life Italian New York gangster named Frank Costello (1891–1973), the character of Frank Costello is based mainly on Irish Boston mobster Whitey Bulger.
37. On the basis of this it would be logical to assume that this scene takes place in the fall of 1982, during which time the growing popularity of The Marvel Comics superhero Wolverine led to a solo, four-issue limited series (September–December 1982). The wolverine is not really a wolf, of course, but a weasel.
38. Joyce, *Portrait of the Artist as a Young Man*. Milton, *Paradise Lost*, 127.
39. Nietzsche, *Beyond Good and Evil*, 68.
40. 15 issues of #711 were published from August 1941 to January 1943.
41. When Colin tells Costello about the irony of his situation — "I gotta find myself" — he does not see the double meaning of that sentence even when Costello points it out to him.
42. Shakespeare, *Hamlet*, 172. My emphasis.
43. No original score was written for *Shutter Island*. Instead, Scorsese asked his longtime friend and associate, Robbie Robertson, to collect classical and popular music from the twentieth century to "create a wall of sound." This works astoundingly well, and Robertson has done an absolutely spectacular job. *Production Notes*, Paramount Pictures, 23.
44. In Lehane's novel, Teddy's fear is traced back to childhood which seems slightly illogical since Teddy Daniels has no childhood. In Scorsese's film it is more plausibly and relevantly linked directly to the two things he is trying to repress in the actual story. However, the book actually begins with a scene between a father and a son, which fits in perfectly with the other Scorsese/DiCaprio collaborations.
45. In the novel we are given Teddy's and Dolores's full names — Edward Daniels and Dolores Chanal — quite early on, so that we might figure out that they are, in fact, anagrams of Andrew Laeddis and Rachel Solando.
46. The mention of HUAC (the House Un-American Activities Committee) instantly introduces much wider political ramifications and adds deeper connotations of fear.
47. *Production Notes*, Paramount Pictures, 12.
48. When I first read John Fowles's *The Magus*, I always imagined Ben Kingsley as Conchis, so it is a real pleasure for me that Scorsese chose him to play the godhead in *Shutter Island*.
49. I am indebted to and deeply in awe of my friend Henrik Frederiksen for figuring this out.
50. When Laeddis has carried his daughter from the lake, he lays her down in the grass and tenderly takes off her little red sandal. This is a reference to Michael Powell's film *The Red Shoes*, in which Vickie, with her dying breath, asks Julian to take off the red shoe. It is also a moment of almost unbearable poignancy in *Shutter Island*.
51. Scorsese handles this scene exquisitely: he first shows us Teddy's delusion of killing Dr. Cawley, then

slides into the true version of what happens. I was so relieved that he decided to refrain from using the squirt gun that is in both the novel and the original screenplay for the film.

52. De Niro played the creature in Kenneth Branagh's 1994 adaptation of Mary Shelley's famous novel.

53. Lehane, *Shutter Island*, 391.

54. In the final film there are two lines on that piece of paper: "The law of 4" and "Who is 67?" But in original version there was only that one haunting line. "Who is 67?"

55. The office of the Devil's Advocate, established in 1587, was significantly reformed by Pope John Paul II in 1983. This facilitated the process so much that John Paul II managed to canonize close to 500 individuals during his 27-year reign, as compared to a total of 98 canonizations by his predecessors in the entire 20th century.

56. James Kaplan, "The Outsider," *New York Magazine*, March 14, 1996, 35.

57. Di Renzo, *American Gargoyles: Flannery O'Connor and the Medieval Grotesque*, 7.

58. Kris Kristofferson, "To Beat the Devil" from *Kristofferson*.

Bibliography

Abramowitz, Rachel. "In the Works." *Premiere* (December 1991): 22.
Agan, Patrick. *Robert De Niro: The Man, the Myth and the Movies*. London: Robert Hale, 1989.
The American Heritage Dictionary of the English Language (3rd ed.). Boston: Houghton Mifflin, 1992.
Arnheim, Rudolf. *Film as Art*. Berkeley: University of California Press, 1984.
Asbury, Herbert. *The Gangs of New York: An Informal History of the Underworld*. London: Arrow, 2003.
Bach, Steven. *Final Cut: Dreams and Disaster in the Making of Heaven's Gate*. New York: William Morrow, 1985.
Barrie, J.M. *Peter Pan*. London: Armada, 1988.
Baum, L. Frank. *The Wonderful Wizard of Oz*. New York: Signet Classics, 2006.
Berry, Jo. "Sit Up Straight, Don't Talk with Your Mouth Full, and Get Your Elbows Off the Table …" *Empire* (February 1994): 64–65.
Bettelheim, Bruno. *The Uses of Enchantment: The Meaning and Importance of Fairy Tales*. London: Penguin, 1991.
The Bible: Authorized King James Version. Oxford: Oxford University Press, 1998.
Bishop, Kathy. "Liotta." *Rolling Stone*, November 1, 1990.
Biskind, Peter, and Susan Linfield. "Chalk Talk." *American Film*, November 1986.
_____, and _____. "Slouching Toward Hollywood." *Premiere* (November 1991): 30–33, 69–72.
Blake, Richard Aloysius. *Street Smart: the New York of Lumet, Allen, Scorsese, and Lee*. Lexington: University Press of Kentucky, 2005.
Blake, William. "The Marriage of Heaven and Hell": *The Norton Anthology of English Literature* (Vol. 2, 3rd ed.). New York: W.W. Norton, 1974.
_____. "The Tyger": *World's Greatest Classic Books*. Ottawa: Corel, 1995.
Bliss, Michael. *Martin Scorsese and Michael Cimino*. Metuchen, NJ: Scarecrow Press, 1985.
_____, and Anthony Slide, ed. *The Word Made Flesh*. Lanham, MD: Scarecrow Press, 1999.
Boorstin, Daniel J. *The Image: A Guide to Pseudo-Events in America*. New York: Harper & Row, 1961.
Brown, Peter Harry, and Pat H. Broeske. *Howard Hughes: The Untold Story*. New York: Time Warner, 2004.
Callahan, Jean. "Ordinary People." *American Film* (October 1983): 62–68.
Campbell, Joseph. *The Hero with a Thousand Faces*. New York: MJF, 1997.
Capote, Truman. *In Cold Blood*. London: Sphere, 1987.
Carroll, Lewis. *Alice's Adventures in Wonderland & Through the Looking Glass*. New York: Airmont, 1965.
_____. *Alice's Adventures Under Ground*. New York: Holt, Rinehart and Winston, 1985.
_____. *The Annotated Alice: Alice's Adventures in Wonderland & Through the Looking Glass*. London: Penguin, 2001.
Casillo, Robert. *Gangster Priest: the Italian American Cinema of Martin Scorsese*. Toronto: University of Toronto Press, 2006.
Chanko, Kenneth M. "The Last Temptation of Christ." *Films in Review* (November 1988): 550–552.
Chaucer, Geoffrey. *The Canterbury Tales*: *The Norton Anthology of English Literature* (Vol. 1, 3rd ed.). New York: W.W. Norton, 1974.
Chevalier, Jean, and Alain Gheerbrant. *The Penguin Dictionary of Symbols*. London: Penguin, 1996.
Chopra, Deepak. *The Path to Love: Renewing the Power of Spirit in Your Life*. New York: Harmony, 1997.
Christie, Ian. "The Scorsese Interview." *Sight and Sound* (February 1994): 10–15.
Combs, Richard. "Gifts of the Magi: New York Stories." *Sight and Sound* (Autumn 1989): 279–282.
_____. "Once a Contender." *Sight and Sound* (Winter 1986–87): 68–69.
_____. "Where Angels Fear to Tread." *Sight and Sound* (Summer 1986): 208–290.
The Complete Bible and Reference Guide CD-Rom. Cinerom, Inc., 1995.
Conard, Mark T., ed. *The Philosophy of Martin Scorsese*. Lexington: University Press of Kentucky, 2007.
Conn, Andrew Lewis. "The Adolescents of Martin Scorsese: The Drama of the Gifted Child." *Film Comment* (May/June 1998): 24–27.
Connelly, Marie Katheryn. *Martin Scorsese: An Analysis of His Feature Films, with a Filmography of His Entire Directorial Career*. Jefferson, NC: McFarland, 1994.

Cook, Pam. "The Age of Innocence." *Sight and Sound* (February 1994): 45–46.
_____. "Scorsese's Masquerade." *Sight and Sound* (April 1992): 14–15.
Corliss, Richard. "Filming at Full Throttle." *Time* (November 11, 1991): 62–63.
Dante. *The Divine Comedy: Paradise* in *World's Greatest Classic Books*. Ottawa: Corel, 1995.
_____. *The Divine Comedy: Purgatory* in *World's Greatest Classic Books*. Ottawa: Corel, 1995.
_____. *The Divine Comedy: The Inferno* in *World's Greatest Classic Books*. Ottawa: Corel, 1995.
De Curtis, Anthony. "The Rolling Stone Martin Scorsese Interview." *Rolling Stone* (November 1, 1990. Issue No. 590): 58–65, 106–108.
Di Renzo, Anthony. *American Gargoyles: Flannery O'Connor and the Medieval Grotesque*. Carbondale: Southern Illinois University Press, 1995.
Dickens, Charles. *American Notes for General Circulation*. London: Penguin, 2000.
_____. *Oliver Twist*. London: Penguin, 1994.
Didion, Joan. *Slouching Towards Bethlehem*. New York: Washington Square, 1981.
Diski, Jenny. "The Shadow Within." *Sight and Sound* (February 1992): 12–13.
Dostoevsky, Fyodor. *The Gambler—with Polina Suslova's Diary*. Chicago: University of Chicago Press, 1972.
Dougan, Andy. *Martin Scorsese*. London: Orion Media, 1997.
Douglas, John, and Mark Olshaker. *Journey into Darkness*. New York: Pocket Books, 1997.
Ebert, Roger. *Awake in the Dark: Forty Years of Reviews, Essays, and Interviews*. Chicago: University of Chicago Press, 2006.
_____. http://rogerebert.suntimes.com.
_____. *Scorsese by Ebert*. Chicago: University of Chicago Press, 2008.
Ehrenstein, David. *The Scorsese Picture: The Art and Life of Martin Scorsese*. New York: Birch Lane Press, 1992.
Errigo, Angie. "The Age of Innocence." *Empire* (February 1994): 20.
Faludi, Susan. *Stiffed: The Betrayal of the Modern Man*. London: Chatto & Windus, 1999.
Fein, Esther B. "Martin Scorsese: The Film Director as a Local Alien." *New York Times* (Sunday, September 29, 1985).
Fitzgerald, F. Scott. *The Crack-Up*. New York: New Directions, 1993.
_____. *The Great Gatsby*. Middlesex: Penguin, 1976.
Ford, Debbie. *The Dark Side of the Light Chasers: Reclaiming Your Power, Creativity, Brilliance, and Dreams*. New York: Riverhead, 1999.
Fowles, John. *The Magus*. London: Pan, 1988.
Francke, Lizzie. "Screen Dreams of Beautiful Women." *The Observer* (January 16, 1994): 14–15.
Frankel, Martha. "Tribeca Stories." *American Film* (October 1990): 41–43.
Franz, Marie-Louise Von. *Shadow and Evil in Fairy Tales*. Dallas: Spring, 1983.
Freud, Sigmund. *The Interpretation of Dreams*. Middlesex: Penguin, 1985.
Friedman, Lawrence S. *The Cinema of Martin Scorsese*. New York: Continuum, 1997.
Gilchrist, Alexander. *The Life of William Blake*. Mineola, NY: Dover, 1998.
Gleiberman, Owen. "Happy Families." *Empire*, March 1992.
Grist, Leighton. *The Films of Martin Scorsese, 1963–77: Authorship and Context*. New York: St. Martin's Press, 2000.
Hamlin, Suzanne. "Remembering an Italian Mother Just as She Would Like." *New York Times*, February 19, 1997.
Haskell, Molly. *From Reverence to Rape: The Treatment of Women in the Movies*. London: New English Library, 1975.
Hawthorne, Nathaniel. *The Scarlet Letter*. New York: W.W. Norton, 1962. London: Penguin, 1987.
_____. *Selected Tales and Sketches*. New York: Penguin, 1987.
Heath, Chris. "Belle Michelle." *Empire* (February 1994): 62–63.
_____. "Good Fellows." *Empire* (February 1994): 56–62.
_____. "She's Arrived." *Empire* (February 1994): 66–67.
Hoberman, J. "Sacred and Profane." *Sight and Sound* (February 1992): 8–11.
Homer. *The Odessey*. London: Penguin, 2003.
Huxley, Aldous. *The Doors of Perception & Heaven and Hell*. London: Chatto & Windus, 1972.
Ibsen, Henrik. *Peer Gynt*. Whitefish, MT: Kessinger, 2004.
Jacobs, Diane. *The Hollywood Renaissance*. New York: Dell, 1980.
Jaehne, Karen. "GoodFellas." *Film Quarterly* (Spring 1991): 43–50.
James, Henry. *The Turn of the Screw and Other Stories*. Middlesex: Penguin, 1977.
Johnson, Kevin Orlin. *Why Do Catholics Do That?* New York: Ballantine, 1995.
Johnson, Robert A. *He: Understanding Masculine Psychology*. New York: Harper & Row, 1989.
_____. *Inner Work: Using Dreams and Active Imagination for Personal Growth*. San Francisco: Harper & Row, 1989
_____. *Owning Your Own Shadow*. San Francisco: HarperCollins, 1991.
_____. *She: Understanding Feminine Psychology*. San Francisco: HarperCollins, 1989.
_____. *We: Understanding the Psychology of Romantic Love*. New York: HarperCollins, 1983.
Joyce, James. *A Portrait of the Artist as a Young Man*. New York: Oxford University Press, 2008.
Jung, Cark Gustav. *The Archetypes and the Collective Unconscious*, in *Collected Works* (Vol. 9, Part I). Princeton, NJ: Bollingen, 1981.
_____. *The Development of Personality* in *Collected Works* (Vol. 17). London: Routledge and Kegan Paul, 1991.

———. *Letters, Vol. 1, 1906–1950*. Edited by Gerhard Adler and Aniela Jaffe. Princeton, NJ: Princeton University Press, 1992.
———. *Man and His Symbols*. New York: Anchor, 1964.
———. *Memories, Dreams, Reflections*. London: Collin Fount, 1977.
———. *Two Essays on Analytical Psychology*. London: Routledge & Kegan Paul, 1974.
Kael, Pauline. *5001 Nights at the Movies*. New York: Henry Holt, 1991.
Kamp, David. "Three on a Match." *Vanity Fair* (October 1999).
Kaplan, James. "The Outsider." *New York Magazine* (March 14, 1996): 32–40, 101.
Kazantzakis, Nikos. *The Last Temptation*. London: Faber and Faber, 1975.
Kelly, Mary Pat. *Martin Scorsese—A Journey*. New York: Thunder's Mouth Press, 1991.
———. *Martin Scorsese—The First Decade*. Pleasantville, NY: Redgrave, 1980.
Keyser, Les. *Martin Scorsese*. New York: Twayne, 1992.
Kirkham, Pat. "Looking for the Simple Idea." *Sight and Sound*, February 1994.
Kolker, Robert Phillip. *A Cinema of Loneliness*. New York: Oxford University Press, 1980.
Lehane, Dennis. *Shutter Island*. London: Bantam, 2006.
LoBrutto, Vincent. *Martin Scorsese: A Biography*. Westport, CT: Praeger, 2008.
London, Jack. *The People of the Abyss*. Middlesex: The Echo Library, 2007.
Lopate, Phillip. "Fourteen Koans by a Levite on Scorsese's *The Last Temptation of Christ*." *Tikkun* (November/December 1988): 74–78.
MacDonald, John D. *The Executioners*. New York: Penguin, 1991.
Manoogian, Haig P. *The Film-Maker's Art*. New York: Basic, 1966.
Marlowe, Christopher. *Dr. Faustus*. New York: Signet Classics, 2001.
McCreary Boyd, Blanche. "The Natural." *American Film* (October 1984): 22–26, 91–92.
McGilligan, Patrick, and Mark Rowland. "The American Film Critics Poll: The 80s." *American Film* (November 1989): 23–29.
———, and ———. "American Film 2nd Annual Critics Poll." *American Film* (April 1991): 28–33.
McGreal, Jill. "Mean Streets." *Sight and Sound* (April 1993): 64.
McIntosh, James, ed. *Nathaniel Hawthorne's Tales*. New York: W.W. Norton, 1987.
McRobbie, Angela. "Cape Fear." *Sight and Sound* (March 1992): 39–40.
Microsoft Bookshelf, 1996–97 Edition CD-Rom. Microsoft Corporation, 1987–1996.
Microsoft Cinemania 97 CD-Rom. Microsoft Corporation, 1992–1996.
Miliora, Maria T. *The Scorsese Psyche on Screen: Roots of Themes and Characters in the Films*. Jefferson, NC: McFarland, 2004.
Millea, Holly, "My Father, Myself." *Premiere* (March 1994): 35.
Milton, John. *Paradise Lost*. London: Penguin, 2003.
Monaco, James. *American Film Now*. New York: Zoetrope, 1984.
Morgan, David. "A Remake That Can't Miss: *Cape Fear*." *American Cinematographer* (October 1991): 34–40.
Morris, Michael, O.P. "Of God and Man." *American Film* (October 1988): 44–49.
Mueller, Matt. "Cape Fear." *Empire* (March 1992): 16–17.
———. "Tattoo You." *Empire* (March 1992): 66–67.
Murphy, Kathleen. "Made Men." *Film Comment* (September/October 1990): 25–27.
Navasky, Victor S. *Naming Names*. New York: Viking Press, 1980.
New English Bible with the Apocrypha. New York: Oxford University Press, 1976.
Nicholls, Mark Desmond. *Scorsese's Men: Melancholia and the Mob*. North Melbourne, Australia: Pluto Press, 2004.
Nietzsche, Friedrich. *Beyond Good and Evil*. New York: Oxford University Press, 1998.
Nyce, Ben. *Scorsese Up Close: A Study of the Films*. Lanham, MD: Scarecrow Press, 2004.
Osbon, Diane K., ed. *A Joseph Campbell Companion*. New York: HarperCollins, 1991.
Paris, Barry. "Maximum Expression." *American Film* (October 1989): 30–39, 54.
Patterson, Patricia, and Manny Farber. "The Power and the Gory: *Taxi Driver*." *Film Comment* (May/June 1998): 30, 35–44.
Pearson, Carol S., *The Hero Within: Six Archetypes We Live By*. New York: HarperCollins, 1989.
Penman, Ian. "Jukebox and Johnny Boy." *Sight and Sound* (April 1993): 10–11.
Pileggi, Nicholas. *Casino*. London: Faber and Faber, 1996.
———. *Casino: Love and Honor in Las Vegas*. United Kingdom: Corgi, 1996.
———. *Wise Guy: Life in a Mafia Family*. New York: Simon & Schuster, 1987.
Poe, Edgar Allan. *The Complete Tales and Poems of Edgar Allan Poe*. London: Penguin, 1982.
———. *Tales of Mystery and Imagination*. Hertfordshire: Wordsworth Classics, 1993.
Poland, Larry W, Ph.D. *The Last Temptation of Hollywood*. Highland: Mastermedia International, 1988.
Pye, Michael, and Lynda Myles. *The Movie Brats*. New York: Holt, Rinehart and Winston, 1979.
Quart, Leonard. "Goodfellas." *Cineaste* (Vol. 18, No. 2, 1991): 43–45.
Rafferty, Terrence. "High Stakes." *Sight and Sound* (Autumn 1986): 264–265.
Rank, Otto. *The Don Juan Legend*. Princeton, NJ: Princeton University Press, 1975.
Reber, Arthur S. *The Penguin Dictionary of Psychology*. London: Penguin, 1985.

Ressler, Robert, and Tom Shachtman. *Whoever Fights Monsters.* New York: St. Martin's Press, 1993.
Richardson, Cheryl. *The Unmistakable Touch of Grace.* New York: Free Press, 2005.
Rickey, Carrie. "Movies." *New Woman Magazine* (December 1986): 22.
Rilke, Rainer Maria. *Letters to a Young Poet.* London: Vintage Books, 1992.
Rosen, Marjorie. "Woman Talk." *Film Comment* (May/June 1998): 29.
Rosenbaum, Jonathan. "Raging Messiah." *Sight and Sound* (Autumn 1988): 281–282.
Rosenbaum, Ron. "The Fall and Rise of Barbara Hershey." *American Film* (May 1986): 20–25.
Rowe, Dorothy. *Beyond Fear.* London: Fontana/Collins, 1987.
Sante, Luc (introduction). *Martin Scorsese's Gangs of New York: Making the Movie.* New York: Miramax, 2002.
Schickel, Richard. *Intimate Strangers: The Culture of Celebrity.* New York: Doubleday, 1985.
Schiff, Stephen. "The Casino Cut." *The New Yorker* (November 27, 1995): 46–50.
Schrader, Paul. "Paul Schrader on Martin Scorsese." *The New Yorker* (March 21, 1994): 124.
Scorsese, Catherine, with Georgia Downard. *Italianamerican: The Scorsese Family Cookbook.* New York: Random House, 1996.
Scorsese, Martin. "Martin Scorsese's 100 Random Pleasures." *Film Comment* (May/June 1998): 50.
_____. "Martin Scorsese's Guilty Pleasures." *Film Comment* (May/June 1998): 46–48.
_____. "Scorsese." *Premiere* (December 1995): 111–117.
_____, and Michael Henry Wilson. *A Personal Journey with Martin Scorsese Through American Film.* London: Faber and Faber, 1997.
_____, and Nicholas Pileggi. *GoodFellas.* London: Faber and Faber, 1990.
_____, and Peter Brunette, ed. *Martin Scorsese: Interviews.* Jackson: University Press of Mississippi, 1998.
_____, Jay Cocks, and Robin Standefer, ed. *The Age of Innocence: A Portrait of the Film Based on the Novel by Edith Wharton.* New York: Newmarket Press, 1993.
Seibert, Perry. *All Movie Guide.* http://allmovie.com
Shakespeare, William. *Hamlet.* New York: Signet Classics, 1963.
Sharrett, Christopher. "The Last Temptation of Christ." *Cineaste* (Vol. 17, No.1, 1989): 28–29.
Singer, Mark. "The Man Who Forgets Nothing." *The New Yorker* (March 27, 2000): 90–102.
Smith, Gavin. "Martin Scorsese Interview by Gavin Smith." *Film Comment* (September/October 1990): 27–30, 69.
_____. "Street Smart." *Film Comment* (May/June 1998): 68–77.
Smith, Lori J. "Willem Dafoe: Center Stage." *American Film* (October 1988): 50–54.
Sotinel, Thomas. *Martin Scorsese.* Paris: Cahiers du Cinéma, 2007.
Stern, Lesley. *The Scorsese Connection.* Indianapolis: Indiana University Press, 1995.
Stuart, Jan. "Scorsese Gets Spiritual." *Otago Daily Times* (Monday, November 15, 1999): 29.
Taubin, Amy. "Dread and Desire." *Sight and Sound* (December 1993): 6–9.
Taylor, Clarke. "Off-Hollywood Producers." *American Film* (September 1985): 28–32, 72.
Thompson, David. "The Director as Raging Bull: Why Can't a Woman Be More Like a Photograph?" *Film Comment* (May/June 1998): 52–63.
_____, and Ian Christie. *Scorsese on Scorsese.* London: Faber and Faber, 1996.
Thompson, G.R., ed. *The Gothic Imagination: Essays in Dark Romanticism.* Washington: Washington State University Press, 1974.
Tolkien, J. R.R. *Tree and Leaf.* London: Unwin Hyman, 1988.
Vadmand, Margrethe. "On the Road to Somewhere: The Feminist Road Movie." Unpublished master's thesis, University of Copenhagen, 1998.
van Daalen, Bill. "After Hours." *Film Quarterly*, Vol. 42, No. 3. (Spring 1988): 31–34.
Vogler, Christopher. *The Writer's Journey: Mythic Structure for Storytellers and Screenwriters.* London: Boxtree, 1996.
Walker, Alexander. "Slowly Burning the Erotic Fuse." *Evening Standard* (Thursday, January 27, 1994): 38.
Weiss, Marion. *Martin Scorsese: A Guide to References and Resources.* Boston: G.K. Hall, 1987.
Wershoven, Carol: *The Female Intruder in the Novels of Edith Wharton.* Rutherford, NJ: Fairleigh Dickinson University Press, 1982.
Wharton, Edith. *The Age of Innocence.* London: Penguin, 1993.
Whitmont, Edward C. *The Symbolic Quest: Basic Concepts of Analytical Psychology.* Princeton, NJ: Princeton University Press, 1991.
Whitty, Stephen. "Driven to Greatness." *Austin American-Statesman* (March 28, 1996): 52.
Williams, Mark. *Road Movies.* London: Proteus, 1982.
Wilmington, Michael. "The Wild Heart." *Film Comment* (May/June 1998): 16–22.
Wood, Robin. *Hollywood from Vietnam to Reagan.* New York: Columbia University Press, 1986.
Wordsworth, William. *The Major Works.* New York: Oxford University Press, 2000.
World's Greatest Classic Books CD-Rom. Corel Corporation, 1995.
Zukav, Gary. *The Seat of the Soul.* London: Rider, 1991.

Selected Documentaries on Martin Scorsese

Hayden, Peter. *Movies Are My Life*, 1977.
Sucher, Joel, and Steven Fischler. *All This Filming, Is It Healthy?* Pacific Film Projects, Inc., in association with Thirteen/WNET, 1990.
Wattis, Nigel. *A South Bank Show Special: Scorsese—The Last Temptation of Christ*. London Weekend Television, 1988.

Index

Numbers in ***bold italics*** indicate pages with photographs.

Abbott, Diahnne 93
Aeschylus 178
After Hours 10, 13, 14, 55, 58–67, ***61***, 68, 82, 132, 164
The Age of Innocence 10, 13, 14, 75, 104, 139, 146, 159–170, ***162***, ***165***, ***169***, 186
"Agony in the Garden" 222
Alice Doesn't Live Here Anymore 58, 67–76, ***69***, ***72***, ***76***, 120, 164
Alice's Adventures in Wonderland 58, 59, 68, 70, 72, 73, 144, 183, 207, 216
Allen, Woody 81
Amazing Stories see "Mirror, Mirror"
Andersen, Hans Christian 100, 211
anima 13, 14, 25, 34, 54, 105, 137, 172, 197; in *After Hours* 58, 65, 66, 67; in *The Age of Innocence* 164, 167, 168, 169; in *Gangs of New York* 185, 186, 187, 188, 189; in *Shutter Island* 217, 220, 223
animus 13, 58, 71, 72
Anthony, Marc 172
Arana, Tomas 103
Argento, Dario 100
Arnheim, Rudolf 35
Arquette, Patricia 172, ***173***
Arquette, Rosanna 59, 108, ***109***
Asbury, Herbert 177, 178
The Aviator 10, 13, 14, 80, 177, 190–203, ***192***, ***199***

Baker, Joe Don 151
Bako, Brigitte 108
Baldwin, Alec 194
The Band 118, 128–132; "Cripple Creek" 130; "Don't Do It" 130; "Helpless" 130; "I Shall Be Released" 131; "Ophelia" 131; "The Shape I'm In" 130; "Stagefright" 130; "The Weight" 130
The Band Wagon 122
Barnes, Johnny 36
Barretto, Ray 25
basements 9, 10, 23, 66, 93, ***94***, 154, 180, 185, 208; *see also* dungeons
Bass, Elaine 148, 161

Bass, Saul 148, 161
"Beauty and the Beast" 115–116
Beckinsale, Kate 195, ***199***
Bergman, Ingmar 10, 11, 20, 106
Bernhard, Sandra 94
Bernstein, Elmer 149
Bernuth, Peter 80
Berryigan, Bunny 80
Bethune, Zina 25
Bettelheim, Bruno 2, 27, 95, 97, 115, 133, 154, 158, 210
Bible 11, 21, 31, 57, 101–102, 183, 184; Job 149; John 41; Matthew 105, 175
The Big Heat 34
The Big Shave 79–80, 198
Blake, William 31, 100, 107
Blanchett, Cate 193
Bloom, Verna 65, 106
Blossom, Robert 104
Body and Soul 35
Bonnie and Clyde 20, 24, 119, 120
Boorstin, Daniel 99
Borrego, Jesse 108
Bouguereau, William-Adolphe 163
Boxcar Bertha 13, 102, 119–120, 187
Boyd, Blanche McCreary 74
Boyle, Peter 20
Bracco, Lorraine 45
Bradbury, Lane 73
Brando, Marlon 135
Braveman, Sarah 79
Bremer, Arthur 80, 83
Brewster, Senator Owen 190
Bringing Out the Dead 13, 14, 80, 139, 170–176, ***173***, 177
Broadbent, Jim 187
Brooks, Albert 84
Brooks, Mel 78, 119
Burstyn, Ellen 68, 69, ***69***, ***72***, 74, 75, ***76***
Bush, Billy Green 69, ***69***
Butch Cassidy and the Sundance Kid 120

The Cabinet of Dr. Caligari 213
Cage, Nicholas 170, ***173***
Cajano, Pasquale ***50***, 53
Campbell, Joseph 2, 3, 5, 7, 8, 9, 66, 101, 118

Cannes Film Festival 121
The Canterbury Tales 109, 130
Cape Fear 1, 10, 13, 55, 139, 146–159, ***148***, ***150***, ***155***, 160, 161, 164, 168, 189
Capote, Truman 20
captivity myth 81, 82
Caravaggio, Michelangelo di ***50***
Carradine, David 119
Carradine, John 119
Carroll, Lewis 10, 68, 70, 71, 72, 135, 207
Casey, Bernie 119
Casino 22, 24, 37, 49–57, ***50***, ***52***, 80, 125, 160, 161, 169
Cassavetes, John 20, 21, 29, 120
Catholic Mass 7, 8, 18, 20, 224
Cavaleria Rusticana 39
cellars *see* basements
Cerdan, Marcel 39
The Chantells 33
Chapman, Mark 98
Chapman, Michael 128, 130
Charon 60, 62, 66
Chaucer, Geoffrey 109, 130
Chesterton, G.K. 171
Chong, Thomas 63
Chopra, Deepak 66
Cinecittà 177, ***179***
Citizen Kane 191
Clapton, Eric 131
Clarkson, Patricia 217
Cobb, Lee J. 35
Cobbs, Bill 136
Cocks, Jay 160
Colasanto, Nicholas 36
The Color of Money 132–138, ***133***, ***137***
color symbolism *see* red
Connelly, Joe 170
Copacabana 37, 38, 45, 57
Coppola, Francis Ford 19, 24, 68, 119
Corman, Roger 29, 119, 120
crucifixion 8, 39, 40, 66, 79, 80, 106, 107, 111, ***111***, 112, 120, 139, 171, 201, 213, 222, 223
Cruise, Tom 133, ***137***
Curtin, Valerie 71
Curtis, Cliff 174

253

Daedalus 194, 200
Dafoe, Willem 103, **107**
Dalai Lama, His Holiness the 139, 140
Damon, Matt 204, **210**
Danko, Rick 128, **129**, 130
Dante 22, 118, 149, 157, 164, 171
The Dark Side of the Light Chasers 7; *see also* Ford, Debbie
death and rebirth 8, 34, 138, 145, 147, 163, 197; *see also* resurrection
DeFazio, Sam 23
De Fina, Barbara 161
De Mille, Cecil B. 102
De Niro, Robert 11, 12, 220; in *Cape Fear* 146, 149, **150**, **155**; in *Casino* 50, **52**, 54, 56, 58; in *GoodFellas* 42, **44**, **46**; in *The King of Comedy* **94**, **97**, 99; in *Mean Streets* 30, 32; in *New York, New York* 121, 123, **124**; in *Raging Bull* 35, 36, 37, **38**, **40**; in *Taxi Driver* 80, **85**, **87**, **89**, 92
De Palma, Brian 119
The Departed 10, 161, 177, 203–212, **203**, **206**, **210**, 213
Devil's Advocate 224
Devil's interval 149
Diamond, Neil 128
Diaz, Cameron **181**, 183
DiCaprio, Leonardo 11, 17; in *The Aviator* 190, 191, **192**, 193, **199**, **202**; in *The Departed* **203**, 204, **206**, 207, **210**; in *Gangs of New York* 177, 178, **181**, **184**; in *Shutter Island* 213, **215**, **221**
Dickens, Charles 171, 178
Dickinson, Angie 26
Didion, Joan 191
DiLeo, Frank 43
The Divine Comedy 22, 118, 149, 157, 164, 171
Dr. Faustus 194
Dr. John 128
Doctorow, E.L. 191
Domino, Fats 29
Don Juan 195
Donovan: "Atlantis" 45
Don't Look Now 219
Dostoyevsky, Fyodor 80, 108, 211
The Double 211
Douglas, Illeana 151
Douglas, John 43, 86
Dracula 211
Dropkick Murphys 204
dungeons 6, 7, 10, 40, 53, 115, 160, 161, 163, 164, 214, 220, 224, 225; *see also* jails
Dunne, Griffin 58, 59, **61**
Dylan, Bob 11, 116, 118, 128, 131; "Like a Rolling Stone" 116

Easter Triduum *see* crucifixion
Ebert, Roger 47, 74, 125, 160, 178
Enya 167

Eurydice 65, 82
The Executioners 146

Fahrenheit 451 91
Fairy tales *see* "Beauty and the Beast"; "Hansel and Gretel"; "Little Red Riding Hood"
Farber, Manny 88
Farmiga, Vera 208
father 177; in *Alice Doesn't Live Here Anymore* 71, 75; in *The Aviator* 192, 194, 196, 200, 201, 202; in *Boxcar Bertha* 119, 120; in *Bringing Out the Dead* 172, 174, 175; in *Cape Fear* 150, 152, 154, 157, 159; in *Casino* 53, 56; in *The Departed* 204, 205, 206, 207, 208, 211, 212; in *Gangs of New York* 178, 179, 182, 183, 184, 185, 186, 187, 188, 189, 190; in *GoodFellas* 43, 47, 48, 49; in *Italianamerican* 15, 16, 17; in *It's Not Just You, Murray!* 24; in *The King of Comedy* 95, 96, 97; in *Kundun* 141, 143; in *The Last Temptation of Christ* 104, 106; in *Life Lessons* 115–116, 118; in *Mean Streets* 33; in *Raging Bull* 35, 36, **38**; in *Shutter Island* 213, 220, 223; in *Taxi Driver* 90; in *What's a Nice Girl Like You Doing in a Place Like This?* 79; *see also* Scorsese, Charles; shadow of father
Faulkner, William 151
Faust 132, 134, 161, 194
Faye, Alice 68, 69, 74
Field, David 170
Fight Club 59
Fincher, David 59
Fiorentino Linda 60
The Fisher King 97, 178
Fitzgerald, F. Scott 51, 191, **192**, 199
Force of Evil 35
Ford, Debbie 2, 7, 49, 159
Ford, John 26, 32, 80, 82, **89**, 208
Foster, Jodie 86, 91, 98
Fowles, John 59, 65, 67
Fox, Billy 39
Frankenheimer, John 20, 213
Frankenstein's creature 136, 220
Freed, Arthur 121
Freud, Sigmund 25, 37, 60, 81, 219
Friedman, Lawrence 86, 89, 120
From Reverence to Rape 67
Fuller, Samuel 213

Gabriel, Peter 103, 114
Gaines, Lenny 125
Gangs of New York 10, 14, 177–190, **179**, **181**, **184**, 192, 203, 204, 205, 212, 220
Gardner, Ava 191
Garland, Judy 121, 127
Garr, Teri 62
The Genies 27
The Ghost Ship 213
Girlfriends 68

Gleason, Jackie 35, 135
Gleeson, Brendan 180
Godard, Jean-Luc 127
God's-eye-view 28, 65, 90, 103, 106, 112, 188
Goethe, Johann Wolfgang von 65
GoodFellas 10, 22, 41–49, **44**, **45**, 49, 50, 56, 57, 160, 161
Goodman, Benny 29
Goodman, John 172
Gothic 9, 66, 108, 146, 213, 217, 224; Southern Gothic 151
Gough, Michael 161
Gounod, Charles Francois 161
Goya, Francisco 7
The Graduate 20
The Great Gatsby 51, 191, **192**
Greeley, Horace 186
The Green Room 138
Gregory, André 104

Hack, Shelley 95
Hades 30, 58, 60, **61**, 62, 63, 65, 66, 67, 82, 171, 178, 207; *see also* Hell; inferno; underworld
Haley, Jackie Earle 217
Hamlet 33, 178, 184, 212
Hammer Studios 77
"Hansel and Gretel" 97
The Harder They Fall 35
Harris, Emmylou 131
Harris, Leonard 86
Harrison, George 47
Haskell, Molly 67
"The Haunted Mind" 6, 53; *see also* Hawthorne, Nathaniel
Hawkins, Ronnie 130
The Hawks *see* The Band
Hawthorne, Nathaniel 6, 10, 51, 53, 146, 150, 212
Heard, John 62
Heaven's Gate 121
Hell 50, 63, 81, 82, 98, 118, **150**, 157, 164, 180, 199, 205; *see also* Hades; inferno; underworld
Hell's Angels 190, 195, 196, 210
Helm, Levon 128, **129**, 130, 131
Henry, Clarence 50
Hepburn, Katharine 191
hero's journey 2, 5, 8–9, 10, 17, 22; in *After Hours* 58–67; in *The Age of Innocence* 159–170; in *Alice Doesn't Live Here Anymore* 67–76; in *The Aviator* 190–203; in *Bringing Out the Dead* 170–176; in *Cape Fear* 146–159; in *Casino* 49–57; in *The Color of Money* 132–138; in *The Departed* 203–212; in *Gangs of New York* 177–190; in *GoodFellas* 41–49; in *It's Not Just You, Murray!* 22–24; in *The King of Comedy* 92–99; in *Kundun* 139–146; in *The Last Temptation of Christ* 102–108; in *Life Lessons* 108–117; in *Mean Streets* 29–34; in *New York, New York* 120–127; in *Raging Bull* 34–41; in *Shutter Island* 212–

224; in *Taxi Driver* 80–92; in *What's a Nice Girl Like You Doing in a Place Like This?* 78–79; in *Who's That Knocking at My Door?* 24–29
Herrmann, Bernard 82, 84, 91, 149, 152, 213
Hershey, Barbara 102, 104, 109, 119, 120
Hinckley, John 83, 91, 92, 98
Hitchcock, Alfred 17, 70, 79, 152, 207; see also Psycho
Hollywood 19, 20, 25, 58, 68, 70, 76, 119, 120, 121, 190, 191, 195, 196, 198
Holm, Ian 196
Holy virgin see Virgin Mary
HUAC (the House Un-American Activities Committee) 216
Hudson, Garth 128, 130, 131
Hughes, Howard 190, 191
Husing, Ted 39
The Hustler 35, 132, 133, 134, 135

The I Ching 139
Ibsen, Henrik 12
Icarus 194, 200
In Cold Blood 20
Infernal Affairs 203
inferno 82, 164, 171, 180, 217; see also Hades; Hell; underworld
The Informer 208
Italianamerican 14–18, **15**
Italianamerican: The Scorsese Family Cookbook 49
It's Not Just You, Murray! 10, 17, 22–24, 37
Ivory, James 160

jails 10, 23, 39, 41, 45, 46, 51, 90, 91, 98, 146, 147, 150, **150**, 156, 157, 163, 206, 208, 217; see also dungeons
Jesus Christ 41, 100, 101, 102, 120, 141, 172, 187, 197, **199**, 200, 222
Johnson, Kevin Orlin 101
Johnson, Robert A. 2, 6, 8, 22, 33, 34, 98, 136, 177, 186
Joyce, James 205
Jules and Jim 19
Jung, Carl Gustav 1, 2, 6, 11, 13, 14, 22, 100, 104

Kael, Pauline 35, 122, 126, 128
Kafka, Franz 59, 64
Kalachakra Mandala 141, 145
Kazantzakis, Nikos 7, 38, 102, 103, 110, 120, 165
Keitel, Harvey 11, 12, 24, **28**, 29, 30, **32**, 71, **72**, **89**, 103
Kelly, Mary Pat 98, 127, 128
keys 9, 26, 34, 42, 43, 50, 51, 54, 55, 57, 60, 63, 64, 67, 151, 168
King, Alan 53
King Arthur 98, 134
King Kong 78
The King of Comedy 10, 12, 17, 42, 92–99, **94**, **97**

King of Kings 102
Kingsley, Ben 215, **221**
Kiss of Death 35
knight in shining armor complex 86, 88, 94, 95
Kolker, Robert Philip 30, 81, 84
Koteas, Elias 217
Kovacs, Laszlo 128
Kristofferson, Kris 11, 73, 74, 75, **76**, 80, 85, 224; "The Pilgrim" (Chapter 33) 75, 80; "To Beat the Devil" 224
Kundun 10, 139–146, **142**, 176
Kuras, Leonard 25

Ladd, Diane 73
La Motta, Jake 35, 41
landscapes 8, 9, 10, 30, 63, 68, 71, 72, 148, 150, 154, 158, 164, 166, 167, 180, 213
Lang, Fritz 34, 59, 86
Lange, Jessica 147, **148**, 152
The Last Temptation (Kazantzakis) 6, 38, 102, 120, 175
The Last Temptation of Christ 3, 6, 10, 39, 58, 74, 101, 102–108, **107**, 110, 112, 117, 118, 120, 122, 140, 41, 143, 144, 161, 169, 171, 172, 173, 175, 223
The Last Waltz 34, 127, 128–132, **129**
Lee, Peggy 70, 127
Lehane, Dennis 213, 214, 222
Lennon, John 92, 98
Leonard, Robert Sean 168
Leven, Boris 128
Lewis, Daniel Day 161, **162**, **165**, 180, **184**
Lewis, Jerry 93, **94**
Lewis, Juliette 147, **148**
Lewton, Val 213
Life Lessons 1, 13, 102, 104, 108–117, **109**, **111**, **114**, 118, 122, 169
The Lion King 178
Liotta, Ray 42, **44**, **46**
"Little Red Riding Hood" 1, 26, 27, 154, **155**, 157, 204
Logan, John 190
Look Homeward Angel 152
The Lord of the Rings 180, 188
Lost Highway 216
Lucas, George 19, 119
Lucifer 107, 149, 151, 161, 179, 180, 205; see also Mephistopheles; Satan; shadow; temptation
Lutter, Alfred 69, **69**
Lynch, David 10, 207, 211, 216

MacDonald, John 146
Madonna (Ciccone) 97, 118
Madonna/whore complex 13, 15, 54, 88
The Magus 59, 65, 67
Mahler, Gustav 215
The Man I Love 121
The Manchurian Candidate 213
Mann, Michael 190
Manoogian, Haig 19, 41

Mantegna, Andrea 222
Manuel, Richard 128
Margolyes, Miriam 167
Marin, Cheech 63
Marlowe, Christopher 194
Martin, Andrea 23
Mary, Mother of Christ see Virgin Mary
mask 11, 22, 31, 34, 53, 54, 57, 153, 204, 205, 207, 209, 210, 211; see also mirror; persona
masochism 23, 36, 39, 41, 53, 55, 70, 80, 112, 134, 135, 171, 193
"The Masque of the Red Death" 174
Mastrantoni, Mary Elizabeth **133**, 134
Mathison, Melissa 140
Mays, Willie 115
Mazursky, Paul 68
Mcclure Michael 130
Mcgowan, Alec 163
McGuffin 59
Mean Streets 11, 12, 14, 18, 19, 22, 24, 29–34, **32**, 54, 55, 58, 68, 75, 80, 89, 103, 120, 123, 134, 140, 160, 161, 169, 178, 183, 186
Mephistopheles 132, 134, 174; see also Lucifer; Satan; shadow; temptation
MGM 121
Michaelis, Zeph 78
Michelangelo 60
Miller, Barry 104
Miller, Henry 59
Milton, John 205
Minnelli, Liza **94**, 121, **124**, 126
Minnelli, Vincente 121
mirror 10, 11, 22, 23, 25, 29, 31, 34, 40–41, 62, 66, 71, 75, 77, 80, 81, 87, 88, 91, 132, 151, 153, 171, **181**, 182, 183, 185, 186, 187, 189, 193, 194, 198, **202**, 203, 207, 211, 214; see also mask
"Mirror, Mirror" 10, 77
Mitchell, Joni 128, 130, 131
Mitchum, Robert 147
Mithras 39
Monahan, William 203
money 25, 30, 31, 33, 45, 47, 49, 51, 54, 55–56, 57, 60, 63, 64, 80, 73, 90, 119, 120, 122, 123, 127, 130, 134, 135, 137, 138, 180, 195, 196, 200, 201, 202, 205, 206
Montero, Zully 156
Mooreeffoc 171
Moriarty, Cathy 36, 37, **38**
Morrison, Jim 10
Morrison, Van 128
Mortimer, Emily 216
mother 9, 10, 13, 177; in *After Hours* 65–66, 67; in *Alice Doesn't Live Here Anymore* 68–69, 69–76; in *The Aviator* 192–193, 194, 195, 196, 197, 198, 199, 200, 201, 202; in *Cape Fear* 158; in *Casino* 49; in *The Departed*

205, 206, 211, 212; in *Gangs of New York* 185; in *GoodFellas* 43, 46, *46*, 48; in *Italianamerican* 14, 15, 16, 17, 22; in *It's Not Just You, Murray!* 23, 24, 25, 26, 27; in *The King of Comedy* 93, 94, 95, 97, 98; in *Kundun* 141; in *The Last Temptation of Christ* 106, 107; in *Mean Streets* 33; in *What's a Nice Girl Like You Doing in a Place Like This?* 79; *see also* Madonna/whore complex; Scorsese, Catherine; Virgin Mary
mother archetype 17, 33, 66
mother complex 13, 17, 33, 66, 98
Music from Big Pink 131–132
myths *see* captivity myth; Charon; Daedalus; Eurydice; Faust; The Fisher King; Hades; Icarus; King Arthur; Mithras; Narcissus; Oracle of Delphi; Orestes; Orpheus; Parsifal; Persephone; River Styx; Theseus; underworld

Narcissus 77
narrators 23, 42, 48, 50, 78, 83, 103, 160, 163, 167, 168
Nausea 80
Navasky, Victor 48
Neeson, Liam 179
New York, New York 34, 120–127, *124*, 128
New York Stories see Life Lessons
Newman, Paul 132, 133, *133*, 135, *137*
Nicholson, Jack *203*, 204
Nietzsche, Friedrich 77, 118, 207
No Direction Home 118
Nolte, Nick 108, *109*, *111*, *114*, 146, *148*
Norma Rae 68
Notes from the Underground 80
#711 208

Oedipal conflicts 26, 71, 95, 97, 115, 154, 195, 196, 201
O'Hara, Catherine 64
Oliver Twist 178
On the Town 122
On the Waterfront 11, 25, 35, 40, 135
O'Neal, Patrick 109
Oracle of Delphi 217, 218
Orestes 178
Orpheus 59, 65, 82
The Outlaw 193
"The Oval Portrait" 113

Parsifal 33, 98, 193
Passion week *see* crucifixion
Patterson, Patricia 88
Patton, Will 63
Peckinpah, Sam 120
Peeping Tom 81
Peer Gynt 12, 153
Pells, Richard 135

Penderecki, Krzysztof 213
Penman, Ian 30
Penn, Arthur 20
Persephone 63, 65, 67, 82
persona 22, 23, 30, 31, 32, 34, 43, 51, *52*, 53, 54, 55, 57, 60, 64, 117, 163, 204, 208, 209, 210, 211, 216, 218; *see also* mask
Pesci, Joe 36, 37, 42, *44*, *46*, 51, *52*, 54, 56, 57
Peter Pan 70, 71, 72
Pfeiffer, Michelle 160, *162*, *169*, 170
Pileggi, Nicholas 41, 42, 49
Poe, Edgar Allan 77, 113, 146, 174, 213
Powell, Michael 7, 81, 100, *101*, 117, 121
Pressburger, Emeric *101*, 121
Price, Richard 117, 132, 133, 136
Primus, Barry 119, 125
Prince, Steven 87
Principe, Father Francis 18
prisons *see* jails
Problem Child 152
Procul Harum 109; "A Whiter Shade of Pale" 109, 113, 114
Proval, David 30
Psycho 17, 70, 79, 80, 81, 83, 91, 152, 156
Puccini, Giacomo 116

Raging Bull 10, 13, 22, 34–41, *38*, *40*, 54, 55, 56, 57, 80, 92, 125, 134, 135, 161, 170, 171, 197, 201, 202, 223
Rank, Otto 195
red 98, 100–101, 108, 113, 126–127, 141, 149, 154, 163
The Red Shoes 100, *101*, 104, 108, 117, 121, 127
redemption 7, 29, 35, 39, 40, *40*, 51, 77, 80, 102, 106, 133, 146, 149, 175, 221, 223
Redford, Robert 70, 73
Reeves, Jimmy 36
Reilly, John C. 196
Renaldo and Clara 131
Requiem for a Heavyweight 35
Ressler, Robert 83, 84, 86, 90
resurrection 8, 51, 57, 91, 102, 171, 176, 198; *see also* death and rebirth
Rhames, Ving 172
Richardson, Cheryl 8
Richter, Max 213
Rickey, Carrie 121
Rio Bravo 25–26
Ritt, Martin 68
River Styx 60, 63, 65, 145, 171
Robertson, Robbie 35, 128, *129*, 130, 131, 132
Robinson, Amy 12, 32, *32*, 58
Roeg, Nicholas 219
The Rolling Stones 30, 128
Romanus, Richard 30
Rosen, Jeff 118
Ross, Herbert 68

Ross, Matt 193
Rossen Robert 132
Rowe, Dorothy 9
Rubin, Ira 23
Ruffalo, Mark 214, *215*, *221*
Ryder, Winona 164, *165*

St. Francis 34, 99, 172, 187
St. John of the Cross 8
St. Matthew Passion (Bach) 50
St. Michael 180, 182, 183, 186, 205
St. Patricks's Old Cathedral 18, 20, 21, 27, 28, *28*, 30
St. Paul 100, 104, 110, 117
St. Veronica 111
Sartre, Jean-Paul 80
Satan 103, 105, 106, 107, 149, 173, 174, 175, 180, 186, 205; *see also* Lucifer; Mephistopheles; shadow; temptation
Scala, Michael 25
Scarface 196, 207
The Scarlet Letter 51
Schoonmaker, Thelma 37, 160, 203
Schrader, Paul 20, 80, 81, 83, 85, 89, 90, 92, 170, 171
Schultz, Cathy 191, 195
Scorsese, Catherine (daughter) 49
Scorsese, Catherine (mother) 14, 15, 16, 17, 18, 22, 23, 24, *46*, 46, 49, 59, 90, 160; *see also* mother
Scorsese, Charles (father) 14, 15, 16, 17, 18, 59, 90, 159, 160; *see also* father
Scorsese, Frank (brother) 18
Scorsese, Martin: alter egos 10–14, *169*, 177; asthma 12, 18, 19, 20, 35, 43; childhood in Little Italy 2, 5, 9, 15, 16, 18–19, 20, 29, 102; New York University 9, 19, 24, 78; priesthood 19, 20, 21, 224; works of: *After Hours* 58–67; *The Age of Innocence*; 159–170; *Alice Doesn't Live Here Anymore* 67–76; *The Aviator* 190–203; *The Big Shave* 79–80; *Boxcar Bertha* 119–120; *Bringing Out the Dead* 170–176; *Cape Fear* 146–159; *Casino* 49–57; *The Color of Money* 132–138; *The Departed* 203–212; *Gangs of New York* 177–190; *GoodFellas* 41–49; *Italianamerican* 14–18; *It's Not Just You, Murray!* 22–24; *The King of Comedy* 92–99; *Kundun* 139–146; *The Last Temptation of Christ* 102–108; *The Last Waltz* 128–132; *Life Lessons* 108–117; *Mean Streets* 29–34; "Mirror, Mirror" 77; *New York, New York* 120–127; *No Direction Home* 118; *Raging Bull* 34–41; *Shine a Light* 128; *Shutter Island* 212–224; *Taxi Driver* 80–92; *What's a Nice Girl Like You Doing in a Place*

Like This? 78–79; *Who's That Knocking at My Door?* 24–29 (see also individual listings)
Scott, George C. 35, 132, 133, 135
The Searchers 26, 32, 80, 82, **89**
The Seat of the Soul 149
Seibert, Perry 190
The Set-Up 35
The Seven Year Itch 96
The Shadow (Andersen) 211
the shadow 2, 6–8, 10, 11, 12, 13, 14, 22, 39, 40, 41, 66, 77, 86, 87, 92, 98, 99, 103, 104, 111, 118, 143, 144, 145, 174, 198, 200; in *The Age of Innocence* 161, 164, 168, 169; in *Cape Fear* 146, 147, 148, 149, 150, 151, 152, 153, 154, 157, 158, 159; in *Casino* 49, 53, 54, 55, 57; in *The Color of Money* 132, 134, 136, 138; in *The Departed* 204, 207, 209, 210, **210**, 211, 212; in *Gangs of New York* 177, 178, 179, 180, 182, 189; in *Mean Streets* 30, 31, 34; in *Shutter Island* 213, 214, 218, 220, 222, 224, 225
the shadow of father 154, 178, 184, **184**, 186–187, 188, 189, 207
Shadows (Cassavetes) 20
Shakespeare, William 131, 178, 184, 212
Shane 101
Shaver, Helen 77, 133
Sheen, Martin 204
Shepard, Sam 11, 74
Shepherd, Cybill 84
Shine a Light 128
The Shining 152
Shock Corridor 213
Shoot the Piano Player 19
Shutter Island 10, 14, 77, 177, 212–224, **215**, **219**, **221**
Sica, Fred 78
Sister of the Road 119
Sizemore, Tom 172
Somebody Up There Likes Me 35
The Sorcerers Apprentice 93, 136
Sorvino, Paul 42, **44**
Spielberg, Steven 12, 19, 119

Springsteen, Bruce 11
A Star Is Born 121
Star Wars 134, 178, 186
Stark, Mimi 78
Steinbeck, John 11, 119
Stone, Sharon 51, **52**
Strangers on a Train 207
Sunset Blvd. 51
Suslova, Polina 108, 112
Symphony #3 (Penderecki) 213

Taxi Driver 10, 13, 20, 54, 55, 58, 75, 80–92, **85**, **87**, **89**, 92, 93, 96, 121, 171, 214
Technicolor 131, 190, 191, 198
temptation 102, 105, 107, 112, 116, 117, 130, 149, 173, 174, 175, 178, 194, 206; see also Lucifer; Mephistopheles; Satan; shadow
Tevis, Walter 132
Thelma and Louise 71
Theseus 5, 82
The Third Man 19
Thomas, Henry 183
Thompson, Bertha 119
Thompson, J. Lee 146
Through the Looking Glass 77
Titanic 177
Tolkien, J.R.R. 171
Touchstone Pictures 132, 140
Tropic of Cancer 59
Truffaut, Francois 19, 91, 138
Turandot 116
The Turning Point 68
Turturro, John 133
Twin Peaks 211
"The Tyger" 31

underworld 59, 60, 63, 65, 82; see also Hades; Hell; inferno
United Artists 170
Universal Pictures 102, 159
An Unmarried Woman 68

Vale, Jerry 29
Vella, Vinny 53
Vicious, Sid 42
Vincent, Frank 42, 53, 56, 57
violence 7, 12, 13–14, 18, 31, 51, 75, 81, 84, 86, 87, 119, 140, 151, 171, 172, 215, 223
Virgin Mary 17, 24, 25, 27, 65, 66, 131, 172
vocation 9, 21, 98, 100–102, **101**, 104, 105, 106, 107, **107**, 111–112, 116, 117, 122, 126, 127, 130, 141, 149, 163, 169, 173
voiceover narrators see narrators
von Franz, Marie-Louise 11, 13, 149, 159
von Sydow, Max 215

Wahlberg, Mark 204, 206
Warhol, Andy 99
Warren, Robert Penn 88
Waters, Muddy 47, 128, 131
Waterston, Sam 77
Wayne, John 25, 82
Weill, Claudia 68
Welles, Orson 191, **192**
Wharton, Edith 160, 161, 164, 168, 170
What's a Nice Girl Like You Doing in a Place Like This? 78–79, 214
Whitaker, Forest 136
Whitmont, Edward 13, 65
Who's That Knocking at My Door? 11, 17, 18, 22, 24–29, **28**, 30, 34, 68, 119
Wiene, Robert 213
Williams, Michelle 215
Wilson, Stuart 163
Winterland Arena 128, 130
Wise Guy: Life in a Mafia Family 41
The Wizard of Oz 58, 59, 63, 66, 68, 70
Wolverine 204, 208
The Woman in the Window 59, 86
Wood, Robin 97
Woods, James 54
Woodstock 128
Woodward, Joanne 160

Young, Neil 128

Zsigmon, Vilmos 128
Zukav, Gary 149

www.ingramcontent.com/pod-product-compliance
Ingram Content Group UK Ltd.
Pitfield, Milton Keynes, MK11 3LW, UK
UKHW050537150426
5217IPUK00026B/1974